THE
GREATEST
STORIES
EVER TOLD

THE LIFE AND MINISTRY
OF JESUS CHRIST

ALLEN
DAVID
BOOKS

THE GREATEST STORIES EVER TOLD

THE LIFE AND MINISTRY OF JESUS CHRIST

GREG LAURIE

KERYGMA™
PUBLISHING

The Greatest Stories Ever Told: The Life and Ministry of Jesus Christ

Production: Mark Ferjulian
Cover Design: Ty Mattson

ISBN-13: 978-1-942090-13-7

Printed in India

1 2 3 4 5 6 7 8 / 21 20 19 18 17 16

ISBN 978-1-942090-13-7

9 781942 090137

TABLE OF CONTENTS

CHAPTER ONE

CHRISTMAS: THE STORY BEFORE THE STORY

I remember waiting in line at the theater back in 1980 to see *The Empire Strikes Back*, the second movie in the classic Star Wars trilogy.

At that point, I didn't have a clue about the plot line. And then some joker who had been in the previous showing walked by with a smirk and said, "Oh, by the way, Darth Vader is Luke's father."

Every head in the line jerked around and we all said, "Noooo!"

Those first three Star Wars movies were really good. But then the creator, George Lucas, came up with the idea of doing a series of three "prequels." Instead of advancing the story, he moved the story back in time, revealing where Luke Skywalker and Obi Wan Kenobi came from—and how Darth Vader ended up on the dark side.

Lucas lost me with those movies. I couldn't get into the lizard-faced character Jar Jar Binks, and I didn't like the prequels at all. Now that Disney has picked up the franchise, we are getting on with the original storyline and finding out what happened to Han Solo, Luke Skywalker, and Princess Leia.

Some prequels—the stories behind the stories—aren't as interesting as the original accounts. But that isn't true of the story of Christmas. Not at all! The main story, of course, begins with the angel coming to Mary, a virgin, and announcing that she would bear a Child who would be called "the Son of God." Then there was the birth in Bethlehem, the shepherds, the angelic choir, and later, the wise men following a star.

We love that true story of our Lord's birth, and I for one never get tired of reading it, hearing about it, singing about it, or just thinking about it.

But in the gospel of Luke there is a prequel to the main story—and it's every bit as good.

The Doctor's Journal

Luke wasn't one of our Lord's disciples. Because of that, he wasn't an eyewitness of the events he recorded in his gospel, as Matthew and John were. It was Luke's desire to capture an overview of the life of Jesus that would be understandable to those outside the Jewish faith and culture. So with educated skill and the attention to detail of a physician—not to mention the heart and artistry of a poet—Dr. Luke gave us highlights from the life of Jesus.

Luke's account is addressed to a man named Theophilus. The only thing we really know about this individual is that his name means "love of God." Presumably, then, he was a believer. It's just speculation, but he might have been the one who underwrote the project—funding Luke's research as the doctor traveled here and there doing interviews, engaging in conversations, and seeking pertinent details.

In his prologue, Luke wrote,

Many have undertaken to draw up an account of the things that have been fulfilled among us, just as they were handed down to us by those who from the first were eyewitnesses and servants of the word. With this in mind, since I myself have carefully investigated everything from the beginning, I too decided to write an orderly account for you, most excellent Theophilus, so that you may know the certainty of the things you have been taught. (Luke 1:1-4, NIV)

I like that word *certainty.*

Luke believed that if the essence of this true story were set down in an accurate and orderly way, the result would create new believers in Jesus. And he was right.

In my experience, I've seen many people reject the message of Christ without even looking to see if it might be true.

"Are you a Christian?" you may ask someone.

"No," she replies.

"Have you ever read the Bible?"

"No."

"Have you ever read the New Testament—or even one of the gospels?"

"No."

"Would you be interested in hearing about Jesus?"

"No."

The fact is, this person has decided to reject something she knows nothing about.

Luke was saying, "I want to put together this orderly account of the Lord's life so you can know your faith is built on a sure foundation. I want you to know with certainty that these things are true."

Already at that time, there were false stories going around about the birth of Jesus and His life and ministry. I don't know if they had tabloids in their markets in those days (the *Jerusalem Enquirer*?), but there were myths and legends floating around. Dr. Luke wanted to set the record straight, giving an accurate presentation of who Jesus was, what He did, and what He said.

And here is how Luke began his account.

"In the Days of Herod . . ."

There was in the days of Herod, the king of Judea, a certain priest named Zacharias, of the division of Abijah. His wife was of the daughters of Aaron, and her name was Elizabeth. And they were both righteous before God, walking in all the commandments and ordinances of the Lord blameless. But they had no child, because Elizabeth was barren, and they were both well advanced in years.

So it was, that while he was serving as priest before God in the order of his division, according to the custom of the priesthood, his lot fell to burn incense when he went into the temple of the Lord. And the whole multitude of the people was praying outside at the hour of incense. Then an angel of the

Lord appeared to him, standing on the right side of the altar of incense. And when Zacharias saw him, he was troubled, and fear fell upon him.

But the angel said to him, "Do not be afraid, Zacharias, for your prayer is heard; and your wife Elizabeth will bear you a son, and you shall call his name John. And you will have joy and gladness, and many will rejoice at his birth. For he will be great in the sight of the Lord, and shall drink neither wine nor strong drink. He will also be filled with the Holy Spirit, even from his mother's womb. And he will turn many of the children of Israel to the Lord their God. He will also go before Him in the spirit and power of Elijah, 'to turn the hearts of the fathers to the children,' and the disobedient to the wisdom of the just, to make ready a people prepared for the Lord." (Luke 1:5-17)

When Luke wrote, "in the days of Herod . . ." it would be like saying in Germany, "in the days of Adolf Hitler." Or in China, "in the days of Mao Tse-tung." Or in Iraq, saying, "in the days of Saddam Hussein." Those words would give immediate context to the people who actually lived in those places and times. In each case, those were dark days. Wicked days. For Israel, also suffering under the brutal heel of Roman rule, it was almost as difficult as their days of bondage in Egypt under Pharaoh.

King Herod was in charge, a puppet king under Roman rule, to whom Caesar had given the title "King of the Jews." Herod was known for his cruelty, fueled as it was by over-the-top paranoia and jealousy. According to historical accounts, this king-in-name-only murdered his wife, her brother, her mother, and several of his own sons, fearing they presented some threat to his rule. It was this Herod who gave the decree to kill all the boys aged two years and under in the vicinity of Bethlehem. One of the popular expressions of the day was "Better to be one of Herod's pigs than a member of his family."

This is the depressing backdrop of Luke's story. To make matters much worse, the people of Israel had not heard from God for four hundred years! In four centuries there had not been a single prophet, a single miracle, or a single angelic appearance. Heaven had gone silent. Luke's narrative, then, found Israel in the midst of a long night of spiritual darkness.

Even so, God had ended the Old Testament with a promise. In the book of Malachi, the closing book of the Old Testament, God had said,

> But to you who fear My name
> The Sun of Righteousness shall arise
> With healing in His wings;
> And you shall go out
> And grow fat like stall-fed calves. (4:2)

God was saying to the faithful in Israel, "A better day is coming. Though it's dark now, the sun will rise again and bring healing." The Bible commentator R. Kent Hughes put it this way: "Great plans laid down in eternal ages past now begin to activate. Angels scurry around visibly preparing for the dawn."

Not only had God promised a better day was coming, not only had God promised a Messiah was coming, but He had also told them they could watch for a forerunner who would announce the arrival of the Messiah and prepare the way for Him. In Malachi 3:1 (NIV), the Lord said, "'I will send my messenger, who will prepare the way before me. Then suddenly the Lord you are seeking will come to his temple; the messenger of the covenant, whom you desire, will come,' says the LORD Almighty."

When John the Baptist, the "messenger" of this passage, arrived on the scene, he was effectively the bridge between the Old and New Testaments. In a sense, he was the last of the Old Testament prophets heralding the arrival of Israel's long-awaited Messiah.

Sometimes people will talk about "the God of the Old Testament" and "the God of the New Testament" as if they were separate beings. We're told that the God of the Old Testament is harsh, judgmental, and intolerant. The God of the New Testament, however, is compassionate, loving, and accepting. But this whole comparison isn't true at all. The God of the Old Testament and the God of the New Testament is the same God. Scripture gives us one continuous revelation of God from Genesis through all sixty-six books of the Bible, culminating in the book of Revelation.

John the Baptist bridged the gap between the Old and New Testaments and addressed Israel's longing for Messiah, for someone to deliver them.

I'm reminded of the lyrics to that ancient Christmas carol:

O come, O come, Emmanuel
And ransom captive Israel
That mourns in lonely exile here
Until the Son of God appear.
Rejoice! Rejoice! Emmanuel
Shall come to thee, O Israel.

God Remembers His Oath

That's the background Dr. Luke gave for that moment when the godly old priest Zacharias went into the temple of the Lord to burn incense. Here is a description of that critical moment in Israel's history from a different Bible translation:

The crowded congregation outside was praying at the actual time of the incense-burning, when an angel of the Lord appeared on the right side of the incense-altar. When Zacharias saw him, he was terribly agitated and a sense of awe swept over him. But the angel spoke to him, "Do not be afraid, Zacharias; your prayers have been heard. Elisabeth your wife will bear you a son, and you are to call him John." (Luke 1:10-13, PH)

Was this a big deal?

Yes, this was a *very* big deal.

Why? Because the angel who showed up in that moment was none other than Gabriel. Remember, it had been four hundred years since any angel had made an appearance in Israel. When God finally sent a heavenly messenger, He didn't send just any angel who happened to be on call at the moment. He sent a mega-angel. This is the same Gabriel, one of only two named holy angels in Scripture, who had appeared to the prophet Daniel to give him a message about the future Messiah. There is no question that this mighty servant of God is uniquely connected to the life and ministry of Jesus. It is Gabriel who would later appear to Mary, telling her that she was to bear a Son and call His name Jesus.

It is interesting that the last appearance of an angel in the Old Testament came to Zechariah the prophet, and the first angel appearance of the New Testament also comes to someone named Zechariah (or Zacharias). The name means "God remembers."

Zacharias and his wife, Elizabeth, were an elderly couple who were childless. Elizabeth's name means "God is an oath" or "my God is an oath." In effect, God would confirm and fulfill the meanings of both of their names.

He was going to keep His oath.

He was going to remember His promise.

What We Can Learn from Zacharias and Elizabeth

What truths can we take away from this godly couple through whom God worked in that amazing moment of transition in Israel? Here are a few principles we might consider:

1. Zacharias was a humble man.

Contrast him with the wicked and powerful Herod, who would in time be cut down. Zacharias was a humble servant of the Lord. What does it mean to be humble? It *doesn't* mean you walk around with your hands folded and your eyes cast down, saying, "I'm just a humble person."

That's not humility. That's just being a wimp. A humble person is a strong person, one who keeps that strength under control. We see that same idea communicated in the word *meekness*, which means great power under constraint. (Think of a mighty war horse being controlled by a bit and bridle.)

Zacharias was humble before God, and God favored him, just as we read in James 4:6, where the apostle said, "God resists the proud, but gives grace to the humble." A humble person is simply someone who sees himself as he really is—a sinner in need of a Savior.

Zacharias was a country priest with a small congregation, similar to being a country pastor of a little flock in some tiny community today. The priest would represent the people to God, interpret Scripture for them, pray for them, counsel them, and render judgment when necessary.

In a real way, each one of us is a priest today.

You say, "What do you mean, Greg? I don't have any clerical collars at home."

Perhaps not, but the Bible tells us in 1 Peter 2:9 (NIV) that we are "a chosen people, a royal priesthood, a holy nation, God's special possession, that [we] may declare the praises of him who called [us] out of darkness into his wonderful light."

You are a priest, and so am I. In the Old Covenant, there was a high priest who would go into the temple to represent the people to God. But now Jesus is our High Priest, and we are all in the priesthood. That means that we, in essence, do what an Old Testament priest did. *We represent people to God.*

Have you thought about it?

God has chosen you as His personal representative. You represent God to the world. You represent God to your city, school, worksite, sports team, or neighborhood. You represent God to your family. If you are married, you represent God to your spouse.

I can hear someone say, "That's a lot of pressure, Greg."

Yes, it is.

But that's what being a Christian is all about.

The fact is, you are the only Bible some people will ever read. A Christian is a walking epistle written by God and read by people. The New Testament expresses it like this: "You yourselves are our letter, . . . known and read by everyone. You show that you are a letter from Christ, the result of our ministry, written not with ink but with the Spirit of the living God, not on tablets of stone but on tablets of human hearts" (2 Corinthians 3:2-3, NIV). Some of the people you rub shoulders with may have never looked up John 3:16 in a New Testament, *but they will read your life.* Count on it!

They will watch the way you treat your husband or wife.

They will watch the way you live as a single person.

They will watch the way you transact your business.

They will watch the way you respond to trials and crises in your life.

And they will make evaluations about God according to your lifestyle.

"But that's not right!" you say. "I don't want that responsibility. I don't want people to do that." Nevertheless, they will.

2. Zacharias was a faithful man.

As the story begins, we see this humble country priest just going about his duty. Back in those days, each priest would leave his local area and go to Jerusalem to serve in the temple twice a year for one week. I can imagine that this would be something they would really look forward to. You have your little rural parish, but twice a year you get to serve in the big city of Jerusalem and offer prayers for the nation and its people. And talk about a privilege; as a priest of the living God you got to walk into the Holy Place, with the Holy of Holies and the ark of the covenant just feet away behind the curtain. Zacharias was just doing his duty when an angel of the Lord appeared to him, standing at the right side of the altar of incense.

Here is a word for you if you desire to be used by God. Maybe you've told the Lord, "I want You to use me!" Perhaps you even feel called into full-time ministry.

That's great. Now get busy and do something.

"Well," you say, "I'm just waiting on the Lord."

But what does that mean? Relaxing in your La-Z-Boy at home and watching TV? That's not how it will get done. You need to get yourself in motion and plunge your hands into the work somewhere. When God called Moses, what was he doing? He was tending his sheep. When David had an encounter with Goliath that changed his life, what had he been doing? Running an errand for his dad, delivering cheese sandwiches to his older brothers who were out on the battle line. God called Elisha when he was out plowing a field. Gideon was threshing wheat when God's angel called him to deliver Israel from bondage to the Midianites. Peter and John were mending their nets with their dad when Jesus called them to be fishers of men.

In other words, they were doing something. They were in motion.

In my experience, it's much easier to steer a car when it's moving down the street than when it's parked in a driveway.

Sometimes the way to find out what you are called to do for the Lord is by first finding out what you have *not* been called or equipped to do. As you roll up your sleeves to do kingdom work, you may find that what you had thought you were called to do hasn't been as productive as you might have hoped. But then as you are out and about offering your services here and there, you may find that you have a gifting you weren't even aware of.

Here is the key: Be faithful in the little things.

And if you are faithful in those small areas of responsibility, God will open up greater opportunities for you. It was Warren Wiersbe who said, "You can never be too small for God to use. Only too big." Just avail yourself to the Lord and watch what He will do.

I felt a call to ministry early in my life. I became a Christian at age seventeen. By age eighteen, I was already sure I was called to serve God. I might have even imagined myself as some kind of preacher or evangelist. With those thoughts in mind, I made an appointment with Pastor Chuck Smith to talk it over. I went in and sat down in his office and said, "Hi, Chuck. I'm Greg Laurie, and I drew this little 'living water' cartoon tract."

"Okay," he said, "that's good."

"I want to serve God. I feel called to the ministry. I could lead a Bible study or something if you want me to."

Chuck said, "Greg, I want you to go meet with Pastor Romaine. He will tell you what to do."

Pastor Romaine? I didn't even know who Pastor Romaine was. But I found out quickly. Romaine was a former drill sergeant in the Marine Corps.

After he had heard my little speech, he pointed to the corner of the room. "There is a broom," he said. "Pick it up and start sweeping over there. When you're done, go over to the bathrooms and clean the toilets. When you're done there, come back and I'll give you something else to do."

I had thought they would ask me to preach! I thought they'd put me to work teaching Bible studies or maybe designing and illustrating printed materials. But no, it seemed to me that they just wanted some free janitorial help.

But I have since figured out that they had something else in mind. This was a way to test me. Did I really want to serve the Lord? Would I be faithful in the little things, doing them to the best of my ability for the glory of God? The truth is, if you can't be faithful in the small things, you will never be faithful in the larger things.

Jesus said, "Whoever can be trusted with very little can also be trusted with much" (Luke 16:10, NIV). The bottom line, then, is that we need to do what is set before us to the best of our abilities, and use the gifts that have been given to us however and wherever we can.

Here is something to remember, however. The gifts of God do not come to us fully formed. Anyone with raw and undeveloped talents can strengthen those gifts of God through use and practice, application and discipline.

When I was a boy, I remember meeting a man who claimed to be an animator for Disney. It blew me away. Being a cartoonist at Disney Studios was the biggest dream of my life. But I wasn't sure about this guy. I said to him, "Prove to me that you're an animator for Disney." So he pulled out a pencil and drew a flawless Donald Duck. I was convinced and in awe!

"How did you do that?" I said.

Holding up his pencil, he said, "Greg, this is a magic pencil. If you will take this pencil and put it under your pillow and go to sleep, in the morning you will be able to draw like I do."

I believed him. With my heart racing, I immediately ran out of the room and stuck that pencil under my pillow. In the morning, I grabbed the pencil and ran to find a piece of paper, drawing something on it the same way I always did. But there was no magic. Nothing had changed with my talents.

As the years went by, however, and as I worked and practiced and spent countless hours with a pencil and paper, I began to develop my gifting and talents. The "magic" was in being faithful to use and perfect the gifts God had given me.

3. Zacharias and Elizabeth were godly people.

The text says "they were both righteous before God, walking in all the commandments and ordinances of the Lord blameless" (Luke 1:6). By the way, to be "blameless" doesn't mean that they were sinless. It means that they consistently followed God.

This couple was getting along in years and were well past the age of having children. Zacharias and Elizabeth had longed for a son and prayed for a son, but no child had come along. And now, seemingly, it was too late.

But it wasn't too late.

In verse 13 the angel said to the old priest, "Do not be afraid, Zacharias, for your prayer is heard; and your wife Elizabeth will bear you a son, and you shall call his name John." The original language seems to imply here that Zacharias had been praying for a son *in that very moment*. While he stood there before the altar of incense, representing the people, he might have been whispering in prayer, "Lord, I don't want to exploit this opportunity. But since I am standing in the Holy of Holies and You are already listening to me, let me just throw in a quick prayer that I've prayed many times before. Lord, please give us a son. I know we're old. I know we're past the age of parenthood. But Lord, I'm just going to ask You anyway. We would like a boy of our own."

Again, the implication of the language shows that God intended to answer that prayer in real time. Right there at that moment, Zacharias's prayer was heard in heaven and God sent an answer.

The same is true of your prayers.

Your prayers are heard in heaven.

"Well, Greg," someone will say to me, "my prayers haven't been answered. God must not have heard me."

Are you sure of that? In Revelation 8:3 (NIV) we read these words: "Another angel, who had a golden censer, came and stood at the altar. He was given much incense to offer, with the prayers of all God's people, on the golden altar in front of the throne."

God stores up all the prayers of His people. Every prayer that is ever prayed is recorded and stored. In fact, since God dwells in a timeless eternity, the prayer you prayed ten years ago is still before Him just as much as the prayer you prayed ten minutes ago.

God always answers our prayers. We just don't like the answers sometimes. He may answer yes or no or "wait," but He will answer.

In this instance, the Lord was saying yes to Zacharias and Elizabeth after years and years of saying "wait." In sending an angel to announce the answer to the priest's prayer, the Lord was saying in effect, "I have noted your faithfulness. I have noted your humility. I have paid attention to the way you live." Some people serve the Lord faithfully behind the scenes and they imagine that no one really notices or cares. That's not true; God notices and cares. And He promises that what we have done in secret for His name will someday be acknowledged openly.

In this passage, God was openly rewarding the faithfulness of Zacharias and Elizabeth and answering a prayer they had probably been repeating for over thirty years. By that time, Zacharias may not have been praying with much enthusiasm or faith. It probably seemed to him that God hadn't really been listening. Then suddenly, an angel came and told him God had heard his prayer, and was about to answer him with the deepest desire and longing of his heart for many years.

And how did Zacharias react?

He reacted with doubt.

4. Zacharias was human and flawed just like us.

In Luke 1:18 he replied to the angel, "How shall I know this? For I am an old man, and my wife is well advanced in years." In *The Message* paraphrase, Zacharias said, "Do you expect me to believe this? I'm an old man and my wife is an old woman."

In reply, the angel said, "I am Gabriel, who stands in the presence of God, and was sent to speak to you and bring you these glad tidings. But behold, you will be mute and not able to speak until the day these things take place, because you did not believe my words which will be fulfilled in their own time" (verses 19-20).

If he had exercised faith in that moment, Zacharias *could* have believed. Instead, he questioned and doubted. He wanted to believe, but he just wasn't sure. Gabriel replied, in effect, "Do you have any idea who you're speaking to? I'm not your garden-variety angel. I stand in the presence of God Himself! I am Gabriel, a super angel with power and authority beyond your comprehension. And you are doubting my word?" As a consequence of this failure of Zacharias's faith, he suddenly became mute and couldn't speak a word.

The truth was, though God was answering this godly couple's heartfelt prayers, there were bigger things afoot than they realized at first. God was setting things in place to reveal His chosen and long-promised Messiah. As the book of Galatians puts it, "But when the set time had fully come, God sent his Son, born of a woman, born under the law, to redeem those under the law, that we might receive adoption to sonship" (4:4-5, NIV). God wasn't just giving Zacharias and Elizabeth a son, he was giving them the greatest prophet who ever lived—the very forerunner of the Messiah Himself.

Jesus said of John, "What did you go out into the wilderness to see? . . . A prophet? Yes, I say to you, and more than a prophet. For this is he of whom it is written: 'Behold, I send My messenger before Your face, who will prepare Your way before You.' Assuredly, I say to you, among those born of women there has not risen one greater than John the Baptist" (Matthew 11:7,9-11).

This means that John was greater than Abraham, Noah, Moses, Ezekiel, Isaiah, Jeremiah, Elijah, and Elisha. But what made him so great? Did John ever write a book of the Bible? No. Did John receive the commandments from God on Mount Sinai? No. Did God ever perform a miracle through John as He did through Elijah and Elisha? No.

Why, then, was John the greatest? Because John and John alone was the direct forerunner of Jesus Christ. His greatness was a result of his closeness to Jesus, and he was given the most wonderful privilege a person could ever receive: to announce that Messiah was coming.

Unlike many prophets of the Lord, John was very popular in his own day and time. Josephus the historian actually wrote more about the life and ministry of John than he wrote about Jesus. To put it into the vernacular, John was a rock star in his culture. Everyone wanted to see John or be baptized by John. His words were the topic of conversation across the land, as he would blast the Pharisees and religious leaders with both barrels.

John had been set apart by God while he was still in his mother's womb. In Luke 1:15 we read, "For he will be great in the sight of the Lord, and shall drink neither wine nor strong drink. He will also be filled with the Holy Spirit, even from his mother's womb."

That's a significant verse when we're talking about the subject of abortion. There are those who say that an unborn child is nothing more than a glob of cells or a "potential human being." But how could a piece of tissue or a glob of cells be filled with the Holy Spirit? According to Scripture, a child in the womb is a *child*, a human person with an eternal soul.

A Bold Statement

Finally the day of John's birth arrived. When the couple's neighbors and friends gathered around to celebrate with them, they all speculated that the baby would be named Zacharias, after his dad. That's when Elizabeth spoke up (because Zacharias was mute and *couldn't* speak up) and told them all that the baby's name would be John. When the relatives and friends heard this, they had a hard time believing it. "John? Seriously? No one in your family has that name! Why would you name him that?" But when they brought Zacharias into the discussion, he took a writing pad and wrote it out in bold letters: HIS NAME IS JOHN.

In the moment he affirmed that truth, the Lord miraculously opened his mouth, activated the vocal chords that had been silent for so long, and he began to praise and glorify God. It was such a wonderful psalm of praise to the Lord that God had it recorded in Scripture for us, and we are able to read it (and join in) even today. Turning to his little infant son, perhaps holding him in his hands, Zacharias prophesied:

> And you, child, will be called the prophet of the Highest;
> For you will go before the face of the Lord to prepare His ways,
> To give knowledge of salvation to His people
> By the remission of their sins,
> Through the tender mercy of our God,
> With which the Dayspring from on high has visited us;
> To give light to those who sit in darkness and the shadow of death,
> To guide our feet into the way of peace. (Luke 1:76-79)

What Do We Learn from This Prequel?

From the lives of Zacharias, Elizabeth, and John, then, we learn that we should be humble, wait on the Lord, and serve Him right where we are. We also learn that we should keep praying and not give up, because our prayers are heard in heaven. God takes note of them and will certainly answer them in His perfect time (and sometimes in totally unpredictable ways). We should also remember to believe what God tells us and act in faith rather than trusting our feelings or our own weak wisdom. And just as John was filled with the Holy Spirit from the womb, so we should submit to the daily filling of the Spirit, living our lives within His power and under His direction.

Sometimes when we look back at people in the pages of the Bible, we imagine them to be like stained-glass images, or that they walked around with halos over their heads. But that isn't correct. There is only one perfect Person who walked this earth, and that is Jesus. Everybody else was flawed. Mary and Joseph were flawed. Zacharias and Elizabeth were flawed. Even John the Baptist had his season of doubt late in life, when times were dark and he was discouraged in heart. Everyone—including Bible characters—has human weaknesses. It's important that we understand that these were people just like us.

Again, Jesus said of John, "Among those born of women there is not a greater prophet than John the Baptist; but he who is least in the kingdom of God is greater than he" (Luke 7:28).

What? Greater than John? How could you and I ever be "greater" than he?

It's all about the covenants under which we live. John lived in the days of the Old Covenant, and we live in the New Covenant. John (and everyone else in that day) approached God through a human high priest, who would enter the Holy of Holies once a year. We can approach God through our High Priest Jesus at any time, any moment, 24/7.

Because of God's Son being born in a manger, living a perfect life, willingly going to the cross for our sins, and rising from the dead, life is radically different for those who have placed their faith in Him and belong to Him. We can actually experience Jesus taking up residence inside us, in the very center of our being.

John didn't have Christ living within him. But as Christians, we do.

The only thing better than that is to actually be with Christ in heaven, and we have that to look forward to as well.

CHAPTER TWO

CHRISTMAS: THE BIG ANNOUNCEMENT

I n a seedy little town known for sin and corruption, a teenaged girl had a most unexpected visitor.

The mighty angel Gabriel, who no doubt could have taken on the whole Roman army single-handedly, appeared to a maiden named Mary in the town of Nazareth. As surprising and awesome as his appearance must surely have been, his message to this girl was more amazing still. He told her she was to have the privilege of being the mother of Israel's Messiah, who would be the Savior of the entire world.

In contrast to Zacharias, who initially doubted Gabriel's words, Mary believed at once. Here is how Dr. Luke, who gave years of his life to chronicle the life and times of Jesus, recorded that moment:

> Now in the sixth month the angel Gabriel was sent by God to a city of Galilee named Nazareth, to a virgin betrothed to a man whose name was Joseph, of the house of David. The virgin's name was Mary. And having come in, the angel said to her, "Rejoice, highly favored one, the Lord is with you; blessed are you among women!"

> But when she saw him, she was troubled at his saying, and considered what manner of greeting this was. Then the angel said to her, "Do not be afraid, Mary, for you have found favor with God. And behold, you will conceive in your womb and bring forth a Son, and shall call His name Jesus. He will be great, and will be called the Son of the Highest; and the Lord God will give Him the throne of His father David. And He will reign over the house of Jacob forever, and of His kingdom there will be no end."

Then Mary said to the angel, "How can this be, since I do not know a man?"

And the angel answered and said to her, "The Holy Spirit will come upon you, and the power of the Highest will overshadow you; therefore, also, that Holy One who is to be born will be called the Son of God. Now indeed, Elizabeth your relative has also conceived a son in her old age; and this is now the sixth month for her who was called barren. For with God nothing will be impossible."

Then Mary said, "Behold the maidservant of the Lord! Let it be to me according to your word." And the angel departed from her. (Luke 1:26-38)

Let's take a closer look at this amazing story in all of its simplicity and glory. Here are a few points to consider.

Mary Lived a Godly Life in an Ungodly Place

This was not the first time a holy angel from heaven was dispatched to a godless city. In the book of Genesis, angels were sent into Sodom to deliver Lot and his family from the destruction that was coming. Sodom and Gomorrah were known as wicked cities in their day, and Nazareth was also known for its sin.

Have you noticed how certain cities have certain nicknames? Rome is called the Eternal City. Paris is called the City of Lights. New York is known as the City that Never Sleeps. And Vegas? Well, "What happens in Vegas stays in Vegas." (But of course it really doesn't.) Nazareth in the first century could have been called Sin City, overrun as it was with Roman soldiers.

Nazareth was one of those towns you go through to get to somewhere else. It was definitely no destination resort. One commentator described it as "a hotbed of corruption." This explains why Nathanael, on hearing that Jesus came from Nazareth, responded in surprise, saying, "Can anything good come out of Nazareth?" (John 1:46).

Let's imagine Jesus was born on earth today, instead of over two thousand years ago. Where would you expect Him to be born? Jerusalem? Maybe in Rome or London or Paris? How about New York City, Boston, or Los Angeles? What if you heard that Jesus had entered this world in Disappointment, Kentucky? That is an actual town. Who would want to live in a place like that? Or what if the Messiah had grown up in Frog Eye, Alabama, or Bald Knob, Arkansas? What would it have been like if He had lived most of His years in San Francisco or Las Vegas? *"The Savior has arrived! Jesus of Las Vegas!"*

Do you see how changing the place changes the way you view the event?

That's what it would have been like for people in much of Israel to hear about "Jesus of Nazareth."

Nevertheless, that is where Mary lived and where she had most likely grown up. She was Mary of Nazareth. Here was a young woman with royal blood in her veins, with a lineage that went back to King David, and she lived in a corrupt, sinful city. Living in an impure environment, she stayed pure. Mary showed that it is possible to live a holy life in an unholy place.

In his second letter, the apostle Peter described the influence of the world on two prominent Old Testament believers: The first was Noah, and the second was Lot. Noah lived an uncompromised life at a place and time where "every inclination of the thoughts of the human heart was only evil all the time. . . . But Noah found favor in the eyes of the LORD. . . . Noah was a righteous man, blameless among the people of his time, and he walked faithfully with God" (Genesis 6:5,8-9, NIV). The world at that time was like an overflowing septic tank. Yet Noah faithfully served the Lord in the midst of that godless, cynical culture. He raised his family as believers, he preached to others, and he maintained a walk of integrity and a close personal relationship with God.

The second man Peter mentioned is Lot, Abraham's nephew, who ended up living with his family in the utterly corrupt city of Sodom. Interestingly, the Bible tells us that although Lot lived in that wicked place, he wasn't comfortable with it. He didn't like it. Peter wrote, "But God also rescued Lot out of Sodom because he was a righteous man who was sick of the shameful immorality of the wicked people around him. Yes, Lot was a righteous man who was tormented in his soul by the wickedness he saw and heard day after day" (2 Peter 2:7-8, NLT).

But even though Lot knew he ought to get his family out of that evil place, he hesitated and was reluctant to leave. Finally God sent a couple of angels to take Lot, his wife, and two daughters by the hands and effectively drag them out of the city. When it came right down to it, they didn't want to go; it was like pulling a kid out of a candy store. Tragically, Lot's testimony had become so weak and ineffective that when he tried to warn his sons-in-law about God's approaching judgment, they laughed right in his face.

There is no power in a compromised life. Compromised people reach no one. Lot eventually escaped the destruction of Sodom and Gomorrah, but his family was ruined in the process.

Here is the question for each of us as we consider the lives of Mary in Nazareth, Noah in a wicked and violent world, and Lot in a corrupt city: *Are you changing your culture, or is your culture changing you?* Are you a thermometer or a thermostat? A thermometer is affected by its surroundings; its mercury goes up or down according to the temperature. A thermostat, however, changes the temperature of a room. Which are you? Do you merely react to what is happening around you, or are you actually making an impact on your surroundings?

Lot was a thermometer. He may not have liked the temperature, but he couldn't or didn't do anything about it. Noah and Mary were thermostats and stood in contrast to their cultures. You and I may sometimes blame our wicked culture for the way we are, but in reality it is our task as followers of Jesus Christ to permeate and affect our culture.

When a Christian walks into a room, the atmosphere should change. In some sense, people in the room should be aware that a follower of Christ has just come in the door. It should affect the conversation. I don't mean that you should come across as overly pious or self-righteous, looking down your nose at people. But if you are walking with Jesus Christ and are filled with His Spirit, you will definitely bring His Presence into whatever room you enter.

Mary was a godly young woman living in an ungodly place. How young was she? Commentators say she may have been as young as twelve and was probably no older than fourteen. Had she been like many other teens of her time, she might have married a poor man, given birth to numerous poor children, never traveled more than a few miles from her home, and died without the world ever knowing her name. Nevertheless, God chose her, and that made all the difference in her life. Even though she was a "nobody" living in a nothing town in the middle of nowhere, God said, "This is the woman I choose for the highest honor of all."

This is a good reminder to us that God uses nobodies to tell everybody about Somebody. God can use you where you are, *whoever* you are.

Mary was handpicked to fulfill a landmark Old Testament prophecy. Isaiah 7:14 says, "Therefore the Lord Himself will give you a sign: Behold, the virgin shall conceive and bear a Son, and shall call His name Immanuel."

As a good Jewish girl, Mary would have known this Scripture from her earliest days. I imagine that in her wildest dreams she would never have dreamed she would be the one actually spoken of in this prophecy. "Who, *me*? I'm going to be the mother of the Messiah? I'm going to carry the Son of God in my womb?"

When that truth finally dawned on her, it must have blown her away.

We read in Luke 1:28, "Having come in, the angel said to her, 'Rejoice, highly favored one, the Lord is with you; blessed are you among women!'" The phrase "come in" implies that Mary was in the house alone. She was probably doing the domestic chores of a twelve-to-thirteen-year-old Jewish girl.

In the King James Version, Gabriel says, "Hail." That does not mean he was offering worship or praise to her. "Hail" is simply old English for "Hi" or "Hello." In Hawaii you say, "Howzit, Bra." If you are in Australia you say, "G' day." If you are in New York or Philadelphia you say, "Yo!"

In other words, it was just a simple greeting, and we shouldn't read anything else into it. Suddenly, an immensely powerful angel was standing in a humble little house in Nazareth, saying, "Hey, Mary. Good morning. You are a very privileged girl. God has extended His hand of grace to you."

And she would need that grace!

In fact, Mary was startled by that appearance and that greeting, just as you or I would have been. One translation says, "She was thoroughly shaken, wondering what was behind a greeting like that" (Luke 1:29, MSG).

As we have noted, seeing any angel of God would drop most of us to our knees, and Gabriel was no ordinary angel. Not by a long shot!

Five Quick Facts About the Messenger

1. Gabriel is mentioned in both the Old and New Testaments.

This mighty angel first appears in the book of Daniel, where he speaks to the prophet about the coming Messiah. It seems that Gabriel's ministry is specifically tied to telling people about Jesus. When he appeared to Daniel, he came with a greeting similar to what he said to Mary. In Daniel 9:23, Gabriel said, "I have come to tell you, for you are greatly beloved."

2. Gabriel stands in the presence of the Lord.

This is how he described himself when he came to Zacharias, who was to be the father of John the Baptist. When the old man expressed doubt about the angel's words, Gabriel replied, "I am Gabriel. I stand in the presence of God" (Luke 1:19, NIV). In other words, this powerful being has immediate access to the Almighty Himself.

3. Gabriel is one of two angels mentioned by name in the Bible.

The other named angel is Michael, the Archangel. Is Gabriel an archangel, too? The Bible doesn't say. Clearly, he is (to this day) a high-ranking angel. Lucifer, "the son of the morning," was also once a holy, powerful angel but lost his place of privilege when he fell and became Satan, or the devil.

4. Gabriel looks like a man.

In fact, the name Gabriel means "man of God." In Daniel's second encounter with Gabriel, the prophet described him as a man. All of this to say, there are no female angels in the Bible. In spite of this fact, however, we usually use the term *angel* in a feminine way. We will say, "She is an angel." When we see angels portrayed in paintings or cartoons, they're often depicted as being women. I know it's a disappointment, but "chick angels" don't exist—at least in the Bible. Angels always appear as men.

5. Gabriel scares people because he is so awesome and powerful.

His first words to Zacharias were, "Don't be afraid." The prophet Daniel related an encounter with Gabriel by saying, "He came up to me, but when he got close I became terrified and fell facedown on the ground" (Daniel 8:17, MSG). In the Luke passage, we read that Mary "was greatly troubled at his words and wondered what kind of greeting this might be" (Luke 1:29, NIV).

Was it the angel's appearance or his message that left her so stunned? Have you ever received a message that left you absolutely stunned? Maybe it was good news or maybe it was bad news, but for a few seconds, you couldn't speak or move. That was the case with Mary in her little home in Nazareth.

Mary Was Surprised at Being Selected

Mary was honestly surprised that God had selected her and not someone else. There was no sense of "I deserve this recognition" or "It's about time! I've earned this!" No, she was completely overwhelmed that the Lord would confer such a privilege on her.

That's the way it is with godly people. When people are truly close to the Lord, you won't hear them boasting about their devotion or trying to draw attention to themselves. You won't hear them talking about what they have done for God; they will always speak of what God has done for them—how kind, merciful, and gracious God has been to them.

This is why John, in his gospel, described himself as "the disciple whom Jesus loved." Does that sound a little self-serving, like John was bragging about being someone Jesus was especially attached to? Not really. And isn't it better than saying, "I am the disciple who loved Jesus"? John was showing his humility with these words. He was saying, in effect, "My love is fickle. My love can vary with the circumstances. But the love of Jesus is constant and never changes. He loves me and He always will!"

John boasted about God's love for him, rather than his love for God.

By the way, this is also the mark of a good testimony—your story of how you came to Christ. Such a testimony will always focus on what Christ gave up to save you, not on what you gave up to follow Him. I've heard people's testimonies that make it sound like their past was more interesting than their present and future. They will say things like, "Well, I used to party and have lots of fun doing wild and crazy things. Then I heard about Jesus and took up the old rugged cross. Now I just read my Bible all day. One day I'll die and go to heaven where I will float around and play a harp."

Really?

Who will be drawn to Christ by words like those? Don't focus on the past you walked away from, focus on the life God has given you today and what He has promised concerning your future. Focus on what God has done for you.

Though Mary was a virtuous woman and a godly woman, she was not a sinless woman. Mary was a sinner just like us. Was she privileged, set apart, and called by God? Yes! But she was also a sinful, fallen human being. In her beautiful song of praise in Luke chapter 1, she began by saying, "My soul magnifies the Lord, and my spirit has rejoiced in God my Savior" (verses 46-47).

Even Mary needed a Savior. Perhaps that was part of her surprise in being selected for such an unbelievable task and privilege. She may not have felt worthy for an honor like that. But who would?

In Luke 1:31-33, Gabriel went on to describe the Child whom Mary would bear:

> *And behold, you will conceive in your womb and bring forth a Son, and shall call His name Jesus. He will be great, and will be called the Son of the Highest; and the Lord God will give Him the throne of His father David. And He will reign over the house of Jacob forever, and of His kingdom there will be no end.*

At that time, "Jesus" was a common name. Many young boys of that era were named Jesus. In Hebrew, it's the name *Joshua*, which means "Jehovah is salvation." But of all the boys and men who were ever called Jesus or Joshua, only one could embody the full meaning of that name, and that is Jesus the Christ.

Gabriel said, "He will be great." The word *great* in the original language comes from the root word *megas*, from which we draw our English word *mega*. We use it in terms like megaphone, mega-church, and mega-store. It conveys the idea of bigness or greatness, and if ever that word applied to anyone, it applies to Jesus. He is great, and the very definition of the word great. People in our culture may belittle His name, scoff at His name, slander His name, or drag His name through the mud. But one day every knee in the universe will bow before that name, acknowledging Him as King of kings and Lord of lords.

Also notice that in verse 32 Gabriel said God "will give Him the throne of His father David." I find that fascinating. David is such a unique figure in Scripture. He is described on one hand as the "sweet psalmist of Israel" and the "man after His [God's] own heart" (2 Samuel 23:1; 1 Samuel 13:14). But we also know of his foibles, shortcomings, and sins.

Two other names connected to David serve well to sum up his whole life: David and Goliath, and David and Bathsheba. In Goliath we recall David's greatest victory, defeating a nine-foot-six-inch Philistine warrior with only a slingshot and a stone. With Bathsheba, David suffered his most profound defeat when he pursued this married woman, had an affair with her, and orchestrated the murder of her husband—who happened to be one of David's most loyal soldiers.

David was a flawed man, and yet Jesus was called "the Root and the Offspring of David" (Revelation 22:16) and "the Son of David." In spite of David's failings, the Lord allowed Himself to be intimately connected with him.

If you imagine that you have a dysfunctional family, take a look at Jesus' family tree!

I was talking to my friend Bob Shank the other day about family trees, and he made this observation: "Someone warned me about not examining the Shank family tree too closely, because I might find a few Shanks hanging from that tree!"

It's true for most of us. We may want to go back and look into our ancestors and our heritage, but we might not like all that we find there. We all want to think we are connected to royalty or some great American historical figure, but we might also unearth a few swindlers and a murderer or two.

It's the same in the Lord's family tree. There are some unsavory characters who made it into the most exclusive genealogy in human history—including prostitutes, liars, cheats, adulterers, and even a murderer.

What does this say to us?

It all points to one thing: Christ came into the world to save sinners. He Himself was sinless, but He was born into a long family line of flawed, sinful, broken people. David committed some terrible sins, yet Jesus, throughout His ministry, was known as "the Son of David."

"How Shall This Be … ?"

Mary's question to Gabriel was both natural and appropriate. In Luke 1:34 (NIV) she said, "How will this be, . . .since I am a virgin?"

This is different question altogether than the doubting response Zacharias gave to the angel. When Gabriel told the old priest that he and Elizabeth were going to have a son, his response was more like, "No, I don't think so. She's too old and so am I. It's not going to happen."

Mary, however, wasn't disbelieving. She was more interested in how God was going to pull this off, since she was a virgin and had never had sexual relations with a man. Gabriel wasn't offended by the question at all, and gave her this beautiful reply: "The Holy Spirit will come upon you, and the power of the Highest will overshadow you; therefore, also, that Holy One who is to be born will be called the Son of God" (Luke 1:35).

We don't know how this actually happened, or how long it took for this amazing event to transpire. But we can sum it up by saying that Mary's womb became the Holy of Holies for the Son of God.

As a man, I'm not sure I understand this at all. But women who have been mothers know what it's like to carry a child in their womb. There is a connection between mother and child that a father can never fully know. But just imagine not only carrying a child within you, but understanding that this Baby was God incarnate.

Incredible? Incomprehensible? Perhaps. But completely true.

Mary Was Completely Obedient

Mary answered the angel, "Behold the maidservant of the Lord! Let it be to me according to your word" (Luke 1:38).

Have you ever said something similar to God?

"Lord, let it be to me according to Your Word."

Even though Mary didn't begin to understand everything these developments meant for her, she was fully obedient and submissive to the Lord. This is the kind of attitude God looks for in His servants: a childlike faith and obedience.

Since they were very little, my grandchildren have been fully willing to jump into my arms. If I ask them to jump, they will jump. I remember when little Christopher was just over a year old. He couldn't even talk yet, but he understood about jumping. I would say, "Okay, Christopher. Ready? One, two, three, *jump.*" And he would just let himself fall. If I hadn't been there to catch him, there would have been trouble. But I was always there to catch him, and he knew that. He completely depended on my being there for him. He demonstrated a complete acceptance that I loved him and wouldn't let any harm come to him.

But what's our response when God says, "Jump"?

Do we fall into His arms, or do we hesitate and hold back? Do we leap into the dark, or do we say, "I'm afraid! What if You drop me?"

And God replies, "I won't drop you. Jump! Come on, just go for it. I will be with you."

That's what Mary did. When God said, "jump," she simply fell into His strong arms. As Corrie ten Boom has said, "Never be afraid to trust an unknown future to a known God."

Many times you and I will wonder about the will of God for our lives. Let me suggest this: *Obedience to revealed truth guarantees guidance in matters unrevealed.* The wind of God is always blowing, but you need to hoist your sail. I would suggest that you simply say, "Lord, I'm willing to obey, even though I don't completely understand what it is You're asking me to do."

In Romans 12:1-2 (NIV), the apostle Paul gave us clear directions on how to know God's will.

> *Therefore, I urge you, brothers and sisters, in view of God's mercy, to offer your bodies as a living sacrifice, holy and pleasing to God—this is your true and proper worship. Do not conform to the pattern of this world, but be transformed by the renewing of your mind. Then you will be able to test and approve what God's will is—his good, pleasing and perfect will.*

Notice that the passage starts out with offering yourself to God. It doesn't say to find out God's will first and then determine if you want to obey it. It says to commit yourself to the Lord. Present yourself as a living sacrifice—and don't let yourself be transformed by the world. Another translation puts it like this: "Don't let the world around you squeeze you into its own mould, but let God re-mould your minds from within, so that you may prove in practice that the plan of God for you is good, meets all his demands and moves towards the goal of true maturity" (PH).

First commit yourself unreservedly to Him, and then He will show you His will.

That's what Mary did. After the angel told her how her whole life would change forever, she said, "Behold the maidservant of the Lord! Let it be to me according to your word."

Even so, her head must have been swimming. Uppermost in her mind must have been, *How am I going to explain this to Joseph? When I tell him what really happened, he will never buy it!* "Um, Joseph . . .I'm pregnant, but it's not what you think. Listen, Joseph, an angel came and spoke to me. It turns out that I am the virgin spoken of in the book of Isaiah. I haven't been unfaithful, I have been chosen by God!"

At first, Joseph didn't buy it.

But God already had that base covered, and spoke to Joseph Himself.

The Unsung Hero

Joseph doesn't get nearly the credit he deserves in the Christmas story.

Matthew 1:19 assures us that he was a righteous man. No doubt he was deeply in love with Mary, his young bride-to-be, and was severely jolted by the news that she was with child. They were engaged at the time, which in that culture was like being married.

In the Hebrew culture of that day, you didn't get to decide whom you would marry, as we do today. Your parents decided, and that was that. Sometimes the two sets of parents would espouse a son to a daughter while the children were still very young. At eight years old, you might already know who your wife or husband would be. Once you entered into the twelve-month engagement or espousal period, this was like being already married, although the man and woman would live in separate houses, and there were no sexual relations involved at this point. The wedding ceremony would come at the end of the twelve months. This was the period in which Mary become pregnant, and her supposed offense was equivalent to being unfaithful after marriage.

Even so, Joseph loved this girl and was probably at his wits end knowing what to do about it. He didn't want to see her publicly shamed or put to death. Finally he concluded in his heart, "I'm going to have to put her away. I'm going to have to end our marriage—and do it as quietly as possible."

Joseph is really a hero in this story. No, there are few songs about him, and if he went missing from our nativity sets we might not even notice. And yet Joseph was chosen for his role as surely as Mary. God the Father in heaven chose Joseph to be a step-father or father figure on earth for Jesus.

You would have thought God would have selected a priest for that honor. But no, He chose a blue-color guy. A hard-working carpenter. And it was no mistake that Jesus grew up in a carpenter's home. Carpenters create new things and fix broken things, and these skills became part of Jesus' heritage. No doubt Joseph taught Jesus how to put his back into a task, how to be responsible, and how to put in a hard day's work.

The greatest crisis in his life, however, had to be those moments when Mary told him of her pregnancy and he was wrestling in his mind and heart, trying to figure out what in the world he should do. One night he fell asleep pondering these things and had an angelic encounter of his own. In Matthew 1:20-21 we read,

But while he thought about these things, behold, an angel of the Lord appeared to him in a dream, saying, "Joseph, son of David, do not be afraid to take to you Mary your wife, for that which is conceived in her is of the Holy Spirit. And she will bring forth a Son, and you shall call His name Jesus, for He will save His people from their sins."

That was all Joseph needed to hear. He was onboard with Mary and Jesus for the rest of his life.

It might not have been that way with someone else. A lesser man might have walked away, even after learning the truth. Do you imagine that the other carpenters at the worksite would accept the story of a virgin birth? Not a chance! Can you imagine Joseph showing up at work with his lunchbox, noticing the glances of his fellow workmen and hearing their whispered comments? He knew he would be laughed at. He knew they would never believe the truth. But Joseph squared his shoulders, set his jaw, and endured it all for the sake of his beloved Mary and her little Son, Jesus.

It was as though Mary had to go through life with a scarlet "A" (for adulteress) sewn on the front of her garment. Though she was pure and had lived a clean and devoted life, Mary had to go through her years with the reputation of a loose woman. Later in the Lord's ministry, some Pharisees threw the old rumors back in His face. They said, "We aren't illegitimate children! God himself is our true Father" (John 8:41, NLT).

This was equivalent to saying to Jesus, "Well, at least we weren't conceived out of wedlock *like You.*" But of course Jesus was not conceived out of wedlock or born of fornication. He was supernaturally conceived in Mary's womb. Even so, Joseph and Mary had to go through life with this slander—with all the attendant whispers and glances included—continually thrown in their faces. It was part of the price they paid for the great privilege that had come to them.

The fact is when God blesses a person, there is a price to pay.

When God uses a person, there is a sacrifice to be made.

When you say—and mean it with all your heart—"Let it be to me according to Your Word," don't imagine that it will put you on an easy path. It probably won't be easy at all, but it could be very, very fruitful. Later in life when you look back, you won't regret it.

The Virgin Birth Is Non-negotiable

How important is it to hold to and believe in the virgin birth of Jesus? Some would say, "You really don't need to believe in the virgin birth of Jesus to be a Christian. You need to simply believe in His death and resurrection."

And yet, of what *value* are the death and resurrection of Jesus if He wasn't supernaturally conceived? Because of the manner of this conception, Christ did not inherit a sinful nature. He was the sinless Son of God, who became "the Lamb of God who takes away the sin of the world!" (John 1:29). As the apostle Paul wrote, "God made him who had no sin to be sin for us, so that in him we might become the righteousness of God" (2 Corinthians 5:21, NIV).

If you doubt the virgin birth, you really have to doubt whether Christ could die for your sins and reconcile you with God. Without the virgin birth, there is no sinless Christ. Without a sinless Christ, there is no atonement. Without atonement, there is no forgiveness. Without forgiveness, there is no hope of heaven. Without a hope of heaven, there is really no hope at all in life. We might as well live for today and selfishly grab all the pleasure that we can.

If you doubt the virgin birth, you have to doubt the truthfulness of God's Word, because it plainly says that Jesus was born of a virgin.

If you doubt the virgin birth, you have to question the character of Mary. If her conception wasn't supernatural, then she was immoral, and Jesus was born out of wedlock.

If you doubt the virgin birth, you can't put any confidence in Christ Himself, because He is a mere man and no Savior at all.

In fact, the virgin birth is central to everything we believe.

Jesus was supernaturally conceived in Mary's womb, lived a perfect life, and died a horrific death on the cross, giving Himself for the sins of the world and then rising again after three days in the tomb.

As hard as it may be to wrap our minds around this truth, Jesus was born to die. The shadow of the cross hung over Him even in the cradle. When He was a little older, the magi from the East came to visit Him, bringing Him gifts of gold, frankincense, and myrrh. That last gift, myrrh, was an embalming element. It would be like giving someone a jar of formaldehyde for their birthday. Why would the wise men give the Christ child such a gift? Because they had insight into the fact that He had been born to die for the sins of humankind.

Looking into the eyes of an amazed and wondering Mary and Joseph in the temple, the old man Simeon held the infant Jesus in his arms and said, "This child is destined to cause the falling and rising of many in Israel, and to be a sign that will be spoken against, so that the thoughts of many hearts will be revealed. And a sword will pierce your own soul too" (Luke 2:34-35, NIV).

Jesus had come on a rescue mission from heaven to save us all from our sins.

"You can take joy in that," Simeon seems to have been saying, looking at Mary, "but He will pay a great price . . .and so will you."

CHAPTER THREE
THE MAN WHO TRIED TO STOP CHRISTMAS

Christmas, so we have assumed, is about love, peace, harmony, and the whole family gathered around a crackling fire sipping warm cocoa. That's the picture we've developed in our culture through the years, but that is not the true essence of Christmas. That's not what the real Christmas story is all about.

Christmas is actually about conflict.

It always has been, and it always will be.

The book of Revelation includes a startling passage (chapter 12) that depicts a pregnant woman being pursued by a powerful dragon, who seeks her death. As she prepares to give birth to the child, the dragon hovers over her, wanting to destroy the baby.

That is Christmas from a heavenly perspective. The woman in that picture is the nation of Israel, the child is the Lord Jesus Christ, and the dragon is Satan. That gives you a big picture of what was really happening when God sent His Son into the world. The devil opposed it, and wanted to stop it, at all costs.

This dynamic is still in play today. In fact, it's growing more fierce (and desperate) as time goes by. You can see this same spirit— this hostility to Christ and Christmas—sprouting up on all sides, and it escalates with each passing year. More nativity scenes are being removed from public places every year. Atheists have been emboldened to put up billboards around the country attacking the Christian faith. The city of Eugene, Oregon, banned Christmas trees in public spaces. This past year in Times Square, a giant, full-color display asked the question, "Who Needs Christ at Christmas?" It then proclaimed the answer: "Nobody!"

These are all symptoms of a trend that will grow more and more intense as we enter our planet's last days.

Mark this: Jesus did not come to bring a mind-numbing, self-indulgent "peace on earth" devoid of truth. Yes, we all remember what the angels declared to the shepherds keeping watch over their flocks on the night Christ was born: "Glory to God in the highest, and on earth peace, goodwill toward men!" (Luke 2:14).

But what does that mean? A better rendering of that passage would read, "Peace on earth, good will toward men among whom God is pleased." In other words, the only way we will have peace on earth is when men and women are pleasing to God.

Peace on earth? Read what Jesus said in Luke 12:51-53 (NLT):

> Do you think I have come to bring peace to the earth? No, I have come to divide people against each other! From now on families will be split apart, three in favor of me, and two against—or two in favor and three against. "Father will be divided against son and son against father; mother against daughter and daughter against mother; and mother-in-law against daughter-in-law and daughter-in-law against mother-in-law."

This may not sound much like a Christmas message, but it is actually better than a Christmas message. It is New Testament Christianity and its sharp division between light and darkness, good and evil, righteousness and unrighteousness.

What we are seeing played out in our culture with these renewed attacks on the name of Jesus and even the celebration of Christmas is in reality a battle of the gods: It is the God of the Bible, the true and living God, against "the prince of this world" (John 16:11, NIV).

So no, we shouldn't be surprised by the conflict we see around us.

What might surprise us is that it is through conflict that we find peace.

Someone may say, "What do you mean, Greg? Isn't that contradictory?"

No, not in the ultimate sense. Here is what I mean: If your family is like most families, it is be made up of both believers and nonbelievers. At times like Christmas, perhaps, you try to avoid subjects that might cause arguments or disagreements, but they inevitably come. Eventually, the topic of faith in Christ comes up, and some harsh words are spoken. Someone in your family might say something like this: "We liked you better the old way. You were a lot more fun when we all drank together and did the things we used to do. Now you're acting pious and holier-than-thou. You've ruined Christmas for the rest of us."

Does this sort of discussion lead to peace? It can!

It's like when someone walks into a room and flips on a light switch, changing the whole dynamic in the room. Some people might say, "Turn that off! We like it dark!" There is such a contrast between light and the gloominess of a dark room that some people would rather pull back into the dim shadows. Sometimes you don't even have to *say* anything to make them uncomfortable. Your very presence as a Christian offends and irritates them.

How do you respond? Just hold your ground and keep praying for the nonbelievers in your family, and don't be upset or disheartened by a little conflict. Those individuals, as they consider your life and contrast it with their own, may be closer to Christ than you would ever guess. The very conflict may eventually lead them into peace with God.

An Age-Old Struggle

This whole battle over Christmas in our culture has its roots all the way back at the beginning of history. After Satan caused the fall of Adam and Eve in the Garden, God spoke the very first messianic prophecy in the Bible. In Genesis 3:15 (TLB), He told the evil one, "From now on you and the woman will be enemies, as will your offspring and hers. You will strike his heel, but he will crush your head."

Through the years, Satan watched for that Coming One with hatred and fear. He wanted to stop the Christ from being born, because he knew the Messiah would be his doom.

Red is the color of Christmas—not because of red candles or a red-suited Santa or red ribbons around a package. Red is the color of Christmas because of the blood of Jesus Christ that would be poured out as the payment for our sins.

The red blood of Jesus tells the story of Satan's furious attempts to at first prevent the birth of Christ, and failing that, to maneuver for His death and destruction by the Roman overlords. Little did the devil realize that Christ's death and resurrection would be the very thing that would seal his doom.

Herod, Satan's Unwitting Ally

History might call him "Herod the Great," but a more accurate title might have been "Herod the Cruel," or maybe, "Herod the Paranoid." This puppet king of Israel reigned in Jerusalem during the births of John the Baptist and Jesus; a portion of his story unfolds in Matthew 2.

Herod was raised in a well-connected family and was destined for a life of ruthless politics and power brokering. At age twenty-five he was named the governor of Galilee, a very high position for such a young man. The Romans had high hopes that he would bring some calm and control over the Jews in that troubling province they called "Palestine."

In 40 BC, the Roman Senate gave Herod the title "King of the Jews," of which he was very proud. He became so attached to that image of himself that he couldn't bear any thought of a challenger to his throne, as we shall soon see.

This was a man who was addicted to power and known for his cold and heartless cruelty. Anyone he perceived as even a distant threat to his rule would be quickly eliminated. History tells us that this blood-stained ruler murdered his brother-in-law, his mother-in-law, two of his own sons, and his favorite wife (he had many). He murdered out of spite to stay in power. Human life meant nothing to him.

There have always been such power-hungry, bloodthirsty rulers in our world. In fact, Herod reminds me of the present-day dictator of North Korea, Kim Jong Un. He recently had his uncle murdered in a barbaric way and has killed many of that nation's citizens for imagined or trivial offenses. There is great persecution of the church of Jesus Christ in that troubled nation. Kim Jong Un is something like a modern-day Herod—with a nuclear arsenal.

The historian Josephus called Herod "barbaric." Another dubbed him the "malevolent maniac." On one occasion he had the most distinguished citizens of Israel arrested, giving orders that upon his death they should be executed. Why would he do such a thing? To guarantee that it would be a day of great mourning in Israel when he died.

Herod was also known to be a great builder. He saw himself as a miniature Caesar, building seven palaces and seven theaters. One of those theaters seated 9,500 people. He constructed stadiums for sporting events, built the beautiful port city of Caesarea, and created the stronghold of Masada. Herod's crowning achievement as a builder was the second temple in Jerusalem. This was the temple that was standing when Jesus was engaged in His public ministry. It took forty-six years to build and was one of the wonders of the ancient world.

Imagine then the shock the disciples felt when Jesus gestured toward that monumental temple and said, "Do you see all these things? . . . Truly I tell you, not one stone here will be left on another; every one will be thrown down" (Matthew 24:2, NIV).

And within just a few years, in AD 70, that prophecy was literally fulfilled.

At the time of Christ's birth, Herod the Great, the so-called King of the Jews, wasn't feeling "great" at all. In fact, he was slowly dying from a terrible disease. Historians tell us that his body was wracked by convulsions, that his skin was covered with open sores, and that he was rapidly losing his mind. Nevertheless, he was still king! And in that day and time, being king counted for a great deal.

It was at this troubled time in Herod's life that word came to him of a party of foreign dignitaries who had come into town from the distant East. This is where Matthew picks up the story.

"Where Is He . . . ?"

Now after Jesus was born in Bethlehem of Judea in the days of Herod the king, behold, wise men from the East came to Jerusalem, saying, "Where is He who has been born King of the Jews? For we have seen His star in the East and have come to worship Him."

When Herod the king heard this, he was troubled, and all Jerusalem with him. And when he had gathered all the chief priests and scribes of the people together, he inquired of them where the Christ was to be born.

So they said to him, "In Bethlehem of Judea, for thus it is written by the prophet:

'But you, Bethlehem, in the land of Judah,
Are not the least among the rulers of Judah;
For out of you shall come a Ruler
Who will shepherd My people Israel.'"

Then Herod, when he had secretly called the wise men, determined from them what time the star appeared. And he sent them to Bethlehem and said, "Go and search carefully for the young Child, and when you have found Him, bring back word to me, that I may come and worship Him also." (Matthew 2:1-8)

We draw so much of what we think we know about these wise men or magi from popular Christmas traditions. Storytellers have given them names, a song, matching outfits, camels, and a precise number: three. We don't know how many there were. It may have been nine or nineteen. These men were essentially astrologers or wizards. They studied the heavens and then gave advice to their kings and rulers about what to do and which course to follow. In that sense, they were influential, highly respected, and very powerful. We call them "kings of the East," but in actuality they were more like the king makers. They influenced the king.

When they came into town they were more than likely astride powerful Arabian horses (and certainly not camels). With their strange Eastern garb and tall conical hats, they would certainly have created a stir in Jerusalem. You didn't see guys like *that* ride into town every day.

If the appearance of these wise men created a stir, their repeated question created an even greater one. *"Where is He who has been born King of the Jews?"* Clearly, they weren't talking about Herod.

For his part, the highly paranoid Herod had his spies everywhere. The words "King of the Jews" must have struck him like a slap on the face. Why hadn't he been informed of this potential threat to his throne? That's why verse 3 reads, "When Herod the king heard this, he was troubled, and all Jerusalem with him." The word translated "troubled" here could also be rendered "to shake violently." Have you ever been around a washing machine when it gets out of balance and starts thumping loudly and lurching around? That was Herod in that moment. He was agitated, and in consequence, everyone was agitated. It's like that old expression, "When Mama ain't happy, ain't nobody happy."

When Herod was angry, people around him were afraid. For very good reason. They knew that heads were going to roll.

All of this may have given the dying, reprobate king a surge of new life. Now he had something to get up for in the morning. Something to work on. Something to do. With a potential threat to his throne out there, he had another person to find and kill. This time, it happened to be a baby.

The first people Herod called in were the clergy, the Jewish scribes and teachers who had made it their business to know the Scriptures. "Do you guys know anything in the Bible about some King being born around here?"

What amazes me is that without missing a beat, they zeroed in on the right verse, Micah 5:2: "But you, Bethlehem Ephrathah, though you are little among the thousands of Judah, yet out of you shall come forth to Me the One to be Ruler in Israel, whose goings forth are from of old, from everlasting."

There was no question. The Messiah would be born in Bethlehem. Animated then not only by his own hatred and paranoia, but also most likely driven by Satan himself, Herod set out to destroy the Child before He could become a threat.

It's interesting to me to think about these magi. These were pagan men, steeped in the occult, yet God came to them in a way they could readily understand: *through a special star*. In contrast, God sent angels to the shepherds out in the fields. They were good Jewish boys who believed in Scripture and knew about angels.

God reaches out to people in a million different ways, touching them and speaking to them in ways they understand. As the Lord told Jeremiah, "You will seek me and find me when you seek me with all your heart. I will be found by you" (Jeremiah 29:13-14, NIV). I believe that if a person is truly seeking God, no matter where they may be in this world, God will (somehow) reveal Himself to them. He will come to them in a way that they understand. The way He touches the heart of a little child will not be the same way He moves in the soul of a teenager or creates a longing in the heart of a scientist.

He knows how to bring people to Himself. And sometimes, He even gives the privilege of touching someone's heart through you or me.

I'd like to add a note regarding the gifts that the wise men brought to the Christ child. First, I'd like to point out that the gifts weren't wrapped. That's because these guys were *wise* men . . . and wise *men*. Most men I know don't like to wrap gifts. When I buy a gift for someone, the first question out of my mouth is, "Will you wrap this for me?" My son Christopher, however, was one of the best gift wrappers I have ever seen. He was meticulous, even to the point of creating hand-drawn wrapping paper and hand-drawn cards. So at least some men through the years have had this skill.

The wise men brought amazing gifts to the Child, including gold, frankincense, and myrrh. Each of the gifts spoke to an aspect of who this Child was, and who He would become. They brought Him gold because He is a King. They brought Him incense because He would be our High Priest. And they brought Him myrrh, an embalming element, because He was destined to die for the sins of the world.

The wise men presented their gifts to a Child, not to a Baby, and they came to a house, not a stable. This was obviously a few months—even up to a couple of years—after the birth of our Lord.

God spoke to the wise men in a dream, warning them not to go back home through Jerusalem, and certainly not to return to the evil Herod with information about the Child. Of course Herod was furious when he found out about it. And that is when "the butcher of Bethlehem" gave the order that all baby boys two years old or under living in the vicinity should be put to death.

Herod will have much to answer for when he stands before his Creator.

Let's take a moment to consider three primary characters in this story. I think you will find yourself in one of the following three categories.

Three Categories of Response

Herod

This is the man who tried to stop Christmas from ever taking place. In spite of all his wealth, power, influence, title, and strategic connections, he came to complete ruin. In the final years of his life his body was wasted by disease, with pain so great that he would scream through the night. In *Antiquities*, his book of history, Josephus wrote that the wicked king died of "ulcerated entrails" with "putrefied and maggot-filled organs." He also suffered from "constant convulsions that neither physicians nor warm baths could heal."

Herod ended up in the Dumpster of history, like dictators before and after him. It reminds us of other dictators on the world scene who fell from great power to a debased and disgraceful end. Hitler went down into his bunker and shot himself as his Third Reich crumbled around him. Saddam Hussein was found hiding in a hole and was eventually hanged by his own people. Muammar Gaddafi was hunted down by his own people, beaten, and then shot to death. These cruel and evil rulers who lived such wicked lives eventually reaped what they had sown. They may blaspheme God, persecute His people, or try to stop the work of God for a while, but they will eventually fail. God's Word will ultimately prevail. One day everyone who has ever lived will have to bow the knee before Jesus Christ and acknowledge Him as Lord.

Herod wanted to be a big man, but he was really only a slave to his own corruption. He wanted to be known as "King of the Jews," but he became the king of fools.

Ironically, Herod pretended to be a worshipper. In Matthew 2:8 he told the magi, "Go and search carefully for the young Child, and when you have found Him, bring back word to me, that I may come and worship Him also." Obviously, it was just talk. He had no intention of doing anything of the kind. There are people like him today, who say they believe in God but live lives that are a contradiction to everything the Scriptures teach. Jesus said, "Why do you call me 'Lord, Lord,' and do not do what I say?" (Luke 6:46, NIV).

Religious scholars and scribes

These men should have known better. They knew the Scriptures inside and out and were the top theological scholars of their day. It was a scribe's job to study the Scriptures and number the letters and the lines to ensure careful copying. Herod was right in expecting them to have an answer about where the Messiah would be born. And they knew the answer immediately.

Their response really puzzles me. They believed in God. They believed in the Scriptures. They knew what the prophet Micah said about where the Messiah would be born. They too had seen the mysterious visitors from the East, who spoke of a star and a newborn King. Bethlehem was only about five miles from Jerusalem, a little more than an hour's walk.

Why didn't they go to see for themselves?

Was it all just dry and academic to them? Didn't they have any desire to see the One who could very well be Israel's Messiah?

Apparently not.

I think it was because they didn't care about a baby King; they wanted an adult monarch who could line their pockets with gold. It's not that they hated Jesus or saw Him as a threat. *They simply didn't care about Him.* They couldn't be bothered. They were too busy and wrapped up in their own little worlds to trouble themselves over such things. They were "religious," but their hearts were ice-cold toward God.

As strange as it may sound, the biggest thing that will keep many people away from Christ is religion. When someone speaks to them about a relationship with the Lord, they say, "I already know that. I've already heard that. Don't waste your time."

Participating in the externals of religion without a living, vital relationship with Jesus can actually dull the spiritual senses to the Word of God and the voice of the Holy Spirit.

One sure way to get sleepy, of course, is to eat a lot of food. On Thanksgiving Day, for instance, we eat all that turkey and then go into a collective coma. Then we wake up and head for the kitchen to make turkey sandwiches! Sometimes it's like that when people are in a good Bible-teaching church, hear the truth over and over again, never put that truth into action, and then fall into complacency. If we're not careful, if we don't take pains to stay alert, we can find ourselves spiritually asleep.

The New Testament warns us against the dangers of this spiritual drowsiness and apathy. In the book of Ephesians we read, "Wake up, sleeper, rise from the dead, and Christ will shine on you" (5:14, NIV). Believers can fall asleep just like the religious scholars and scribes did in Jesus' day—even to the point of knowing the truth, but not really caring anything about it. They missed out on one of the greatest events in all of history. We can act in the same way if we "celebrate" the birth of Christ but never give our relationship with Him a passing thought.

Wise men

As we've mentioned, these men were occultists. But God reached into their dark world with a star to bring them to their Creator. These were followers of the stars who met the Lord Jesus Christ who created the stars. Matthew 2:2 says, "We have seen His star in the East and have come to worship Him." And that's exactly what they did. Verse 11 says, "When they had come into the house, they saw the young Child with Mary His mother, and fell down and worshiped Him."

Everyone worships something at Christmas. It doesn't matter if they are Christians, atheists, skeptics, lawyers, or college professors. It may not be God they are worshiping, but they *are* worshiping.

Some people worship material things, which they never seem to have enough of. Others worship pleasure. Still others worship their own bodies. Some might even worship their families. Another might worship some god of his own making.

Everyone worships at Christmas. The wise men showed themselves to be very wise indeed by worshiping Jesus Christ.

What does it mean to worship God? Christians toss that word around a lot. The word comes from the old English term "worth-ship." It means to ascribe worth or value to something or somebody. A god of our own making, however, isn't worthy of our worship. All of these lesser gods in our lives will eventually disappoint us and let us down. But the true and living God is worthy of our praise.

Two words are often used in Scripture to define worship. One means "to bow down and do homage," which speaks of reverence and respect. Another word, however, means "to kiss toward," which speaks of intimacy and friendship. Obviously, we would never kiss a stranger (unless we wanted to get slugged in the face). We would only kiss someone we are very close to. This is why it was such a despicable act for Judas to betray our Lord with a kiss. He turned what seemed to be an act of reverence and worship into a cruel, deceitful thing.

We come into God's presence and we stand in awe of Him. We respect and reverence Him, and at the same time there is a closeness and intimacy because of what Jesus has done to bring us into relationship with the Father.

As Paul wrote in Galatians, "But when the set time had fully come, God sent his Son, born of a woman, born under the law, to redeem those under the law, that we might receive adoption to sonship. Because you are his sons, God sent the Spirit of his Son into our hearts, the Spirit who calls out, 'Abba, Father'" (4:4-6, NIV).

How can we worship? One way, of course, is to sing His praises right out loud. It's not the only way to worship, but it's certainly an important one. In fact, worshiping in song is something we will do both on earth and in heaven. Revelation 5:9,12 (NLT) says of the residents of heaven that "they sang a new song," and "they sang in a mighty chorus."

And what was the song they sang, angels singing right alongside redeemed men and women?

Worthy is the Lamb, who was slain,
to receive power and wealth and wisdom and strength
and honor and glory and praise! (verse 12, NIV)

The fact is, however, we don't always *feel* like worshiping, do we? This is why the book of Hebrews speaks of bringing a "sacrifice of praise" to the Lord (13:15). We should praise the Lord simply because He deserves it. The Bible doesn't say, "Give thanks unto the Lord because you feel good." It says, "Oh, give thanks to the LORD, for He is good!" (Psalm 106:1). I praise Him because it is the right thing to do—not because I happen to feel in the mood.

When was the last time you said words like these to God? "Lord, I love You. I recognize all You have done for me, and I thank You." If you love someone, you need to tell them.

Of course there are other ways to worship as well. Serving others can be an act of worship. One of the ways the word *worship* is translated in Scripture carries the meaning of serving and ministering to others. In our Lord's encounter with the devil in the wilderness, one of His replies to Satan was, "You shall worship the LORD your God, and Him only you shall serve" (Matthew 4:10). Why did Jesus say that? Because He understood that worship *leads* to service. Inevitably, you will serve whatever it is you worship. As you make it a practice to worship God with all your heart, you will find yourself looking for opportunities to serve Him. Hebrews 13:16 (NLT) reminds us, "Don't forget to do good and to share with those in need. These are the sacrifices that please God."

Sometimes the simplest tasks done for others with Christ in mind become an act of worship to the Lord. I remember being in the home of Billy and Ruth Graham a number of years ago and noticing a sign that Ruth had placed over the kitchen sink. It read: "Divine service done here three times a day." If you want more joy in your life this Christmas season, that's something to keep in mind:

You are serving and worshiping the King as you extend a helping hand to those in need.

I think what we really long for at Christmas isn't the holiday, but it is Christ Himself. The fact is, you and I were designed by God to know Him and be with Him and walk with Him. You were designed—prewired when you emerged from the womb—to worship.

Let's do that with our songs, with our words of praise, and with willing hands that help and serve others for the sake of the King.

CHAPTER FOUR
THE GREATEST STORY EVER TOLD

A newspaper article reported on a scientific survey that asked, "Who was the most important and influential person in all of human history?" Ten names surfaced in the survey, and according to this poll, the number one person in human history was (and is) Jesus Christ.

It makes sense, doesn't it?

But do we really need a poll to tell us that? It's simply stating the obvious.

Years ago, John Lennon was quoted as saying that the Beatles were more popular than Jesus Christ. But who, dear John, is more popular now? Jesus remains the most influential person of all time, to this very day.

Why is that?

What is it about the Galilean carpenter that so fascinates and mystifies people? He was the most extraordinary, influential, and, yes, even revolutionary individual to ever stride the stage of human history. More books have been written about Jesus than any other man who has ever lived. More music has been composed about Christ than any man or woman throughout time. More dramas have been staged about Jesus than anyone who ever breathed the air of planet Earth.

Why is this?

Why does one Man occupy such a unique and unforgettable place in human history?

By the way, the nine other names in the "most influential" survey, in order, were:

2. Napoleon Bonaparte
3. William Shakespeare
4. Mohammed
5. Abraham Lincoln
6. George Washington

7. Adolf Hitler
8. Aristotle
9. Alexander the Great
10. Thomas Jefferson

But none of these other men—significant, famous, or infamous as they may be—even hold a candle to Jesus Christ. Why is this? Because Jesus wasn't merely a good Man, a great Man, or even the greatest Man. Jesus Christ and He alone is the *God*-Man. And that is why He stands apart from all the others.

Even though the Lord Jesus tops the most-influential-people list, however, His earthly beginnings were anything but significant, at least from a human point of view. The "influential" people of the day didn't even recognize Him. But from God's point of view, everything proceeded exactly according to plan.

When the Time Was Right

When did Jesus Christ arrive on the scene? We might pinpoint His birth at two thousand plus years ago. But there's the broader answer: Jesus Christ came at the appointed time. The perfect time. The right time. Galatians 4:4-6 (NLT) says, "But when the right time came, God sent his Son, born of a woman, subject to the law. God sent him to buy freedom for us who were slaves to the law, so that he could adopt us as his very own children. And because we are his children, God has sent the Spirit of his Son into our hearts, prompting us to call out, 'Abba, Father.'"

He came just in time, at the precise, right, and best time.

It also happened to be a time of darkness and distress for Israel— and almost as difficult as their bondage under Pharaoh in Egypt. They were living under the iron tyranny of Rome and Rome's puppet king, Herod. To make matters worse, Israel had not heard from God for four hundred years. Four hundred years without a single word from a prophet or an angelic appearance or a single miracle.

Then the silence was broken and a miraculous chain of events was set into motion with the appearance of the angel Gabriel to an elderly country priest in the temple who was presenting sacrifices for his people. His name was Zacharias, husband to Elizabeth. In that dramatic encounter, Gabriel revealed the amazing news that Zacharias was going to be the father of a son. What a stunner! This was what he and his wife had been praying for throughout the long years of their marriage, and now—even at this late date—God was about to answer their prayer.

And He was about to answer in a way that this godly couple could have never predicted or imagined.

Their coming son would become a prophet. In fact, he would be the prophet of prophets. According to Christ Himself, Zacharias and Elizabeth's son would become the greatest prophet who ever lived. And he would be known as John the Baptist.

It was almost time for this forerunner to appear, which meant the Messiah was on His way.

On a Mission

Gabriel, who had already brought good news to Zacharias and Elizabeth, was soon standing in front of Mary, a young peasant girl living in Nazareth—a rough, nondescript town known for its wickedness. Mary was a nobody living in a nothing town in the middle of nowhere. But Mary lived a godly life, and heaven took notice. She was told she would be a fulfillment of Bible prophecy and actually become the mother of Israel's long-awaited Messiah.

Luke 1:28-30 (NLT) says, "Gabriel appeared to her and said, 'Greetings, favored woman! The Lord is with you!' Confused and disturbed, Mary tried to think what the angel could mean. 'Don't be afraid, Mary,' the angel told her, 'for you have found favor with God!'"

Mary obeyed, as did Joseph. She didn't have to, and God didn't force anything on her. She could have said, "Lord, I really don't want this mission." She would certainly have to suffer for this great privilege. When Mary and Joseph went to dedicate their newborn in the temple, they were met by a godly old man named Simeon, who told Mary, "A sword will pierce your very soul" (Luke 2:35, NLT).

How did a sword pierce Mary's soul? For starters, Mary, a pure and moral girl, had to live the rest of her life under the suspicion that she was an immoral woman and that she had conceived Jesus out of wedlock. Then later in her life, as Jesus pulled away from her and went about His public ministry, the sword went in a little deeper. But it pierced the deepest of all when she stood at the foot of the cross and saw the young Man she had loved and nurtured hanging there in front of her, a bloody pulp hardly recognizable as a person.

Even so, though she couldn't have known all these things at Gabriel's visit, she humbly accepted this call and mission.

And so did Joseph.

Remember, it wasn't easy for him, either.

He was a carpenter, and when he showed up at the worksite he had to endure the knowing glances and sneers of men who assumed he had been immoral with Mary, conceiving a son before their marriage.

He may have told them, "But you don't understand. This was something supernatural. It isn't what you think!"

And they would have said, "Yeah, Joseph. *Right.*"

But they both accepted the mission. Joseph and Mary would bring Jesus into the world.

The Road to Bethlehem

When Mary was nine months pregnant, God needed to get them to Bethlehem, where Jesus was to be born, according to Old Testament prophecy.

And it came to pass in those days that a decree went out from Caesar Augustus that all the world should be registered. This census first took place while Quirinius was governing Syria. So all went to be registered, everyone to his own city.

Joseph also went up from Galilee, out of the city of Nazareth, into Judea, to the city of David, which is called Bethlehem,

because he was of the house and lineage of David, to be registered with Mary, his betrothed wife, who was with child. So it was, that while they were there, the days were completed for her to be delivered. And she brought forth her firstborn Son, and wrapped Him in swaddling cloths, and laid Him in a manger, because there was no room for them in the inn.
(Luke 2:1-7)

Of course, these are very familiar words, and most of us have read or heard this story many times before. But take note for a moment of how precise this record is. Dr. Luke, the author, was a stickler for facts. He had not been an eyewitness to the life of Jesus as Matthew and John had been. In fact, he was a physician who came to faith from a non-Jewish background. Before writing his gospel, he carefully researched the whole story of Christ, conducting first-person interviews with the principal characters. Luke wanted his account to be understandable to those outside the Jewish culture. He wanted his readers to grasp that these were actual, historical events. The story of Jesus wasn't a fairy tale or legend. It happened in real time to real people.

In Luke 1:1-4 (MSG), he wrote to a man named Theophilus:

So many others have tried their hand at putting together a story of the wonderful harvest of Scripture and history that took place among us, using reports handed down by the original eyewitnesses who served this Word with their very lives. Since I have investigated all the reports in close detail, starting from the story's beginning, I decided to write it all out for you, most honorable Theophilus, so you can know beyond the shadow of a doubt the reliability of what you were taught. (emphasis added)

Theophilus, whose name means "lover of truth," apparently sponsored Luke's project, and we can be very glad he did!

Note how Luke pinpointed the birth of Jesus in Luke chapter 2 verses 1 and 2, mentioning Augustus and Quirinius. From the historical record, we know that Caesar Augustus was the first real Roman emperor. His actual name was Gaius Octavius, the great-nephew of Julius Caesar, who had fought his way to the top by defeating both Antony and Cleopatra. The Roman republic, governed by a senate, was now a thing of the past. Now the Roman Empire was emerging, and it would be ruled by Caesars from then on.

Gaius Octavius gave himself a fancy new name, adding the word "Augustus" to the title of Caesar, meaning "of the gods." In other words, this was the first Caesar to declare himself a deity and demand worship from his subjects. Archaeologists have found an inscription about Caesar Augustus that declares, "He is the savior of the whole world."

With this in mind, consider the message of the angels to the shepherds in Luke 2:11: "For there is born to you this day in the city of David a Savior, who is Christ the Lord."

It's as though these angels were saying, "Augustus is not the savior of the world. The real Savior has just been born, and He is Jesus!"

At a time when a man wanted to be God, God became a man. But He didn't come as a monarch draped in gold and silk, He came as a Baby wrapped in rags.

The story of Jesus is not a rags-to-riches story. It is a riches-to-rags story. He left the glory of heaven for this dark, unhappy planet. He went from being the Sovereign of the universe to a Servant of humanity. From the glory of God to a stable filled with animals. Think about what Jesus left to come and be our Savior!

Meanwhile, of course, this Roman Caesar was imagining himself to be "large and in charge." When he woke up in the morning and looked in the mirror, he thought of himself as the most powerful man in the world. But here's the truth: Kings, queens, prime ministers, dictators, and Caesars come and go on the world stage. Through it all, however, it doesn't matter who sits on earthly thrones, who gets voted into office, or who has the largest army. God is in control. Proverbs 21:1 (NLT) says, "The king's heart is like a stream of water directed by the LORD; he guides it wherever he pleases."

Caesar-so-called-Augustus was just a little pawn in the hand of God Almighty.

In fact, he wasn't very big at all. Historians tell us he was five feet seven inches tall. (That's about the height of Tom Cruise.) The Lord nudged this little man who was so big in his own mind. Though Caesar had established something later called Pax Romana (Latin for "Roman peace"), which was the forced rule of Rome on all his subjects, God directed him to accomplish His purposes.

And Caesar did exactly what God wanted him to do.

It's amazing to consider that both Quirinius and Caesar Augustus thought they were hot stuff. And now, who even remembers them? The only reason the name "Caesar Augustus" sounds familiar at all is because he ended up in the gospel of Luke! He's just a footnote—in tiny little print—in the greatest story ever told. Now we name our dogs after Roman emperors—Caesar and Nero—and name our sons after apostles—James, John, Peter, and Andrew.

Jesus is the most influential person in all of human history. Caesar is known for a great salad. It's a strong reminder that all of history is *His story*.

Too Busy for Jesus

Caesar Augustus, who imagined himself to be a god, sent out a decree that all of the Roman world should be taxed. Because Joseph was a descendent of David, he went to the boyhood town of David, which is Bethlehem, to pay his tax to Rome.

As Mary and Joseph came into Bethlehem, the town was crowded with other taxpayers. Could you have picked them out in a crowd? Probably not, because they didn't look the way religious artwork through the centuries has portrayed them. Whenever we see Mary and Joseph in a painting, Mary is always wearing blue. Other people in the picture will be dressed in peasant garb, but Mary will always have her cool blue outfit on. And, of course, they always have halos over their heads in the paintings—and so does Jesus. In pictures and images of Him as a child, He's wearing a halo, too—sort of a baby halo.

But that's not the way it was. They looked like what they were—a young, impoverished couple. The innkeeper took them in at a glance and said, "Sorry, I have no room for you." The word used here for *room* or *inn* is translated two ways in the New Testament. One speaks of what we would call a hotel, though it was still very primitive. There would be food, a fire, and an enclosure of some kind over the top of the room. Just a basic place to shelter in. The other word used for inn simply meant an enclosure. It was basically four walls, no roof, and no other accommodations. Actually, it was a place to keep animals. And that was the kind of place Mary and Joseph were turned away from. They weren't refused entrance to a hotel, they were turned away from the garage! They were sent off to the parking lot, or even worse.

Through history, people have wanted to vilify this innkeeper, though the Bible says nothing about him. The text simply says there was no room for them in the inn. If there was such an innkeeper, he was probably like so many people are today. Just too busy. You could write on our tombstones, "Hurried. Worried. Buried." The United States is the only nation in the world that has a mountain called "Rushmore." This is never more evident than at the Christmas season, when the lines in the malls are long and the tempers of people are short.

The innkeeper missed the ultimate opportunity. Imagine if he had taken them in! We would be preaching sermons about him to this day. He would have been held up as an icon of hospitality all over the world. But he just didn't want to deal with one more intrusion that night, so he turned them away. He is an illustration of so many of us—not unlike people who say, "I would like to make time for God, but I'm just too busy. I can't find time in my schedule. I would like to go to church, but there's no time for it. I would like to read the Bible, but I just can't fit it in somehow."

That's nonsense, of course. We find time for whatever is important to us.

I read recently that Americans spend twenty-three hours a week online and texting. Thanksgiving is a day when we come from across the country and gather in one room—so we can look at our phones!

I recently went to lunch with a group of people. As we sat down, they all pulled out their phones. I sent them all a text with these words: BE HERE NOW. They all looked up at me. Someone said, "Did you send that?"

"Yes," I said. "Can we have a conversation *here*? With the people who are *here*?"

Bottom line, we become so busy so much of the time that we don't have time for God. The innkeeper in this story, of course, missed the ultimate opportunity.

Losing Jesus

A little later on in the book of Luke we have the story of Mary and Joseph losing Jesus altogether on one occasion. The Bible doesn't tell us much about the boyhood of Jesus, but Luke does allow us one tiny glimpse. When Jesus was twelve years old, He went to Jerusalem to worship the Lord with His parents. As they were journeying back home, they didn't realize they had left Jesus behind. Men and women traveled separately in those days, and somehow Joseph assumed Jesus was with Mary, and Mary assumed Jesus was with Joseph. But then they discovered He was missing.

Filled with fear (as any parents would have been), they made their way back to Jerusalem to look for Him. After three days they found Him in the temple, sitting with the teachers and elders, asking questions.

But can you imagine Mary and Joseph running around town asking acquaintances and strangers, "Where is Jesus? Have you seen Jesus? We can't find Him!" And, no, Jesus didn't glow in the dark. He was a normal-looking twelve-year-old, and He had somehow faded into the masses of people in the crowded city.

We can be the same way sometimes, especially, perhaps, at Christmas. We can be so busy celebrating Christmas that we lose Jesus. We string our lights, trim our trees, and buy presents for people we like (or possibly don't like at all), and then in the middle of it all realize with a start that we haven't thought about Jesus for hours and hours. Maybe even days.

Christmas can be such a letdown. There is so much buildup to it and so much hype that you can actually imagine the day itself will bring you a measure of happiness. But then reality kicks in, the bills start arriving, and you feel empty and depressed. Experts tell us that calls to psychiatrists and emergency rooms go up at this time of the year. That's because Christmas cannot possibly live up to its romanticized, highly marketed image.

The solution? I suggest you forget about the clutter of X-mas and "Happy Holidays" and replace it with the Christ of Christmas. Then it will be something very, very special. Because the day is not about Christmas presents, but rather the *presence* of Jesus in your life and in your home.

The message of Christmas isn't "let it snow" or even "let us shop."

It is "let us worship."

Deity in Diapers

Where was the Lord Jesus born? We all know the answer. He was born in Bethlehem. The Creator of the universe was born in a stable in Bethlehem. As with everything else surrounding Christmas, we have romanticized this, too. We sing, *"O little town of Bethlehem, how still we see thee lie."* But the reality of it wasn't romantic at all. Joseph and Mary were scared and probably felt sick about the idea of having the Baby on the dirty floor of a barn or perhaps even a cave. Can you imagine your baby being born in a filthy garage? Or how about in an animal shed with manure lying all around? Talk about unsanitary!

It would have been very cold, with no comforts at all.

But it was there that the Son of God was born into our world, a helpless infant. As Augustine observed, "Unspeakably wise, He is wisely speechless. He is the Word without a word." He wasn't super baby, flying around the room. And he wasn't born talking, saying, "Hey, Mary and Joseph. Good to see you. I am a baby, but I can speak." He was like any other baby, needing to be cradled, nurtured, and protected. The Bible commentator R. Kent Hughes has observed, "It was clearly a leap down. . . . As if the Son of God rose from His splendor, stood poised on the rim of the universe irradiating light, and dove headlong, speeding through the stars over the Milky Way to earth's galaxy, where He plunged into a huddle of animals. Nothing could be lower."

Jesus was deity in diapers. He who was larger than the universe became an embryo. He who sustains the world with a word chose to be dependent on a young girl. G. K. Chesterton wrote, "The hands that had made the stars were too small to reach the huge heads of the cattle that surrounded Him. Too small to change His own clothing or to put food into His own mouth. Amazing God in infant helplessness."

Jesus could have been born in the most elegant mansion on the ritziest boulevard in Rome. He could have had aristocratic parents boasting of their pedigree. He could have worn the finest clothes from the most exclusive shops. He could have called legions of shining angels as an army to respond to His every whim. But He had none of that. He humbled Himself. As Paul wrote in 2 Corinthians 8:9 (NIV), "Though he was rich, yet for your sake he became poor, so that you through his poverty might become rich."

The Announcement

Who was the first to know about His arrival?

When your first baby was born, whom did you tell first? You probably told those who were waiting right outside the room. I was present for the birth of both of our sons—and for all of our grandchildren as well. We heard the cry of the newborn, and we were excited. We wanted our immediate family and closest friends to hear the news, just as you probably did.

Can you imagine running outside the hospital to give the news to a total stranger, someone you had never met before? No, of course not. With news like that, you would want to tell people who were close to you.

But what did God do when His Son was born in a manger in Bethlehem? Who was first to get the announcement? If it had been me, I would have dispatched an angel to the court of Caesar Augustus in Rome. "Hey, Caesar, how's it going? You call yourself the savior of the world, but check this out: The *real* Savior of the world has just been born." Or maybe I would have sent that angel to the high priest, scribes, and scholars in Jerusalem, telling them, "The Messiah is born!"

But that's not what God did. God gave this message to whom? To *shepherds*, keeping watch over their flocks at night.

Like everything else in the Christmas story, we have romanticized and glamorized these shepherds through the years. But we need to understand that to be a shepherd at that time and in that culture was to be at the very bottom of the social ladder. Shepherds were mistrusted and despised in those days—even to the point that the testimony of a shepherd was not allowed in a court of law. Shepherds did the work nobody else would do. They worked hard, had dirt under their fingernails, and smelled like the sheep that they cared for day and night.

When the angelic announcement came to them, they probably felt right at home to hear about a baby being born in a cave full of animals. They related to this; it seemed right and natural to them for a child to be born in the open air. God was speaking their language.

This, of course, became the mode of operation for Christ throughout His ministry. He went to the outcasts, and they loved Him and related to Him. He went to the hurting. The rejected. Ordinary people trying to make a living in a difficult world.

People like the woman at the well, in John 4, who had to draw water in the middle of the day because nobody else wanted to be around her. She was ostracized because of her multiple marriages and divorces.

People like Zacchaeus, who was hated by his fellow Jews because he collected taxes from them for Rome.

People like the woman caught in the act of adultery, who was thrown like a piece of garbage at Jesus' feet.

Our Lord always had time for people like that—so much so that He was described as "the friend of sinners" (see Matthew 11:19 and Luke 7:34). So it only made sense that the announcement of His birth would come first to the scruffy, humble shepherds out in the hills watching over their sheep.

Let's pick up the account in the gospel of Luke:

Now there were in the same country shepherds living out in the fields, keeping watch over their flock by night. And behold, an angel of the Lord stood before them, and the glory of the Lord shone around them, and they were greatly afraid. Then the angel said to them, "Do not be afraid, for behold, I bring you good tidings of great joy which will be to all people. For there is born to you this day in the city of David a Savior, who is Christ the Lord. And this will be the sign to you: You will find a Babe wrapped in swaddling cloths, lying in a manger."

And suddenly there was with the angel a multitude of the heavenly host praising God and saying:

"Glory to God in the highest,
And on earth peace, goodwill toward men!"

So it was, when the angels had gone away from them into heaven, that the shepherds said to one another, "Let us now go to Bethlehem and see this thing that has come to pass, which the Lord has made known to us." (2:8-15)

These shepherds—and all of Israel—were living in frightening times. They existed under the reign of the Roman puppet king, Herod, who was a bloody tyrant. Their land was occupied by foreign troops. Would Rome ever leave? Would they ever be free again? Would the promised Messiah ever come?

And then suddenly, He did. He came. And the sky blazed with angels announcing His birth.

When you read about this, don't minimize how frightening this experience must have been. Angels are powerful, awesome beings, radiant with the reflected glory of God. And on that night there were *multitudes* of them! How many—a thousand? Ten thousand? Who really knows?

By the way, that's why the first thing that usually comes out of an angel's mouth when he appears before people is "Don't be afraid." In other words, "Don't freak out. It's okay. You're not going to die."

I haven't checked this out, but someone once told me there are 365 occasions in the Bible where the phrase "fear not" is used. If that's true, it means there is a "fear not" for every day of the year. I like that! Don't be afraid. The message of Christmas is fear not and have joy. The commentator Ray Stedman once said, "The chief mark of the Christian ought to be an absence of fear and the presence of joy."

It's hard to have joy in this world because we are surrounded by so much sadness. We hear about it every night in the evening news: shootings on school campuses, acts of terrorism, the threat of war, and the breakdown of families and lives all around us. How can we enter into these "tidings of great joy" we read about in the Christmas story?

I can think of three strong reasons for joy.

1. We have a Savior.

No matter what happens in life, remember this: You have a Savior. That means you have been saved. Saved from what? You have been saved from death. You have been saved from eternal punishment in hell. You have the hope as a Christian that when you die, you will go straight to heaven.

You might be reading those words and thinking, "Well, that's nice. One day I think I will really appreciate that." But if you are reading those words and lying on your deathbed, I can assure you that you will be hanging on to that hope with everything in you. No matter what happens in this life, we have an unimaginably wonderful future waiting for us in heaven, just over the horizon. That is the promise of our Savior.

2. We have a Christ.

Luke 2:11 says, "There is born to you this day in the city of David a Savior, who is Christ the Lord." The word *Christ* means "anointed one" or "messiah." Jesus was the fulfillment of God's promise to send His Son to earth as the Messiah. It is a reminder that God keeps His promises.

What has Jesus promised me? He has promised me as a Christian that He will never leave or forsake me (see Hebrews 13:5). Whatever I go through in life I am never alone. He will never leave me. He will never abandon me.

What else has He promised? He has promised that He will work all things together for good to those who love Him and are called according to His purpose (see Romans 8:28). Whatever you may be facing in life, whatever circumstances you find yourself, He has promised to work those things together for good.

What else has He promised? He has promised that He will come again and receive us to Himself (see John 14:3). Just as surely as the Lord fulfilled His promise to come the first time, He will come back again.

Some people might say, "Well, then, where is He? Isn't He a little late?"

The Bible says,

I want to remind you that in the last days scoffers will come, mocking the truth and following their own desires. They will say, "What happened to the promise that Jesus is coming again? From before the times of our ancestors, everything has remained the same since the world was first created."

. . . The Lord isn't really being slow about his promise, as some people think. No, he is being patient for your sake. He does not want anyone to be destroyed, but wants everyone to repent. (2 Peter 3:3-4,9, NLT)

God knows who that last person is, the last man or woman He is waiting for before He calls us to meet Him in the air and take us to heaven. Can you imagine how you would react if you knew who that person was? What if it were revealed to you that the person sitting next to you at work or in school or at church was the very one the Lord was waiting for—and as soon as that person believed, He would call us all home in the Rapture? Do you think you might be tempted to apply a little pressure, asking that person if he or she is ready to believe in Jesus?

Only the Lord knows who that person is, and when he or she believes, we will be caught up to meet the Lord in a moment, in the twinkling of an eye (see 1 Thessalonians 4:16-17). But until that day He wants to reach more people and bring them into His kingdom.

3. We have a Lord.

"There is born to you this day in the city of David a Savior, who is Christ the Lord." When I became a Christian, God took control of my life. He directs me in the way I should go and protects me along that pathway. Then, when that journey is done, He will welcome me into heaven.

All of these promises, of course, are for believers in Christ, for those who belong to Him. At Christmastime we may wrack our brains trying to think of gifts for people on our lists. Yet the ultimate gift of Christmas in not the gift we give to someone else; it is the gift God has given to us. That gift is waiting for you, and there will be no bill coming for it next week.

The price for this gift has already been paid.

You just need to reach out and accept it.

CHAPTER FIVE
HEART TO HEART

hat could a late-night, first-century conversation between a young Jewish carpenter and a prominent religious leader have to do with someone in the 21st century?

The answer is *everything*.

It has everything to do with our contemporary world, today's headlines, and all the trending news of the day. Why? Because it wasn't just a conversation between two people. It was a conversation between God and man, and it has made an impact on both time and eternity.

If we were going to nominate someone to represent humanity to God in that after-hours rooftop dialogue, we couldn't find a better representative than the man Nicodemus. He was the finest this world had to offer, the closest a person could come to being what we would call a good individual. He was intelligent, cultured, respected, and moral. He was a well-known religious leader and a significant man in his country.

But he also had a hole in his spirit about a mile wide and deep. Probably no one else on earth knew it, but Nicodemus felt a deep emptiness in his life. And the words Jesus spoke to Nicodemus that night in Roman-occupied Judea have unlocked the mystery of life for countless millions of people throughout the centuries.

And they may even unlock the mystery of life for you.

The Backdrop

As you open your Bible to the book of John, you may notice that John chapter 2 comes before John chapter 3. When the Bible was originally given to humankind, however, it didn't have chapters and verses. Those were added later to help us find our way around. So chapters 2 and 3 of John really flow together, with no break.

In John 2:23-25 we read, "Now when He was in Jerusalem at the Passover, during the feast, many believed in His name when they saw the signs which He did. But Jesus did not commit Himself to them, because He knew all men, and had no need that anyone should testify of man, for He knew what was in man."

Another way to translate this more simply would be, "They believed in Him, but He did not believe in them." Or, "They trusted Him, but He did not trust them." Why? Because Jesus the Son of God is omniscient; He knows everything about everyone. Jesus knows every individual and what each one is all about.

The people who supposedly "believed in His name" were fickle followers and fair-weather believers. They were dazzled by His miracles, but their faith wasn't genuine. Because of that, Jesus didn't reveal Himself to them. But with Nicodemus it was different. Jesus did reveal Himself to Nicodemus because He knew the man's heart; Nicodemus was really seeking the truth and honestly looking for answers.

God wants us to believe in Him, but He wants that belief on His terms. It's not a matter of thinking good thoughts about Jesus or admiring Jesus, but really understanding what it means to believe and put the full weight of our hope and trust in Him.

Face to Face

The conversation in John 3 has three primary movements. The first movement is in verses 2-3, where Jesus and Nicodemus initially encountered one another. I call this *face to face*. In the second movement, verses 4-8, Jesus and Nicodemus were *mind to mind*. Then finally, in the third movement, verses 9-21, the two of them were *heart to heart*.

But here is where it began:

There was a man of the Pharisees named Nicodemus, a ruler of the Jews. This man came to Jesus by night and said to Him, "Rabbi, we know that You are a teacher come from God; for no one can do these signs that You do unless God is with him."

Jesus answered and said to him, "Most assuredly, I say to you, unless one is born again, he cannot see the kingdom of God."

Nicodemus said to Him, "How can a man be born when he is old? Can he enter a second time into his mother's womb and be born?"

Jesus answered, "Most assuredly, I say to you, unless one is born of water and the Spirit, he cannot enter the kingdom of God. That which is born of the flesh is flesh, and that which is born of the Spirit is spirit. Do not marvel that I said to you, 'You must be born again.' The wind blows where it wishes, and you hear the sound of it, but cannot tell where it comes from and where it goes. So is everyone who is born of the Spirit."

Nicodemus answered and said to Him, "How can these things be?"

Jesus answered and said to him, "Are you the teacher of Israel, and do not know these things?" (verses 1-10)

As John 3 begins, Jesus and Nicodemus came face to face. In the first verse, we learn something very significant about this man who sought out Jesus by night. He was a Pharisee. We usually think of Pharisees in a negative light, but there were positive things about them as well. These were men who took the law of God very seriously and sought to apply the Ten Commandments to every area of their lives. Every Pharisee took a solemn vow before three witnesses that he would devote every waking moment of his entire life to obeying these commandments. At this time, there may have been around six thousand Pharisees in Israel. They were the theological conservatives of their day, believed in miracles and the resurrection of the dead, and held tightly to the authority of Scripture.

Nicodemus was not only a Pharisee. He was a leader of the Pharisees and belonged to the highly prestigious ruling body of Israel known as the Sanhedrin. This was a group of men who wrote laws and conducted trials, equivalent to the Supreme Court in the United States but even more powerful. Nicodemus had dedicated his life to the study of Scripture and was a member of the most powerful ruling elite in Israel at that time.

He was also famous. Something of a celebrity. Jesus called him "the teacher of Israel." Nicodemus was quite possibly the best-known teacher in all the land. Yet despite the fact that he was famous, powerful, educated, and religious, there was something missing in his life—and he knew it.

That "something missing" brought him to Jesus at night.

That Nicodemus came during the hours of darkness is mentioned more than once in Scripture. It's worth noting. Why did he come after dark? Was he concerned about what people would think or say if he visited with this controversial young rabbi in broad daylight? People might whisper, "Why is the most celebrated teacher in all of Israel—this distinguished, highly educated man— going to speak to this outspoken son of a carpenter?" Was Nicodemus worried about the possible gossip?

Possibly. Then again, maybe he went to Jesus by night because our Lord's schedule was so full, and He was so often surrounded by a crowd. We don't really know why he came by night, but the important thing is that he came. The fact is, Nicodemus turned out to be one of the most courageous followers of Jesus Christ. He is a reminder that it's better to have a great ending and a poor beginning than a great beginning and a poor ending. Nicodemus had a strong final chapter to his story, but he may not have started so well.

Maybe you look back on your own life and say, "I wish I had become a Christian when I was younger instead of wasting so many years of my life." Perhaps. But if you are a Christian now, you have *today*, and today is a precious gift of God. God can do incredible things with *today* if you will place it completely in His hands. Life is like a race where the finish means everything, regardless of when or how well you started. Even if you have stumbled and fallen, get up and finish this race of life well as a follower of Jesus Christ. Far better that than the person who started with such promise only to crash and burn and never get up again.

In John 19:38-39, after the death of Jesus on the cross, we read, "After this, Joseph of Arimathea, being a disciple of Jesus, but secretly, for fear of the Jews, asked Pilate that he might take away the body of Jesus; and Pilate gave him permission. So he came and took the body of Jesus. And Nicodemus, who at first came to Jesus by night, also came, bringing a mixture of myrrh and aloes, about a hundred pounds."

These verses point out that Nicodemus came out publicly for Christ in the end. He might have initially come to Jesus at night, but in the end he claimed the right to honor Jesus in front of Jerusalem's highest Roman authority.

"A teacher come from God"

Nicodemus had great respect for Jesus. Note how the conversation began that night: "Rabbi, we know that You are a teacher come from God; for no one can do these signs that You do unless God is with him" (John 3:2).

That was a significant statement for a man with the stature of Nicodemus. He was essentially acknowledging Jesus as an equal. Of course they weren't really equals at all, because this Pharisee was talking to the Son of God. But I don't think he realized that at this point.

Because Nicodemus was a careful student of the Scriptures, he would have read the prophecies of Daniel about Messiah. If he understood those prophecies, he would have realized that the Messiah was alive at that moment, and he may have even recognized Jesus as that Messiah. But he would have also learned from Daniel's prophecies that the time would come when the Messiah would be cut off (see Daniel 9:26). In other words, he might have known that time was short and that he, perhaps getting on in years, needed to act quickly. In John 3:4, he said to Jesus, "How can a man be born when he is old?" So he was probably an elderly man when this conversation took place.

Most people come to Christ before the age of twenty-one, and the longer a person waits after that, the more difficult it becomes. But that doesn't mean it's impossible.

Years ago we had a Harvest Crusade in Santa Barbara at an outdoor amphitheater. When the invitation was given for people to receive Christ, a ninety-year-old man walked forward at the urging of his granddaughter. The man's wife, a Christian, had died a few years before. She had prayed for him throughout her entire life, but he refused to believe in Jesus. On her deathbed his wife pleaded with him to come to Christ. She wanted her husband to know the love and peace that she had experienced. But he turned her down.

But there he was, at age ninety, attending a Harvest Crusade. As the service came to a close, I gave the invitation for people to come to Christ.

"Grandpa," his granddaughter said to him, "do you want to go forward?"

"No, I don't," he answered.

"Come on, Grandpa," she said. "I will go with you!"

"No. It's cold down there. I don't want to go down there."

"But Grandpa," she said, "I think you are going to like what you find when you get down there."

He turned to her and said, "What do you think it is that I'm going to find when I get down there?"

"I think," she said, "that you are going to find love and peace and life."

At that, the old man got out of his seat, made his way forward, and prayed the prayer to receive Jesus. Afterward he said, "Now I know what my wife was talking about all those years. Now I know that I will see her again."

God can still work in a life, no matter what the age. Don't write anyone off regardless of their years.

Something about verse 2 amuses me a little. The Pharisee said, "We know that You are a teacher come from God." *We* know? Who are the "we"? It was just Nicodemus and Jesus there that evening. Nicodemus had come alone, not with a group. Of course, Nicodemus could have been speaking about the leadership of his fellow Pharisees. Maybe there really was a sense that God was working through this mysterious Galilean teacher. On the other hand, maybe Nicodemus used the word *we* because he wasn't yet comfortable using the word *I*. He couldn't quite bring himself to say, "*I* know that You are a teacher come from God." It's like when we say to someone, "This friend of mine has a question" when our "friend" is really ourselves.

But with one sharp and penetrating phrase, Jesus sliced through all the layers of rules and legalistic attitudes that had accumulated around the mind of Nicodemus: "Most assuredly, I say to you, unless one is born again, he cannot see the kingdom of God" (verse 3).

You might have expected Jesus to make a little polite small talk, saying, "First of all let me say that it's an honor to meet you, Nicodemus. I really appreciate your taking time to visit with Me, and I just want to thank you."

There was none of that. Instead, the Lord went right to the bottom line. In essence, He was saying, "I know why you are here, because I am God and know everything. Listen very carefully to this, Nicodemus. If you want to go to heaven, you need to be born from above."

Sadly, the term *born again* has lost much of its meaning. The term has been pirated, mocked, dragged through the gutter, and given back to us minus its power. Today when people say they are "born again," we don't even know what they mean. They might even be talking about New Age mysticism instead of biblical Christianity.

What does it mean to be born again? It means having our spiritual eyes opened and embracing Christ as Savior and Lord. We really can't explain this transformation to nonbelievers; God has to touch them Himself, draw them, and open their eyes.

Jesus was saying, "Buddy, listen to Me. You need to be born again. Born from above. Your education and title and religious beliefs aren't going to do it for you. None of those things has brought you any closer to heaven—and deep in your heart, you already know that, don't you?"

This may be a controversial statement, but I believe religion has kept more people out of heaven than all the other sins combined.

By "religion" I mean man's attempt to reach God. To be honest, I don't even consider myself a religious person.

"But Greg," someone may say, "you're a preacher. Of course you're religious."

I hope not. I certainly try not to be. Because the fact is, I hate religion. I hate it because it blinds people to their need for God. You might be talking to someone about faith in Christ and she will reply, "Oh, I was raised Presbyterian."

I want to reply, "So what do you want? A medal?"

Someone else will say, "I was raised Catholic," or "My grandfather was a preacher," or "I got baptized when I was a kid."

But none of those things will save you. None of those things will gain you entrance into heaven. People will go through religious rituals and think they've earned the favor of God, but that's not the way it works. Nicodemus was as good a man and religious a man as you would ever hope to meet. But Jesus told him, "You won't see the kingdom of God unless you are spiritually reborn."

Religion is a deception and a distraction, keeping people from doing real business with God. I desperately do not want to become a religious person, but with all my heart, I do want to be a follower of Jesus Christ. And there is a big difference between the two.

Sometimes we may hear people say, "I am a Christian, but I'm not one of those 'born agains.'" But here is the newsflash from John chapter 3: You cannot be a Christian without being born again.

Mind to Mind

The conversation escalated quickly from face to face to mind to mind. Jesus was going to prompt Nicodemus to think deeply about things. In verse 4 Nicodemus said, "How can a man be born when he is old?" In other words, he was saying, "I accept this concept in premise. But how? What's the process? How does a person start over? Can a man or woman really change at this time of life?"

We've all tried to change things about our lives on our own, and most of us haven't been very successful. We make New Year's resolutions—in all sincerity—but the change barely makes it into

February. The fact is, we can change some exterior things about ourselves, but that doesn't really affect the interior.

Years ago my mom owned an old Ford Galaxie Starliner. What a supercool car that was. I wish I still had it. On one occasion my mom decided to get it painted, so we went to Earl Scheib, who advertised that he would paint any car for $29.95. So in a matter of minutes it seemed, our Starliner went from a powder blue to a deep metallic blue.

It looked really nice, but you know what? It was still the same car. It still smelled the same on the inside. It still ran the same. It might have looked new, but it was just a thin coat of paint on an old body. It's the same for us, isn't it? We can change our style or change this or that about our appearance, but we're still the same person on the inside.

We have to change the inside. We have to be born anew.

As the two men conversed, possibly up on the flat rooftop of someone's house, a cooling breeze may have swept across them, rustling the fronds of surrounding palm trees. Jesus looked at Nicodemus and said, "The wind blows where it wishes, and you hear the sound of it, but cannot tell where it comes from and where it goes. So is everyone who is born of the Spirit" (verse 8).

Jesus was saying, "Do you get it, Nicodemus? Think about it! You can feel that wind on your face right now. But can you see the wind? No. But you can see its effects. You know it's there. And so it is with everyone who is born of the Spirit. It's an invisible but undeniable reality that something changes when God comes into a life."

Heart to Heart

Now we come to the third phase of the conversation. It began with *face to face,* progressed to *mind to mind,* and is just about to move to *heart to heart.* In verse 9 Nicodemus said to Jesus, "How can these things be?"

He was being honest and open at this point. "Break it down for me, Jesus. What's the process here? I'm an old man and set in my ways. How can I make such a drastic change? How can I be born again?"

John 3:10 tells us, "Jesus answered and said to him, 'Are you the teacher of Israel, and do not know these things?'"

In other words, "Come on, Nick, everyone knows who you are. You're the go-to-guy in Israel for spiritual information. How can you not know these things?" Then Jesus, speaking heart-to-heart with this man who had sought Him out, began to explain things to him. In essence, He was giving him the ABCs of the gospel: "As Moses lifted up the serpent in the wilderness, even so must the Son of Man be lifted up, that whoever believes in Him should not perish but have eternal life" (verses 14-15).

As an expert in Jewish history, Nicodemus knew exactly what Jesus was referring to. The Old Testament book of Numbers gives the account of the Israelite nation out in the wilderness, before they arrived at the Promised Land. They had begun bitterly complaining to Moses about everything, saying things like "Why did you bring us out of Egypt to die in this forsaken place?"; "We're sick of this stinking manna God gives us for food"; "We never have enough water!" On and on it went, until the Lord unleashed an army of deadly, venomous snakes among the population.

I once had a hobby as a snake-keeper, believe it or not, and have handled (and been bitten by) many different snakes—but never by a venomous one. The snakes in this story may have been saw-scaled vipers. They are only about three feet at the longest and very aggressive. This sort of viper will strike with such force that it actually leaves the ground. So a bunch of these snakes seemingly appeared out of nowhere and began leaping up and biting the Israelites. Many were bitten and were going to die unless God intervened. Moses prayed for the people, and God gave him the cure—the antivenin.

God told Moses, "I want you to get a tall pole, make a serpent out of brass, and wrap it around the top of that pole. Then hold it up high where everyone can see it. Whoever looks up to see the serpent on the pole will live. You do your part, and I will do mine."

So Moses obeyed and held the pole high for all to see. Those who looked at the pole were healed and didn't die. Those who refused to look at the pole died from the snakebites.

I'm very sure Jesus had Nicodemus's full attention at that point as He explained how God's Messiah, "the Son of Man," would also be lifted up—on a pole, on a cross. And everyone who looked to Him for salvation and eternal life would find it!

That's how it was on that dark Friday when Jesus was crucified on Calvary. The centurion looked up at Him and said, "Truly this was the Son of God." Jesus' mother, Mary, looked up at Him. So did John. So did many others. But others mocked Him and walked away. In fact, several Roman soldiers threw dice, gambling for His only earthly possession, while He was dying for their sins and the sins of the whole world.

People had a choice on the day Jesus died. They could look and live or they could look and leave. In Isaiah 45:21-22, God put it like this: "There is no other God besides Me, a just God and a Savior; there is none besides Me. Look to Me, and be saved, all you ends of the earth! For I am God, and there is no other."

With Nicodemus still processing these words, Jesus spoke to him and gave him what has become the most well-known verse in all the Bible: "For God so loved the world that He gave His only begotten Son, that whoever believes in Him should not perish but have everlasting life" (John 3:16).

This verse has been called the Hope Diamond of Scripture.

In the last interview I did with the late Pastor Chuck Smith, I asked him, "Chuck, if you had one last sermon to give before you went to heaven, what would your text be?"

"John 3:16," he said. "Because the gospel is in it."

Max Lucado says of John 3:16, "It is a 26-word parade of hope, beginning with God, ending with life, and urging us to do the same. Brief enough to write on a napkin or memorize in a moment, yet solid enough to weather 2,000 years of storms and questions. If you know nothing of the Bible, start here!"

What does it say?

"For God so loved . . ." Some people have a concept of God as a cosmic killjoy out to ruin our lives, but nothing could be further from the truth. God longs for a relationship with us. And whom does God love?

"For God so loved the world . . ." It doesn't say, "For God so loved really nice people." It doesn't say, "For God so loved Christians." It says, "For God so loved the world." That includes everyone. Thieves. Adulterers. Terrorists. Murderers. Republicans. Democrats. Homosexuals. His love is for every person who ever lived and who ever will live.

The thief on the cross next to Jesus was most likely a murderer. We call him a thief, but the word in the original language could speak of someone who had committed a more serious crime—possibly an act of insurrection against Rome. He may very well have murdered a Roman soldier or official. In today's world, we might refer to him as a terrorist. Yet Jesus extended complete forgiveness to him and took him to heaven that very day.

Some people with a Calvinist point of view might say that Christ died only for "the elect," and only "the elect" will believe. People of this persuasion believe God has predestined certain people to go to heaven and other people to go to hell, and we have nothing to say about it!

I don't believe that. Not for a moment. I don't believe Jesus died for an elect few. I believe He died for the whole world. He died for every man, every woman, every boy, every girl, and every sinner. As D. L. Moody once said, "Lord, save the elect—and then save some more!"

This offer is for everyone.

". . . He gave His only begotten Son . . ." The world reaches up to God through religion and ritual, but God reaches down to humanity through Christ. The verse could be better translated, "God gave His one and only Son," His unique, one-of-a-kind Son.

". . . that whoever believes in Him should not perish . . ." Who can be forgiven? Everyone. Everyone who believes in Him. No matter what they have done, no matter how many sins they have committed. Whoever believes will not die in their sins, but will enter into eternal life. No one you know is beyond the reach of God. You are not beyond the reach of God, no matter who you are, where you are, or what your circumstances.

But you have to be born again. You have to be born anew in Christ.

"But Greg," you say, "I've always been a moral person. I've even been religious." That's good, but if this story in John 3 tells us nothing else, it tells us that none of these things will get you into heaven.

One dark night, a good, moral, religious man named Nicodemus came to Jesus with a crushing emptiness in his soul. He took a chance, risked his reputation, and opened his life to a Galilean carpenter, possibly young enough to be his son, who also happened to be the Son of God.

It may be the best conversation ever recorded, and it was certainly the best night in Nicodemus's life.

We're still reflecting on it two thousand years later.

And to anyone who wants to come to Jesus by night—or by day or whenever—the door is still wide open.

CHAPTER SIX
SATISFACTION FOR THE SPIRITUALLY THIRSTY

harlene McDaniel was one of the nine children of Charles and Stella McDaniel, who made their home in Friendship, Arkansas.

Charlene was strikingly beautiful. In fact, she was so pretty that people would tell her, "You look just like Marilyn Monroe."

Charles and Stella were Christians and took their children to church every Sunday. But Charlene didn't like church, didn't like what the Bible had to say, and didn't care at all for the "constraints" of the Christian life. As soon as she was able, she rebelled against the rules of her Christian home and began to pursue a lifestyle of drinking and partying with friends. If anyone ever challenged what she was doing, she would bristle, completely rejecting their words.

She figured the best way to escape her parents' rules would be to get married. So when a handsome young guy came along and proposed to her, she accepted. This would be the first of seven, perhaps eight, marriages she would find herself in as the years passed by.

She divorced this first husband shortly after she married him. They'd had a son together, her first of two. Then she married another man and became pregnant again and gave birth to a stillborn child. She was so disillusioned by that event that she went back to the party scene more than ever and decided that marriage wasn't for her.

As time went by, she had a fling with a guy she met in Long Beach and became pregnant again. Because it wasn't in vogue to have a baby out of wedlock in those days (as it is today with the Hollywood elite), she married another man and asked if he would put his name on the birth certificate as the father of the child, which he agreed to do, and she had her second son.

They nicknamed this second son "Pogo," because he was mischievous like that cartoon character in the strips drawn years ago by Walt Kelly.

So Charlene McDaniel was a beautiful woman going from marriage to marriage, from divorce to divorce, on a quest for fulfillment, looking for meaning, looking for purpose in her life. Eventually, she sent Pogo to live with her parents—his grandparents—for a few years. He also went to military school and lived with various aunts and uncles. Eventually Charlene realized she couldn't keep passing Pogo from family member to family member, so he lived with her for a time.

It was pretty frightening for a young boy to see his mom come home at four in the morning after a night of drinking. It was stressful to see her in abusive relationship after abusive relationship. On one occasion, one of Charlene's lovers almost killed her, hitting her across the head and leaving her for dead. Pogo had to call the police and an ambulance.

Charlene continued her lifestyle, her empty quest for meaning in life, with circumstances sliding from bad to worse.

But something unexpected happened to Pogo . . . or I should say . . . me.

An Unexpected Conversion

Charlene was my mom. And when I gave my life to Jesus Christ at the age of seventeen, I longed for her to come to faith as well. But she rebelled against my influence just as she had rejected the influence of her parents as they raised her in the church.

As I became a pastor and evangelist, I knew she was proud of me and of my accomplishments. But she didn't want to make that commitment to Christ herself, and she would clam up whenever the subject arose. She still had her beauty, and she still drew men.

But one day when she was driving under the influence she got into a head-on collision with a car on Jamboree Boulevard in Newport Beach, and it almost killed her. It also disfigured her once beautiful face. Her legendary beauty was fading, and the lifestyle she had chosen was taking its toll on her health.

She was still resistant to the gospel, but we were beginning to see some hopeful signs. She was just beginning to soften a little bit. For instance, we would go out for a meal, and I would always pray before the meal, whether I was with believers or nonbelievers. She began to like those prayers and even wait for them. After a while, I realized she wouldn't eat her food until we prayed. And if I forgot to pray, she reminded me. That was a hopeful sign.

She would come to our crusades, but I never saw her make a commitment to Christ.

One month before her death I sat down with her and asked her about her roots. I also cleared up a few things about my own youth and who my real father was. As it turned out, I've had almost a full-time job ministering to my mom's former husbands. But this time we finally had our conversation about faith in Jesus Christ. She said she had believed in Him, and I told her she needed to make a re-commitment of that decision, which she did.

Soon after that, she was in the presence of God.

It was a glorious thing that my mother came back to the faith she had left as a teenager. But it was also sad that she had spent most of her years looking for a man, a marriage, a relationship to fill the great void in her heart. And it never worked.

A Biblical Parallel

Why do I bring up my mother's story? Because it so closely parallels the story told by the apostle John in the fourth chapter of his gospel. This is the story of a very empty woman, a woman who thought romance and sex would fill the empty places in her life. Like my mother, Charlene, this was a woman who went from husband to husband, hoping to find her prince. Apparently, after her fifth husband, she just gave up.

The woman in John 4 had been used and abused and disillusioned.

We can assume this woman, whom we know as the woman at the well, had once been beautiful—perhaps strikingly so. But we can well imagine that at this point in her life, after five husbands, her beauty was beginning to fade. The husbands were gone, and friends of days gone by had abandoned her. She was now living with a man to whom she seemed indifferent. She was basically a woman alone—until she had an encounter with Jesus Christ and her life was turned around. In this story we not only see how the spiritual thirst of a person can be satisfied but we see how to effectively reach a person who is searching.

Meeting at a Well

So [Jesus] left Judea and returned to Galilee.

He had to go through Samaria on the way. Eventually he came to the Samaritan village of Sychar, near the field that Jacob gave to his son Joseph. Jacob's well was there; and Jesus, tired from the long walk, sat wearily beside the well about noontime. Soon a Samaritan woman came to draw water, and Jesus said to her, "Please give me a drink." He was alone at the time because his disciples had gone into the village to buy some food.

The woman was surprised, for Jews refuse to have anything to do with Samaritans. She said to Jesus, "You are a Jew, and I am a Samaritan woman. Why are you asking me for a drink?"

Jesus replied, "If you only knew the gift God has for you and who you are speaking to, you would ask me, and I would give you living water."

"But sir, you don't have a rope or a bucket," she said, "and this well is very deep. Where would you get this living water? And besides, do you think you're greater than our ancestor Jacob, who gave us this well? How can you offer better water than he and his sons and his animals enjoyed?"

Jesus replied, "Anyone who drinks this water will soon become thirsty again. But those who drink the water I give will never be thirsty again. It becomes a fresh, bubbling spring within them, giving them eternal life."

"Please, sir," the woman said, "give me this water! Then I'll never be thirsty again, and I won't have to come here to get water."

"Go and get your husband," Jesus told her.

"I don't have a husband," the woman replied.

Jesus said, "You're right! You don't have a husband—for you have had five husbands, and you aren't even married to the man you're living with now. You certainly spoke the truth!"

"Sir," the woman said, "you must be a prophet." (John 4:3-19, NLT)

At the beginning of this account, the Bible tells us Jesus "had to go through Samaria on the way." Under normal circumstances, *no* orthodox Jew would *ever* go to Galilee through Samaria. In fact, he would go miles and miles out of his way to avoid Samaria altogether. Most of the Jews of Jesus' time who wanted to travel from Judea to Galilee would take the long way around. This would make for a journey of about five days, even though there was a direct route that passed through Samaria that would take half the time.

Why would they do that?

One simple answer: prejudice.

The Jews wanted nothing to do with the Samaritans, and the feeling was mutual. They hated one another—not unlike the passionate hatred between Israelis and Palestinians today. But the gospel writer told us Jesus *had* to go.

Jesus, a good Jew, had to go through Samaria? Why?

Was it because He wanted to take the shortcut to save some time? No. He had to go through Samaria because there was a miserably unhappy, burned-out woman on a search for meaning in life. And unbeknownst to her, she had an appointment with God on that particular day.

The Lord and His Detour: What Does This Teach Us?

What can we learn from the deliberate detour Jesus took through Samaria?

We need to reach out to people who aren't necessarily like us.

The conventional wisdom for sharing my faith might go something like this: I need to find someone who looks and maybe thinks just like me and go talk to him because I can relate to him. (By that logic, I'm only going to speak to really handsome bald men.) In other words, for the most part I'm going to avoid approaching someone who is a little different from me, because we might not relate to one another.

Obviously, there is some validity to that line of thinking, but it can also put you in a position of limiting God.

I believe in the power of the Word of God to cross *every* barrier.

There is a trend in churches today for leadership to actually custom design their ministry to fit a certain demographic. For instance, some might say, "We want to have an affluent suburban church. Therefore, this is our target audience, and we will develop programs, our style of music, and everything else to reach this target audience in hopes that they will come." Another group might say, "We want to reach bikers. We want to talk a lot about bikes— Harleys and all those big, gnarly motorcycles."

Others see themselves as a surfer church.

Or a cowboy church.

Or a black church.

Or an Asian church.

I believe the church should reach *all* of these people—and reach them in the same congregation. Bikers next to surfers. Blacks next to whites. Asians next to Hispanics. All of us worshiping together and setting aside our differences because we are brothers and sisters in Christ and part of God's family.

To me, the beauty and the genius of the church Jesus started is that when a nonbeliever walks in he doesn't see a bunch of people who are the same age, same race, and same socioeconomic background. He will see people who are different from one another and yet have become one because of their faith in the Lord.

In Galatians 3:28 (TLB) we read, "We are no longer Jews or Greeks or slaves or free men or even merely men or women, but we are all the same—we are Christians; we are one in Christ Jesus."

I remember standing at the back of our church some time ago, talking to a guy who seemed to be an obvious "biker dude," dressed in all the biker leather and gear.

He introduced me to a sweet little old woman. Smiling, he said, "We just led her to the Lord the other day."

I'm looking at this big, rough biker and this tiny, elderly woman, and I'm having trouble processing the situation. I said, "How on earth would you ever even meet each other?"

"It was after our Easter service," he said. He and his biker buddy had been in a Jack in the Box restaurant, getting a meal, when they decided to go over and talk to this eighty-year-old woman, Bonnie, and her ninety-two-year-old husband, Tippy. The bikers invited the elderly couple to church, they came, and both of them made a commitment to Christ. The four of them have been the best of friends and have been walking with the Lord together for over two years.

These men were willing to cross a barrier, just as Jesus was willing to cross a barrier.

Jesus met this Samaritan woman at noon by the town well. Most of the women would have come to the well earlier in the day, before the sun got hot, to exchange the latest gossip and draw some water. But she came alone in the heat of the day, because she was a social outcast. She had been ostracized and she had no friends.

It must have been quite surprising for her to come to the well and see a visitor—someone she didn't recognize. And not only that, but He was clearly a *Jew*. A rabbi! She could tell these things by the way He dressed. A rabbi's robe had a thin strip of blue along the bottom edge, and it may have been that Jesus had that strip, too.

As a result of what she saw at the well, this Samaritan woman undoubtedly braced herself for a confrontation. Or at the very least a hateful sneer and stony silence.

Can you imagine her surprise when this rabbi approached her and said, "Will you give Me something to drink?" He was deliberately engaging her, and He'd had to cross a huge barrier to do even that.

We have to go where people are.

Jesus went to Samaria, into this woman's world, to reach her on that level. And that is what we need to do. We want to go to where people are living and walking and functioning, and invade that place with the gospel message.

Our crusades have been on many Christian TV networks and stations, but we recently went on a major secular station in Los Angeles—a station that had no other Christian programming. Why are we doing it? Because we want to go where people are. We want to "invade their space" with the message of the gospel.

We need to care about the people we speak to.

Again, John 4:4 (NLT) says, "He had to go through Samaria." Why did He have to go? Because He had a burden for this lost woman.

We need to keep at it even when we are tired.

John 4:6 (NLT) tells us that "Jesus, tired from the long walk, sat wearily beside the well about noontime."

What a picture! Here is God in human form, exhausted, wiped out! You know the feeling, don't you? We've all experienced times when we've said, "I can't go another step farther. I've got to sit down for a minute and rest."

The disciples had said, "Lord, we're going into town to get some food. Do You want to come?"

And Jesus would have essentially replied, "No, guys, you go on ahead. I'm just going to sit here by this well for a while."

If I had been God in that moment, I would have been hugely tempted to simply speak food into existence. Waiting for food is always hard for me. I'll order something in a restaurant and want to eat it right away! I will say, "When is the food coming?" When my wife is cooking a meal, I'll walk into the kitchen and say, "When will it be done?"

If I had been as weary and hungry as Jesus was surely weary and hungry, I would have spoken an In-N-Out burger into existence. But Jesus never used His miraculous powers for His own benefit. That is what the devil tempted Him to do during the temptation in the wilderness. After Jesus had been fasting for forty days, the evil one said to Him, "Hey, why don't You take this rock and turn it into a nice, fresh piece of bread if You're so hungry?" But Jesus refused that temptation. He never did a miracle for His own benefit.

When Luke wrote that Jesus was tired from the journey, we can be sure He was really exhausted. When we read the Gospels, we realize Jesus hardly ever had a moment to Himself. It wasn't only the physical strain of all that walking, those meager meals, and sleeping on the ground. He must have also had to deal with a tremendous spiritual and emotional drain. That's why He would spend long nights in prayer—to spiritually recharge, so to speak.

We have all kinds of advisors and counselors these days warning us about burning ourselves out with too much busyness. And, yes, there is some truth in what they say.

But at the same time, there is nothing wrong with getting tired in the service of the Lord. I've been a pastor for over thirty years, and I will tell you I have been tired. I have been tired *in* ministry, but never tired *of* ministry. What greater thing could I ever do than serve the Lord?

There are many worse things you could be tired from.

You could be tired from partying all night and not getting your rest.

You could be tired from trying to cover up your sins or escape from your own lies.

You could be tired from running around in a frenzy trying to have fun.

I'd rather be tired in the Lord's work!

I'd rather be tired from a long prayer meeting.

I'd rather be tired from counseling a troubled soul.

I'd rather be tired from helping people with a need.

People will say, "Hey, man, take it easy." But where does it say that in Scripture? Nowhere in the Bible are we told to slow down and take it easy. Oh, I know that's what we say to one another: "Hey man, take it easy." But the Bible tells us we are to press on, to not grow weary in well doing, and to run the race. In the book of Romans, Paul wrote, "Let us not allow slackness to spoil our work and let us keep the fires of the spirit burning, as we do our work for God" (12:11, PH). Our greatest recreation and rest will come later when we are in heaven.

Oswald Sanders once said, "The world is run by tired men." And I think you will find that effective ministries are run by tired pastors, and effective outreaches are run by tired, weary Christians.

In 1 Thessalonians 2:9 (NLT) Paul said, "Don't you remember, dear brothers and sisters, how hard we worked among you? Night and day we toiled to earn a living so that we would not be a burden to any of you as we preached God's Good News to you."

We must share the truth of God with tact and love.

Notice how Jesus made conversation with this woman and bridged the great gap between them.

"Please give Me a drink."

"Why would You, a Jew, ask for water from me, a Samaritan woman?"

"Ma'am, if you knew who it was speaking to you, you would have asked Him and He would have given you water that's alive."

"Water that's alive? What are You talking about? Are You greater than our ancestor Jacob?"

It was a *dialogue*. He wasn't lecturing her, He was engaging her. He had piqued her curiosity and arrested her attention. He spoke and He listened.

Often when we share our faith it's more like a monologue. "I'm going to preach a sermon to you, so shut up and listen, and I won't let you get a word in edgewise."

That's not effective communication. Learn to listen. Ask questions. Pay attention to what the other person is saying and respond appropriately. Show how the Word of God has everything he needs in life. Ask questions that get her to think about her life. That is what Jesus was doing. He was appealing to the woman's inner spiritual thirst.

In John 4:10 (NLT), He threw out the bait: "If you only knew the gift God has for you and who you are speaking to, you would ask me, and I would give you living water."

Initially her response was sarcastic and flippant—perhaps even cynical. She was verbally jousting with this Stranger—possibly because of her general attitude toward men. Men are all the same. *They're all dogs. Corrupt. Selfish. They don't care. So who is this guy? What's His angle?*

As she continued to converse with Jesus, however, she knew in her heart that something made Him different. She could see that He cared.

In the course of their brief dialogue, Jesus gave this woman three important facts. He told her who He was, what He had to offer, and how she could receive it.

Jesus Gives Her Three Facts

1. He told her who He was.

In verse 12, the Samaritan woman asked, "Are You greater than our father Jacob?" This is almost humorous to me. Jesus could have said, "Jacob? Jacob? Let Me tell you a little bit about Jacob. I know him pretty well. Remember the incident described in Genesis when Jacob wrestled all night with a mysterious Stranger? When it was all over, Jacob named the place 'Peniel,' because he said, 'I have seen God face to face.' Listen to Me. I was the One who wrestled with Jacob that night. And do you know what else? I whipped him."

He could have said that, but He didn't. He let the Jacob comment go right on by. She wasn't ready for that kind of information right then, so He didn't share it with her. It was too much.

When we share the gospel with someone, we need to

remember to keep it simple and to avoid rabbit trails. We also need to bear in mind that a non-Christian won't understand everything about the truth of the gospel.

One of the things I have so admired about Billy Graham's preaching through the years is his laser-beam simplicity with the essential gospel message. There are certain elements that must be in any gospel message—and many other side trips that need to be left out!

My objective is not to sway someone to my political views.

My objective is not to move someone toward my worldview.

My objective is not to focus on multiple lifestyle questions.

What I want to do before anything else is to help them move toward God to have their sins forgiven—regardless of their lifestyle, regardless of what they've been involved in to that point. Then, once they have met Christ and begin to study the Word, I believe the Lord Himself will begin to change their outlook and habits of life.

Sometimes in the church we get the cart before the horse. We are almost proclaiming political viewpoints or contemporary moral issues before Christ Himself.

I want people to hear the gospel and come to faith in Jesus. That is what the Lord was doing with the woman at the well.

At one point in the conversation, the Samaritan woman tried to get Jesus off on a rabbit trail regarding the right place to worship God. "We think it's in Samaria," she told Him, "but you Jews claim it's in Jerusalem."

Jesus brought her right back on message, telling her that whoever worships God must worship Him "in spirit and truth" (verse 23). That returned the conversation to the essential message He had been giving her: "I will satisfy your deepest spiritual thirst."

This was a woman who had been in and out of marriages, which isn't uncommon in our times, either. Someone will feel an initial sense of euphoria upon meeting someone else and will imagine they are "in love." They will call it "falling in love" or maybe "love at first sight."

"Oh—I have butterflies in my stomach. My mouth goes dry and my mind goes blank. I don't know what to say. I'm just so excited when I'm near her (or him). My heart is just aflutter."

If you married that person, would you really want to repeat that experience every single day? I have been married to my wife for over thirty years, and I can truthfully say I love her now more than the day I married her. But I don't want to have those initial experiences rerun every single day. If I came down the stairs and said, "Cathe, my mouth has gone dry and my mind is blank and my heart is aflutter," she would think I was having a heart attack and call 911.

Genuine love has to deepen and grow through the years. You understand that you have made a commitment, you have given your vows to that person for better or for worse, for richer or for poorer, in sickness and in health.

So many people say such words at their wedding and then quickly abandon those promises when they encounter difficult times. Someone has said, "What's so remarkable about 'love at first sight'? It's when the same two people have been looking at each other for years and years that love becomes remarkable."

I love the definition of married love that C. S. Lewis gave:

[Love] is not merely a feeling. It is a deep unity, maintained by the will and deliberately strengthened by habit; reinforced by . . . the grace which both spouses ask, and receive, from God. They can have this love for each other even at those moments when they do not like each other. . . . They can retain this love even when each would easily, if they allowed themselves, be "in love" with someone else. "Being in love" first moved them to promise fidelity: this quieter love enables them to keep the promise. It is on this love that the engine of marriage is run: being in love was the explosion that started it.[1]

Real love requires real commitment, but for whatever reason, the Samaritan woman wouldn't keep that commitment. As soon as the initial euphoria and excitement of a new relationship wore off, she was off to a new conquest, off to a new guy. The years went by, and the men in her life used her and abused her—including the one she was currently living with.

Jesus said to her, "Whoever drinks of this water will thirst again" (verse 13).

When He made that statement, He knew that the same thing could be said over all the "wells" in her life.

It's true for you and me, as well (no pun intended).

You could write it over the well of success. You could write it over the well of possessions. You could certainly write it over the well of pleasure. *If you drink of this water, you will thirst again.* You always want what you haven't got.

2. He told her what He had to offer.

One of the many diets I will try now and then is the Atkins diet—where you're allowed plenty of proteins and fat, but have to avoid carbohydrates. My problem is that I go on the diet . . . for a while. Then I weaken and go off it. My wife has actually said to me, "I think you're on a weight-gain diet right now, because you eat all of the fattening stuff on Atkins and then you go and you eat carbs."

It is possible to lose weight on this diet. I have lost pounds—but then gained them right back. Over and over. The first day on the diet is really cool. I can eat a cheese omelet with bacon on the side. I can actually have two chicken breasts for dinner and munch on cheese in between meals.

But after three or four days on the diet I start dreaming of carbs. I will say to my wife, "I dreamt about pizza last night." I remember telling her at one point, "I have an emptiness in my life that only carbs can fill!"

After another couple days I don't care about bacon. I don't want any more cheese. I don't want any more meat. I want *bread*. I want French fries. I want cereal. I want pancakes.

That's a poor illustration, perhaps, of those who have excluded God from their lives. No matter what they might say or insist about themselves, they have a craving for God—a deep inner longing for their Creator.

In Isaiah 26:9 (NIV), the prophet cried out to the Lord, "My soul yearns for you in the night; in the morning my spirit longs for you."

That's how it was for this Samaritan woman, and Jesus knew it immediately. So He began telling her what she needed to do to quench that deep inner thirst.

In John 4:14, He spoke of what He had to offer, saying, "Whoever drinks of the water that I shall give . . ." What did He mean by "living water" (verse 10)? He was basically describing water that moved—like a stream or river—as opposed to water that is stagnant.

3. He told her how to get it.

Jesus had been speaking to her of something more than physical water, and she knew it. But she was still playing coy with Him, and said, "Please, sir . . . give me this water! Then I'll never be thirsty again, and I won't have to come here to get water" (John 4:15, NLT).

From that point on, the conversation took a more direct turn.

Jesus said, "Why don't you call your husband and come back?"

She answered, "I don't have a husband."

And He essentially answered, "That's right, girl. You don't have a husband. You've been married and divorced five times, and now you're living with a guy."

I can imagine her mouth dropping open at that point. That woke her up.

Why did Jesus make that statement? Because she had been playing games with Him, and it was time for her to take the conversation seriously. He was saying, in essence, "I know what's going on with you. And before you can drink of the living water, before you can get right with Me, this sin needs to be identified and repented of."

This reminds us of the essential fact that there can be no conversion without conviction and repentance.

Some people want to bring Jesus in as a wonderful additive in life. They say to themselves, "I'll keep living the way I've been living and do what I want to do, but I'll add Jesus to the mix and everything will be great."

No, it won't.

Not knowing how else to reply, she said to Him, "Sir . . . you must be a prophet" (John 4:19, NLT). And of course He was and is far more than a prophet; He is the very Son of God.

With the truth beginning to dawn on her, she said cautiously, "I know the Messiah is coming—the one who is called Christ. When he comes, he will explain everything to us" (verse 25, NLT).

That's when Jesus dropped the bomb.

"I AM the Messiah!" (verse 26, NLT).

Boom! The Samaritan woman believed right on the spot. And in that moment she became the first female evangelist in the New Testament. The biblical account says, "The woman left her water jar beside the well and ran back to the village, telling everyone, 'Come and see a man who told me everything I ever did! Could he possibly be the Messiah?' So the people came streaming from the village to see him" (verses 28-30, NLT).

Even though her newfound faith was only moments old, she just had to tell others.

A Final Question

Returning to where I began this chapter, with the story of my mother, it's clear to me now that for many years she had been trying to satisfy a spiritual thirst with something or someone other than Jesus Christ.

She had been raised in the church, and deep down she knew what was true. And she discovered very late in the game that what she had been searching for her whole life was very near at hand. She was like the prodigal son in Jesus' story: He realized that everything he had been searching for in life was right there in his father's house.

Have you discovered that yet?

Nothing this world has to offer will satisfy your deepest spiritual thirst.

If you drink of the well of possessions, you will thirst again. Jesus said, "What will it profit a man if he gains the whole world, and loses his own soul?" (Mark 8:36).

If you drink at the well of pleasure, you will thirst again. The

Bible says that sin may be pleasurable for a season (see Hebrews 11:25, KJV), but it also flatly declares that "the wages of sin is death" (Romans 6:23).

You can drink at the well of what seems to you to be the "perfect relationship." But the woman in this story undoubtedly had high hopes, too—yet she went from marriage to marriage, from divorce to divorce. Only God can fill that void.

The Samaritan woman ran back into town, telling everyone she met, "Come and see a man who told me everything I ever did."

Jesus offers the same invitation to you. He says, "Come and see. Come and see for yourself who I am."

CHAPTER SEVEN
HOW TO EFFECTIVELY RESIST TEMPTATION

oing on a diet is a fine idea . . . until you get hungry.

Anyone can fast . . . on a full stomach.

But when you are hungry—really ravenous—the whole idea of that diet book you bought seems absurd. You walk through a grocery store to pick up a bunch of celery and a carton of tofu and you make the mistake of walking by the deli. Man does that stuff look good! *Mac and cheese. Swedish meatballs. Barbequed ribs.* Then you happen to stroll by the bakery, where they've just put out fresh doughnuts, and nothing in all the world smells like a fresh doughnut. Suddenly your desire for food puts a move on you like a champion wrestler.

In the same way, Satan, the enemy of our souls, knows how to package his temptations in ways that appeal to us. He knows how to market his wares in a way that makes bad things look not so bad at all.

Forbidden things, after all, have a certain charm, don't they? Someone says, "This thing is really bad. Stay away from it. Don't even look at it." And something inside us says, "I want to have a little look at that. I want to see what's so bad about it." And we are drawn to the very thing we know we ought to shun.

It happened to Eve in the Garden of Eden. God had given her and her husband complete freedom over the whole garden—and presumably, the place must have been vast. But He had given only one small restriction: Don't eat the fruit from one particular tree. And what happened? She was drawn to *that* tree like a magnet. With all the thousands and tens of thousands of beautiful trees in Eden, why did she find herself standing next to that particular tree, talking to the serpent? It was the wrong place at the wrong time with the wrong person.

Temptation, however, isn't sin. Everyone will be tempted. In fact, if you *aren't* being tempted there's something wrong with you. It was Matthew Henry who said, "The best of saints may be tempted to do the worst of sins."

So there is no sin in being tempted. It isn't the bait that constitutes temptation, it's the *bite*. It is giving in to that impulse. The fact is, if you find yourself being barraged by temptations lately, that could be an indication that you are doing something right, rather than doing something wrong. When the enemy sees you as a threat to his kingdom, he will try to bring you down. If you're no threat to him and he knows it, he will probably leave you alone.

In this chapter, we will consider six questions about temptation, and where it comes from.

Where Does Temptation Come From?

Then Jesus, being filled with the Holy Spirit, returned from the Jordan and was led by the Spirit into the wilderness, being tempted for forty days by the devil. And in those days He ate nothing, and afterward, when they had ended, He was hungry.

And the devil said to Him, "If You are the Son of God, command this stone to become bread."

But Jesus answered him, saying, "It is written, 'Man shall not live by bread alone, but by every word of God.'"

Then the devil, taking Him up on a high mountain, showed Him all the kingdoms of the world in a moment of time. And the devil said to Him, "All this authority I will give You, and their glory; for this has been delivered to me, and I give it to whomever I wish. Therefore, if You will worship before me, all will be Yours."

And Jesus answered and said to him, "Get behind Me, Satan! For it is written, 'You shall worship the LORD your God, and Him only you shall serve.'"

Then he brought Him to Jerusalem, set Him on the pinnacle of the temple, and said to Him, "If You are the Son of God, throw Yourself down from here. For it is written: 'He shall give His angels charge over you, to keep you,' and, 'In their hands they shall bear you up, lest you dash your foot against a stone.'"

And Jesus answered and said to him, "It has been said, 'You shall not tempt the LORD your God.'"

Now when the devil had ended every temptation, he departed from Him until an opportune time. (Luke 4:1-13)

Where does temptation come from? In a broad sense, it clearly comes from the devil. But the fact is, we play a key role in our own temptation. Satan needs our cooperation for us to give in. The enemy works within the context of our own desires.

Have you ever noticed how telemarketers always seem to call at dinnertime? Is that intentional? I guess they figure that's when we're at home. Sometimes when we get one of those calls, my wife answers and she's very polite to them.

I say to her, "Cathe, just hang up! Don't talk to telemarketers."

Not long ago the phone rang and I picked it up. Cathe looked at me, saw me nodding, and heard me say, "Oh really?"

She said, "Greg, who are you talking to?"

"A telemarketer."

"Hang up the phone!"

"You're right," I said, and hung up.

"Why were you talking to that person? You always tell me to hang up on those calls."

"Well, yes," I explained, "but this time they were offering something that was interesting to me. A better deal on cable TV!"

That's how it is with Satan and temptation. He sizes you up, figures out your vulnerabilities, and then brings a temptation across your path that will be attractive to you. It takes two to make a successful temptation—and you are one of the two.

The apostle James explained how it works:

But each one is tempted when he is drawn away by his own desires and enticed. Then, when desire has conceived, it gives birth to sin; and sin, when it is full-grown, brings forth death. Do not be deceived, my beloved brethren. (James 1:14-16)

Step One: "Each one is tempted . . ."

Each person is tempted; that's a given. (It may be true that opportunity only knocks once, but temptation beats on the door every single day, doesn't it?) So the temptation comes to you. That evil thought knocks on the door of your imagination.

What should we do with that temptation? The best thing to do is keep the door closed. We get into trouble when we think about opening it even a crack.

Step Two: "He is drawn away by his own desires . . ."

We are drawn away by our own desires, as James wrote, when we check out the temptation just a bit, maybe try it on for size, think about taking it for a little test drive. People who slide into this second step say to themselves, *Of course I would never actually DO this, but just for the sake of research I need to know a little bit more. . . .*

Frankly, the whole battle can be won or lost in those first few seconds. What makes temptation so difficult for so many people is they don't want to discourage it completely. They don't immediately embrace the temptation, but they let it hang around, thinking they can toy with it a little.

Step Three: "And enticed . . ."

By the time we are "enticed," it's almost too late. We're almost hooked.

Now we've moved from toying with the temptation to really giving it our attention. We've almost fallen into sin, but there is still a way out. There is still time to make a quick retreat. We can hang up the phone. We can walk out the door. We can shut down the computer. We can push that red "off" button on the remote. Those are the steps we need to take, and doing so may save us from getting tangled up in sin and grieving the heart of God.

Step Four: "When desire has conceived, it gives birth to sin . . ."

At this point the hook is set. The temptation has come and we have looked at it, thought about it, pursued it a little, and then suddenly say, "I'm going for it." *Chomp!* We bite down, the hook is in, and we experience a very temporary euphoria.

All too soon, however, the repercussions of sin start to kick in.

Step Five: "And sin, when it is full-grown, brings forth death . . ."

Death comes in a thousand little ways. Guilt and remorse flood in after the euphoria vanishes. We feel dead inside, and we begin dealing with the consequences or repercussions of our actions.

That is when we need to go immediately to the Lord and say, "Lord, I fell. I am sorry. I repent." And we get right with Him as quickly as we can. We *run* back to Jesus.

We have three enemies to contend with as Christians: the world, the flesh, and the devil. The world with its allure is the external foe. The flesh with its evil desires is the internal foe. And the devil with his enticements is the infernal foe. These are our opponents, and this is the warfare that never stops until we step through the gate of heaven.

"Frenemies" with the World?

I think the problem is that we become *frenemies* with the world. A "frenemy" is a person whom you normally wouldn't get along with, but you patch things up with them temporarily if it serves both of your purposes. In other words, you have developed a love-hate relationship; sometimes you're on, and sometimes you're off, depending on the circumstances.

Being frenemies might also describe a relationship that is essentially poisonous and drags you down spiritually, but you have allowed it to continue anyway. The person is not a friend, and is really more like an enemy. Some of us have become frenemies with this world. First John 2:15-16 tells us more:

> Do not love the world or the things in the world. If anyone loves the world, the love of the Father is not in him. For all that is in the world—the lust of the flesh, the lust of the eyes, and the pride of life—is not of the Father but is of the world.

If you are a friend of the world, you are God's enemy. The word *world* here is not a synonym for "earth." It's okay to love the earth. It's okay to get excited about sunsets and rainbows and crashing surf and snowcapped mountains. The Bible isn't speaking about God's creation here. The term refers to a system, a mentality, a pervasive philosophy that infects everything everywhere.

Listen to another translation of 1 John 2:15-17:

> Don't love the world's ways. Don't love the world's goods. Love of the world squeezes out love for the Father. Practically everything that goes on in the world—wanting your own way, wanting everything for yourself, wanting to appear important— has nothing to do with the Father. It just isolates you from him. The world and all its wanting, wanting, wanting is on the way out—but whoever does what God wants is set for eternity. (MSG)

Yes, the world—with all its glitter, sparkle, and glamour—can appear very enticing at times. But in order for its pull to work, we must desire what it is offering. Jesus said, "For out of the heart proceed evil thoughts, murders, adulteries, fornications, thefts, false witness, blasphemies. These are the things which defile a man" (Matthew 15:19-20). The problem is within. We have ourselves to thank when we give in to temptation. It's just our nature.

Where Does Temptation Come From?

The short answer: It comes from our own sinful nature!

I'm reminded of the classic story of the scorpion and the tortoise. One day there was a tortoise sitting by a pond sunning himself. A scorpion walked up to him and said, "Hello, Mr. Tortoise. I was wondering if you would give me a lift across the pond."

The tortoise replied, "I don't think I should do that. You would sting me, and then I would drown."

The scorpion replied, "My dear tortoise, if I were to sting you I would go down with you. Now where is the logic in that?"

"That is true," said the tortoise. "All right. Hop on." And as they made their way across the pond, the scorpion stuck his stinger into the tortoise's neck, and they both began to sink.

Before he went under, the tortoise said, "Do you mind if I ask you something?"

"Ask away," said the scorpion.

"You said there was no logic in stinging me. Now we're both going to drown. Why did you do it?"

The scorpion replied, "It has nothing to do with logic, tortoise. It's just my nature."

That's how it works with us, too. Why do we do the stupid stuff we do sometimes? It's just our sinful human nature that we inherited from our parents, and they inherited from their parents, all the way back to Adam.

I'm thinking right now of a particular family. God had blessed them, and both husband and wife were raising their children to love the Lord. Why did that husband betray his wife and his family and his Lord to commit adultery? Why did he act in such an insane, damaging, hurtful, and irrational way? Why did he destroy his marriage and his family? It makes no sense! But that's the point. It has nothing to do with sense or logic. *It's just our nature.*

So we have to be aware of that. We have to be cognizant of the unruly, combustible, evil sinful nature that makes its home inside every one of us, with no exceptions.

Sometimes we blame God. We say, "It's God's fault. He gave me more than I could handle." No, He didn't! James 1:13 says, "Let no one say when he is tempted, 'I am tempted by God'; for God cannot be tempted by evil, nor does He Himself tempt anyone."

Or someone else will say, "The devil made me do it."

No, he didn't make you do it. You cooperated. You willfully engaged in the temptation that landed in front of you.

When Does Temptation Come?

The broad answer to that question is simple: It comes all the time. We are never truly free from it.

But there are certainly times when it becomes more intense.

I believe one of the times when we have to be most on our guard against temptation is after a time of great blessing.

When did Satan hit Jesus with his first recorded barrage of temptation? It was immediately after Jesus' baptism in the Jordan River. It's such a glorious moment in the life of Christ—and I'm sure it meant more to Him than we can begin to comprehend.

> *Just as Jesus was coming up out of the water, he saw heaven being torn open and the Spirit descending on him like a dove. And a voice came from heaven: "You are my Son, whom I love; with you I am well pleased." (Mark 1:10-11, NIV)*

The sky was "torn open"? Yes, Mark used a term in the original language that means to split, sever, or tear open. Something *very* dramatic happened in that moment.

And then Jesus heard those incredibly affirming words from His Father as the Holy Spirit in the form of a dove descended on Him. It was a Trinity moment, and how can we calculate how joyful that must have been for Jesus?

That's why the very next verses in Mark are so significant: "At once the Spirit sent him out into the wilderness, and he was in the wilderness forty days, being tempted by Satan" (verses 12-13, NIV).

Immediately after the dove came the devil.

Immediately after the affirmation came the testing.

This is often the way it happens in our lives as well. After a time of blessing, after we have had the strong sense that the Lord has used us in a positive way, we get hit with a drone strike from hell.

It might be right after church or a Bible study or a significant spiritual conversation. I have seen the pattern repeated over and over in my life, and many others would say the same thing.

Remember the story in Scripture of the Transfiguration of Jesus? The Lord and His three closest disciples were up on a mountaintop when the disciples suddenly saw Jesus transformed before their very eyes: "His face shone like the sun, and His clothes became as white as the light. And behold, Moses and Elijah appeared to them, talking with Him" (Matthew 17:2-3).

Wow, talk about a mountaintop moment! Moses and Elijah? For a Jew it doesn't get much better than that! But then they went back down that mountain of blessing, and the first thing they encountered was a child possessed by a powerful demon.

That's how it so often is; after the blessing comes the attack.

But mark this: Temptation will also come *when we think we are the strongest*. Sometimes people say, "I could potentially fall in area A, B, or C, but I would never fall in area D."

Don't say stuff like that.

The fact is, you don't know what you are capable of doing in your sinful nature. You could do the worst thing imaginable. *Anyone* could. As the old hymn says, "Prone to wander, Lord I feel it. Prone to leave the God I love."

That's all of us. We are prone to wander. Never doubt it! In the book of Jeremiah, the Lord describes the human heart as "deceitful above all things, and desperately wicked; who can know it?" (17:9).

Remember that it was immediately after Simon Peter began boasting about his great devotion to the Lord that he stumbled badly and fell. It was Simon Peter boasting of his great devotion to the Lord that led to his fall. As Solomon wrote, "Pride goes before destruction, and a haughty spirit before a fall" (Proverbs 16:18).

To Whom Does Temptation Come?

As we have noted, temptation comes to everyone; we are all susceptible. Even so, the enemy often focuses his attention on those who are young in the faith and those who are making a difference in the kingdom.

Young believers are particularly vulnerable to Satan's deceptions and attacks. I think of my little granddaughters. When they were babies, they would grab things without any idea what they were grabbing. They would try to stuff random things into their mouths that had no business being in their mouths. They didn't know any better. In their innocence, they would wave to and chatter at any stranger who walked by. The fact is, young children need to be nurtured, loved, and protected, because the world can be a hostile, hurtful place.

Newborn Christians need the same kind of care. At our church, we give out copies of *The New Believer's Bible* to everyone who receives the Lord. We tell our people, "If you see someone carrying that Bible, it's a good indication that they have recently come to Christ. Take time to introduce yourself to them. Ask them how they're doing. Ask them when they committed their lives to Jesus, and how it's been going. Offer to pray with them and for them. Remind them that God will be faithful to them and help them, even when the inevitable attacks come."

We need to help and encourage new believers whenever and however we can.

But there is another "target" group on Satan's hit list, and it is those who are truly making a difference for the kingdom of God. Do you imagine that if you stand up and say, "Lord, I will do what You want me to do and go where You want me to go," that you will get a standing ovation in hell?

Hardly. It's more likely that you will acquire a target on your back. So, stay very alert and keep your guard up. As Vance Havner wrote, "If you have not been through the devil's sifter, you are probably not worth sifting."

Someone may say, "Greg, I can't even remember the last time I was tempted."

That may not be good news! You don't kick a dead horse. The devil looks at such a person and says, "Why should I bother attacking him? He's no threat to me. I'm going to save my attacks for this person over here who keeps being used by God. She's really getting on my nerves!"

How Does Temptation Come?

Temptation comes primarily through the doorway of our minds.

Paul wrote, "I am afraid that just as Eve was deceived by the serpent's cunning, your minds may somehow be led astray from your sincere and pure devotion to Christ" (2 Corinthians 11:3, NIV).

Beware of those flaming arrows aimed at your mind. Beware of allowing ungodly thoughts to gain any traction. You can't stop them from coming, but you can dispose of them as soon as they arrive!

In 2 Corinthians 10:5-6 (MSG), Paul told us,

We use our powerful God-tools for smashing warped philosophies, tearing down barriers erected against the truth of God, fitting every loose thought and emotion and impulse into the structure of life shaped by Christ. Our tools are ready at hand for clearing the ground of every obstruction and building lives of obedience into maturity.

Fill your mind with God's Word!

I recently filled the hard drive on my computer, mostly with photographs. It wouldn't let me load even one more picture. So I had the drive replaced and a larger hard drive installed. Until I did, my hard drive was too full to absorb any new information.

Wouldn't it be great if the devil couldn't fit any evil thoughts into your mind because it was already filled up with the Word of God?

Philippians 4:8 (MSG) says, "Summing it all up, friends, I'd say you'll do best by filling your minds and meditating on things true, noble, reputable, authentic, compelling, gracious—the best, not the worst; the beautiful, not the ugly; things to praise, not things to curse."

Temptation comes to us because we're not strict with ourselves about shutting evil thoughts out of our minds. Someone may say, "Yes, I agree with you that sin would hurt me, but I don't really intend to buy anything. I just want to do a little window shopping and see what's out there." So we allow ourselves to do a little browsing, and then next thing we know we're hanging out with the wrong people at the wrong places and end up doing the wrong things.

Satan has an amazing marketing strategy for sin. You think all of those ad agencies on Madison Avenue are clever? They can't hold a candle to Satan's marketing. The key is, don't listen to even the first words of his pitch. Shut him down. As James 4:7 (PH) says, "Resist the devil and you'll find he'll run away from you."

Where Is the Best Place to Be When Temptation Comes?

The best place to be is in God's will.

In other words, don't put yourself in places where you don't belong. Don't hang out with people who aren't good for you and who lead you into doing things you shouldn't.

Let's imagine you have a severe coffee allergy, and have to give up coffee altogether. But you have always loved coffee. Every time you smell it brewing, you want to get a cup of it, even though you know you'll pay a heavy price. So don't go anywhere near a coffee shop! Don't tell yourself that you'll order tea or just get a cookie and a juice. Stay away from coffee as best as you can in this coffee-crazy culture of ours.

The best place to be when temptation comes is smack-dab in the middle of God's will, doing the things He has asked you to do, and being with people who will build you up and encourage you in your faith.

Yes, Jesus faced intense temptation in the wilderness, but the Spirit of God led Him there. And when it was over, angels came and ministered to Him. Jesus was in the very center of His Father's will when He went one-on-one with Satan and turned back every one of the enemy's attacks with Bible verses He quoted from memory.

To sum up, being in God's will and being in God's Word won't keep you from temptations or Satan's attacks. In fact, Satan might quote some Scripture right back at you—out of context.

In one of Satan's last temptations of Jesus, we read that he transported Him to Jerusalem, set Him on the pinnacle of the temple, and said, "If You are the Son of God, throw Yourself down. For it is written: 'He shall give His angels charge over you,' and, 'In their hands they shall bear you up, lest you dash your foot against a stone'" (Matthew 4:6).

Satan was quoting from Psalm 91 verses 11-12. Yes, the devil apparently knows the Scriptures well and may quote from them when it serves his purposes. But he quoted it out of context. God will certainly protect us with His angels, but He doesn't promise to shield us from deliberate self-destruction.

Satan was using Scripture, but not in the way it was intended.

I heard a story not long ago about the comedian W. C. Fields, whose whole shtick was playing an inebriated man. Sadly, his real personal life seemed to reflect his public image, because Fields was an alcoholic. According to the story, someone actually saw W. C. Fields leafing through the pages of a Bible once.

"W. C. Fields reading the Bible?" the person said wonderingly. "Why on earth would you be reading the Bible?"

"Looking for loopholes!" Fields deadpanned.

That's the way Satan reads the Bible. Looking for loopholes. Looking for ways to misuse it, misquote it, or rip it out of its proper context. Our best defense, of course, is to know its context and to be conversant with its content, so we can defend ourselves when we're hit by someone who twists and misuses the Bible.

The book of Acts tells us about a group of believers who pursued that very course. We read, "Now the Berean Jews were of more noble character than those in Thessalonica, for they received the message with great eagerness and examined the Scriptures every day to see if what Paul said was true" (17:11, NIV).

Which brings us to our final point.

What Is the Primary Weapon We Should Use to Resist Temptation?

The Word of God.

It's great to carry a Bible in your briefcase or purse or have it loaded on your smartphone or tablet. But the best place to carry the Word of God is in your heart. You need to know the Word of God and memorize it. Psalm 119:9 says, "How can a young man cleanse his way? By taking heed according to Your word." Verse 11 says, "Your word I have hidden in my heart, that I might not sin against You."

Are you memorizing the Bible?

"I can't memorize," you say. "It's just too hard. I'm not very good at remembering things."

Really? We all have so much information in our brains—much of it totally useless. It is astounding what the brain can retain. I've talked to some guys who know the scores of their favorite sports teams going back twenty years. Many of us can quote those mindless jingles from ads we heard on TV decades ago. Some people know the codes for certain video games so they can gain an advantage. Others know all kinds of trivia about the entertainment world or minutia about people they admire.

But you can't memorize the Word of God?

Yes, it takes some time and some discipline. But when you find yourself under attack by the evil one and his minions, you will be glad you equipped yourself to emerge victorious.

For instance, when the devil whispers in your ear, "You've really blown it this time. God is so disgusted with you He might never forgive you!"

Instead of panicking or falling into depression, you quickly say back to him, "No! That is a lie. First John 1:9 says, 'if we confess our sins, He is faithful and just to forgive us our sins and to cleanse us from all unrighteousness.'"

Or maybe Satan says, "God condemns you for what you have done. You're under His condemnation!" Again, you say, "Not so! Romans 8:1 tells me that 'There is therefore now no condemnation to those who are in Christ Jesus.'"

Satan might say, "You'll never make it as a Christian. You're going to fall away, and God will give up on you."

And you reply, "Get out of here, Satan. That's not true. Philippians 1:6 tells me, 'Being confident of this very thing, that He who has begun a good work in [me] will complete it until the day of Jesus Christ.'"

When tragedy hits your life, as it inevitably will, the devil may say, "That's it. Your life is over. It's ruined. God has abandoned you."

"Oh, no, He hasn't!" you reply. "Because Romans 8:28 says that 'All things work together for good to those who love God, to those who are the called according to *His* purpose.'"

When a Christian loved one dies, Satan may whisper, "That's it. They're gone. You'll never see them again."

Again, you reply, "That's a lie and you are a liar, Satan. Jesus said in John 11:25-26, 'I am the resurrection and the life. He who believes in Me, though he may die, he shall live. And whoever lives and believes in Me shall never die.'" And then you quote 2 Corinthians 5:8, which says that to be absent from the body is to be present with the Lord.

Temptation will be part of our lives until we finally arrive home in heaven. Even so, it can be effectively resisted while we're on earth as we memorize Scripture, stay close to God and His people, and stay away from the ungodly influences that hurt us and drag us down.

Paul summed it up well in his words to his young friend Timothy: "Run from anything that stimulates youthful lusts. Instead, pursue righteous living, faithfulness, love, and peace. Enjoy the companionship of those who call on the Lord with pure hearts" (2 Timothy 2:22, NLT).

Flee from temptation, and follow the Lord. Flee and follow.

And don't leave a forwarding address.

CHAPTER EIGHT
DEAD MAN WALKING

ears ago I took scuba diving lessons in Hawaii and, believe it or not, became a certified scuba diver.

During those days of training, a friend of mine wanted to go on a deep-water dive—something I'd never attempted before. The greatest depth I had achieved to that point was around thirty feet. Just off the island of Molokai, however, there is a dive that goes down a hundred feet—which is just a little bit scary for a beginner. When you're diving at thirty feet, for instance, you can push a little button that will inflate a vest and take you right to the top. But if you get yourself into trouble at a hundred feet, the vest isn't going to be much help.

We were making our dive that day with an instructor who told us, "If you run out of air, come right over to me." He gave us all the signals to use underwater, because talking isn't much good, either. Running out of air, however, was the last thing on my mind.

It shouldn't have been. About twenty minutes into the dive, I suddenly realized I was in serious trouble. Apparently, I'd been so excited and breathing so fast that I'd used up all the air in my tank. A quick glance at my air pressure gauge confirmed what I already knew: I was deeper in the ocean than I had ever been before, and *I was out of air*. Somehow, this wasn't the way I had imagined myself dying.

Turning to my instructor, I gave the universal sign for "out of air." He gestured for me to swim over to him and pointed at his back. It was time to employ "the octopus." He had told us about this little emergency breathing device with a short hose that hooked into the instructor's tank. I tapped into it immediately and had to breathe off that little piece of equipment for the rest of the dive.

Yes, I was very grateful to have air, but it was so humiliating. I had to use shallow, short strokes and keep up with him without bumping into him. Where he moved, I had to move, hovering over him and feeling embarrassed and absurd. It was the deepest dive of my life and, in another sense, one of my lowest moments. I was completely dependent on the instructor; if he didn't give me that air, I was a dead man.

Have you ever been in a situation like that—one that left you feeling overwhelmed and helpless? Maybe you had set certain goals for your life—like financial success—but somehow your dreams came up empty and you started to lose hope.

The truth is, just as people can't live very long without air, they also can't live very long without hope.

I read a newspaper article not long ago about an attractive, successful, young woman named Autumn Radtke, who became a rising star in what's known as the virtual currency world. She had been groomed working for Apple and other Silicon Valley tech firms, and incredibly, by age twenty-eight, she had become the CEO of her own multimillion-dollar company. Imagine the shock and dismay of everyone who knew her when they read in their morning newspaper that she had jumped from the balcony of a sixteen-story apartment building. Her death, according to the article, was one of eight suspected suicides in the financial sector in 2014 alone. That list included a thirty-three-year-old J. P. Morgan financial pro who leaped off his firm's building in Hong Kong. A few weeks earlier, a vice president with that same company jumped off the bank's Canary Wharf tower in London.

What in the world is going on? Here are bright, intelligent, young men and women, brilliantly successful in their field, who became so despondent that they couldn't bear to face even one more day of life.

This reminds me of an article I read in 2009 about a German billionaire. After enduring a series of financial setbacks, he felt a deep sense of hopelessness and took his own life. At the height of his success, he'd had assets worth 9.2 billion dollars. And how much did he lose? A billion or two? What if it had been half his fortune? Well, he would have still been worth something like 4.5 billion. And what if it had been even worse, and he only had a billion dollars left to his name? Actually, most people I know could live rather well on a billion dollars.

It's so sad. So insane.

Before Autumn Radtke took her own life, she had posted a link on her Facebook page about entrepreneurs suffering depression. And she added this comment: "Everything has its price."

How true. Jesus said, "For what profit is it to a man if he gains the whole world, and loses his own soul? Or what will a man give in exchange for his soul?" (Matthew 16:26). I wish with all my heart someone could have shared the gospel of Jesus Christ with every one of those despondent people before they allowed their despair to destroy them.

In Luke chapter 5, we encounter the stories of two nearly hopeless men in two seemingly impossible situations.

But there was a difference with these men. They encountered Jesus.

Despair and Hope

Luke 5 identifies the first desperate man as a leper, afflicted with this incurable disease in its last terrible stages. One translation says he was "full of leprosy."

But rumor had it that Jesus, the prophet from Nazareth, was passing through his town, and this man entertained a sudden wild hope that Jesus could—and just might—heal him. The other individual in this passage was paralyzed and unable to walk. But he had four very persistent friends who would not take no for an answer, and determined to bring him before Jesus.

Again, these were two men who found themselves in two very different situations. But their need was the same. They were on the edge of despair, and they needed Jesus.

What's your situation? Do you have some insurmountable walls in your life? Do you feel trapped at a dead end with no way out? Are you facing circumstances you have no idea how to handle or where to turn? This chapter might contain the answers you've been looking for. What happened to the two despondent, desperate men in Luke 5 could also happen to you.

Before we go on to open up the Scriptures, I'd like to make this one point: It's so important for those of us who know the Lord and have tasted and experienced His hope and peace and joy to let that light shine from our lives wherever we go. There is a place I go every now and then to get coffee with my family. Right next to it is a little sunglasses store, and I'll sometimes walk in and look around while I'm waiting for my coffee. On one such occasion I struck up a conversation with a young woman who worked there. Before long, I began to share the gospel with her. Every time I went to get coffee in that place, I'd walk around the corner and talk to her a little bit more. One time I gave her one of my books.

Then one day I noticed she wasn't working there anymore.

Last week I went back to the coffee shop with a friend and the sunglasses girl walked through the door.

"Hey, how are you?" I said. "I haven't seen you for a long time. Do you still work in that store?"

"No," she said, "I don't work there anymore." She was wearing this huge smile and said, "But guess what happened?"

"What?"

"I became a Christian!"

"Really? That's wonderful! Tell me how that happened."

"I just looked at you and your family," she said, "and saw how happy you were whenever you came in. I looked at some other Christians I know, and they were all so happy, too. I thought, *Why do they get to be happy and I'm not happy? I want what they have!"*

So she committed her life to Christ, and I could tell from her face—her whole countenance—that she had found what she had been looking for.

I tell that story just to make the point that what happened to the two needy, seemingly hopeless people in Luke 5 is still happening today, all over the world, as people turn to Jesus in their unhappiness and despair. But as Paul said, "How, then, can they call on the one they have not believed in? And how can they believe in the one of whom they have not heard? And how can they hear without someone preaching to them?" (Romans 10:14, NIV).

Let's dip into the passage now for a closer look.

A Desperate Situation

And it happened when He was in a certain city, that behold, a man who was full of leprosy saw Jesus; and he fell on his face and implored Him, saying, "Lord, if You are willing, You can make me clean."

Then He put out His hand and touched him, saying, "I am willing; be cleansed." Immediately the leprosy left him. And He charged him to tell no one, "But go and show yourself to the priest, and make an offering for your cleansing, as a testimony to them, just as Moses commanded."

However, the report went around concerning Him all the more; and great multitudes came together to hear, and to be healed by Him of their infirmities. So He Himself often withdrew into the wilderness and prayed. (Luke 5:12-16)

Again, verse 12 says that this man was "full of leprosy." Other translations say he was "covered with leprosy." This means that this disfiguring disease had almost completely run its course. It was about as bad as it gets.

Leprosy today is more often referred to as Hansen's disease. It was once thought that leprosy was a flesh-eating disease, but more recent research reveals that the disfigurement of the body comes from afflicted individuals losing their sense of touch and not being able to feel pain. For instance, if you were to wash your face with scalding water you wouldn't even know it, because you couldn't feel it. In Third World countries there have been lepers who have fallen asleep and woken up with fingers or toes missing, because vermin have come in the night and eaten them away. But the sleeper never awakened and never felt anything.

When you were a leper in New Testament times, you had to shout, "Unclean, unclean" wherever you went. People with leprosy were ostracized in the worst possible ways. For instance, if a leper stuck his head inside a person's house, the whole house had to be pronounced unclean. You weren't allowed to even greet a leper. One Jewish historian said lepers were treated as if they were, in effect, dead people.

Dead men walking.

Dead women walking.

That's a phrase that's also used to describe someone who is on their way to their execution, walking to the electric chair, the lethal injection gurney, or a hangman's noose. The guards would say, "Dead man walking" as that person made his way to the place of execution. But in this passage, the dead man walking was in the final stages of a terrible disease.

You might be reading this, thinking, "Greg, I really don't know anybody with leprosy. I don't really need to hear any more about this."

Leprosy, however, has some things to teach us about the effects of sin in our lives. In what way?

Leprosy starts small.

Think about it. The disease might start with a little scab on your hand, arm, or leg—so small it hardly seems worth bothering about. But, in fact, it is a warning. Sin is the same way. Little did Eve, in the Garden of Eden, know the pain and sorrow that would come to this planet as a result of that one quick bite of the forbidden fruit. But that's how sin works. Very rarely do we take time to think through the cause and effect of our actions. We don't say to ourselves, "If I do *this*, then *that* may happen . . . and if *that* happens then *this other thing* will happen. And if that other thing happens, then all these *many other things* will happen."

Instead, we just live in the moment. We say to ourselves, "Hey, this will be fun." Even the Bible says sin is pleasurable for a time (see Hebrews 11:25). In that instant, it's exciting. We feel like we're getting away with something—a forbidden pleasure. But it always comes with a hefty payment afterward. And Romans 6:23 states very clearly that "the wages of sin is death"—not immediate death perhaps, but death in all of its terrible and depressing forms.

Sin starts small. But a few moments of passion can lead to a lifetime of regret. That one little fling, that so-called one-night stand, can result in an unplanned pregnancy, a sexually transmitted disease, or even AIDS. But we don't think about that; we think about the immediate pleasure and close our minds to possible consequences.

Leprosy works almost imperceptibly.

Leprosy can barely be perceived in its initial stages. The disease is difficult to track. It might start with a bright spot on a leg. And then another one appears on the neck—followed by more here and there on various parts of the body. You try to cover it up to keep it hidden. But the time comes when you can't hide it any longer.

Naaman, the Syrian general in 2 Kings 5, tried to cover his leprosy. He wore his armor all the time because he didn't want anyone to see his true condition. In fact, his own troops were shocked when, at the command of Elisha the prophet, he stripped off his armor to immerse himself in the Jordan River seven times. For the first time, his men would have realized, "Whoa! General Naaman is a *leper!*"

We do the same with our sin. We cover it up. We hide it. We think no one will ever see it. And we have no idea how quickly it is spreading. Sin works through our lives and infects us. It's contagious! That's why we need to give careful thought to whom we choose to spend time with. The Bible says, "Do not be yoked together with unbelievers. For what do righteousness and wickedness have in common? Or what fellowship can light have with darkness? What harmony is there between Christ and Belial? Or what does a believer have in common with an unbeliever?" (2 Corinthians 6:14-15, NIV).

Maybe you are a single woman dating a non-Christian guy. You call it "missionary dating" and entertain hopes of eventually leading him to Christ. Can I let you in on a little secret? A plan like that is just as likely to end with you falling away as with him coming to faith. If I've seen it once, I've seen it a thousand times. It's a lot easier for a nonbeliever to pull a believer down than it is for a believer to pull a nonbeliever up. In 1 Corinthians 15:33 (NIV), Paul wrote, "Do not be misled: 'Bad company corrupts good character.'"

Leprosy was a state of living death, causing loss of sensation, discoloration of the skin, and impaired vision. In the same way, the Bible says that before we came to Christ, we were dead in trespasses and sin (see Ephesians 2:1). Scripture says of the woman who lives for pleasure that she is dead even while she is living (see 1 Timothy 5:6). Those who allow sin to remain in their lives lose their sense of touch. They're not able to feel things. They become hardened.

I'm reminded of the story of the man who went to see the doctor with two severely burned ears. The doctor shook his head and said, "I have never seen anything like this! Please, tell me, how did this happen?"

"I was ironing," the man said, "and I had my phone next to the iron. Then, when the phone rang, I answered the iron instead of the phone."

"Oh, that's horrible!" the doctor replied. "But how did you burn your other ear?"

"Well," he said, "they called back!"

That can happen to us. Our heart or our conscience is cauterized or rendered insensitive. We can become numb to the conviction of the Holy Spirit.

At my house, we used to have an overly sensitive smoke alarm on the ceiling in the kitchen that went off if it even thought it smelled smoke. You couldn't make a piece of toast or fry an egg without that thing shrilling and driving everyone crazy. I'd have to grab a broom and poke at that little button in the middle of it to turn it off. Finally I couldn't take it anymore. I pulled up a chair and ripped it right off the ceiling. Then we replaced it with a new one that wasn't quite as particular.

You can have an overly sensitive conscience that responds too much, but you can also have a conscience that's been seared as with a hot iron and doesn't feel anything anymore (see 1 Timothy 4:2).

Leprosy was incurable.

In the past, once you contracted leprosy, there was no hope. It was a virtual death sentence. Now, the disease is treated with antibiotics. However, the person with leprosy must take the antibiotics for the disease to be stopped. The same is true of sin. There is no cure apart from the forgiveness of God. You can't run from it. You may change your appearance, your job, your friends, or your location, but you still take yourself with you wherever you go. Nothing can change you but God alone, through the blood of Jesus Christ.

"If You Are Willing . . ."

The man with leprosy had a realistic awareness of his condition. In Luke 5:12 he said, "Lord, if You are willing, You can make me clean." He acknowledged before the Lord that he was unclean and that he couldn't do anything about it in his own strength. He was saying, in effect, "Lord, we both know what my condition is. We both know I have no hope apart from You."

And he added the words, *"If You are willing . . ."*

I love this statement. There was no sense of expectation or entitlement here. He was just saying, "Lord, I know You can do this; that isn't the issue here. I'm just asking if it's in Your will to do this. Would You do it for me?"

That is the way to pray, adding "if it is Your will" to your prayers. Even Jesus prayed that way in the Garden of Gethsemane as He was anguishing over the impending death He faced on the cross. With His heart breaking, He prayed, "My Father, if it is possible, may this cup be taken from me. Yet not as I will, but as you will" (Matthew 26:39, NIV). In other words, "Father, I really don't want to do this, but if You want Me to I will do it. Your will be done."

Jesus also taught us to pray in this way in the Lord's Prayer, which is effectively a template for all prayer. "Our Father in heaven, hallowed be Your name. Your kingdom come. Your will be done on earth as it is in heaven. Give us this day our daily bread" (Matthew 6:9-11). Notice that before you get to the part where you start asking for things, you say, "Lord, I want Your will."

Many times, He will say yes to your requests; He will provide for you or pull you out of a bad situation that you're in. But at other times He will say, "Not now. I have a work I want to do in your life. I have some changes I want to bring into your life through these circumstances. I love you too much to shortcut the process." God has purposes in everything He does.

Jesus will touch those who come reverently and in desperation to Him.

The man who was full of leprosy, with no earthly hope of healing, saw Jesus and fell on his face before Him. By the way, that's a good place to be when God is near. On your face. When God came to Abraham, Abraham fell on his face. When the prophet Ezekiel saw heavenly visions, he fell on his face. When the elders in heaven saw the throne of God, they too fell on their faces.

Have you ever fallen on your face before God? I'm speaking very literally here. Have you ever found yourself lying flat on the dirt or carpet or grass in complete desperation before God? Have you gone that low?

I have. I will tell you the very day. It was on July 24, 2008, when I heard the news that my son Christopher had died. Our house was immediately filled with well-wishers who all had something to say. Some of those words were helpful, and some weren't. But I remember thinking, *I need God right now. If God doesn't come through for me, I don't know how I can get through this at all.*

I fell on my face before God, and said, "God, help me!"

And He did. He came through for me, and He continues to come through for me. He will come through for you as well.

Matthew's gospel says the leper knelt before Jesus (see 8:2, NIV). I don't know if he started out on his face and then got up into a kneeling position, or if it was the other way around. But we know he was on his face before Jesus.

I think sometimes people are a little too flippant, a little too casual, when they come to God. Yes, certainly He is our Friend. And, yes, He is our Father who loves us. *But this is God.* This is the all-powerful One, the majestic Creator of everything. Don't forget that. This is why we read in Scripture, "Don't be hasty in bringing matters before God. After all, God is in heaven, and you are here on earth. So let your words be few" (Ecclesiastes 5:2, NLT).

Don't prattle on and on, especially in an irreverent way. This man was reverent, and he cried out to Jesus.

His faith was active.

We read that "he fell on his face and implored Him, saying, 'Lord, if You are willing, You can make me clean'" (Luke 5:12). In the parallel passage in Mark's gospel, the text implies that the man repeated this a number of times. Over and over again. Was that really necessary? Well, it sure impressed Jesus.

There is a time when we just refuse to back down in our prayers. Jesus said, "Ask and it will be given to you; seek and you will find; knock and the door will be opened to you" (Luke 11:9, NIV). In the Greek, that statement could be translated, "Keep on asking, keep on seeking, keep on knocking."

The man dying of leprosy was determined to press forward with his request. If the Lord had said no, or "I am *not* willing," that would have been the end of the matter. But until Jesus said that or walked away, the desperate man was going to keep reaching out for mercy and healing. This was a remarkable display of faith that touched the heart of Jesus. According to Mark's record of the same incident, Jesus was "moved with compassion" (1:41), and He reached out and touched this man.

Luke 5:13 says Jesus "put out His hand and touched him." The man with leprosy probably hadn't felt human touch for a long, long time. He might have been a husband at one time and known the touch of his wife. As a father, he might have known the touch of his little ones. Or perhaps he could remember the strong embrace of a friend. But that was all before leprosy invaded his body, and he hadn't experienced anyone's touch for possibly years and years. But Jesus didn't hesitate; He moved close to him and touched him. And immediately, the healing power of God flowed through his body. The disfigurements melted away. The right color came back to his skin. The fingers and toes and facial features grew back. The sensations that had been dead for so long returned.

What an amazing miracle!

A Second Desperate Man

In this same chapter of Luke, we come across another hopeless man, another man in a desperate situation. Like the first man, he'd heard that Jesus was in town, and he wanted to see Him. In fact, he knew which house Jesus was in at that very moment. But there was a problem: He was paralyzed. He couldn't go anywhere unless someone carried him.

And that is exactly what four very determined friends of his did.

Now it happened on a certain day, as He was teaching, that there were Pharisees and teachers of the law sitting by, who had come out of every town of Galilee, Judea, and Jerusalem. And the power of the Lord was present to heal them. Then behold, men brought on a bed a man who was paralyzed, whom they sought to bring in and lay before Him. And when they could not find how they might bring him in, because of the crowd, they went up on the housetop and let him down with his bed through the tiling into the midst before Jesus.

When He saw their faith, He said to him, "Man, your sins are forgiven you."

And the scribes and the Pharisees began to reason, saying, "Who is this who speaks blasphemies? Who can forgive sins but God alone?"

But when Jesus perceived their thoughts, He answered and said to them, "Why are you reasoning in your hearts? Which is easier, to say, 'Your sins are forgiven you,' or to say, 'Rise up and walk'? But that you may know that the Son of Man has

power on earth to forgive sins"—He said to the man who was
paralyzed, "I say to you, arise, take up your bed, and go to your
house."

Immediately he rose up before them, took up what he had
been lying on, and departed to his own house, glorifying God.
And they were all amazed, and they glorified God and were
filled with fear, saying, "We have seen strange things today!"
(Luke 5:17-26)

There was a major sensation when Jesus came into a town or village. Everyone wanted to catch a glimpse of Him, hear Him speak, or possibly watch Him perform a miracle. Try to imagine if this event had taken place today. What if you knew for sure that Jesus Christ Himself would be at your church as a guest speaker on a given Sunday? Do you think there would be any empty seats? Of course not! There would be people in the balcony, on the floor, on the platforms, crowding up to every window and door, with an incalculable crowd outside trying desperately to get in. Every square inch of space would be taken.

The four friends had their buddy on a cot or a stretcher and they wanted to get him in to see Jesus. But it seemed impossible. Even so, these guys refused to take no for an answer. Men who were less determined, who were less concerned about their friend, would have given up. They would have taken one look at the house surrounded by a great mob of people, and said, "Well, we tried. It was a good idea and we meant well, but it's just too hard. It wasn't meant to be today."

But not these men!

Do you have friends like that? Some of us can't really count that many people we call true friends. However, if you could count loving, loyal friends like that on ten fingers, you would have a great many.

The fact is, many people find their way into the presence of Jesus because they were brought by a friend. In our Harvest Crusades, we have found that 85 percent of those who make a profession of faith to follow Christ at our crusades were brought by a friend. They went forward to receive Jesus and stood on the field in front of the platform because a believer had taken the time to invite them and go with them.

These four friends in Luke 5 display three particular characteristics we can admire:

1. They were concerned about their friend and wanted to see him helped.

2. They had faith to believe that Jesus would meet their friend's need, but they did more than pray about it. They put feet to their prayers and did something.

3. They worked together and dared to do something different.

When they realized the house was packed out, they looked at each other and said, "We can't let this stop us. We've got to get our friend to Jesus *today.*" Let me assure you of something: When you make a commitment to get someone to Jesus, you will face opposition—just as these guys did. Obstacles will loom in your path. Doors will be firmly closed in your face. That's par for the course! When you decide to be used by God, please don't expect a standing ovation in hell. No, you need to expect opposition, lots of it, and from quarters you never expected.

In Mark 9 we read the story of a man who had a demon-possessed child and brought the boy to Jesus. Verse 20 (NLT) says, "But when the evil spirit saw Jesus, it threw the child into a violent convulsion, and he fell to the ground, writhing and foaming at the mouth."

That's how it works. The devil throws a hissy fit when you try to take one of his people away from him. Just understand in advance that it's not going to be easy. But that doesn't mean you shouldn't do it! In fact, you have to seize the moment, opposition or no opposition.

Here's something to consider. I think sometimes we "spiritualize" a situation and say, "Well, the Lord closed the door," when the truth is we have simply turned away from the door. We knocked once and nothing happened, so we walked away. Or maybe we ran into a little opposition and told ourselves, "Well, this must not be God's timing." There are times when we need to keep going forward in spite of closed doors and opposition, and not back off so quickly and easily.

These four friends faced a closed door and a seemingly insurmountable obstacle and said, "Well, if we can't get in the front door, we'll go in through the roof." They were persistent and even daring in their faith.

Back in those days the roof of a house was flat, like a floor. The family would even spend time together up on the roof. When it was hot they might sleep out under the open stars. In most homes, there would be an outside stairway leading up to the roof. The four friends had their buddy on a cot, and when they got to the rooftop, they immediately started making a hole in the roofing. It wasn't like one of our houses today, with a pitched roof covered with shingles or tiles. The roof was soft, with straw and pitch laid in between the beams.

Can you picture the scene? Jesus was teaching inside the house when suddenly there was a commotion up above Him. Roofing material started falling down, followed by a shaft of light. Everyone looked up as the hole grew bigger and a couple of faces peered in. I imagine Jesus must have looked up, too, as the hole kept getting larger and larger. People were looking at each other and saying, "What in the world is going on up there?"

After a few minutes, when the hole was pretty large, a man on a cot suspended by ropes came down. People could hear the guys on the roof saying, "Easy now, take up the slack. Don't drop him!"

And then the paralyzed man was lying directly in front of Jesus, looking up at Him. I can imagine him saying something like, "Hello there. Actually, this wasn't totally my idea. Am I in trouble?"

How did Jesus react to having His teaching interrupted by a rooftop invasion?

He loved it. Luke 5:20 says, "When He saw their faith, He said to him, 'Man, your sins are forgiven you.'"

Sometimes we in the church get hung up on our methodologies and traditions. Someone will say, "This is the way it has to be done," or "This is the only kind of music that's appropriate for worship."

I can remember when the Internet was first becoming part of our culture (yes, I'm that old). Many younger people can't imagine a world without an Internet, but those of us who are older remember when it was only a strange-sounding concept. And those of us in ministry began to see the potential in it.

I remember in the early 1990s when a missionary somewhere in Africa figured out how to receive our live Sunday webcast on his computer, hooked up to a funky little modem. He had set it up with a group of people watching, and later told me how many in that group had come to Christ through watching the webcast. Right then and there I thought, "We have to go with this. This is something God will use!"

Now, as the speed of the Internet has improved and more people have devices that can access the information on it, it's becoming a ministry mainstay. But I can still remember people who scoffed at the idea, called computers "toys," and insisted that God would never work through a setup like that.

Yes, He will work through any means He pleases, and His Word will not return to Him void. Let's not get hung up on certain "traditional" ways of doing things. Let's be flexible where we can be flexible.

That's what the guys in this story did. When they saw that one method wasn't working (going in through the front door), they said, "Okay. We'll try something different. We will go in through the roof." And Scripture says that Jesus "saw their faith."

How did He do that? Can you see my faith? Can I see yours? The only way I can see if you have faith is *by what you do*. The four men took the trouble and risk to lower their friend through the roof because they believed Jesus could and would do something about his condition. The Bible says that "faith without works is dead" (James 2:20). Works or actions won't save anyone, but they are a good *evidence* that a person is saved. If there is no evidence of any change in your life—no "fruit," as the New Testament puts it—then how can anyone know if you are really a Christian? You can talk all day about how much you love Jesus, but the people around you are looking for results.

Jesus saw their faith. How did He see it? He saw it when they invited the paralyzed man to hear Him preach. He saw it when they took the corners of the cot and struggled down the street with it. He saw it when they labored up the stairs with their friend. And then when they dug through the roof, Jesus just looked at them and said to Himself, "I love these guys. These guys are awesome."

God blesses people like these. And He will bless you if you take the risk, the time, and the trouble to bring a friend to Jesus. No, it might not be easy. You might run into some rejection, some mockery, some obstacles, or some opposition you never expected. But it will be worth everything when Jesus touches that man or woman, sees their faith, and says, "Your sins are forgiven."

Only God Can Forgive Sins!

How did the religious leaders of that day react to this encounter between Jesus and the man on the stretcher?

As you might expect, they freaked out.

In Luke 5:21 we read, "And the scribes and the Pharisees began to reason, saying, 'Who is this who speaks blasphemies? Who can forgive sins but God alone?'"

They were actually right. They were theologically correct in noting that only God can forgive sins. But that was the point! This was a clear proclamation of Jesus' deity. He was saying, "Do the math, guys. Only God can forgive sins, and I just forgave sins. Therefore, I am the Son of God. And just so you will know I have the power and authority to forgive sins, I say to this man in front of you, 'Get up, pick up your cot, and go home.'"

And that is exactly what happened.

Are your sins forgiven?

At the beginning of this chapter I spoke about people who had lost hope—even to the point of taking their own lives. Even though they were successful and seemed to have everything, they had an emptiness in their lives they couldn't escape—an emptiness that threatened to swallow them up in complete despair.

The two men described in Luke 5 found themselves in overwhelming, seemingly impossible situations, completely beyond their own ability to solve or navigate. But then they turned to Jesus, one on his own and one with the help of some loving friends.

They needed Jesus, and when they found Him, everything else in their lives fell into place.

And that's the way it can be for you, too.

CHAPTER NINE
HAPPINESS: WHAT IT IS AND HOW TO FIND IT, PART 1

How do you define happiness?

Years ago cartoonist Charles Schulz wrote a book titled *Happiness is a Warm Puppy*. For my granddaughters, I think we could change that to "happiness is a warm rabbit." They have a little bunny, and when they pull him out of the cage and hold him they squeal with delight. Happiness for the rabbit, however, probably begins when he gets gently returned to the safety of his hutch.

Albert Schweitzer said, "Happiness is nothing more than good health and a bad memory." Comedian George Burns observed, "Happiness is having a large, loving, caring, close-knit family . . . in another city." Milton Berle said, "A man doesn't know what true happiness is until he gets married. Then it's too late."

What exactly is happiness, and where do you find it?

First of all, let me tell you where you will not find it. You won't find it in this world or in our culture. The fleeting happiness people chase after comes and goes, depending on fluctuating, ever-changing circumstances. If things are going well, we are reasonably happy. When things aren't going well we are unhappy.

It has been said, "There are two sources of unhappiness in life. One is not getting what you want. The other is getting it." Many people imagine that money will bring them happiness. (Look at the lines to buy lottery tickets each week.) In reality, there are some things money can give you—and many more things that money can't give you.

Money can buy you books, but it can't buy you brains.

Money can buy you a house, but it can't buy you a home.

Money can buy you medicine, but it can't buy you health.

Money can buy you amusement, but it can't buy you happiness.

To quote St. Paul, St. John, St. George, and St. Ringo, money "can't buy me love."

How can we be truly happy people? Surveys by Gallup, The National Research Center, and the Pew Organization conclude that "Spiritually committed people are twice as likely to report being happy than the least religiously committed people." Isn't that an interesting statistic? It basically says that happy people are spiritual people. Or let me take it a step further: happy people are godly people.

The Bible says, "Happy are the people whose God is the LORD!" (Psalm 144:15). According to the Bible, if we will seek to know God and discover His plans for our lives, the end result will be happiness—the very happiness that has eluded us for so long.

Ironically, happiness doesn't come from seeking happiness. Happiness comes from seeking God. C. S. Lewis made this statement:

> God designed the human machine to run on Himself. He Himself is the fuel our spirits were designed to burn, or the food our spirits were designed to feed on. There is no other. That is why it is just no good asking God to make us happy in our own way without bothering about religion. God cannot give us a happiness and peace apart from Himself, because it is not there. There is no such thing.[2]

Here is the good news: God wants us to be happy. We need to know and remember that. Some people, however, seem to prefer being miserable. They're like Eeyore in the *Winnie the Pooh* stories—always negative, always cynical, always upset about something. They seem to habitually focus on the one thing wrong in their lives, completely missing all the positive things that might be happening. God wants even people such as these to be happy persons. That's the good news. The no-so-good news is that His definition of happiness is probably different from our definition.

What Jesus Said About Happiness

In His well-known Sermon on the Mount, Jesus Himself dealt with the topic of happiness in what we call the Beatitudes. How do I know? Because the word *blessed* in Greek could also be translated "happy." When we say, "Blessed are the poor in spirit" or "blessed are the peacemakers," we could just as easily say, "Happy are the poor in spirit" or "happy are the peacemakers." Jesus was telling us here how to be happy.

In a broader sense, Jesus Christ was giving us His worldview in this passage. It's His take on how we should see this world we live in. Below I will quote all nine of the Beatitudes, but in this chapter we will focus on the first four.

The Headwaters of Happiness

Blessed are the poor in spirit,

For theirs is the kingdom of heaven.

Blessed are those who mourn,

For they shall be comforted.

Blessed are the meek,

For they shall inherit the earth.

Blessed are those who hunger and thirst for righteousness,

For they shall be filled.

Blessed are the merciful,

For they shall obtain mercy.

Blessed are the pure in heart,

For they shall see God.

Blessed are the peacemakers,

For they shall be called sons of God.

Blessed are those who are persecuted for righteousness' sake,

For theirs is the kingdom of heaven.

Blessed are you when they revile and persecute you, and say all kinds of evil against you falsely for My sake. Rejoice and be exceedingly glad, for great is your reward in heaven, for so they persecuted the prophets who were before you. (Matthew 5:3-12)

Blessedness or true happiness occurs independently from circumstances—whatever may or may not be happening in your life right now. You might say, "Hey, I really *am* blessed. The bills are paid. Our health is good. The family is fine and the future is rosy. Everything's looking great." Then again, maybe things aren't going so well for you right now. You're having problems in your marriage or with your children. Your health has taken a sudden turn for the worse. Some relationships that are very important to you have turned south. And you might say, "I am not blessed anymore. I was blessed yesterday, but I am not blessed today."

No, you are *still* blessed. The apostle Paul said, "I have learned the secret of being content in any and every situation" (Philippians 4:12, NIV). This blessedness, this happiness described in the Bible, is dependent only on a holy God, not on the happenings in your life. It doesn't flow from your situations, it flows from your relationship with God.

Can you imagine what the Beatitudes might sound like if our culture were to rewrite them? They certainly wouldn't sound like the ones we just read. In fact, they might read something like this: *Blessed are the beautiful, for they shall be admired. Blessed are the wealthy, for they shall have it all. Blessed are the popular, for they shall be loved. Blessed are the famous, for they shall be followed.*

The Beatitudes Jesus gave, however, begin with a bombshell that must have left a few people scratching their heads. He said, "Blessed are the poor in spirit, for theirs is the kingdom of heaven."

"Blessed are the poor in spirit."

What in the world could this mean? First of all, it has nothing to do with anyone's financial situation. To be poor in spirit is to recognize our state before a holy God. It is to realize that we are sinners hopelessly separated from Him by a chasm wider than the Grand Canyon. It is to see our spiritual poverty and to finally admit that we are spiritually destitute.

Some people have a difficult time admitting this. Instead, they will say, "I'm really a pretty good person." And maybe that individual is right, to a degree. Even so, "pretty good" isn't good enough to get through the front door of heaven.

The classic example of this in Scripture is the story of Naaman, a high-ranking general in the powerful Syrian army—who also happened to have leprosy. Naaman was no doubt something of a celebrity, famous and highly regarded in his nation. When he was told about a prophet named Elisha who could possibly heal him of his leprosy, he made a special trip to Israel to call on this man of God. It must have been quite a scene when the general rumbled up in front of Elisha's humble dwelling in his gleaming chariot, surrounded by his entourage in gleaming armor.

Naaman knocked, but he was shocked when Elisha wouldn't even emerge from the house to greet him. Instead, Elisha sent his servant to answer the door. The servant told Naaman, "Elisha says go down to the Jordan River, take off your armor, immerse yourself in the river seven times, and your leprosy will be gone."

The general was outraged, insulted beyond words that this Hebrew prophet wouldn't even meet with him. And if there was one thing he didn't want to do, it was to immerse himself in the Jordan River. Bitter with disappointment he said, "Let's get out of here. Bathe in the Jordan? No way! We've got better rivers than that back home in Syria. Why should I dunk myself in that muddy little stream?"

Elisha knew that step one for this proud man was to humble himself before God. I don't imagine that many of Naaman's men even knew he was a leper. He hid it well under his armor and royal robes. Then one of his servants said, "Master Naaman, think about it for a minute. What do you have to lose? Just go for it. Give it a try. If it doesn't work, it doesn't work. But what if it does? Now that you've come all this way, you may as well find out."

Naaman didn't like it one bit, but he reluctantly agreed. He walked down the bank to the Jordan and stripped off his armor.

For the first time, some of his men saw the disfiguring effects of that terrible disease, and they probably gasped in amazement. They saw it on his arms and legs—and perhaps all over his body.

The general had to humble himself. He had to follow God's prescription for healing. And what a wonder! He really was healed that day. The Bible says "his flesh was restored like the flesh of a little child, and he was clean" (2 Kings 5:14). Humbled and chastened, he came back to thank Elisha, saying, "Indeed, now I know that there is no God in all the earth, except in Israel" (verse 15). Naaman wasn't just saying that Elisha's God was real, he was declaring that God is the only true God in the whole world. What a transformation! And it began with a painful humbling. He went home a very happy man.

It's the same with us. We all have armor we hide behind. We all have our façade. We all have those things we don't reveal to others. Here is what God says to those who want to be happy: *Humility is the point of entry.* We have to admit our spiritual state before God—that we are sinful and incapable of helping or saving ourselves. When we are poor in spirit, we see ourselves as we really are. Until we do, the healing will never come.

Here is a way to look at it that might sound strange at first: *Misery is the key to happiness.* When we look at ourselves, see ourselves for what and who we really are, finally realizing there is nothing we can do to change our condition, we become miserable. And that's step number one! We are on our way to happiness because we have finally turned from the futility of seeking it on our own terms. Instead, we humbly ask God to help us. The great British preacher Charles Haddon Spurgeon once said, "Those that rise in the kingdom have to first sink in themselves."

It starts there. We admit our weakness. That is the beginning of true happiness.

"Blessed are those who mourn, for they shall be comforted."

Jesus said, "Blessed are those who mourn, for they shall be comforted."

Point two, then, is that happy people are unhappy people. Or said in another way, "Happy are the unhappy." We have seen our state before God, and we mourn over it. The word *mourn* that Jesus used here is the most severe of all nine Greek words used for grief in Scripture. It is usually reserved for mourning over the dead.

I know something about mourning, because I mourn every day. I mourn the loss of my son, who died in a traffic accident at age thirty-three back in 2008. Father's Day is always difficult for me, because I know I will never hear him say, "Happy Father's Day" again. Even though years have passed, I still feel the pain and loss. I still think about him, miss him, and mourn for him. I know I will see him and be with him someday in heaven, but in another sense I will never "get over" or "move on from" that loss. It will always be with me.

Jesus said, "Happy are those who are sad." What did He mean? How do those two emotions go together? Let's look at it like this: When we have someone taken from us through death—especially if it happened suddenly—we gain a new perspective. We realize how fragile life is and how quickly it can end. We all "know" this theoretically. But when someone close to us is taken, someone who was with us just yesterday, it hits home in another way.

It's like a reality check. We say, "That could have been me." As David once said when he was being hunted by Saul, "There is just a step between me and death."

Someone may say, "That sounds morbid. A person shouldn't think that way."

No, a person *should* think that way. The Bible encourages us to think this way and to remember these things. Moses prayed, "Teach us to number our days, that we may gain a heart of wisdom" (Psalm 90:12). In a similar way, David prayed, "LORD, remind me how brief my time on earth will be. Remind me that my days are numbered—how fleeting my life is" (Psalm 39:4, NLT).

Back in ancient times they would write this notation over all their documents: *Memento Mori.* It means "think of death." Why? To give perspective. To compel people to admit reality. Whatever we are doing is short-lived, and then comes eternity. Paul, however, summarized the good news for every Christian, saying, "For to me, to live is Christ, and to die is gain" (Philippians 1:21).

This open-eyed, realistic perspective on life and death has put a strong longing in my heart for heaven. I talk about heaven, think about heaven, and probably preach about heaven more than I used to. When we think about heaven more, we see this earth more for what it really is—a brief staging area for eternity. And we are reminded how temporary and shallow so many things of earth really are.

Don't get me wrong. I enjoy my life very much. I like to have fun, joke around, savor the moment, and usually eat like a pig. I think most people would recognize me as a balanced, happy person. What I'm saying is that we need perspective to really enjoy life to the full, and mourning can be good for us.

Blessed are those who mourn. Blessed are those who cry and shed tears as they understand their real condition before God. They *will* be comforted. God will comfort us in our pain, our difficulty, our hardship, and our feeling of devastation when we see ourselves as we really are. Whatever your grief, whatever the ache in your heart, you need to know that you are not alone in your pain. Jesus Himself has been there and knows firsthand what it is like. That's why the prophet Isaiah called Him "A Man of sorrows and acquainted with grief" (Isaiah 53:3).

Some people laugh when they ought to mourn. That's why the Bible says, "Let there be tears for the wrong things you have done. Let there be sorrow and sincere grief. Let there be sadness instead of laughter, and gloom instead of joy. Then when you realize your worthlessness before the Lord, he will lift you up, encourage and help you" (James 4:9-10, TLB). The apostle James wasn't saying we should be miserable all the time or walk around with slumped shoulders, dragging our feet. But he was saying that if we're happy about the wrong stuff, we need to stop and rethink that.

Let me illustrate. Let's say you go into a restaurant and see a table full of people who are having a reasonable conversation. Then they start ordering drinks. After the first round of drinks they're all laughing. After the second round they're laughing very loudly. After a little bit more they're laughing uncontrollably. What are they laughing at? They don't even know, and they won't remember tomorrow when you ask them.

Solomon went down that road during one season of his life. He tried out bingeing on sin for a while and tasting everything this world has to offer. Then he wrote about it in his journal: "I said to myself, 'Come on, let's try pleasure. Let's look for the "good things" in life.' But I found that this, too, was meaningless. So I said, 'Laughter is silly. What good does it do to seek pleasure?'" (Ecclesiastes 2:1-2, NLT).

We need to be sad over our sin. There's nothing wrong with that. On the contrary, it is a good and wholesome train of thought. I think the problem is that some people are too flippant when it comes to confronting sin in their lives. Yes, God will forgive our sins when we confess them and forsake them. But that doesn't mean we get to dodge all the repercussions. We still have to walk through the wreckage, absorbing the consequences of what we have done.

I've heard people say, "God wants me to be happy." No, my friend, God wants you to be *holy.* If you think you can do whatever you want because "God wants you happy," you have been seriously misled.

I've also heard people say, "God knows my heart." Yes, He does, and that's the problem. The Bible says "the heart is deceitful above all things and beyond cure. Who can understand it?" (Jeremiah 17:9, NIV). We tend to minimize or rationalize our sin. We tell ourselves, "It will be okay," and we don't think about the repercussions of our sinful words and actions. Or to put it another way, the chickens will come home to roost.

That is what happened to David. After he committed adultery with Bathsheba and arranged for her husband Uriah's battlefield death, David just went on living in sin for a while. He practiced denial, pretended that everything was okay, and didn't confess his sin for several months. But oh, how miserable he was! Here is a description of how he felt while he lived with unconfessed sin: "I recognize my rebellion; it haunts me day and night" (Psalm 51:3, NLT).

Does this describe you right now? Are you doing something that you know is wrong before God? Maybe you haven't been caught or found out yet, and you haven't confessed it to the Lord. But does it "haunt you day and night"? If you answer, "Yes, it does," then that's a good thing. It shows you are a child of God and have a functioning conscience.

Not long ago we had a smoke alarm go off in our house. Why do they always go off at three in the morning? Is that a law somewhere? Couldn't it go off at three in the afternoon? It woke me up out of a dead sleep. My heart was pounding and I clomped downstairs to check on things. But there was no problem. No smoke. No emergency. The alarm had just decided to start screaming for no reason. I yanked it off the ceiling and put it under a pillow. Alarms are fine in their place, but this one was way too sensitive.

Sometimes we are in sin and that inner alarm in our lives isn't working at all. It ought to be chirping or shrieking, but it is dead quiet. Someone might say, "I am living in sin and I'm having a great time. It's a lot of fun and I don't feel any guilt. I am not haunted."

Frankly, that would scare me. That would make me wonder if you are truly a child of God. If God isn't disciplining you, are you really His child? You'd better get that right.

David was certainly a child of God, because he was tormented and miserable with what he had done. Finally, he was confronted by the prophet Nathan and admitted his sin. David said to the Lord, "Against you, and you alone, have I sinned; I have done what is evil in your sight" (Psalm 51:4, NLT). He confessed his sin and agreed with God about what a horrible transgression it had been. Then and then only was he able to say in Psalm 51:12 (NLT), "Restore to me the joy of your salvation."

We all want that joy, don't we? And it will flow again in our lives as we mourn over our sins, see ourselves for who we are, and confess our sins to God, refusing to make excuses for them or blame them on someone else. Then God will forgive us. Then we will know the true blessed happiness Jesus promises.

"Blessed are the meek, for they shall inherit the earth."

Jesus said, "Blessed are the meek, for they shall inherit the earth."

A happy person will be a meek person. Seeing ourselves as we really are produces a vital—and often misunderstood—spiritual quality: *meekness*. We are meek when we are no longer inflated with pride, when we realize we are sinners just like everybody else.

Some people think meekness means being quiet and so soft-spoken that people can't even hear you when you speak. But that is not what it means. Meek doesn't mean mousy. A meek person is not a wimp.

The word *meekness* means "strength under control." It comes from a word used to describe the breaking of a powerful stallion. Horses are beautiful animals, but also just a little bit scary. A horse is a mighty beast that pretty much does what he wants to do unless he is required to submit to his trainer's authority.

That's the idea with meekness. Something powerful under control. A horse that has been broken is not a horse that has lost its will or lost its power. It is rather a horse that has voluntarily chosen to surrender to the will of its rider. In context, we are saying that a meek person is one who controls himself or herself under the authority of God. When we are meek, we have surrendered ourselves to Him.

By contrast, our world values aggression. Our culture says, "Speak up for yourself. Assert yourself. Demand your rights. Be strong." But the truth is, it takes more strength to hold your tongue than to speak your mind.

How different the worldview of Jesus is from that of our culture! Here is what Jesus was saying in summation: *Last is first. Giving is receiving. Dying is living. Losing is finding. Weakness is strength. Mourning leads to happiness. Insults for following God are a badge of honor.* It's all upside down from the world's point of view. It's the very opposite of what we hear around us all the time.

In the book of Genesis, Joseph gives us a classic example of meekness. He had been betrayed by his jealous brothers and sold into slavery. After years of suffering and trials, in God's providence he ended up becoming one of the most powerful men in the world, second only to the pharaoh of Egypt. With Joseph in charge of the world's food supply during a great global famine, his brothers came to Egypt to obtain food for their starving families. At first, they had absolutely no idea that the brother they had betrayed years before now stood before them in power and authority.

If this story had been a Hollywood film, Joseph would have used this moment to get the ultimate revenge. He would have said, "You're all going to die today." Most of us like movies like that, where the hero gets beaten down within an inch of his life, but comes back to stomp on all his enemies. But that's not what Joseph did. Instead, he forgave his brothers. Comforted them. Wept over them. Provided and cared for them and their families. He had the power to destroy them a thousand times over, but he treated them with kindness instead. That is meekness.

Are you a meek person? It's not an easy thing to be. We need God's help to pull that off. The ultimate example of meekness is Jesus Christ Himself. He was a man's man. Today He would have been a blue-collar worker, a construction guy. He was a carpenter, and that didn't mean He built bird houses or little pieces of furniture. It meant He chopped down trees, framed housed, hauled wood around, and did other physical tasks. He was very strong.

When He was arrested in the Garden of Gethsemane, He could have easily escaped. He could have snapped His fingers and summoned a vast army of angels. He could have spoken His attackers right out of existence. In John 18, when the mob came to arrest Him and haul Him away, Jesus said, "Whom are you seeking?" They answered, "Jesus of Nazareth." When Jesus replied, "I am He," John wrote that "they drew back and fell to the ground" (verses 4-6).

Jesus was uttering the same words God had said to Moses, when Moses asked Him, "Whom shall I say sent me?" God answered, "I AM THAT I AM." It was the very name of God, and when the Son of God spoke it in Gethsemane that night, it sent out a wave of power and authority that literally knocked people off their feet.

But He submitted to the arrest. He submitted to the chains. He submitted to the beatings and the indignities. He submitted to the spitting and mockery. He submitted to the cross, and He did it for you and me. That was meekness. In His only autobiographical statement, Jesus said in Matthew 11:29 (KJV), "I am meek and lowly in heart."

"Blessed are those who hunger and thirst for righteousness, for they shall be filled."

Those who know me understand that I'm pretty much always hungry. You could set a clock by my stomach. When I walk by a Krispy Kreme doughnut shop and catch the fragrance of those hot doughnuts rolling out of the oven, I feel like I could eat a dozen of them at one sitting. On Thanksgiving Day, with the incredible scents of turkey, cornbread dressing, and pumpkin pie wafting through the house, I get totally ravenous. I find myself praying that the people we have invited won't be late.

Now, take that idea of physical hunger and bring it into the spiritual realm. Jesus was saying that if we see ourselves as we really are, if we are truly sorry for the condition of our hearts and lives and have repented of it, we will become meek and humble people. And we will also find ourselves with a new hunger. Instead of chasing after what used to satisfy us, we will chase after God, trying to find ways to please Him and honor Him. It is a hunger and thirst for righteousness.

Do you come to church hungry? I don't mean that you've skipped your breakfast and your stomach is rumbling. I mean, do you come really hungry for the Word of God and for an experience with God? Maybe you're still hungry when you leave. You say, "That was good, but I really want more. I want to study more, learn more, worship more." You feel like there is never enough.

One of the songs we used to sing began, "This is the air I breathe . . . Your holy presence living in me. . . . I am desperate for You, I am lost without You." Jesus said that people who are truly desperate for God, people who are ravenously hungry for Him, will find what they are looking for! As God said, "You will seek me and find me when you seek me with all your heart. I will be found by you" (Jeremiah 29:13-14, NIV). Only God—and nothing or no one else—will satisfy a deep spiritual hunger.

Summing It Up

Let's put it together. How can you be a happy person?

Be poor in spirit. See yourself as you really are, a man or woman who is spiritually and utterly bankrupt before a holy God. The answers to life don't come from within you; the problem is within, and it is sin. Admit that you are a sinner in need of a Savior.

Mourn for your sin. Be sorry for what you have done. Let some tears fall. The Bible says that "godly sorrow produces repentance" (2 Corinthians 7:10).

Experience a change in attitude. The old arrogance and self-reliance will make way for a new humility—the result of seeing life as it really is. You're not better than anyone else. You may be better off, but certainly not better.

Ask God to make you hungry and thirsty for Him and His ways. You will find that He will fill vast areas of emptiness in your soul that you hadn't even been aware of. God will bring a happiness into your life that nothing in this world can come close to duplicating.

CHAPTER TEN

HAPPINESS: WHAT IT IS AND HOW TO FIND IT, PART 2

hy are we alive on this world of ours? What is the purpose of our existence?

Some would say we are here to pursue happiness.

Is this a uniquely American mindset? After all, we're familiar with what it says in our founding document, the Declaration of Independence: "We hold these truths to be self-evident, that all men are created equal, that they are endowed by their Creator with certain unalienable Rights, that among these are Life, Liberty, and the pursuit of Happiness."

You might be surprised to learn that this pursuit of happiness is not unique to America. Two thousand years ago the Greek philosopher Aristotle said, "Happiness is the meaning and purpose of life, the aim and the end of human existence."

Humankind has been seeking happiness for a long time. How has that worked out for us? Usually, not all that well. In fact, it was the contemporary philosopher Eric Hoffer who wrote, "The search for happiness is one of the chief sources of unhappiness." He might have something there. It seems to me that some of the most unhappy people I know are the people who want to be happy the most.

Conventional wisdom, of course, says that if you want to be happy you need to be handsome or beautiful in addition to being rich and famous.

Is that really true? Clearly, it isn't. A singer named Lana Del Rey shot to fame at the age of twenty-seven. A couple of years ago, after the release of her new album "Ultraviolence," she granted an interview to a reporter. When she was asked about her perspective on that whole experience, she admitted, "I never felt any of the enjoyment. It was bad. All of it." She went on to describe her life as (and I paraphrase) "a messed-up movie." She didn't want to live anymore. In fact, she has the words "die young" tattooed on her ring finger.

Her last record project was called "Born to Die." In the interview she said, "I wish I was dead already."

You would think that with her beauty, fame, and money she would be happy. Conventional wisdom says she certainly *should* be very happy. But she is not. And conventional wisdom is wrong.

Comedian and actor Jim Carrey once said, "I hope everybody could get rich and famous and have everything they ever dreamed of, so they will know that is not the answer."

USA Today did an article on the topic of happiness some years ago. After interviewing hundreds of people and experts who had studied the topic for years, here is what they came up with:

- Family and friends provide the best antidote to unhappiness. They said that marriage makes most people happier, and a close family inoculates many kids against despair. They also said that happy people all seem to have at least one good friend.

- Things don't make you happy. One psychologist said, "Materialism is toxic for happiness. Even rich materialists aren't as rich as those who care less about getting and spending."

- If you want to be happy, be grateful for what you already have. Psychologists say that gratitude has a lot to do with life satisfaction. Talking and writing about what one is grateful for amplifies a person's happiness. Also, the smallest pleasures can bring great happiness.

- Forgiving people are happy people. Christopher Peterson, a University of Michigan psychologist, said, "Forgiveness is the trait most strongly linked to happiness. In fact it is the queen of all virtues and hardest to come by."

Finally, they said that Scandinavians are the happiest people on earth, with Americans coming in second behind them. Putting it all together then, here's a portrait of a happy person: *family, friends, expressing gratitude, granting forgiveness, not expecting things to satisfy, and being Scandinavian.*

Did you notice how many of the so-called secrets these psychologists discovered are actually biblical principles? God gives us the family and describes how to live in one. Forgiveness is a strong biblical principle, as is not seeking fulfillment in material things. It seems like these researchers could have saved a lot of time by simply searching through the pages of Scripture.

As we saw in the last chapter, Jesus spoke of happiness in what we call the Beatitudes in Matthew 5:3-12. We noted how the word *blessed* could be interchanged with the word *happy*. In the nine Beatitudes, Jesus effectively gave us the keys to happiness.

Let's pick up right where we left off in the last chapter.

"Blessed are the merciful, for they shall obtain mercy."

Beginning with the progression we discussed in the last chapter, if we see ourselves as sinners and weep over our sin, allowing that sorrow to produce in us a humility and a hunger and thirst to know Christ and become more like Him, we will become individuals who are merciful to others. In other words, if I realize that I'm not better than anyone else, and that I'm basically just one beggar telling another beggar where to find bread, then I will be someone who shows mercy and compassion to others.

This was not a popular concept in the first century (or any century, for that matter). The Roman culture did not value the virtue of mercy. In fact, one Roman philosopher called mercy "a disease of the soul." The Romans worshiped power, might, and strength. Mercy was regarded as a weakness. In fact, when a child was born in the Roman world, the father of that child had the right of *patria potestas*, which meant that he held the child's life in his hands. If he wanted the newborn baby to live, he held his thumb up. If he wanted the child to die, he held his thumb down and immediately the child was drowned. That's how the Romans viewed life. Mercy was mocked and laughed at.

But are we really so different? Does our culture value mercy? We speak a lot about "justice," but more often what we want is revenge and retribution. God, however, highly values mercy. What does it mean to be merciful? In Matthew 6:3, the word for *mercy* is used to describe alms-giving—presenting your offering to the Lord or helping someone in need and rescuing the miserable. Mercy involves a sense of pity married with a practical desire to relieve the suffering. Mercy is meeting a need, not just "feeling" it. Mercy is pity plus action.

If you are walking down the street, pass someone who is destitute, and say, "That is so sad," you aren't being merciful. You are just sad. Mercy means you reach down into their world and say, "How can I help you? Let me get you to a meal or take you to a shelter where you can find some help. Let me do something for you."

The great example of mercy in Scripture is the story of the Good Samaritan in Luke 10:30-37. A man had been savagely beaten by robbers, stripped of his belongings, and left on the side of the road to die. Several others, who ought to have been concerned, simply passed him by. But a despised Samaritan stopped, attended to the wounded man, and took time to transport him to an inn where he could be cared for, stepping up to pay all the expenses. That is mercy.

Notice that Jesus said, "Blessed are the merciful, for they shall obtain mercy." As we have stated earlier, a forgiven person should *be* a forgiving person. If you are not, if you harbor grudges and wish ill on those who have harmed you, the bitterness will consume you. Refusing to forgive someone is like drinking rat poison and then waiting for the rat to die. The rat won't be inconvenienced at all, but the poison will take a toll on you. We've all been there, haven't we? We imagine that withholding forgiveness from someone will somehow hurt them for the harm they've done us. But in the process, we will do far more damage to ourselves.

We've all been hurt. We've all been disappointed, let down, abandoned, or even betrayed by someone who had seemed close to us. Do they *deserve* forgiveness and a clean slate with us? Probably not. But haven't you and I received rescue and grace and kindness and provision from God that we didn't deserve and couldn't have merited in a billion years?

Yes, of course we have. We have been forgiven when we didn't deserve it, and we need to forgive others when they don't deserve it. We need to forgive as God in Christ has forgiven us. When we truly do, happiness will begin to whisper its way back into our lives—like fresh, rain-washed air through an open window. Suddenly, when we're not expecting it, it will come.

"Blessed are the pure in heart, for they shall see God."

We use the word *heart* quite a bit in our culture, but do we really know what the Bible means here? We commonly use the term to describe emotion. We say, "My mind tells me one thing, but my heart tells me another." We might refer to an emotional person as someone who "wears his heart on his sleeve." When we are sad we will say, "I am heartbroken."

And think of how we use the word *heart* in our music. We could go back and forth all day naming songs with that word in the title. The Eagles sang about "Heartache Tonight." Bruce Springsteen had "A Hungry Heart." Neil Young is "Searching for a Heart of Gold." Billy Ray Cyrus said he had that "Achy Breaky Heart" (not to mention a certain daughter who needs to come back to Jesus).

These songs teach us that hearts get broken and then become unbroken. That's a lot of trauma for the heart! Maybe that's why Stevie Nicks sang, "Stop Dragging My Heart Around." It would also explain why the Bee Gees sang, "How Can You Mend a Broken Heart?" All of these musicians will probably end up with Elvis at the "Heartbreak Hotel." But they won't have to worry, because Celine Dion reminds us that "The Heart Will Go On."

When the Bible speaks of the heart, it isn't just referring to emotions. *It is speaking of the mind and the will as well.* Proverbs 23:7, for instance, tells us that as a man "thinks in his heart, so is he." The phrase "pure in heart" in this Beatitude could actually be translated "singleness of heart." Later on in the Sermon on the

Mount, Jesus said that if a person's eye is "single," their whole body will be full of light (see Matthew 6:22, KJV).

To be single or pure in heart indicates a single-minded devotion to Jesus Christ. The pure in heart are not fragmented, divided, or conflicted. They know where they stand and to whom they belong. As the psalmist wrote, "Unite my heart to fear Your name" (Psalm 86:11). If we want to live happy lives, we need to live holy lives, pure lives, with single-minded dedication to follow Jesus.

We don't exalt purity in our culture. In fact, the term is even used in a derisive way. When a person says, "She's as pure as the driven snow," the expression on that person's face is typically one of disgust.

Though the mention of purity may cause some to roll their eyes, our God values purity. When Jesus said, "Blessed [or happy] are the pure in heart," He meant it.

Martin Luther once said, "Seek righteousness and you will discover you are happy. It will be there without your knowing it, without your seeking it."

"Blessed are the peacemakers, for they shall be called sons of God."

Of all the Beatitudes, this is the one that probably meets with the most approval from all sides. It is often quoted by nonbelievers. But what does it really mean to be a peacemaker?

I think most of us want peace in our world. Our planet has been plagued by war since its very beginning. In the last four thousand years of history, less than three hundred of those years have been without a major war. It seems as though "peace" is comprised of those brief glorious moments in history when everyone stops to reload.

Why is there war? Albert Einstein had an interesting insight on this question. He said, "It is not a physical problem. It is an ethical one. What terrifies us is not the explosive force of the atomic bomb but the power of the wickedness of the human heart. It is an explosive power for evil."

Einstein was right, of course. It all comes back to the heart. The apostle James wrote, "Where do you think all these appalling wars and quarrels come from? Do you think they just happen? Think again. They come about because you want your own way, and fight for it deep inside yourselves. You lust for what you don't have and are willing to kill to get it. You want what isn't yours and will risk violence to get your hands on it" (James 4:1-2, MSG).

What was Jesus talking about when He said, "Blessed are the peacemakers"?

It wasn't about world peace.

It's about personal peace with God.

Jesus was speaking about our relationship with God, and the effect that will have on our relationships with others. Before we became Christians, whether we realized it or not, we were at war with God. It is God's desire to have that war cease and bring peace to troubled souls. In fact, the Bible says that we experience peace after we are justified through Jesus Christ. The gospel is called the good news of peace through Jesus Christ.

After I find personal peace with God, I become a peacemaker, helping others end their self-destructive wars with the One who loves them. I do everything I can in every way I can to maximize every opportunity I can to bring others into a relationship with the Lord, so they can have peace, too.

Be forewarned, however. Peacemakers are often troublemakers.

Some people don't want to hear this message of peace with God. They hate it. And when we share the gospel, they will revolt. The fact is, sometimes people get mad at us before they are happy with us. Jesus explained it in Matthew 10:34-36 (NLT), when He said, "Don't imagine that I came to bring peace to the earth! I came not to bring peace, but a sword. 'I have come to set a man against his father, a daughter against her mother, and a daughter-in-law against her mother-in-law. Your enemies will be right in your own household!'"

Wait a second! This is actually telling me that if I am to be a peacemaker I must first be troublemaker? Yes, and here's an example of how that works. Let's say you have an unbelieving family, where nobody is a Christian. For the most part, they all get along in their basic nonbelieving, dysfunctional, weird way. Then you become a Christian, and that wrecks everything for them. There they are at the next family gathering, drinking, partying, and cussing. Then you, Mr. Christian, show up. Maybe you even brought your Bible.

The thing is, you're different, and everyone knows you're different. Your very presence at the gathering is like rain on their parade. You begin talking about the Lord and your faith, and people groan or roll their eyes. Then it's time to eat, and everybody wants to chow down. But, oh no, Mr. Christian wants to pray first.

As a representative of Jesus Christ in a dark place, your presence causes friction. Others will say that the family was better off before you came in with that Jesus stuff. Better off? No, all of them were separated from God and on their way to judgment. In actuality, the friction you cause as a Christian in their midst could ultimately produce a wonderful and joyous unity if the family turned to Jesus Christ.

Fast forward three years, when the family has turned to the Lord. Now you are a Christian family, praying before meals, raising your children in the way of the Lord, and passing on a godly legacy. It's like a little piece of heaven, but there had to be trouble before there was peace.

We don't like the trouble part. We don't enjoy the conflict and tension. But it is simply a fact of life in our world, because Satan doesn't let go of his influence and possessions without a fight. But those who persevere and lead their friends and loved ones to Christ will have a special designation in this life and in the life to come: *sons and daughters of the living God.*

The book of Daniel puts it like this: "Those who are wise will shine like the brightness of the heavens, and those who lead many to righteousness, like the stars for ever and ever" (12:3, NIV).

"Blessed are those who are persecuted for righteousness' sake, for theirs is the kingdom of heaven."

Jesus went on to say, "Blessed are you when people insult you, persecute you and falsely say all kinds of evil against you because of me. Rejoice and be glad, because great is your reward in heaven, for in the same way they persecuted the prophets who were before you" (Matthew 5:11-12, NIV).

A happy person will be a persecuted person.

If you are living a godly, uncompromising life, hungering and thirsting for a closer walk with God and sharing the gospel whenever you can, the persecution will come. You may not be that excited about it, but it's part of the package of following Jesus.

Why do I say that? Because He said so.

It won't be a matter of "if," but rather "when" and "how much."

We all love to claim the promises of God, don't we? We will quote Matthew 6:33: "Seek first the kingdom of God and His righteousness, and all of these things shall be added to you." Amen! We like that one, and we should like it.

But what about 2 Timothy 3:12? "All who desire to live godly in Christ Jesus will suffer persecution." Maybe we don't quote that one quite as much. We don't have it printed on our coffee cup or stitched on cloth in a frame above the fireplace.

Perhaps not, but it is just as true as the earlier verse.

Jesus used the word *blessed* or "happy" twice in Matthew 5:10-11. He was emphasizing the generous blessing given by God to those who are persecuted. He was effectively saying, "Doubly blessed are the persecuted," or perhaps, "Happy, happy are the persecuted."

But take note of this. The Lord said, "Blessed are those who are persecuted *for righteousness' sake.*" He didn't say, "Blessed are those who are persecuted for *self*-righteousness' sake." Nor did He say, "Blessed are those who are persecuted for being obnoxious . . . or tactless . . . or condemning . . . or mean . . . or ridiculous." To be very candid with you, I have seen Christians persecuted not because they are righteous but because they are jerks.

I'm speaking here about Christians who are mean, condemning, short-tempered, negative, usually in a bad mood, or who are quick to find fault with others. These people are lousy ambassadors of Jesus Christ. Then, when someone pushes back against their bad manners or negative attitude, they will say, "Hallelujah, I'm being persecuted for being righteous!"

No, they're not. They're being persecuted because they are difficult to get along with, inflexible, and unkind. They need to change.

Sometimes we think Christianity produces these people. Not me. I think these people were always difficult, and they are just "saved difficult." Jesus Christ will not deliver them from their "difficultness," He will deliver them from their sin. Hopefully, as they study the Word of God and allow His Spirit to fill them, they will become more compassionate, loving, and discerning.

If we are being persecuted, we want to make sure it's for the right reason.

The word *persecution* means to be chased, driven away, or pursued. In an article titled "The War on Christians," author Paul Marshall writes, "From Africa, to Asia, to the Middle East, they are the world's most persecuted religious group. The Pew Forum on Religion and Public Life finds that Christians are suffering in more places today than any other religious group. . . . They were targeted for harassment in 151 countries—three quarters of the world's states. Similar findings are reported by the Vatican, *Newsweek*, the *Economist*, and Open Doors."

All of these organizations are coming to the same conclusion. The most persecuted people in the world today are Christians. In some Islamic countries people are put to death for converting to Jesus Christ. In communist nations such as North Korea, people can be imprisoned for years or even executed for speaking of their faith in Christ.

In the United States? Yes, there is persecution here, too. It may be violent, but more often it's just mockery. It rears its ugly head in many ways. And if you are a true follower of Jesus, you will taste it and experience it at some time and at some level.

What should you do if you are persecuted? How should you react? In Matthew 5:12, Jesus said, "Rejoice and be exceedingly glad." A better translation would be "Jump and skip with happy excitement."

I love that. Someone attacks you for your faith and you say, "Yes! Thank You, Lord. What a privilege." In the Greek language, when Jesus said "rejoice," it is a *command*. That's how He wants us to respond. He wants us to wear persecution as a badge of honor.

If you have been on the receiving end of some persecution and you are feeling down about it, don't feel down. Feel encouraged! You're doing your job. Let me put it another way: If you can't remember the last time you were persecuted for being a believer, ask yourself, "What's wrong with me?" Because if you are living a godly life, according to Jesus, you will be persecuted—and have a great reason to be happy.

God will use any persecution against you as a follower of Jesus for His own glory. In fact, there is a reward waiting for you. Verse 12 says, "Great is your reward in heaven, for so they persecuted the prophets who were before you." What is this great reward? Who can say? But you will be very glad, for all eternity, that you possess it.

Persecution for being a Christian, then, has its distinct benefits. It's a confirmation that you are a child of God. And it causes you to cling closer to Christ and be reminded that this world is not your true home.

Someone might say, "You talk about being a Christian and how persecution will come. Why would anyone want to be a Christian?"

The truth is, it's not easy to be a Christian in this day and age. The culture is changing fast, and people of faith will be more and more looked down on and excluded. Wimps need not apply! So if you want to get along with everybody, never offend anyone, fit in with the crowd, and march in lockstep with the rest of this culture on the road to destruction, you can certainly do that. But if you want to think for yourself, get to know the God who created you, and find lasting and true happiness, give your life to Jesus, follow Him, and be assured that whatever comes your way, He will be with you. He will get you through it.

No other object, relationship, or experience can offer this to you. No other religion in the world can offer this to you. Only a relationship with Jesus Christ can bring you this hope. As the Scripture says, "Happy are the people whose God is the LORD!"

CHAPTER ELEVEN
AMERICA, THIS IS YOUR WAKE-UP CALL

I heard a story about a young lady who was walking down the beach when she saw a shiny object embedded in the sand. She reached down, pulled it out, and dusted it off.

It was a lamp, and a genie came out when she rubbed it.

The genie said, "Oh master, I will grant you one wish. Whatever you want, I will give it to you."

"One wish?" the girl said. "Whatever happened to three wishes?"

"Well, you know how it is," the genie said with a shrug. "Times are hard. We had to cut back. So what's your one wish?"

"Well, genie, I was just looking at this map of the Middle East. You see these countries?" The genie nodded, looking over her shoulder.

"Yes, I am familiar with them."

"Well, they're always *fighting*. Always in turmoil. My wish is that they would have peace and no longer fight. As a matter of fact, I want world peace. I want peace all around the globe."

The genie was appalled. "Are you out of your mind?" he said. "There's no way I can grant a wish like that. These people have been fighting in this region forever. World peace? Forget it. It can't happen. Come up with another request."

She thought about it for a moment. "Okay, genie. Here goes. I have always wanted a good man. I've never found the right one. You know—one who likes to cook and can help with the housecleaning. A guy who won't sit around on the couch and watch sports all day. A guy who will get along with my family and smother me with affection. If I can't have world peace, that's what I want. I want the perfect man."

The genie sighed and said, "Let me see that map again."

Some things just seem impossible. And yet the Bible tells us that with God nothing is impossible. So, is it possible for our country to change, to turn back to God? Is it possible that America's best days are in our future and not only part of the distant past?

I believe it is possible. Why? Because we don't serve a genie in a lamp; we serve the all-powerful God of the universe.

And that's what I want to talk about in this chapter. Our country, the state we are in, the role we play as Christians, and how we can turn our country around.

What we need in the United States of America is a wake-up call.

Two Options: Judgment or Revival

Years ago I was in Anchorage, Alaska, with Richie, an old friend who is also a Calvary Chapel pastor; I was speaking and he was singing. It was really fun to have that ministry opportunity together, and we ended up goofing around in the hotel and playing tricks on each other like a couple of teenagers on a youth retreat.

On the day I left, I went down to the hotel's front desk and ordered two wake-up calls for Richie's room, one at 4:00 a.m. and another one at 5:00 a.m. the next morning. I knew he was leaving that day—but not that early!

"Okay, sir," the desk clerk said. I was actually surprised they would do it.

I left, arrived home, and got a call from Ritchie the next day.

"Do you know what happened?" he asked me.

"No, what happened?"

"I got the first wake-up call and knew right away you had done it. So I said, 'Fine, thank you,' and hung up. But somehow the front desk thought I had an important meeting. So instead of giving me a second wake-up call, they came into my room and *shook me* while I was in bed asleep! 'Sir,' they said, 'you need to get up. You have a meeting!'"

Of course that really made me laugh. I pumped the air with my fist and said, "Yes!" Sometimes things just work out.

Is that what it will take for America? Do we need to be shaken in our bed to wake up to the reality of what is taking place? I believe we have two options before us as a nation right now: judgment or revival.

Of course judgment will come to the USA as it will come for all nations. We know that a time of terrible tribulation is coming upon the earth. We know that the Antichrist will arise. All of that is in our future, but we don't know when—maybe sooner or maybe later.

I am praying that before that time comes, our nation will experience at least one more great spiritual awakening, a revival.

Peter Marshall, former chaplain to the U. S. Senate, once made this statement: "The choice before us is plain. It is Christ or chaos. Conviction or compromise. Discipline or disintegration." How true that is.

Here is the question: Are we to just throw up our hands and say there's nothing we can do, or *can we really make a difference?*

I believe we can. And the "how-tos" can be found in the Sermon on the Mount.

Salt and Light

You are the salt of the earth; but if the salt loses its flavor, how shall it be seasoned? It is then good for nothing but to be thrown out and trampled underfoot by men.

You are the light of the world. A city that is set on a hill cannot be hidden. Nor do they light a lamp and put it under a basket, but on a lampstand, and it gives light to all who are in the house. Let your light so shine before men, that they may see your good works and glorify your Father in heaven. (Matthew 5:13-16)

Salt and light. Why did the Lord use these two word pictures? Because the world is corrupt and the world is dark. The world needs salt because it is corrupt and the world needs light because it is getting darker by the day. The true biblical worldview of this culture is that it is dark and will continue to get darker. By its very nature, it cannot get anything but worse, because there is no inherent goodness in mankind to build on.

Man has increased in scientific, medical, historical, educational, psychological, and especially technical knowledge to an outstanding degree. But he has not changed his own basic nature. He has not improved society. His confidence has increased, but his peace of mind has diminished. His accomplishments have increased, but his purpose has all but disappeared.

General Omar Bradley, in a 1948 armistice speech, made this incredible statement: "We have grasped the mystery of the atom and we have rejected the Sermon on the Mount. The world has achieved brilliance without conscience. Ours is a world of nuclear giants and ethical infants."

Instead of making things better in the world, humankind has only made things worse for the whole planet. Modern man has come up with ingenious new methods to destroy himself. We go from war to greater war. From crime to greater crime. From perversion to greater perversion. From immorality to more terrible immorality. The spiral is downward not upward.

In response to this, some Christians want to withdraw. They say, "There's nothing we can do. The world is going to hell in a handbasket. Let's just build a Christian city, live in Christian houses, drive Christian cars, go out to eat in Christian restaurants, and wear Christian clothes. And let's not forget, we will have Christian dogs and Christian cats." (Well, maybe not cats.)

The philosophy of some is to evade the culture. To isolate. But that is virtually impossible. We can try to remove ourselves and our children from the culture, but the culture will find us. We won't be able to create a Christian subculture and withdraw into a Christian bubble.

But that isn't what Jesus called us to do anyway.

He has not called us to isolate but to infiltrate. To permeate. To saturate. Not to evade but to invade. To impact culture without being compromised by it. And that is a tricky balance, for sure.

Sometimes I think we want to "Christianize" nonbelievers more than we want to convert them. We want them to act and think like Christians when they are *not* Christians. That's getting the cart before the horse. We want to change their behavior before their hearts are changed. But the fact is, when we are around nonbelievers, they just naturally do the things nonbelievers do. They use profanity. They drink. They smoke. They tell lies. They commit adultery when they get a chance.

When I am around nonbelievers and they use profanity, I don't correct it. I don't say, "Please don't say that word in my presence. I have never heard such words." But I have heard such words, and I used such words—before I came to Christ. What I recognize is that if I can get to their hearts and if they will come to Jesus, *then* their behavior will change. But not until.

No, we don't like being exposed to the corrupt stuff in our world. It grates on the ears. We strongly disagree with the attitudes and outlooks and values of those outside of Christ. But how will we influence these people unless we are around them? Paul was right when he declared, "I have become all things to all people so that by all possible means I might save some. I do all this for the sake of the gospel" (1 Corinthians 9:22-23, NIV).

The idea here is that we have to be around people and adapt to become salt and light to them.

Behind Enemy Lines

As Christians, we are like soldiers or agents behind enemy lines.

I watched a World War II movie not long ago. In one scene, the commanding officer speaks to paratroopers from Easy Company who have parachuted behind enemy lines. The commander says to them, "A Panzer division is about to cut you off. You will be surrounded."

The lieutenant in command of Easy Company makes this classic reply: "We are paratroopers, sir. We're *supposed* to be surrounded."

I love that line. I thought, *That is what we are as Christians. We are paratroopers, dropped behind enemy lines. We are in hostile territory. Everywhere we turn the enemy is at work.*

What do we do? We infiltrate. We invade. We are *supposed* to be surrounded. As the apostle John put it, "We know that we are children of God, and that the whole world is under the control of the evil one. We know also that the Son of God has come and has given us understanding, so that we may know him who is true. And we are in him who is true" (1 John 5:19-20, NIV). What a fantastic summary of the world we live in! The whole world is under the control of Satan, but God's Son, the True One, has come. We belong to Him and live in Him and understand life through Him.

For years our country had what you might describe as a "civil religion." Though never completely Christian, the country supported the basic Christian worldview—that there is evil in the world, that the Bible is the Word of God, that the Ten Commandments are absolute truth (and could even be posted in courtrooms or on classroom walls), that parents are to be respected and apply discipline when necessary, that the family unit and the roles of fathers and mothers are honored. You could see those values reflected in the lives of people portrayed on TV shows in the 1950s and early 1960s, such as *Leave It to Beaver, Father Knows Best, The Donna Reed Show,* and *Ozzie and Harriet.*

The idea most often communicated was that the father was a wise man. If you were a kid and you had messed up, he would call you into his den and have a talk with you. He would teach you life lessons. Kids would learn from adults about morals and values, such as kindness and honesty. That was when our nation followed, or mostly followed, this unspoken civil religion loosely based on Christian principles.

That day is gone. The Ten Commandments have become largely irrelevant. The family has been redefined. The Bible is looked at as a book of myths—mostly useless and possibly dangerous. Along with those things we have rampant divorce, suicide, drug and alcohol addiction, and epidemic, violent crime—even mass shootings.

The Bible predicted all of it. As the Old Testament prophet put it, we "sow the wind and reap the whirlwind" (Hosea 8:7, NIV).

In the place of proper faith we have what we might describe as "spirituality," where people effectively make up their own idea about God. *USA Today* did a cover story not long ago on this topic. The article said, "For decades if not centuries America's top religious brand has been Protestant. No more. Where did they go? Nowhere actually. They didn't switch to any new religious brand, they just let go of any religious affiliation or label. This group called the Nones is now the nation's second largest category after Catholics, and outnumbers the top Protestant denomination, the Southern Baptists."

They are called the Nones. What do they believe? Nothing in particular. They are just "open to spirituality." People of this category will say things like, "I'm not into organized religion. I am just a spiritual person."

Allow me to loosely paraphrase what they really mean: "I worship myself and make up the rules as I go along. I will decide what is right and wrong—for me." This is a slippery slope that effectively leads to idolatry—which is putting someone or something in the place of God.

Years ago, G. K. Chesterton made this statement: "When a man stops believing in God, he doesn't then believe in nothing. He believes in anything."

What Should We Do?

How should we respond to this cultural change as Christians? What should our position be? Let me suggest a few ideas.

We need to stand for truth, whether it is popular and politically correct or not.

This is a non-negotiable. On every topic, every issue, we stand where the Bible stands. There is no wavering here. We state (calmly and with conviction) that the Bible—*all* of the Bible—is the Word of God. We believe what the Bible teaches about Jesus Christ being the only way to the Father. We believe what the Bible teaches about the sanctity of life, that life begins at conception, and that *every* child has a right to live. We believe in marriage between one man and one woman.

You pick the topic. We stand on what Scripture says. This is not a time to back down. This is a time to stand up and be counted and to be bold and strong. This is not a time to retreat, it is a time to advance. It is not a time to apologize, it is a time to be an apologist and give a defense for our faith.

We must speak in a language that people understand.

If people don't even know what we are saying, they won't listen to us. When I go into a different country where they speak another language, I have to work through an interpreter (which means cutting my sermons in half, because it takes twice as long to give them). It can be a little disconcerting, because sometimes I say something I think is very serious, but after the interpretation people laugh. Or I will say two sentences and the interpreter will talk for about four minutes. And I think, *What's going on here? I hope he's saying what I want to say and not what he wants to say.* But it's all part of the interpretation process. It's what's necessary to get through the language barrier.

We have to get over the language barrier in our own country—and I'm talking about the English language. Sometimes in our attempts to preach the gospel we use strange or outdated terms that nobody even understands anymore. Or we answer questions no one is asking, instead of the questions that actually burn in *their* hearts.

Sometimes the verbiage we use goes right over their heads. We say, "You need to be washed in the blood and sanctified and justified and become part of the body of Christ." To somebody who doesn't know those terms, you will sound like a crazy person. Even a simple statement like "You need to receive Jesus into your life" doesn't necessarily make sense to people. I'm not suggesting that we do away with biblical terminology, but I am saying we shouldn't assume we're being understood. We need to speak in a way that people can readily grasp. As Paul said in 1 Corinthians 9:22 (TLB), "Yes, whatever a person is like, I try to find common ground with him so that he will let me tell him about Christ and let Christ save him."

A good paraphrase of that key passage puts it like this:

I have voluntarily become a servant to any and all in order to reach a wide range of people: religious, nonreligious, meticulous moralists, loose-living immoralists, the defeated, the demoralized—whoever. I didn't take on their way of life. I kept my bearings in Christ—but I entered their world and tried to experience things from their point of view. (verses 20-22, MSG)

We see this played out in Scripture when Jesus spoke with the woman at the well, a loose-living immoralist, and appealed to her inner thirst. When Jesus spoke to Nicodemus the devout Pharisee, He was speaking to a meticulous moralist. When Paul spoke on Mars Hill, he was addressing a group of pagan intellectuals. When Peter spoke on the Day of Pentecost, he was speaking to people who were religious. In each of these circumstances, Jesus, Paul, and Peter adapted their messages to the people they were speaking to.

We need to bring them the message of the gospel.

When we do this, some will respond favorably and come to faith. Others will not. Paul summed it up like this in 2 Corinthians 2:14-16 (TLB): "Now wherever we go he uses us to tell others about the Lord and to spread the Gospel like a sweet perfume. As far as God is concerned there is a sweet, wholesome fragrance in our lives. It is the fragrance of Christ within us, an aroma to both the saved and the unsaved all around us. To those who are not being saved, we seem a fearful smell of death and doom, while to those who know Christ we are a life-giving perfume."

Our lives are like a fragrance. I happen to be allergic to most colognes and perfumes. When I walk into a department store and someone at a counter wants to spray something on me, I will quickly hold up my hand and say, "No, thank you." If I get some of that cologne on me I will be clearing my throat every thirty seconds for the next hour. Some people wear a lot of cologne. These are the people who hug you, and then you smell like them for the next two days.

There are other scents, of course, that aren't so attractive. The other day my son Jonathan was in the kitchen making garlic cheese bread. Nothing smells better than garlic when it's being cooked. I had one piece, and that was fine. Then I had a second. After my third piece I had a severe stomachache. And for the rest of the day, I must have been knocking people down with my breath.

The gospel is really just like that. When some people hear the gospel, because the Holy Spirit has prepared their hearts, the gospel smells very sweet to them. You tell them about the love of Jesus and they say, "I love this. I want this. Tell me more about this." Other people will hear the same message and say, "This is wrong. This offends me. *You* offend me." The message that is like a sweet-smelling savor to some is an offensive smell to others.

Our job is to faithfully keep living it and presenting it, no matter what the response.

Before we can effectively speak the message, we must live it.

Nothing is worse than a hypocritical Christian. You might be surprised to hear me say this, but to some people I would say, "Please don't preach the gospel." If you are going to consistently contradict what you believe by the way you live, if you aren't seeking to live as a follower of Jesus, then do us all a favor and keep it to yourself.

"Salt of the Earth"

Jesus summarized how His followers are to live in this corrupt world of ours with the dual word picture of salt and light.

How are we to be salt?

He says, "You are the salt of the earth. But if the salt loses its saltiness, how can it be made salty again? It is no longer good for anything, except to be thrown out" (Matthew 5:13, NIV).

It's hard for us to understand how valuable salt was in the first century. To us, salt is something very common, ordinary, and inexpensive. We use it every day but really don't hold it in high regard. Back in the first century, however, is was a valuable commodity. The Romans believed that, except for the sun, nothing was more valuable than salt. In fact, Roman soldiers were sometimes paid in salt. That's where we get the old expression, "He's worth his salt."

There are a few things that salt does that we as Christians should be doing in our culture.

Salt preserves.

Because they didn't have refrigeration in New Testament days, people would rub salt into meat to preserve it. Then they would cut the meat into slender strips and soak it in a salt solution that would keep it edible for a long time. In the same way, we as Christians are a preservative in this world. It is Christians who usually stand up for what is true. When something wrong or immoral is happening in our communities, we stand up and speak out, as we should. When there is a crisis somewhere in the world, it is Christians who step up to the plate and are often the first with boots on the ground, bringing help to those in need.

On a personal level, the presence of a Christian can sometimes change a conversation. Maybe some of your coworkers are telling a dirty joke. Then you walk into the room and the joke suddenly stops. It's a little awkward for them. They wait until you leave the room before they finish.

You just created a little tension in the room by your simple presence. And that is good. Although it may have never occurred to your coworkers in these terms, when you walked in you were a representative of Jesus Christ, and that had a preserving effect, resisting corruption.

If you think things are bad in this world now, wait until all of the salt is suddenly removed—when the church is taken out of the world at the Rapture. Right now, the church of Jesus Christ has a preserving, restraining effect on the culture. The Holy Spirit works through us to stop corruption. Scripture tells us, "For the mystery of lawlessness is already at work; only He who now restrains will do so until He is taken out of the way. And then the lawless one will be revealed, whom the Lord will . . . destroy with the brightness of His coming" (2 Thessalonians 2:7-8). This passage is saying that Antichrist cannot be revealed until the church is first removed from the earth. The Holy Spirit working through the church is a restraining force in the world today.

Salt stimulates thirst.

Someone once said, "You can lead a horse to water, but you can't make him drink." His friend replied, "That may be true. But you can put salt in his oats!" We've all had the experience of eating something really salty and becoming very thirsty afterward. Take those huge buckets of popcorn they sell you at the movies. Do they really have to be that big and cost a hundred bucks? No, but eating that much salty popcorn will probably prompt you to buy a drink with it (which will cost another hundred bucks or so!).

If you are a real follower of Jesus, you will stimulate in others a thirst for God. When I am around certain people for any length of time, I have a desire to be more Christlike. There's something about them—the way they talk, the way they live, the way they *are*—that stirs something in me, making me want to be closer to God.

Have you ever met someone like that? Have you ever *been* someone like that to someone else? If you are living as you should, you will stimulate thirst in them.

But what happens when salt loses its saltiness? It's worthless, isn't it? Jesus said it was good for nothing but to be "trampled underfoot by men." What good is it? It's like tepid coffee or uncarbonated Coke. Who needs it?

"Unsalty" salt is a picture of a believer who isn't walking with God, or has been so compromised by the world that people can no longer even tell if he or she is a Christian. It's a believer with no zing. No tang. No flavor of Christ. And the person becomes useless to the Lord.

A little pinch of real salty salt, however, goes a long way.

Jesus can do a lot with a few salty Christians. A believer in the right circumstances at the right time can make all the difference in the world.

"Light of the World"

Jesus said, "You are the light of the world. A town built on a hill cannot be hidden. Neither do people light a lamp and put it under a bowl. Instead they put it on its stand, and it gives light to everyone in the house. In the same way, let your light shine before others, that they may see your good deeds and glorify your Father in heaven" (Matthew 5:14-16, NIV).

Notice the order here: salt and then light.

First you are to be salt, and then light.

Salt is hidden, subtle. Light is obvious. Salt works secretly; light works openly. Salt works from within; light works from without. Salt is the indirect influence of the gospel, while light is its more direct communication. In other words, you *live* it and then you *share* it. The greatest compliment a nonbeliever can pay you goes something like this: "There is something about you. The way you live. Your attitude. Your disposition. The way you work. Everything. I don't know what you have, but I want it, too."

Oh man! What an open door to share your faith! You gained that opportunity by being salt, earning the right to be light.

What does light do? Light exposes things. It exposes the darkness, and a little light goes a long way. Have you ever been in a movie theater and some guy pulls out his cell phone? You can see it all over the theater. One source I read said that on a dark night, the unaided human eye can see a single candle flame flickering up to thirty miles away![3]

Light exposes darkness, and people who love the darkness don't appreciate that at all. The apostle John wrote, "Everyone who does evil hates the light, and will not come into the light for fear that their deeds will be exposed" (John 3:20, NIV).

In the same way, when a Christian is living as he or she should, it may make people uncomfortable. Sometimes they will come under the conviction of the Holy Spirit, and that is a good thing. That is what we pray for.

Jesus said in John 3:19-20, "This is the condemnation, that the light has come into the world, and men loved darkness rather than light, because their deeds were evil. For everyone practicing evil hates the light and does not come to the light, lest his deeds should be exposed."

Light not only exposes the problem, it shows the way out of the darkness. If I'm in a dark, unfamiliar room and I don't know how to get out, I start groping for a light switch so I can find the door. In the same way, we as believers will tell people what is wrong, but then we show them what is right and how to know God. The door is Jesus Christ, and that's where they need to go.

In Matthew 5:13-14, Jesus said, "You are the salt of the earth. . . . You are the light of the world." A better translation would be, "You *and you alone* are the salt of the earth. You *and you alone* are the light of the world." Think of it this way. What kind of world would we live in if every Christian behaved just like you? How many would be attracted or turned off by the gospel? What kind of opinion would people have of Christianity if you were its sole representative?

You might say, "Greg, that's a lot to lay on one person." But wait a second. You truly are the sole representative of Jesus Christ in certain situations. That's no exaggeration. You may be the only Christian people see. You may be the only Christian in that workplace or classroom or gym or neighborhood. You are the only one, and those around you are literally evaluating how they feel about God by observing and thinking about you.

"That's too much pressure," you say.

Deal with it. You are His representative, so do everything you can to be a good one.

Summing Up

We pray for our nation, asking God that our whole country would turn toward Him. Is there historical precedent for that? Has anything like that ever happened on such a scale?

In fact, there is such a precedent—in the nation of Syria and the city of Nineveh. As you may remember from reading the Old Testament, Nineveh was notorious for being a violent, wicked, barbaric city, and for the cruel, bloodthirsty ways they would deal with conquered peoples. It was a very large city for that day, with up to a million people. What's more, they were a military superpower in their day.

At the preaching of Jonah, however, the whole nation turned to God. Almost overnight. How Jonah arrived in that city and took on that ministry assignment is a story in itself, and it is captured in the Bible book of Jonah. As soon as he entered the city he began walking through the streets crying out, "Forty days and Nineveh will be overthrown!"

Jonah had never wanted the job of evangelizing this bitter enemy of Israel, and he would have been perfectly happy if they had rejected his message and then been fried to a crisp.

But something else happened. Something he didn't expect.

The people actually heard the message, believed it, and turned to God for mercy. The king himself repented and led the people of the city to put on sackcloth and cover themselves with ashes.

And then God forgave them. A whole generation of Ninevites turned from evil and embraced God. It was one of the greatest revivals in the history of the world, and God used a reluctant preacher with a negative message to pull it off.

All this to say, yes, it is possible. God can turn a nation around.

And what's our part? What should we do? Let me go back and touch on three things.

First, we need to infiltrate and not isolate, invade and not evade. Yes, God has dropped us behind enemy lines and we are surrounded. We are supposed to be surrounded. Let's be salt and light, making use of every opportunity God gives us.

Second, we need to pray. The words God spoke to His people in 2 Chronicles 7:14 still apply today: "If My people who are called by My name will humble themselves, and pray and seek My face, and turn from their wicked ways, then I will hear from heaven, and will forgive their sin and heal their land."

When God talks about having a nation turn around, He begins by addressing His own people and says, "This is where it starts. With My people. In the house of God." Revival starts with you and me. It's easy for us to say, "I think the church should do this or that," or "Politicians need to start doing X, Y, and Z." Well, maybe they do. But what about you?

Do you have any "wicked ways" you need to turn from? Do you have any sin you need to repent of? Are there things you are doing as a follower of Jesus that you should not be doing? Maybe you are part of the problem. Instead, become part of the solution, turn from your sinful actions and attitudes, and get right with God.

Third, we need to preach the gospel. This is the message America needs to hear. America needs to see and hear the gospel. On TV or in stadiums or on the Internet? Yes, in all of those ways. But most importantly, they need to see it in you and hear it from you.

As Jesus told us, "You and you alone are the light of the world."

That's not pressure, and that's not a guilt trip.

That is an open door.

CHAPTER TWELVE
WHAT JESUS TAUGHT ABOUT ANGER, HATRED, AND LUST

One thing this digital, interconnected world of ours doesn't lack is commentary on world events.

If you want opinions about the events in today's news, you can have them by the truckload. All kinds of experts, retired experts, would-be experts, and familiar talking heads share their views on Twitter, Facebook, websites, cable TV, radio, podcasts, and countless other media outlets.

But they all have their own slant on things, don't they? They all have their own soapbox and agenda to promote. We get opinions from the left and from the right and from people with all kinds of biases and prejudices.

So, whose worldview is right? Whom are we supposed to believe?

There is One who always has it right.

You can't go wrong with Jesus Christ, the Son of God. This is the One who said, "Heaven and earth will pass away, but my words will never pass away" (Mark 13:31, NIV). His words endure. His viewpoint matters today, and it will matter when the earth as we know it passes away.

And we don't have to wonder about it. We don't have to try to guess His worldview. It is captured for us in Matthew 5–7, in the extended Bible passage we know as "the Sermon on the Mount." It has also been called "the greatest sermon ever preached." And if you want to know what Jesus really thinks about life and living, about priorities and dangers and opportunities, this is the place to camp out for a while.

You might call it the official manifesto of the King of kings and Lord of lords.

A Message for Disciples

And seeing the multitudes, He went up on a mountain, and when He was seated His disciples came to Him. Then He opened His mouth and taught them, saying . . . (Matthew 5:1-2)

In the opening of this message, we are told for sure who these words were meant for. The message was directed to Jesus' disciples, not to the multitudes or the culture or society in general.

The phrase "He opened His mouth" is an expression in Greek used to describe something solemn, grave, and dignified. He was about to say something very important, directed at those who followed Him. And that's the point: The only people who can actually live by the Sermon on the Mount are followers of Jesus.

Back then, as now, Jesus had His fair-weather followers. When He was performing miracles, casting out demons, and providing a free lunch they were "in" with Him. When He spoke of sacrifice and commitment, they were gone with the wind. The words of the Sermon on the Mount are mind-boggling and beautiful. They are also impossible without the help of the Holy Spirit.

No one can live by these standards without God's help.

Sometimes I hear people say, "All the religion I need is found in the Sermon on the Mount."

I reply, "Really? It's that important to you? Quote something from that sermon. Quote anything."

"Umm. Well, . . . 'Judge not lest ye be judged.'"

That is every nonbeliever's favorite verse.

The fact is, you cannot live by the Sermon on the Mount. It is harder to live by than the Ten Commandments, because it deals so much with the heart. Nonbelieving people can make a show of external obedience to a set of rules and standards. But when it comes to the heart? That is a very difficult thing to control. You can be doing the right thing outwardly, but inwardly wanting very much to do the wrong thing. As the little girl who had been told to sit down once said, "I may be sitting down on the outside, but I am standing up on the inside!"

This sermon deals with motives—why we do what we do. You might sum it up by saying, "The heart of the matter is the matter of the heart."

In this chapter, we will focus in on three very difficult, very troubling heart issues that Jesus highlighted in His sermon. Jesus came from heaven and would return to heaven, but we could never say He had His "head in the clouds." He dealt with real-life, front-burner issues in the lives of those who chose to follow Him.

Front-Burner Issues

You have heard that our ancestors were told, "You must not murder. If you commit murder, you are subject to judgment." But I say, if you are even angry with someone, you are subject to judgment! If you call someone an idiot, you are in danger of being brought before the court. And if you curse someone, you are in danger of the fires of hell.

So if you are presenting a sacrifice at the altar in the Temple and you suddenly remember that someone has something against you, leave your sacrifice there at the altar. Go and be reconciled to that person. Then come and offer your sacrifice to God.

When you are on the way to court with your adversary, settle your differences quickly. Otherwise, your accuser may hand you over to the judge, who will hand you over to an officer, and you will be thrown into prison. And if that happens, you surely won't be free again until you have paid the last penny.

You have heard the commandment that says, "You must not commit adultery." But I say, anyone who even looks at a woman with lust has already committed adultery with her in his heart. So if your eye—even your good eye—causes you to lust, gouge it out and throw it away. It is better for you to lose one part of your body than for your whole body to be thrown into hell. And if your hand—even your stronger hand—causes you to sin, cut it off and throw it away. It is better for you to lose one part of your body than for your whole body to be thrown into hell. (Matthew 5:21-30, NLT)

Jesus dealt with three areas of sin that are very widespread in our culture. In every movie theater in America, you will see these three themes being played out on the big screens: anger, hatred, and lust.

Again, Jesus was dealing with the heart. Sin deceives me into thinking that if I haven't done the actual deed, but only *thought* it, I'm all right. People both then and now would tell themselves, "If I haven't actually murdered that person I hate so much, and if I haven't committed the physical act of adultery, everything is good." But here's the truth: If you still want to do these things in your heart, the murder and adultery really haven't gone away. The dark roots are still there.

Anger, Hatred, and Envy

Anger is murder in the heart. Like a surgeon with a sharp scalpel, Jesus uncovered it: "But I say, if you are even angry with someone, you are subject to judgment!" (verse 22, NLT).

Is there no place in our lives, then, for anger?

Yes, there is. And this text is not saying that a Christian can't be angry. In fact, there are certain things that *should* anger us. Ephesians 4:26 says, "Be angry, and do not sin." There is a place for what we sometimes call "righteous indignation." Jesus was angry at times, as was the apostle Paul. But that's not what the Lord is talking about here. The word used for anger here in Matthew 5:22 means a "settled anger." It is a malice that is nursed inwardly, kept alive and smoldering. This isn't describing a person who maybe gets irritated, flies off the handle, and then apologizes.

This is a person who has become bitter by developing a grudge and feeding it.

This is a person who throws gasoline on the fire of anger.

This is a person who has become consumed with anger.

Many people have held on to an anger that has settled so deeply into the cracks and crevices of their souls that they truly desire to see the hated person dead. Do you feel that way about anyone? If you do, the Bible has a word for you: "Anyone who hates a brother or sister is a murderer, and you know that no murderer has eternal life residing in him" (1 John 3:15, NIV).

Scripture says that you cannot be a follower of Jesus and live with a boiling, seething, settled anger that you feed and fuel every day. There is no place for it. The word *hate* means to habitually despise. Again, we're not talking about a transient emotion—a dark cloud that passes over, letting the sunshine back in again. No, this is a deep-seated loathing. When you see this person you just despise them and are bitter toward them.

How do we get into such a state? Sometimes anger is rooted in envy. Remember the story of Cain and Abel in the book of Genesis? Cain killed his brother—the first murder in recorded human history—because he was envious of him.

What is envy? It has been defined as a discontent or uneasiness at the sight of another's good fortune—accompanied with some degree of hatred and a desire to possess equal advantages. It's not as though this person has harmed you personally or done something to you; it is simply a person who has succeeded in a big way. Maybe it's monetary success. Maybe they married someone you wish you could have married. Maybe they have accomplished something you wish you could have accomplished. Maybe they got that position you felt you should have received. Maybe they have a natural, easy confidence about them and seem absolutely comfortable in their own skin, but you struggle even trying to make conversation. Whatever it is, you are envious of that person, and if you're not careful, your envy can morph into something even worse.

Thomas Fuller said, "Envy shoots at another and wounds itself." The only person who suffers when you are envious is you.

In Matthew 5:22 Jesus said, "Whoever is angry with his brother without a cause shall be in danger of the judgment. And whoever says to his brother, 'Raca!' shall be in danger of the council. But whoever says, 'You fool!' shall be in danger of hell fire."

We really don't know what "Raca" means. You probably can't even remember the last time you rolled down the window of your car and yelled, "Raca!" at someone. Back in first-century culture, however, the word carried a lot of weight. Is there a modern equivalent? Maybe something like "brainless idiot" or "bonehead," but we can't be sure. We do know, however, that it was a phrase of arrogant contempt for someone who seemed beneath you or inferior to you.

The word *fool* denoted an obstinate, godless person. It was a condemnation of someone, the act of totally writing someone off. I don't think it was the actual words "Raca" or "fool" that Jesus was condemning as much as the attitude behind them. Speaking or thinking of someone in that way reveals a deep, poisonous, bitterness of heart. In Matthew 12:34 (NIV) Jesus said, "For the mouth speaks what the heart is full of."

Lust

Again in Matthew 5:27-29 we read, "You have heard that it was said to those of old, 'You shall not commit adultery.' But I say to you that whoever looks at a woman to lust for her has already committed adultery with her in his heart."

The Lord wasn't speaking here of a casual glance; He had in mind a continual act of looking. Sometimes it's that *second* look, isn't it? You see an attractive woman—or guy, if you're a woman. (We tend to think of this as a problem for men, but it applies to women, too.) They walk through your line of vision, and how can you help but notice? You might even think, "That's a good-looking woman," or "That's a handsome man." That's not a problem. The problem comes if you lock in on the individual like a laser and allow yourself to desire that person. The idea being conveyed here is of intentional and repeated gazing with a purpose of lusting, going beyond simply admiring beauty to desiring to possess.

This is speaking of someone who goes out of their way to stare at someone and to lust after them. Obviously, if you look at pornography, you will be violating this commandment. Why? Because you are intentionally looking at images that will stimulate lust. Rather than looking at someone as a person, someone God loves and Jesus died for, you are looking at them as an object for your own pleasure.

Probably the best—and saddest—example of this in the Bible is the story of David and Bathsheba. In 2 Samuel 11, David was up on his rooftop one evening getting some air. Back then rooftops functioned more like terraces or decks, where people could relax in the cool evening breezes. David was just hanging out by himself that night, looking over his balcony at the city. That's when he caught sight of the beautiful Bathsheba taking a bath.

The Bible affirms that she was beautiful—an incredibly attractive woman without any clothes on. David took that first look, which wasn't a problem. Instead of turning away, however, as he should have done, he kept looking for a long time. And then, since he had the power to do it, he commanded that this married woman be brought up to his palace, where he had sex with her.

If David was careless that night, was Bathsheba being careless, too? Possibly. No modest Hebrew woman would ever bathe in public. Did she know she was in eyeshot of the palace? Had she ever seen David out on his roof before at a certain time of night? Did she position herself? If she did, the Bible never mentions it or holds her accountable. David was the most culpable in this sin because he misused his authority and position. But she was culpable, too. Because, king or not, she could have said no.

My point is that this can be a two-way street. If lustful looking is bad, then those who dress and expose themselves with the desire to be looked at and lusted after are guilty, too. If men need to guard against that second, lustful look, then women need to think carefully about what they wear (or don't wear) as they leave the house.

"But Greg," some woman will say, "how do I know what will trip someone up?"

You might think of it this way. What if Jesus were picking you up at your house to take you to church or out to dinner? What would you put on before He came? Modesty is a good thing, and you don't want to wear something that will stimulate lust.

You reply, "Greg, some guys would lust after a tree!"

That's true. But I think most women understand how this works, and what it means to be a little more careful, a little more thoughtful.

David's sin was a continuous look followed by dramatic action.

Lust, of course, starts in the mind. And that's the place where we have to be on guard. How far does this problem go back in history? Right back to the earliest days on earth. In what may be the oldest book in the Bible, Job said, "I made a covenant with my eyes not to look lustfully at a young woman" (Job 31:1, NIV).

How does this work in real life? Let's say you are in a movie, and there is a sex scene that you didn't know about. You say, "I didn't know this was in the movie! What should I do?" *You could walk out.* Yes, even if you paid too much money for the ticket. What if a suggestive scene flashes across your TV screen? If the kids were watching, you would turn it off. *Turn it off anyway.* Let's say you're walking down the street and an attractive girl is coming your way. Okay, you've noticed. *Now look somewhere else.* Some people want to be looked at, and that's what they're all about. But you don't have to cooperate. Don't let your mind go to that place.

If you're in a conversation with someone of the opposite sex and it starts getting a little edgy, a little suggestive, *terminate it.* Did you know that most adulterous affairs begin in the workplace, where men and women work closely together? It's good to be a cordial, friendly person. But we have to be very, very careful with our conversations and relationships with those of the opposite sex, because one thing can easily lead to another.

In 2 Corinthians 10:5 (NIV) Paul gave us good counsel for all such scenarios. He wrote, "We take captive every thought to make it obedient to Christ."

The solution Jesus gave sounds pretty drastic. "If your right eye causes you to sin, pluck it out and cast it from you" (Matthew 5:29).

Was He being literal? No. You could pluck out your right eye and still lust with your left eye. That's no solution. You could be blind and lust. You could cut off your left arm and still sin with your right arm. You could sin with no arms! No, Jesus was saying that sometimes you may need to take drastic action, giving up whatever is necessary to keep from falling into sin.

Someone may say, "I have a real problem with Internet pornography. I just can't overcome it." Then drop the Internet. Get rid of your computer if you have to. Yes, you can still survive. People survived and thrived for thousands of years before either one was invented.

You may have heard the story of Aaron Ralston. He was rock climbing by himself in Utah when a shifting boulder pinned his hand. Ralston knew how to use his equipment, and tried ropes and his anchors and everything he had to move the boulder and pull out his hand. But nothing worked.

After a couple of days, he ran out of water and it was cold. He had to do something, or he would simply die in that isolated place. So he did the unthinkable. He pulled out his pocketknife and somehow managed to cut off his own arm. After that, he rappelled seventy-five feet to the canyon floor and walked out. This whole ordeal lasted five days.

A radical solution? Yes. But he is alive today to tell his story.

In the same way, we have to cut off whatever it takes in our lives to live the lives God has called us to live. Anything that morally or spiritually entangles us and causes us to fall into sin or stay in sin must be eliminated, quickly and completely.

Hebrews chapter 12 tells us to "throw off everything that hinders and the sin that so easily entangles. And let us run with perseverance the race marked out for us" (verse 1, NIV).

These temptations and tendencies, of course, vary from person to person. Some people are more vulnerable in one area than others are. We have to look at our own lives and take action wherever it's needed. And the Lord will give us strength and help us as we do (see 1 Corinthians 10:13).

Dealing with Enemies

You have heard the law that says the punishment must match the injury: "An eye for an eye, and a tooth for a tooth." But I say, do not resist an evil person! If someone slaps you on the right cheek, offer the other cheek also. If you are sued in court and your shirt is taken from you, give your coat, too. If a soldier demands that you carry his gear for a mile, carry it two miles. Give to those who ask, and don't turn away from those who want to borrow.

You have heard the law that says, "Love your neighbor" and hate your enemy. But I say, love your enemies! Pray for those who persecute you! In that way, you will be acting as true children of your Father in heaven. (Matthew 5:38-45, NLT)

These are very high standards: Turn the other cheek, go the extra mile, love our enemies. Are these the standards, then, by which we should govern society? If so, how can we justify a military or police force? In a book called *What I Believe*, the nineteenth-century Russian novelist Leo Tolstoy spoke about reading and rereading the Sermon on the Mount. He then concluded, "Christ forbids the human institution of any court, because they resist evil and even return evil for evil. He believed criminals love good and hate evil as I do." Tolstoy went on to say that he didn't think a Christian should be involved in the military, police force, or courts of law. One man who was profoundly impacted by the writings of Tolstoy was Mahatma Gandhi. He believed that by practicing these teachings a society could bring about a perfect state, where punishment would end and prisons would be turned into schools.

Here's a newsflash: Tolstoy and Gandhi were wrong.

They misunderstood these teachings of Jesus.

The Sermon on the Mount was not given as a blueprint from which to govern a society. A society is governed by what Jesus quoted in Matthew 5:38: "You have heard that it was said, 'An eye for an eye and a tooth for a tooth.'" The quote from Exodus 21:23-25 goes on to say, "Hand for hand, foot for foot, burn for burn, wound for wound, bruise for bruise" (NIV).

This is the same expression as "tit for tat," and this was the Hebrew justice system. What was its purpose? According to Deuteronomy 19:20 (NIV): "The rest of the people will hear of this and be afraid, and never again will such an evil thing be done among you."

Criminals don't love good and hate evil. All people have sinful hearts and every one of us every day of our lives is drawn in the wrong direction.

When someone breaks the laws, there has to be a punishment. This punishment is never carried out by the victim, but by the legal system. For us to survive as a nation, we need law enforcement and the military. Government as an entity was created by God Himself. Paul made this unmistakably clear in the book of Romans:

> Obey the government, for God is the one who has put it there. There is no government anywhere that God has not placed in power. So those who refuse to obey the laws of the land are refusing to obey God, and punishment will follow. For the policeman does not frighten people who are doing right; but those doing evil will always fear him. So if you don't want to be afraid, keep the laws and you will get along well. (13:1-3, TLB)

I have a friend who is a chief of police. Sometimes we meet for coffee and he brings along another officer. These guys are in uniform, including the "Sam Brown"—a heavy utility belt that holds all of their equipment, including their radios, guns, and handcuffs.

It's funny to be there in the coffee shop with them and watch how people react. When they order coffee, everyone gets a little nervous. Why? Because they are authority figures. They wear badges. When they walk into a room in uniform, the dynamic of the room changes.

According to the book of Romans, these officers have been placed in authority by God. What if they aren't Christians? They were still placed there by God. Many people respect those uniforms and what they represent. If you are obeying the law, you don't fear the police. You're happy to see them show up. But if you are breaking the law, you don't want to be anywhere near these officers.

Speaking of the police and the military, Scripture says that "the one in authority is God's servant for your good. But if you do wrong, be afraid, for rulers do not bear the sword for no reason" (Romans 13:4, NIV).

"But Greg," someone will say, "what about a corrupt nation with corrupt police officers?" In that case, we as Christians have a higher principle that we obey. When the apostles were strictly ordered by their nation's authorities to stop preaching the gospel, what did they do? They went out and preached the gospel. Peter and John looked those rulers in the eyes and said, "Whether it is right in the sight of God to listen to you more than to God, you judge. For we cannot but speak the things which we have seen and heard" (Acts 4:19-20).

If our government were to pass a law tomorrow that said you could no longer practice your faith or pray, what should you do? You should practice your faith and pray. In that case, where the civil government runs counter to what God says, we go with God. We have a higher law. In Babylon, when a law was passed that no one could pray to God openly, Daniel prayed openly.

We're not talking here about opposing laws because we don't like them. Someone might say, "My taxes are too high. I'm not sure I should pay them." Pay them. Obey the law. Your alternative is to vote for someone who will lower your taxes next time. That's the privilege we have with our form of representative government. But we have to obey the law, even if we don't always agree with it.

The apostle Paul actually used soldiers on several occasions to illustrate how to live and function as a follower of Christ. Paul, it seems, spent quite a bit of time with soldiers because he was so frequently arrested and imprisoned by them. On some occasions, he spent time chained to them. Outgoing man that he was, I can imagine that the apostle became friends with some of these military guards and learned all about their armor and weaponry. In Ephesians

6 he used the metaphor of armor to describe a Christian's spiritual protection in Christ. In 2 Timothy 2:3-4 (TLB) he wrote, "Take your share of suffering as a good soldier of Jesus Christ, just as I do; and as Christ's soldier, do not let yourself become tied up in worldly affairs, for then you cannot satisfy the one who has enlisted you in his army." God would never choose a dishonorable profession as a positive illustration for how a Christian ought to live.

Some people like to think Jesus was the ultimate pacifist, the first hippie, with a lamb wrapped around His neck, throwing flowers and saying, "Peace and love, man." Yes, the Jesus of the Bible was loving, forgiving, and compassionate. The children recognized those qualities and came to Him. But He also administered justice. What do you think He was doing when He made a whip and drove the moneychangers out of the temple? As the days grew more dangerous for the disciples, He told them they might need their swords (see Luke 22:36-38). Why would they need swords? For shish-kabob? No, they were for self-defense.

Christians are entitled to defend themselves and those they love. In the same way, a nation in entitled to defend itself against those who would do it harm. There is a place for both self-defense and national defense.

With these things in mind, what does it mean to "turn the other cheek" and to "go the extra mile"? Jesus was giving specific advice for a believer who is enduring persecution. These aren't literal, mechanical rules but rather general principles for meeting the personal wrongs that come to those who follow Him. There may be times when, for the sake of Christ's kingdom and the soul of the one who wants to persecute us, we take the hit or walk the extra mile.

In Jesus' day, when a Roman soldier was out marching he could requisition a citizen to carry his backpack and gear for him. He would say to some stranger, "Here, you, carry my backpack for me," and by law that individual would have to do it—for the space of one mile.

Jesus was saying, "Do the unexpected. Serve even more than what is expected." I imagine a conversation something like this:

The soldier says, "Okay, we've gone a mile. You're done. You can go back."

The Christian replies, "No problem. I've got it. I'll go another mile with you because that will give me a little more time to tell you about Jesus."

In Matthew 5:39 (NIV), Jesus said, "But I tell you, do not resist an evil person. If anyone slaps you on the right cheek, turn to them the other cheek also." In the culture of that day, striking someone in the face was among the most demeaning and contemptuous of acts. Even a slave would rather be struck on the back than on the face. It was a deliberate, calculated insult. Maybe a contemporary equivalent would be someone spitting in your face or gesturing at your with their middle finger.

Jesus was speaking of someone who absorbs the insult and doesn't immediately strike back. Is this an easy thing to do? Not at all. Even the great apostle Paul struggled with this. When Ananias, the high priest, ordered that Paul be struck on the mouth, he shot back, "God will strike you, you whitewashed wall!" (Acts 23:3). Paul was angered by the unexpected and unfair attack. In other words, he was human, like you and me.

The point is, this idea of forgiving and going the extra mile and refusing to retaliate isn't easy for anyone. We've all been wronged at various times. Most of us have been slandered, mistreated, misunderstood, and taken advantage of. Was Jesus saying that we should be the doormat for the planet and never defend ourselves? No, not necessarily. But His bottom line still goes against the grain of our natural, fleshly response: "But I say, love your enemies! Pray for those who persecute you! In that way, you will be acting as true children of your Father in heaven" (Matthew 5:44-45, NLT). We are not to strike out at those who oppose us, but rather to pray for them and love them in a positive way.

Abraham Lincoln once said, "The best way to destroy an enemy is to make him a friend." This selfless spirit is found in many of the people God has used. It was the spirit of Abraham when he gave the best land to his undeserving nephew Lot. It was the spirit of Joseph when he kissed—and then cared for—the brothers who had so mistreated him. It was the spirit of David when he refused to take the opportunities offered him to kill King Saul, who had become his enemy. It was the spirit of Stephen when he prayed for the very people who were stoning him to death. It is the spirit every one of God's children should have.

May God help us to turn the other cheek, go the extra mile, and refuse to retaliate against those who have deliberately slandered or harmed us. May He enable us to have a change of heart so that we no longer harbor hatred and lust.

These are marks of God's children.

These are characteristics of those who love and follow God's Son.

CHAPTER THIRTEEN
WHAT JESUS TAUGHT ABOUT MONEY, POSSESSIONS, AND GIVING

If travel was ever a novelty for me, the attraction wore off years ago.

Being a preacher with opportunities to speak in many different places means a lot of time in airports and wrestling with luggage. I mention luggage because after all these years of traveling, I still have trouble with packing. When I am scheduled to speak somewhere, I always try to find out what the weather will be, so I know what clothes to bring. If I'm traveling to a warm location, I want to wear light stuff. But if I'm bound for a place that might be chilly, I take extra sweaters and jackets and longed-sleeved clothes, so I won't be cold.

But somehow it never turns out right. The hot places turn cold as soon as I get there, and the cold places have a sudden heat wave right after I arrive. So I've found a solution: I pack everything so I'll be ready for anything.

My wife just shakes her head when she sees all the stuff I carry around. "Why do you bring all of that junk?" she says. "You never wear it. You wear three things the whole time you're gone."

I know that. But I still over-pack.

We do that in life sometimes, too. We haul along a lot of extra things we don't use and don't need. It's cumbersome and we don't enjoy it all that much, but we hang onto our stuff. In fact, we become obsessed with our possessions.

In Luke 12:13-21, Jesus told a story about a man who had become addicted to excess. He had way more than he needed, and told himself he liked it that way. When he acquired even more abundance and didn't know where to put it all, he came up with a solution. He decided to tear down all his storage facilities (that had become too small) and build new and bigger ones that would accommodate all his added wealth. And then, he told himself, he would kick back and take it easy.

It was a bad idea.

After he had made all those plans and was feeling quite satisfied with himself, he had a late-night visitation from Someone he really hadn't thought of.

It was God.

The Lord came to that man in the night and said, "You fool!"

By the way, that's not the word you want to hear from God waking you up from a sound sleep at two in the morning. But the message went on: "You fool! This very night your life will be demanded from you. Then who will get what you have prepared for yourself?" (Luke 12:20, NIV).

Jesus wrapped up His story with this statement: "This is how it will be with whoever stores up things for themselves but is not rich toward God" (verse 21, NIV). In other words, "Life is not measured by how much you own" (verse 15, NLT).

What then, is real life measured by?

That's the subject of this chapter.

"You Are Not Your Own"

You might be surprised to know that 15 percent of everything Jesus said when He walked in our world relates to the topic of money and possessions. This is more than all His teaching on heaven and hell combined.

The moment we hear these things, however, we begin to disengage.

We say, "I don't want to hear this. My money is mine."

But is it? Remember, you belong to God. The very breath you draw into your lungs right now is from God. Every beat of your heart is from God. Everything you've ever had, have now, or ever will have belongs to the Lord Himself.

In his first letter to the church in Corinth, Paul wrote these life-defining words: "Or do you not know that your body is the temple of the Holy Spirit who is in you, whom you have from God, and you are not your own? For you were bought at a price; therefore glorify God in your body and in your spirit, which are God's" (1 Corinthians 6:19-20).

Jesus highlighted that very point with a group of Pharisees one day. A group of them had approached Him with another of their thinly veiled verbal traps they kept trying to spring on Him. Let me paraphrase their conversation.

"Jesus, we have a question for You."

"Okay, what is it?"

"Is it lawful for us to pay taxes to Caesar or not?"

They thought they had Him that time—right on the horns of a dilemma. If He said, "Pay the taxes," then people would turn from Jesus in disgust, because taxes were so high and so unfair. But if He said, "Don't pay the taxes," that was a form of rebellion against the Roman government, and they would turn Him in. How would He answer? It seemed to them that they had Him coming and going.

Jesus said, "Can someone bring Me a coin?"

The Pharisees glanced at each other, and someone dug in a coin purse, pulled one out, and handed it to Him. He held it a moment. Turned it around in His hand. The crowd grew very quiet.

And then He said, "Whose image is on this coin?"

"Well," they said, "Caesar's."

He nodded and said, "Then give to Caesar the things that are Caesar's, and give to God the things that are God's."

And what is it that belongs to God? I do. My life. My time. My resources. My energy. My family. My love. My everything. I give these things to God, because they are His, and on loan to me.

"Wait a second, Greg," you might say. "I worked hard for what I have. I will spend it the way I want. That's the way it's going to be." We may imagine that everything we have achieved has been accomplished on our own. Yet the Bible clearly says, "Remember the LORD your God, for it is he who gives you the ability to produce wealth" (Deuteronomy 8:18, NIV).

Whatever you have, however successful you have been, you have to give the glory to God because God opened those doors for you. God gave you those opportunities.

The psalmist said,

No one from the east or the west
or from the desert can exalt themselves.
It is God who judges:
He brings one down, he exalts another. (Psalm 75:6-7, NIV)

With that established, someone might say, "Hold on. This doesn't apply to me because I don't have that much money." Really? It's a matter of perspective, isn't it? Did you know that the very lowest rung on America's economic ladder would be considered rich by a good portion of the rest of the world? One man wrote these words: "If you have money in the bank and your wallet and spare change in a dish somewhere, you are among the top 8 percent of the world's wealthy."

What does the Bible say to a person who has resources? We read in 1 Timothy 6:17-18 (TLB):

Tell those who are rich not to be proud and not to trust in their money, which will soon be gone, but their pride and trust should be in the living God who always richly gives us all we need for our enjoyment. Tell them to use their money to do good. They should be rich in good works and should give happily to those in need, always being ready to share with others whatever God has given them.

What then, do we learn from these passages?

Don't be arrogant or put your hope in wealth.

I've often said, "You have never seen a hearse pulling a U-Haul trailer." But then I got an e-mail not long ago from a guy who said, "I did. I actually saw a hearse pulling a U-Haul trailer, so you are wrong."

Okay, but where were they taking the stuff? It wasn't into the next life, I can promise you that. Malcolm Forbes, one of the wealthiest men who ever lived, said shortly before his death, "The thing I dread most about death is I know I will not be as comfortable in the next life as I was in this one." Well, that depends. If Mr. Forbes knew Christ and entered heaven, he forgot all his earthly trinkets in about 1.3 seconds. If he didn't know Christ, he still gained a whole different perspective on those things.

I heard the story of a very wealthy man who was near death. He had worked very hard for his money and, like Malcolm Forbes, didn't like leaving it all behind. One night he was talking to God and said, "I know the rules. I know I can't take anything to heaven, but I'm asking You to make an exception in my case. I want You to let me take one suitcase to heaven."

"A suitcase?" God said. "What do you want to put in it?"

"Gold bars," the man said. "I want to fill it with gold bars."

"Okay," God said, "if that's what you want."

The man arrived at heaven's gate, lugging his heavy suitcase after him. Of course he was met by Simon Peter, who opened the case, checked out the contents, and closed it up again. Word got around about the incident, and an angel came over and asked Peter, "What was in that guy's suitcase?"

"It's the weirdest thing," Peter said, shaking his head. "He came to heaven with a suitcase full of asphalt!"

The point being, of course, that gold in heaven is simply the stuff they pave the streets with. Our perspective on wealth and possessions will be very, very different on the other side.

Enjoy what God has given you, whether little or much.

The passage we just read from 1 Timothy tells us to enjoy what God has given us. Verse 17 (NIV) says, "God . . . richly provides us with everything for our enjoyment." It's okay to appreciate and take pleasure from the good things God has placed in your life. There is no special virtue in poverty. The Bible teaches that God can and will bless a person in every area of life, including finances. If you work hard, save, and invest wisely, you may have acquired some wealth over the passing of time. Abraham had wealth. So did David. Joseph of Arimathea, Barnabas, and Mary of Bethany all had resources.

Jesus didn't extol poverty as some great spiritual condition of life. He told the rich young ruler to sell everything and follow Him, but He never said that to anyone again. It was a message for a young man who wanted to follow Jesus, but had allowed His money and holdings to become a stumbling block to him.

God can bless us with material wealth if He chooses, or He can choose to bless us in many other ways. If we have the Lord but don't have much of this world's stuff, we are still blessed. Wherever we are in life, we should give thanks for it. In his letter to the Philippians, Paul wrote, "I have learned to be content whatever the circumstances. I know what it is to be in need, and I know what it is to have plenty. I have learned the secret of being content in any and every situation, whether well fed or hungry, whether living in plenty or in want. I can do all this through him who gives me strength" (4:11-13, NIV).

We need to get to that place, to learn that secret, to tap into that strength, no matter what our present circumstances.

Some will say, "Money is the root of all evil. It says so in the Bible."

No, it really doesn't. Here is what it does say: "For the love of money is a root of all kinds of evil. Some people, eager for money, have wandered from the faith and pierced themselves with many griefs" (1 Timothy 6:10, NIV).

Money is neutral, neither good nor bad. It can be used for good to the glory of God, or it can be bad if spent in the wrong way for the wrong reasons. In 1 Timothy 6:18 (NIV), Paul wrote, "Command them to do good, to be rich in good deeds, and to be generous and willing to share." We can tell a lot about a person's spirituality by their giving. One way to determine whether a person is really living for God is to take a tour of their checkbook. That will reveal their real value system. As Jesus said, "For where your treasure is, there your heart will be also" (Luke 12:34). How we handle our possessions is really a test of faithfulness.

The beauty of giving in secret.

When Jesus taught about money and possessions in the Sermon on the Mount, He directed His words to the disciples gathered at His feet. But he used the Pharisees as examples in His teaching.

> *Watch out! Don't do your good deeds publicly, to be admired by others, for you will lose the reward from your Father in heaven. When you give to someone in need, don't do as the hypocrites do—blowing trumpets in the synagogues and streets to call attention to their acts of charity! I tell you the truth, they have received all the reward they will ever get. But when you give to someone in need, don't let your left hand know what your right hand is doing. Give your gifts in private, and your Father, who sees everything, will reward you. (Matthew 6:1-4, NLT)*

The Pharisees were men who majored on the externals in their religion and missed the point entirely. They prided themselves that they would never commit adultery, but Jesus told them their hearts were filled with lust. They prided themselves that they didn't murder people, but Jesus showed them how their hearts were full of hatred. And it was the same with their giving.

Everything was done for show. Everything was done to impress others. If one of them wanted to give a big gift to the temple, he made it into a Hollywood production. He might actually blow a trumpet to announce what he was about to do. It would be like someone walking up to an offering box in church and pulling out a bullhorn. "ATTENTION! ATTENTION! I WANT EVERYONE TO TAKE NOTE THAT I AM DROPPING A LARGE CHECK INTO THE BOX. THANK YOU, YOU MAY GO BACK TO YOUR WORSHIP NOW."

The Pharisees wanted to be praised for their generosity. They basked in the good feelings and admiration of others. But from God's point of view, it was all wrong.

In verse 1 (NLT) Jesus said, "Watch out! Don't do your good deeds publicly, to be admired by others, for you will lose the reward from your Father in heaven." The phrase "to be admired" is related to the term from which we get our word *theater*. It means to put on a show or a performance. Jesus was saying, "Stop performing. Stop acting and looking for applause. If you're going to give, do it for the glory of God, not to impress others. If you're playing to the crowd, you've already had your reward." In other words, if you give your time or resources in such a way as to draw attention to yourself, that's all the reward you will get. There won't be any from God.

Don't announce it. Don't talk about it. Don't drop little hints. Just do it for God's glory.

Verse 4 (NLT) reminds us, "Give your gifts in private, and your Father, who sees everything, will reward you." It comes down to this: If we give something to God and remember it, God will forget it. But if we forget what we've given and just move on, God will remember. Sometimes we may do something for the Lord, and no one seems to notice or value what we did or the sacrifice we made. No one patted us on the back or said, "Atta boy." We don't need to worry about that. One day our Father, who knows and sees all things, will do better than "Atta boy." He will say, "Well done, good and faithful servant. Enter into the joy of your Lord."

God loves a cheerful giver.

The apostle Paul had some very revealing things to say about money and possessions—viewed from an eternal perspective—in 2 Corinthians 9:

> Remember this—a farmer who plants only a few seeds will get a small crop. But the one who plants generously will get a generous crop. You must each decide in your heart how much to give. And don't give reluctantly or in response to pressure. "For God loves a person who gives cheerfully." And God will generously provide all you need. Then you will always have everything you need and plenty left over to share with others. As the Scriptures say,.

"They share freely and give generously to the poor.
Their good deeds will be remembered forever."

For God is the one who provides seed for the farmer and then
bread to eat. In the same way, he will provide and increase
your resources and then produce a great harvest of generosity
in you.

Yes, you will be enriched in every way so that you can always
be generous. And when we take your gifts to those who need
them, they will thank God. So two good things will result from
this ministry of giving—the needs of the believers in Jerusalem
will be met, and they will joyfully express their thanks to God.
(verses 6-12, NLT)

There are a number of places in Scripture where we learn what God hates. In Proverbs 6 we're told that God hates evil, slander, sowing discord, and lying, among other things. That's enough of a clue for me to stay away from those activities. If I read that God hates something, I don't want anything to do with it.

But the Bible also underlines some things God loves. I'd like to be involved in *those* things—all wrapped up in activities and attitudes that give God great pleasure and joy. And one of the things God specifically loves is a cheerful giver. This is someone who gives because they want to and find happiness in doing it. Jesus highlighted this truth when He said, "It is more blessed to give than to receive" (Acts 20:35).

Have you discovered that yet? For some people, it's all about receiving.

I heard about a mom who took her little girl to church. She wanted to teach her daughter how wonderful it was to give to God. She said, "I'm going to give you a dollar and a quarter. You can decide which one you want to place in the offering box by the door, okay?"

"Okay, Mom," the girl said.

They attended the service, and when they went out the mom couldn't wait to find out how her daughter had responded to the lesson on giving. "Okay, sweetheart, what did you give to the Lord?"

"Well, Mom," she answered, "I was going to give the dollar. But when I heard the preacher say that God loves a cheerful giver, I was much more cheerful about giving the quarter."

Are we any different? What's one of the first words that a child learns? *"Mine!"* Do you ever remember sitting down on the floor with a toddler and teaching your child or grandchild to say "mine"? Probably not. But somehow they learned it—and fast!

But it's different for us grownups, right? Maybe not so much. Have you ever been in a store considering an item you've looked at several times? You've been saying to yourself, "That's a good deal. It's on sale. I might buy that." But before you can make up your mind, someone grabs it and marches away with it. What do you do? Do you feel like saying, "Hey, I wanted that! *Mine!*" Or how about when someone quickly pulls into a parking place you had been angling for? Maybe we're not quite as grown up as we imagined.

Back in 1970 the Beatles were breaking up and were at odds with one another—and in litigation as well. George Harrison wrote a song summing up what all that discord felt like. A bit of the lyrics included the words, "All through the day I me mine, I me mine. All through the night I me mine, I me mine."

That's pretty true for a lot of people, isn't it? *I me mine.* They hold onto everything with a white-knuckle grip, unwilling even to offer it to the Lord or to help anyone else in need.

Why would we do that? Why would we compartmentalize our relationship with God in that way? We believe what the Bible says about marriage. We believe what the Bible says about heaven and hell. We believe what the Bible says about the last days. But when it comes to the subject of money, we're not sure if we agree with those biblical principles.

How quickly we forget. We are not the owners of what we have. We are the *stewards* of what we have. God gives us use of these resources, but they still belong to Him.

It was Martin Luther who said, "Three conversions are

necessary. The conversion of the heart, the mind, and the purse" (or the wallet).

The story is told of General Sam Houston, hero of the history of Texas, who came to Christ late in his life. The preacher was getting ready to baptize him in a little river and told the general to remove his valuables and put them on the riverbank. So Houston took off his glasses, pulled some papers from his vest pocket, and handed over his pocket watch. But the pastor noticed that Houston still had his wallet in his pocket.

"General Houston," he said, "you'll want to take that wallet out, too."

But the old general responded, "If anything needs baptizing, it's my wallet."

We need to understand what a *joy* it is to give. If we haven't discovered that, we have missed out on a major source of encouragement and blessing in the Christian life. In Exodus 36, when the people of Israel were building the tabernacle in the wilderness, they got so caught up in the excitement they had to be restrained from giving. Eventually, Moses had to send out a command that went through the camp: "Send no more materials! You've already given more than enough."

I haven't seen that happen in too many churches. But the truth remains that if we will give to the Lord, He will give back to us. Second Corinthians 9:8 (NLT) reminds us, "God will generously provide all you need. Then you will always have everything you need and plenty left over to share with others."

Every farmer knows that if you sow a little seed, you get a little crop. If you sow more seed, your crop will be larger. If, however, you want to stubbornly cling to "what's yours" and hold onto what you've got, God will not force you to give. That's why Paul said, in effect, "Don't give because you are under pressure or feel the weight of someone's expectations. Give joyfully."

We all know people who are cheapskates. You go out to a meal with someone like that, and when everyone is pitching in on the bill, that person mysteriously disappears. "Oh, sorry, I was in the bathroom. Did the bill come?"

Let me ask you a question. When you want to do something nice for someone, is that stingy person the first person on your list? No, more than likely the person you want to bless is the person who has been consistently kind and generous toward you. It seems like they're always the first to pitch in, the first to volunteer, the first to give even when they can't really afford it. They just jump in there and do it, and you can see that it gives them joy. So if you have the opportunity to help someone or to be with someone, who are you drawn to? You are drawn to the generous, selfless person every time.

It's the same with God. When He sees someone giving generously and sacrificially, it's as though He says, "Do you see that generous person over there? Look at the way he is giving. Look at the way she shares what she has. I love that so much! They are giving more, and I am going to bless them with more."

As many of us who have edged into our senior years have noticed, life goes by at an incredible speed. Before we know it, it's almost time to check out of this life and move on to the next one, the one that will last forever. We looked at 1 Timothy 6, earlier, and I'd like to come back to verses 18-19 (NIV): "Command them to do good, to be rich in good deeds, and to be generous and willing to share. *In this way they will lay up treasure for themselves as a firm foundation for the coming age,* so that they may take hold of the life that is truly life" (emphasis added).

We may not know much about the life to come, the life in heaven that waits for us just around the bend. But we do know that how we give and share and sacrifice in this life will have a direct bearing on the next one. I'm not sure what Paul meant about acquiring a "firm foundation" in heaven, for the coming age, but it certainly sounds like something worth having.

Whatever we let go of *here* can't begin to compare with what we will gain *there*.

CHAPTER FOURTEEN
WHAT JESUS TAUGHT ABOUT PRAYER, PART 1

On September 11, 2001, Todd Beamer was a passenger onboard United Flight 93 from Newark, New Jersey, to San Francisco when it was hijacked by terrorists with knives and box cutters. By this time, the twin towers of the World Trade Center in New York City had been struck by two similarly hijacked jets, and had collapsed in a heap of rubble. In Washington, D.C., yet another hijacked plane had slammed into the Pentagon.

Todd knew something was happening on his flight, but he wasn't quite sure what. He called the operator on an air phone, and she confirmed that his plane had also been hijacked and had changed course for another destination that would surely also become a target.

The operator said to Todd, "Could we pray together?"

Todd, a Christian and a graduate of Wheaton College, said, "Yes."

They prayed this prayer: "Our Father who art in heaven. Hallowed be Your name. Your kingdom come, Your will be done on earth as it is in heaven. . . ."

After they were done praying, Todd turned to the other men who had agreed to help him storm the cockpit and said these words: "Let's roll."

Together, they attacked and overcame the hijackers in the cockpit. During the violent melee, however, the plane plunged out of the sky and crashed into a field in Pennsylvania, killing all onboard. But the action of Todd Beamer and those who assisted him probably saved thousands of lives. The terrorists had probably intended to crash into the White House or U.S. Capitol.

Isn't it interesting that Todd and an unknown telephone operator, in a moment of great stress and danger, repeated the very words Jesus taught His disciples to pray over two thousand years before?

The prayer we know as the "the Lord's Prayer" in Matthew 6:9-13, however, isn't just a prayer to repeat in times of great need—although it is certainly fine to do that. In fact, this prayer is the template for all prayer. It was the Lord's way of showing what prayer is and how to go about praying.

What Is Prayer?

Prayer is listening to and communicating with God. There are many ways to pray mentioned in the Bible, which brings us to Paul's words in Ephesians 6:18 (NLT): "Pray in the Spirit at all times and on every occasion. Stay alert and be persistent in your prayers for all believers everywhere."

Paul's first word in this passage is *pray*. There are many different ways to do this. We can pray publicly or privately. We can pray out loud, or silently in our minds. We can pray kneeling, standing, sitting, lying down, walking, or running. We can even pray driving—if we remember to keep our eyes open. Speaking of eyes, we can pray with eyes open or closed.

My wife, Cathe, and I have four grandchildren—three girls and one boy—and we have been teaching them how to pray. When we sit down to a meal, we say, "Let's pray." They fold their hands and close their eyes. The other day I opened my eyes for a moment to notice little Stella eating a French fry with her eyes closed.

The main thing is just to pray—no matter what the posture, place, circumstances, or time of day. You can literally pray anywhere. Daniel prayed in a lions' den. David prayed in a field and in a cave. Peter prayed on *and* under the water. Jonah called on God from the belly of a great fish. God will hear your prayer wherever you are.

The phrase "at all times" in Ephesians 6:18 reminds us that this needs to be a constant activity rather than an occasional one.

Just pray. And pray a lot.

You might have a time in prayer where you get down on your knees and close your eyes. You might be driving by yourself and begin speaking to the Lord out loud. You might be heading into a meeting, and say, "Lord, please go before me into this meeting. I need Your wisdom. I need the right words to say." *Pray always.* That's the idea. Pray in the morning, afternoon, evening, and when you wake up in the middle of the night.

Scripture tells the story of a man who prayed to God when it was illegal. In fact, it had become a capital crime. What would you do if prayer was suddenly declared illegal in the United States? Anything is possible. It happened to Daniel, one of the king's advisors, in Babylon. The other royal advisors resented Daniel because of his influence with the king, and they determined to dig up dirt on him and bring him down.

The problem was, there was no dirt to dig. Daniel had no sordid secrets or skeletons in his closet. Finally, they reasoned that the only way they could get him in trouble was over his faith in God. Their research had revealed that Daniel prayed to God every day— morning, afternoon, and evening, with his windows wide open. That gave them an idea. They said, "Let's persuade the king to sign a decree that no one can call on any god but him. Then we can nail Daniel for his prayers to the God of Israel."

The vain king went along with the decree and signed it into law. After that, the word went out that any prayer, unless offered to the king himself, was illegal. In fact, it was punishable by death. What would you have done?

Here is what Daniel did. He went to his house at the usual time, opened his windows in the usual way, and got down on his knees and prayed. Daniel 6:10 (NLT) says, "But when Daniel learned that the law had been signed, he went home and knelt down as usual in his upstairs room, with its windows open toward Jerusalem. He prayed three times a day, just as he had always done, giving thanks to his God."

Does it encourage you to hear other Christians pray in public places? I think it's great—most of the time. Just do it in the right way. I was in a restaurant not long ago when a large, nice-looking family sat down together. When their meal came they all bowed their heads to pray. I remember thinking, *I love that.* As I was leaving the restaurant, I stopped at their table to thank them for their strong testimony.

Some Christians, however, get weird about praying in a public place. They will pray really long or really loud, and it becomes an embarrassment and a distraction rather than an inspiration. A good rule of thumb to keep in mind when you are praying is to keep your public prayers short and your private prayers long!

Notice one other thing about Daniel's prayer. He didn't pray, "O God, help me! I'm in trouble! Get me out of this mess and deliver me from these evil people who hate me." No, the text says that Daniel gave thanks to God. Whenever you pray, it's important to remember that God is on the throne, and that He is in control. We call this *the sovereignty of God*. Scripture says, "Give thanks to the LORD, for He is good! For His mercy endures forever" (Psalm 107:1).

No matter what our circumstances or situation, we remind ourselves that our sovereign, powerful, good God is in control and holds our lives in His hands. David wrote, "But I trust in you, LORD; I say, 'You are my God.' My times are in your hands" (Psalm 31:14-15, NIV). No matter what, we give thanks when we pray.

Why Do We Need to Pray?

We should pray because Jesus told us to.

In Luke 18:1, Jesus said that "men always ought to pray and not lose heart." Really, do we need any more reason than that? Jesus the Lord told us to pray, so let's do it. At the same time, however, He also gave us an example to follow. Jesus, who was fully God yet also fully man, regularly took time to pray. He would often spend the night hours in prayer, out under the stars He created, while the others were sleeping. In the Garden of Gethsemane, in the greatest crisis of His life to that point, He prayed to the Father, saying, "O My Father, if it is possible, let this cup pass from Me; nevertheless, not as I will, but as You will" (Matthew 26:39).

When He was about to raise Lazarus from the dead, we read in John 11:41-42: "Jesus lifted up His eyes and said, 'Father, I thank You that You have heard Me. And I know that You always hear Me, but because of the people who are standing by I said this, that they may believe that You sent Me.' Then Jesus shouted, "Lazarus, come forth!" (verse 43).

When Jesus fed the five thousand—the only miracle that appears in all four gospels—we read that He looked up toward heaven and asked God's blessing on the food. Mothers brought their children to Jesus, wanting Him to lay hands on them and pray for them. Even when He was hanging on the cross in indescribable pain, Jesus prayed, "Father, forgive them, for they do not know what they are doing" (Luke 23:34, NIV).

If this is what Jesus did, we certainly ought to do the same.

We should pray because prayer is God's appointed way of obtaining things.

There is nothing wrong with bringing your needs and requests before God. As a matter of fact, there may be things in your life that you don't have simply because you have never asked your heavenly Father. The Bible clearly says, "You do not have because you do not ask God" (James 4:2, NIV). Someone may say, "I've dealt with this physical condition for so long. I've been to all of these doctors, but nothing ever seems to change." Have you asked God? Have you spoken to your Father about it? Could it be that God wants to heal you, and you have simply not asked?

"Why is it that I can never find out the will of God for my life?"

Have you prayed about it?

"Why don't I ever lead people to Christ? Why don't I have those opportunities?"

Have you spoken to God about it? Have you asked Him to open doors for you?

I got into a cab recently for a ride to the airport. As I slid into the seat, I sent up a silent prayer: *Lord, if you want me to share the gospel with this guy, just open a door for me.*

As we drove down a particular road we noticed a "ghost bike"—a bicycle painted white and left in a location where a bicyclist had been killed.

I said to the driver, whose name was Tom, "Why do people get hit on this particular road so often?" We talked about that. He said, "I had a friend who was riding on this road and was hit. The person who hit him just drove off."

"That's horrible."

"Yeah."

Then I said, "Tom, what do you think happens after we die?"

With a little nervous laugh he replied, "Well, I believe you come back in another life-form. I believe—depending on how you have lived—you will come back again."

"Huh," I said.

"Well," he replied, "what do *you* think?" And that was the wide open door I was looking for. I said, "Well, Tom, I believe that when you die, you live on. I believe that if you put your faith in God you will go to heaven. One day heaven will come to earth. I believe God will give us a new body, because these old bodies are wearing out."

"You know what?" he said. "I like your version of the afterlife better than mine."

"It's not my version, Tom. It's Jesus' version. This is what He says"—and I quoted John 14:2-3 to him—"'In My Father's house are many mansions; if it were not so, I would have told you. I go to prepare a place for you. And if I go and prepare a place for you, I will come again and receive you to Myself; that where I am, there you may be also.'"

He listened to the Scripture. Then I said, "A guy named Thomas said, 'Lord, we do not know where You are going, and how can we know the way?'" (verse 5). At that point, Tom the cab driver said, "Thomas! That's my name."

"It is, isn't it?"

"My wife always says I am a doubting Thomas."

"You know, Tom, I like to think of Thomas in the Bible not as a doubter, but as more of a skeptic. Maybe you are just a skeptic."

"Yeah. Maybe I am."

The ride was over and I got out. All I'd had time to do was plant a few seeds. But I continue to pray for Tom, that the seeds will germinate and take root in his heart.

Pray for openings. Pray that God will use you. Prayer is God's method of obtaining things. Will He always say yes? Of course not. He may not want you to have all of your desires, because He knows that they wouldn't be good for you at this particular time in your life. He won't always heal you in the way you want. He may not give you all the money you think you need in a given situation. But at least cover that base and bring it to the Father. Let Him decide.

Prayer is the way by which we overcome our anxiety and worry.

Even the best life has its hardships, anxieties, and worries. Our country faces a great deal of trouble battling Islamic terrorism in all its cruel and hideous forms. We face intractable enemies in nations like Iran and North Korea—both seeking to build nuclear weapons and the missiles that will carry them to our shores. Strange viruses like Ebola and Zika threaten to slip past all of our medical defenses. Life presents a constant menu of things to worry about, and each of us has our own personal set of troubles and concerns. Perhaps you have family troubles, health concerns, or financial issues.

What do we do with all of these issues that buzz around us like bees? We pray. It has been said, "If your knees are shaking, kneel on them."

Paul gave us these wonderful, very familiar words:

Don't worry about anything; instead, pray about everything. Tell God what you need, and thank him for all he has done. Then you will experience God's peace, which exceeds anything we can understand. His peace will guard your hearts and minds as you live in Christ Jesus. (Philippians 4:6-7, NLT)

In other words, *turn your worries into prayers*. Here's how it works. Let's say you are hit with a worry that suddenly tightens on you like a vise. You say to yourself, *What if this happens? What if that happens?* Don't talk to yourself in that moment; let that concern become a prayer. *Lord, I'm scared about this right now. I offer that to You. Help me, Lord. I need Your wisdom, Your perspective, Your protection.* Don't allow those worries to seep like acid into the crevices of your soul; take them immediately to God.

Prayer is one of the ways we make ourselves ready for the return of Christ.

Jesus said, "But take heed to yourselves, lest your hearts be weighed down with carousing, drunkenness, and cares of this life, and that Day come on you unexpectedly. . . . Watch therefore, and pray always" (Luke 21:34,36). We need to be in prayer, asking the Lord to keep our minds clear and our hearts ready for His any-minute return.

Speaking of His imminent coming, Jesus said in the gospel of Mark, "But about that day or hour no one knows, not even the angels in heaven, nor the Son, but only the Father. Be on guard! Be alert! You do not know when that time will come" (13:32-33, NIV).

What if God Doesn't Answer?

Someone may say, "What about those times when I prayed for something and God didn't answer me?"

Could it be that He actually did answer, but you didn't *like* His answer?

Remember, "no" is also an answer.

Here is something I like to remember: Sometimes God says *no*. Sometimes God says *slow*. Sometimes God says *grow*. Sometimes God says *go*. In other words, if the timing is right, the request is right, and you are right, God will give you a green light. When He says "Wait," or "Not now," it is for your own good.

When you look back on your life and think of the things you've asked God to give you, aren't you glad He said no to some of them?

When I was eighteen years old and still a new Christian, I met a girl and told the Lord, "This is the one for me! This is the girl I should marry. I'm sure of it. O Lord, please show her!"

Apparently, she never got that message. She wanted nothing to do with me.

Not long after that I met Cathe. I've been married to her for forty years and love her with all of my heart. Not long ago I was somewhere with my beautiful wife and I ran into that girl I thought I had loved at eighteen. I looked at her, smiled, and said, "Nice to see you again." Then I looked at my wife and breathed a silent prayer, *O God, thank You!*

(By the way, if you happen to be that girl, I don't mean you. It was someone else.)

Don't Pray Like a Hypocrite

Jesus began His teaching on prayer in the Sermon on the Mount with this one piece of advice: Be real when you are speaking to God. Don't put on a show for others.

> *And when you pray, you shall not be like the hypocrites. For they love to pray standing in the synagogues and on the corners of the streets, that they may be seen by men. Assuredly, I say to you, they have their reward. But you, when you pray, go into your room, and when you have shut your door, pray to your Father who is in the secret place; and your Father who sees in secret will reward you openly. And when you pray, do not use vain repetitions as the heathen do. For they think that they will be heard for their many words.*
>
> *Therefore do not be like them. For your Father knows the things you have need of before you ask Him. (Matthew 6:5-8)*

In verse 5, Jesus referred to the Pharisees as "hypocrites." People throw that word around a lot. Sometimes when a Christian messes up or falls into sin, people will call him or her a "hypocrite." But just because a Christian sins doesn't make them a hypocrite; it makes them human. Everyone sins. Everyone fails. The book of James says that "we all stumble in many ways" (3:2, NIV). A hypocrite is something different. In the Greek language, it was just another word for *actor*. Drama and theater started in Greece, and in those days the actors would hold masks in front of their faces to portray different characters or different emotions. If an actor wanted to portray sadness, he held up a sad mask. If it was the time to express joy, he held up a happy mask.

But that won't cut it with God. Jesus was saying, "Don't be an actor when you come into God's presence to talk to Him. Be real." A hypocrite, then, is a person who pretends to be someone they really are not. They want to come off as a holy or devoted individual, when they are secretly living a life that contradicts everything they claim to believe.

Be genuine before God, Jesus was saying. Open your heart to Him. Show Him everything. Tell Him everything.

And while we're at it, why don't we teach our children to pray in the same way? Sometimes people will give their children little prewritten, formula prayers they are supposed to memorize and repeat back to God.

A parent says, "Okay, honey, now say your prayers."

And then the child prays the prayer the parent has taught them, or says, "Now I lay me down to sleep, I pray the Lord my soul to keep. . . ." That may be cute, but is it really prayer? Teach your children how to talk to God, just as they would talk to you. Teach them how to tell God what's in their hearts.

Jesus said in Matthew 6:7-8 (TLB), "Don't recite the same prayer over and over as the heathen do, who think prayers are answered only by repeating them again and again. Remember, your Father knows exactly what you need even before you ask him!"

That last sentence is really interesting. The Father already knows exactly what we need before we even think about praying. He is sovereign, in control, and He will always accomplish His will and purposes. So, why should we even pray?

Do we really think we're going to change God's mind or bring God over to our viewpoint of things? Prayer isn't getting our will in heaven; prayer is getting God's will on earth. If you want to know the secret to answered prayer, it is this: *Your objective is to align your will with the will of God.* When you do that, you will see your prayers answered in the affirmative.

Let's imagine you are in a little boat out on a lake and you want to get to the dock. So you take your rope and throw it over one of the pilings and begin pulling yourself right up beside the dock.

Here is the question: Are you pulling the dock to you, or are you pulling your boat to the dock? When I pray, my objective isn't to pull God my way; it is to pull myself His way. Jesus said, "If you abide in Me [or, have a living communion with Me], and My words abide in you, you will ask what you desire, and it shall be done for you" (John 15:7).

That is an exciting promise. It's kind of a blank check. Jesus was saying that if you maintain a living communion, friendship, and closeness with Him, and if you are biblically literate and praying according to the will of God, then you can ask Him for whatever you will, and it will be done.

Why? Because you will be praying for what God wants to give you already.

"Our Father . . ."

As Jesus taught His disciples a model prayer, what we have come to know as "the Lord's Prayer," He began with four very significant words: "Our Father in heaven."

It's a reminder, of course, of whom we are speaking to. This is the great God in heaven. We ought to approach Him with a sense of awe and wonder and respect. We never want to take this privilege He has given us lightly, or take our access into His presence for granted. At the same time, we are reminded that He isn't just our *God* in heaven, He is our *Father* in heaven.

Sometimes we might find ourselves thinking of God the Father in the same way we think about our earthly fathers. That could be a good or bad comparison. Some of us grew up with stingy fathers. Or maybe they were weak, vacillating, angry, petty, passive, or even violent. I never even met my real father, so in my case, he was nonexistent. But God is a perfect Father. He loves to bless us and give us what we need. We can count on His character, His truthfulness, His love, His compassion, and His wisdom. When we need Him and call on Him, He will be there. As David once prayed, "God is our refuge and strength, a very present help in trouble" (Psalm 46:1).

The Lord's Prayer, then, starts with the bigness of God. We don't have a small god, we have an inexpressibly BIG God. That's comforting to know when we find ourselves with big problems, big heartaches, big dilemmas, big crises, and big perplexities in the course of our lives. This is a God big enough to tackle any and all of those things. If we understand how great He really is, our problems will come into proper perspective.

In his book *Before Amen: The Power of a Simple Prayer*, my friend Max Lucado writes these words: "People suffer from small thoughts about God. In an effort to see Him as friend, we have lost His immensity. In our desire to understand Him, we have sought to contain Him." Max concludes, "The God of the Bible cannot be contained."

So we see God in His greatness and majesty, never forgetting how vast and mighty and incomprehensible He truly is. He is awesome. He is holy. But He is also our Father in heaven.

Paul put it this way—with words that ought to keep us in a perpetual state of wonder: "For as many as are led by the Spirit of God, these are sons of God. For you did not receive the spirit of bondage again to fear, but you received the Spirit of adoption by whom we cry out, 'Abba, Father.' The Spirit Himself bears witness with our spirit that we are children of God, and if children, then heirs—heirs of God and joint heirs with Christ" (Romans 8:14-17).

Abba, Father!

Jews living under the Old Covenant had a great fear of God and would never call Him "Father." In the New Covenant, after Jesus died and rose again, we are now actually invited to do that very thing. As Jesus said to Mary after He rose, "I am ascending to My Father and your Father, and to My God and your God" (John 20:17). It's one thing for Jesus to call God "Father," because He is the only begotten Son. But now Jesus was saying, "Check this out. Because of My death and resurrection, My Father is now *your* Father, too! Now you can talk to Him. You can reach Him through Me."

Why? Because He has adopted you.

Paul used an interesting term in Romans 8:15: "We cry out, 'Abba, Father.'" *Abba* is just another word for "daddy" or "papa"—or whatever your call you own father. My sons called me "Dad" when they were growing up. My grandchildren call me "Papa." And if I am talking to a group of people at church or somewhere else and one of my grandkids runs up to me and says, "Papa!" the conversation stops. I am going to kneel down and talk to that child. My grandkids have access to me any time, and they will have my full attention the moment they approach me.

That is our relationship with God. We say, "Papa. Abba. Father."

And He replies, "Yes, I am listening. You are My son. You are My daughter. I love you."

I don't know what your dad was like—or is like. Maybe your earthly father is warm, affectionate, and affirming. Maybe he is aloof, distant, and uncommunicative. Maybe he hurt you or abused you. Or maybe he was just never there. I really don't know what your earthly dad was like. But I do know what your heavenly Dad is like. He likes you. He loves you. You can approach Him at any time. You need to own that truth and thank God for that.

It is a wonder beyond all wonders.

And it's all because of Jesus.

CHAPTER FIFTEEN
WHAT JESUS TAUGHT ABOUT PRAYER, PART 2

I went to a mall the other day with my two granddaughters, Stella and Lucy. There is a fountain at this mall and the girls like to throw coins into the water.

I'm not very fond of this idea because it seems like a waste of money. So what I usually do is repurpose other people's coins. I reach into the water, pull out a handful, and give them to the girls to throw back in again. Is that a bad thing? Do you think it voids the wishes of the people who threw them in originally? I really don't think so.

On this particular day, however, I thought I would splurge and give the girls some fresh coins—twelve pennies each. I said, "Remember to make a wish with each coin you throw in."

Lucy went first, and tossed in her pennies. "Lucy," I said, "what did you wish for?"

She said, "I wish every day was my birthday." I thought that was a well-placed wish. When Stella had tossed in all her coins, I said, "Girls, what is the difference between a wish and prayer?"

Stella thought about it. "A wish," she said, "is really to ourselves. But a prayer is to God." And I think she nailed it.

What a privilege prayer is! To think that we can approach God—the Creator of the universe—at any time with our requests, or just to talk to Him. Prayer should be a vital part of every believer's life. It was Martin Luther who said, "To be a Christian without prayer is no more possible than to be alive without breathing."

As we noted in the last chapter, Jesus told His disciples to "always pray and not give up" (Luke 18:1, NIV).

Who was a greater example of this than Jesus Himself? Despite the fact that He was God walking this earth in human form, He felt the need to spend hours in prayer with the Father. Often He would pray while the others were asleep. Or He would get up early in the morning while it was still dark and find a private place to speak to His Father.

Observing this, His disciples came to Him one day and said, "Lord, teach us to pray." In response, He gave them what we have come to know as "the Lord's Prayer." That's just tradition, of course, because it's not called by that name anywhere in the Bible. In fact, it's a prayer Jesus Himself would have never prayed. He would have never had to say the words, "Forgive us our sins as we forgive those who have sinned against us." Christ never had any sins that needed to be forgiven! We could more accurately describe this as "the Disciples' Prayer," because He gave it to them (and us) to use as a model for all prayer. If you want to read the real Lord's prayer— the prayer only Christ Himself could pray—read John 17.

In Matthew 6, however, we have what the church has called and treasured as the Lord's Prayer for over two thousand years.

In this manner, therefore, pray:

Our Father in heaven,
Hallowed be Your name.
Your kingdom come.
Your will be done
On earth as it is in heaven.
Give us this day our daily bread.
And forgive us our debts,
As we forgive our debtors.
And do not lead us into temptation,
But deliver us from the evil one.
For Yours is the kingdom and the power and the glory forever.
Amen. (verses 9-13)

A Pattern and a Model

Part of the universal appeal of this prayer is that it deals with our past, present, and future. It speaks to our past when we say, "Forgive us our debts, as we forgive our debtors." It deals with our present when we pray, "Give us this day our daily bread." And it addresses our future as we say to the Father, "Your kingdom come. Your will be done on earth as it is in heaven."

"Our Father . . . "

In the last chapter, we spoke about how the prayer begins—speaking to a great God who also happens to be our great Father.

What is this Father like?

He is like Jesus.

Jesus gives us a snapshot of God. I think you could even call it a "selfie" of God. Jesus told Thomas, "Anyone who has seen me has seen the Father" (John 14:9, NIV). In other words, if we want to know what kind of Father we have in heaven, we can just take a long look at the Lord Jesus. In John 8:19, Jesus told His adversaries, "If you had known Me, you would have known My Father also."

Let's think for a moment about Jesus taking the little children into His arms and blessing them. Think about Him getting down on His hands and knees to wash the disciples' dirty feet. Think about Him feeding the multitudes, forgiving the woman taken in adultery, honoring the wedding feast of a young couple by creating fine wine, weeping over the tomb of Lazarus, His friend. What is the Father like? He is like Jesus.

"Hallowed be Your Name . . ."

It's important to note that in this model prayer for the ages, the template for prayer given by the Son of God Himself, Jesus told us to begin with adoration and praise. Don't cut to the chase and go right to your grocery list. That has its place and will come in time. There is a place for petition in prayer, but that's not the place to begin. Start with honoring His name. Start with worshiping God.

Have you ever heard of the ACTS acronym? It's a little mental handle that helps us remember how to order and prioritize our prayers. In the acronym, "A" stands for *adoration*; "C" stands for *confession*; "T" stands for *thanksgiving*; and "S" stands for *supplication*.

So we begin by just adoring and worshiping the Lord, remembering who He is and all the wonders wrapped up in His name and His character. Then comes confession, where we admit and take ownership of our personal sin. We follow this with thanking Him for all He has given us and all He has done for us. Then we conclude by praying for others and praying for ourselves.

Are there exceptions to this model? Yes, if you have climbed an eighty-foot-tall tree and find yourself slipping off one of the topmost branches, it would be okay to start with a little supplication. As in, "Lord, help!" I'm sure He would honor that prayer.

If you have a bit of time set aside for praying, it's very good to actually remember who you are speaking to. Many times we just wade right into our list. We say, "Hello, Father. Praise Your name. Hallelujah. Here's what I need. . . ." When we do this, we might as well be saying, "our Santa who art in heaven" or "our Butler who art in heaven" or "our Vending Machine who art in heaven."

Don't be in such a hurry. Take time to worship your God. Bask in His presence. Praising the Lord has the effect of lifting our gaze from our own problems and needs. We get caught up in the wonder and beauty of who He is. We remember that this God is supremely powerful and able to tackle our knottiest problems and seeming impossibilities.

What does it mean to say, "Hallowed be Your name"? It means acknowledging that His name is set apart, higher and brighter and more beautiful and glorious than any other name on earth. It means we want to set this God of ours apart in everything we say and do—in our lives, our character, our actions, and our words. We want to set it apart for Christ and we want to live holy lives.

Every now and then I take stock of my life and look at the things I'm interested in, have ambition for, and am passionate about. Then I ask myself this question: Can I write "Hallowed be Your name" over these things? Can you? Can you write "Hallowed be Your name" over your career choice? Over the boyfriend or girlfriend you are involved with? Over the friends you have chosen to be with? Over your choice of entertainment and the way you spend your time and energies? If you can't write "Hallowed be Your name" over these things, then perhaps you should reconsider your choices.

Martin Luther said, "How is God's name hallowed among us? When both our doctrine and our living are truly Christian."

"Your kingdom come. Your will be done on earth as it is in heaven."

This is a multilevel request with multiple shades of meaning. When we pray, *"Your kingdom come,"* we are in effect praying for the return of Jesus Christ to this earth, to rule and reign. It's interesting that the word used here for "kingdom" doesn't primarily refer to a geographical territory, but rather to a sovereignty and dominion. What we are really saying is, "Lord, I want Your rule to come back to planet earth! Come back really soon!" That's a good thing for every Christian to pray. As John cried out at the close of the New Testament, "Even so, come, Lord Jesus!" (Revelation 22:20).

Can you pray that with a full heart in your life right now? *Lord, come! I am ready.* Or do you say, "Lord, come in a little while. Not right now. Could You postpone it just a bit? There are a few things I'm involved with now that I shouldn't be doing."

No, you should be able to pray at any moment of your day or night, "Come, Lord Jesus." That belief in the imminent, any-moment return of Christ has a purifying effect in your spiritual life. In his first New Testament letter, John wrote these words:

> *Oh, dear children of mine . . . have you realised it? Here and now we are God's children. We don't know what we shall become in the future. We only know that, if reality were to break through, we should reflect his likeness, for we should see him as he really is! Everyone who has at heart a hope like that keeps himself pure, for he knows how pure Christ is.* (1 John 3:2-3, PH)

Praying for the return of Christ keeps our lives focused on ultimate realities.

It is also a personal request. When I pray, "Your kingdom come. Your will be done on earth as it is in heaven," I am saying, *Lord, rule in my life! I want Your kingdom in my life. I want You to be in charge of my life.* And remember this: You can't really pray, "Your kingdom come" until you first pray, "My kingdom go."

There isn't room for two kings or two kingdoms in our lives.

When we pray, "Your kingdom come," it is also a request for the salvation of those who don't know the Lord. What is the kingdom of God? It is the rule and reign of Christ. Jesus said on one occasion, "The kingdom of God is in your midst" (Luke 17:21, NIV). What He was saying is, "Guys, I am God! I am here, and therefore the kingdom is here." Wherever Christ is present and reigning, that is where the kingdom of God is. So as we pray for men and women who don't know Jesus, that they will come to know Him and receive Him as Lord of their lives, we are praying for God's kingdom to be extended in this world.

Don't give up in those prayers for the people in your life who don't know Jesus! Sometimes we grow impatient because we think nothing is happening. But this is no time to throw in the towel. Jesus said, "Ask, and it will be given to you; seek, and you will find; knock, and it will be opened to you" (Matthew 7:7). However, the Greek language here implies continuous action. We could read this verse, *"Keep on asking* and it will be given; *keep on seeking* and you will find; *keep on knocking* and it will be opened to you." So be faithful and persistent in praying for that friend or loved one and bringing him or her before the Lord every day.

Jesus modeled this prayer. We are told in Isaiah 53:12, "He bore the sin of many, and made intercession for the transgressors."

He did, didn't He? Even on the cross. And He didn't do it just once. He said it over and over again. "Father, forgive them. They don't know what they are doing." He said it after the first spike went through His hand. He said it after the spike went through His other hand. He said it after they pounded the spike through His feet.

Some weeks later, Stephen prayed a similar prayer as he was being martyred: "Don't hold this sin to their charge."

We need to be praying for those who don't know the Lord— even those who have been unkind or hateful to us—that they will come to believe in Him and find His forgiveness.

Candidly, it isn't always easy for me to pray, "Lord, Your kingdom come. Your will be done." Why? Because I don't always *like* God's plans. I haven't always agreed or felt happy about His plan for my life. Well, here's a newsflash: Even Jesus struggled with the will of the Father on one occasion. He knew He would be betrayed. He knew He was facing scourging and a terrible death on a cross. He knew He would carry the weight of all the sins of the world for all time on His shoulders. He knew He faced a break in fellowship with His Father. He knew those things, and in Gethsemane He struggled mightily with that prospect ahead of Him.

Think about the worst thing you've ever eaten—and how the very thought of it turns your stomach. Jesus knew He was about to drink a cup full of the wrath of God, and drain it down to its dregs. In Gethsemane He prayed, "Father, if it is possible, let this cup pass from Me. If there is any other way around this, that's what I want. Nevertheless, not My will but Yours be done." That is how He prayed, and that is how we need to pray.

There are times when God's will doesn't make much sense to us. But we say to Him, "Lord, I don't get it. To be honest, I don't even like it. But I know You are God, I know You are in control, and I know You love me. Not my will, but Yours be done." Never be afraid to commit an unknown future to a known God. Your Father who loves you has your best interest at heart—even when it doesn't make earthly sense.

Yes, our family has faced some storms, and so has yours. But the fact remains: I would rather be in a storm with Jesus than anywhere else without Him.

Just recently I spoke with a couple after the memorial service for their son. We were talking about the strange, unfeeling things people sometimes say to those who are grieving over the death of a loved one. I asked them, "What was the worst thing someone said to you?"

The mother of the boy who died replied, "Someone said, 'You need to just get over this and get on with life.'"

I told them, "Clearly, they have never lost a child. The truth is, you never get over it. But you will get through it. You will get through it day by day with God's help. It's going to be hard and it's going to be painful. But God will be there for you, and He will give you strength."

"Give us this day our daily bread."

Bread was a staple of the first-century Jewish diet. They ate bread every meal with just about everything. If you have ever had pita bread and dipped it into hummus, you get the idea. (It's not quite chips and salsa, but it's close.) Bread was a staple.

When it comes to foods I love the most, hot, freshly baked bread has to be right at the top of that list. I could say no to a dessert or no to some fattening dish, but if you bring me hot bread right out of the oven, slathered with some butter, I will never say no. I can't resist it, and really don't want to resist it.

In the first century, however, when they spoke of bread, they weren't talking about any kind of bread in particular. It meant all food.

When you take this part of the Lord's Prayer in its broad application, you could loosely paraphrase it like this: "Lord, give me all the things I need in life. Give me the food I need on my table. Give me the clothes I need on my back. Give me the roof I need over my head. Give me transportation. Give me health. Lord, I ask You and depend on You for these things so necessary to life."

When I am saying, "Give me this day my daily bread," I'm not only asking God to provide it in the future, I am acknowledging that He has given it to me in the present. It's an affirmation that everything we have comes from God. James 1:17 (NIV) says, "Every good and perfect gift is from above, coming down from the Father of the heavenly lights, who does not change like shifting shadows."

Someone might say, "Wait, Greg. I worked hard for my money. I have invested wisely." That's good—but God still gave it to you. Ultimately you have to understand that it came from God's hand. Deuteronomy 8:18 (NIV) says, "Remember the LORD your God, for it is he who gives you the ability to produce wealth."

If you have a need, there is nothing wrong with coming to God with your need. We are told in James 4:2, "You do not have because you do not ask." Bring your requests to the Lord day by day, and ask Him to provide for you. Charles Spurgeon once said, "Whether we like it or not, asking is the rule of the kingdom."

We pray for His provision because He has told us to. Nothing is too big for God to attend to, and nothing is too small. If it concerns you, it concerns Him. In Philippians 4:19, the apostle Paul said, "And my God shall supply all your need according to His riches in glory by Christ Jesus." Notice that he said, "all your *need*," not "all your *greed*."

In other words, we shouldn't sit around being inactive and ask the Lord to provide for us. We need to work hard and be responsible and diligent. But if you will do your part, God will do His.

This promise of His provision is also tied to our giving. The Bible says that if we are faithful in the giving of our resources, bringing our tithes and offerings to Him, He will be faithful to take care of us. In Malachi 3:10 (NIV), He gave us this amazing promise: "'Bring the whole tithe into the storehouse, that there may be food in my house. Test me in this,' says the LORD Almighty, 'and see if I will not throw open the floodgates of heaven and pour out so much blessing that there will not be room enough to store it.'"

"Forgive us our debts, as we forgive our debtors."

We could also translate this, "Forgive us our sins, our trespasses, and the wrongs we have done." This is an everyday prayer, because we sin and need forgiveness every day of our lives.

Have you ever noticed that when you wear white pants you always spill something on them? My theory is that we spill the stuff anyway; it just shows up more on white pants. We are always getting dirty in the course of a day.

In the same way, we sin in ways we don't even realize. Sin is defined as "crossing a line." It's similar to the word *trespass*. If you see a sign in the park on newly planted grass that says "No Trespassing," you trespass when you step over that line. The word *sin* could also be defined as "missing the mark." And since God's standard is perfection, I fall short, miss the mark, and trespass again and again in the course of a day.

In this model prayer Jesus gave us, we are taught to ask God for forgiveness every day. But notice that it doesn't stop there: "Forgive us our debts, as we forgive our debtors." According to

Jesus, our forgiveness of others should always be the natural outflow of remembering how God has forgiven us.

Forgiven people should be forgiving people. Forgiveness is the key to all healthy, strong, and lasting relationships. As fatally flawed people, we will continue to sin, saying things we shouldn't have said and doing things we shouldn't have done. At the same time, people near to us will inevitably say and do things that hurt us. If we're going to live the way Jesus wants us to live, if we really want to follow Him through this life, we have to learn to forgive and to forget. If we don't, that unforgiveness will fester, settling into a deep root of bitterness in our heart and making us miserable! Hebrews 12:15 (NIV) says, "See to it that no one falls short of the grace of God and that no bitter root grows up to cause trouble and defile many."

Have you ever noticed how bitter people can't seem to keep their bitterness to themselves? It just comes out of them—in their comments, in their expressions, almost out of their pores. They will say, "I really don't like that person. What do *you* think about it?" In this way they involve others in their bitterness, in their offense, and the bitterness spreads like an infection.

C. S. Lewis once said, "Everyone says forgiveness is a lovely idea until they have someone to forgive." Isn't that the truth! But there are many benefits of living this way—besides the fact that the Lord directs us to do it. Studies show that harboring unforgiveness is actually detrimental to your health. Research has shown that those who refuse to forgive others have higher blood pressure, bouts of depression, and problems with anger, stress, and anxiety. One doctor revealed that there are robust physiological differences between forgiving and non-forgiving states. She said, "Forgiveness is not about absolving the perpetrator. It is about healing the victim."

Is it easy? No, sometimes it can seem like a very high mountain to climb. In fact, forgiving someone who has wronged us or wounded us may actually be impossible for us in our own strength. We need the indwelling power of Jesus Christ Himself to pull it off. And that's why we need to include it in our prayers every day of our lives.

"Do not lead us into temptation, but deliver us from the evil one."

Someone once put it this way: "Lord, lead me not into temptation—I can find it for myself." What we are saying when we pray this part of the Lord's Prayer is, "Lord, don't let me be tempted above my capacity to resist. Don't give me more than I can handle."

We can count on God to hear us in that prayer. In 1 Corinthians 10:13 we read, "No temptation has overtaken you except such as is common to man; but God is faithful, who will not allow you to be tempted beyond what you are able, but with the temptation will also make the way of escape, that you may be able to bear it."

We have all been tempted and we have all fallen to temptations. But if we are honest, we have to admit that there was a way out, an escape hatch out of the situation, if we had been willing in that moment to take it.

Sometimes it's as simple as walking out the door.

Or terminating a conversation.

Or hitting the off button on the computer.

Whatever door the Lord provides for you in the moment of temptation, *take it*. Even if it seems awkward or embarrassing, take the way out that God gives you. And the Lord will bless you for doing that.

Temptation always starts with something small and ends with something big. That's why I think legalizing marijuana is such a huge and tragic mistake. When I was a teenager, before I became a Christian, I used to smoke pot quite a bit. I know what it did to me in those days; I know how my life started unravelling in so many ways. I know how I became apathetic and disconnected. My grades went down the tubes, and my personality was going down with them.

Is it a gateway drug? Of course it is! I wanted to try something beyond marijuana, and then something beyond that. That's the way it works.

That's the way sin works, too. The devil isn't stupid; he knows how to package his stuff. If he can persuade you to take that first nibble, that first taste, that first look, that first listen—he knows that's how you'll get pulled deeper into his snare.

In this phrase from the Lord's Prayer, we pray for protection from those things. We're saying, "Lord, please help me not to go down that road. Help me to turn this temptation away before it gets a handhold or foothold in my life."

I've always loved the old expression: Sin will take you further than you want to go, keep you longer than you want to stay, and cost you more than you want to pay. We need God's help to not even take the first step down that road.

To Summarize

The Lord's Prayer is the template or pattern for all prayer.

Once again, here's how it works.

First, we come into God's presence and pause for a moment to think about who we're speaking to. We are about to enter into a conversation not with the mayor or governor or president, but with the Creator of the universe. That is amazing. What is even more amazing is that He has adopted us into His family circle, and invites us to call Him Dad. As we approach Him, we ask Him to keep us in His will and help us to please Him and bring Him glory in all we say and do. We bring our requests and the concerns of our hearts before Him, transferring the weight of those burdens from our shoulders to His. We ask for His forgiveness from all our sins—known and unknown, conscious and unconscious—and in that moment we deliberately extend our own forgiveness to those who have offended us. Before we leave our time of prayer, we ask Him to keep us from temptation—refusing to even entertain it in our minds.

If we live this way, we will find our spiritual sweet spot in life. And I don't think most of us have any idea how truly sweet—joyful and peaceful—that spot really is.

This isn't just a template for prayer.

This is a template for living as a follower of Jesus Christ.

CHAPTER SIXTEEN
HURRIED, WORRIED, AND BURIED

When I was in Australia a number of years ago for one of our crusades, I picked up an expression that I like very much. I would be talking to an Aussie and ask a question, maybe asking for directions. The person would begin by saying, "No worries, mate."

Maybe that's just habit for Australians now—something they say without even thinking about it. Even so, it's a good expression. And it's also good theology for people who belong to Jesus Christ.

We do get loaded down with worries, don't we? We worry about what we will eat, what we will wear, or where we will live. We worry about our employment, our family, our health, and a host of other things. Sometimes we even worry when life has been trouble free, because we wonder when things will turn bad.

That great theologian Charlie Brown once made this statement about worry: "I have developed a new philosophy. I only dread one day at a time."

Now let me quote a real theologian. Dr. Martin Lloyd-Jones once said, "The result of worrying about the future is that you cripple yourself in the present."

There's an old fable that speaks to the dangers of excessive worry. As the story goes, Death was walking toward a city one morning. A man stopped Death and said, "Where are you going?"

"I am going into that city," said Death, "to take one hundred people."

"That is horrible!" the man responded.

"But that is what I do," Death replied.

The man ran ahead of Death to warn everyone he could, but his warnings fell on deaf ears. When evening came, the man met Death once again, this time coming out of the city. "I thought you were only going to take a hundred people," he challenged. "Why did a thousand people die?"

"I kept my word," Death responded. "I only took a hundred people. Worry took the rest."

That is how life can be for us. Worry can get to us and do us serious harm. According to some surveys, 75 to 90 percent of all visits to primary care physicians are stress-related disorders.

Ironically, most of what we worry about never actually happens. Dr. Walter Calvert reported a survey on worry that indicated only 8 percent of the things people worried about were legitimate matters of concern. The other 92 percent of worries were either imaginary or never happened.

How can we overcome fear and worry?

Jesus Christ Himself addressed this topic in His Sermon on the Mount.

What Jesus Teaches About Worry

Therefore I say to you, do not worry about your life, what you will eat or what you will drink; nor about your body, what you will put on. Is not life more than food and the body more than clothing? Look at the birds of the air, for they neither sow nor reap nor gather into barns; yet your heavenly Father feeds them. Are you not of more value than they? Which of you by worrying can add one cubit to his stature?

So why do you worry about clothing? Consider the lilies of the field, how they grow: they neither toil nor spin; and yet I say to you that even Solomon in all his glory was not arrayed like one of these. Now if God so clothes the grass of the field, which today is, and tomorrow is thrown into the oven, will He not much more clothe you, O you of little faith?

Therefore do not worry, saying, "What shall we eat?" or "What shall we drink?" or "What shall we wear?" For after all these things the Gentiles seek. For your heavenly Father knows that you need all these things. But seek first the kingdom of God and His righteousness, and all these things shall be added to you. Therefore do not worry about tomorrow, for tomorrow will worry about its own things. Sufficient for the day is its own trouble. (Matthew 6:25-34)

Let's consider three important truths from Jesus' teaching about worry.

1. The believer should not worry.

Was Jesus teaching a head-buried-in-the-sand approach to life, where we stop being concerned about our basic necessities? Was He saying we should just "live for today" and never think or plan for the future?

No, because that would go against much of the teaching of Scripture. The Bible encourages us to provide for our family, to work hard, to save our money, and to be aware of dangers and hazards on the horizon. Yes, He was telling us to be aware. Be alert. Keep both eyes open. *But don't worry.*

Verse 25 says, "Do not worry about your life." Another way to say this would be, "Don't be anxious about the issues of life." The Greek term translated "worry" here indicates something that divides, separates, or distracts us. The English word *worry* comes from an old English word that means "to choke." And that's what anxieties in our lives do to us; they choke us. They cut us off from life.

In the Greek language, this command of Christ to not be anxious includes the idea of stopping what has already been done. Effectively, Jesus was saying, "Stop worrying about your life. Stop it! You've been doing it up to this point and you need to stop doing it right now."

The trouble is, some of us have elevated worry to a kind of virtue. We worry, we tell people, because we care so much. But Scripture doesn't make a virtue of worry at all. In fact, worry can be a sin. Why are fretting and anxiety potential sins? Because they grow out of a lack of trust in God. What we are really saying when we worry is that God isn't in control; God isn't taking care of us in this situation; we can't trust in the goodness and providence of God in this circumstance.

But thoughts like those run directly counter to what God says—again and again. Those who belong to Jesus Christ and believe the Bible know deep down that God is in control of all circumstances that touch our lives, and that there are no accidents in the life of a Christian.

Corrie ten Boom put her finger on the real problem with worry. She said, "Worry does not empty tomorrow of its sorrows. It empties today of its strength." William Ralph Inge called worry "interest paid on trouble before it comes due."

Daniel, a prophet and hero of the Old Testament, was someone who certainly could have worried, but he chose not to. His enemies hatched a plot to have him killed because they were envious of his influence with the king. Unwittingly, the king signed into law a decree that no man could pray to any god but the king. Because Daniel was a man of prayer (and everyone knew it), he was quickly caught and condemned to die in a den of hungry lions.

One of the things that amazes me about this story is that the king worried all night about Daniel in that den of lions, while there is no record that Daniel worried at all! The next morning when the king hurried out to check on him, Daniel was alive and well. From the dark depths of that lions' den he looked up at the king and said in a calm voice, "May the king live forever! My God sent his angel, and he shut the mouths of the lions. They have not hurt me, because I was found innocent in his sight" (Daniel 6:21-22, NIV).

The Bible doesn't say Daniel slept soundly that night, but it wouldn't surprise me. He probably used one of those suddenly docile lions as a big pillow!

That's how it is when we walk in a right relationship with God. We can just kick back and rest in Him. The Bible even says, "He grants sleep to those he loves" (Psalm 127:2, NIV). In 1 Peter 5:7 we are told to cast all our cares on Him, because He cares for us. The idea of casting, of course, is to throw something. Imagine you just got off a plane, you are bone tired, and you are lugging a big carry-on backpack in addition to a roller bag and a briefcase. Your friend who meets you at the gate says, "Hey, let me take that load for you," and you gladly hand him that backpack that had been cutting into your shoulder.

He takes the load from you. And that's what Peter was saying. Take your worries and toss them on God. Throw them on Christ.

I like what Martin Luther said. "Pray, and let God worry." God of course, won't worry, but prayer truly is the secret. In the book of Philippians we read, "Don't worry about anything; instead, pray about everything. Tell God what you need, and thank him for all he has done. Then you will experience God's peace, which exceeds anything we can understand. His peace will guard your hearts and minds as you live in Christ Jesus" (4:6-7, NLT). What an incredible promise! It doesn't get any better than that.

The bottom line? *Turn your worries into prayers.* The next time you are gripped by fear and worry, wondering, *What if this happens? What if that happens?* turn it immediately into a conversation with God. Don't let anxiety take root. Don't frown. Don't let your stomach tie itself into a knot. Go straight to Him.

"Lord, I don't know what this means and I don't know how to get through this, but I am trusting in You RIGHT NOW. You are in control, and I commit this to You."

We need to be looking to the Lord in this way and letting Him give us His peace.

Jesus said to His disciples, "Check out the birds. Check out the flowers. Think about what you see!" (see Matthew 6:26-30). Remember, He was giving this message on a hillside in Galilee. All around Him as He spoke were birds chirping away and wildflowers nodding in the breeze, and He used them to make His point. "Look at the birds—right before your eyes! Have you ever seen a stressed-out bird? Birds wake up every morning with a song, and end the day that way, too. Birds are happy being birds. No bird has ever been given the promise of eternal life or the hope of heaven, and yet they sing with everything in them, giving glory to God."

Then there are the flowers. In verses 28-29 Jesus said, "So why do you worry about clothing? Consider the lilies of the field, how they grow: they neither toil nor spin; and yet I say to you that even Solomon in all his glory was not arrayed like one of these." When Jesus spoke here about lilies, He was not speaking of big, cultivated, hot-house Easter lilies. These were little wildflowers growing in the meadows and pastures of Galilee. They were simple, humble, and pretty.

Jesus then addressed worry about clothing. Men and women apparently worried about that in the first century and they worry about it today. We live in a culture that is obsessed with external attractiveness. People are always looking for ways to approve their appearance or look more like the celebrities on magazine covers. The problem is, even the people on the magazine covers don't look like the people on the magazine covers. Most of the glamorous images you see in magazines have been photoshopped or otherwise altered and don't even exist in real life.

With cosmetic surgery, you can become almost anyone. Some time ago, I read an article titled "Beauty Junkies: Examining a Society Obsessed with Appearance." The author writes, "Feel cheated in the looks department? With enough money you can nip and tuck your way to a whole new you. You can redo your teeth, plump your lips, reshape your nose, and reduce your thighs. Medicine allows us to enhance cheekbones, shorten toes to fit into designer stilettos, improve a chin, increase breast size and freeze the forehead so that wrinkles no longer appear there."[4]

It's a good thing to want to look your best on the outside, but don't neglect your soul. You can have a chiseled body and a dying soul. The Bible even addresses this, speaking to women in particular. The apostle Peter wrote, "What matters is not your outer appearance—the styling of your hair, the jewelry you wear, the cut of your clothes—but your inner disposition. Cultivate inner beauty, the gentle, gracious kind that God delights in" (1 Peter 3:3-4, MSG).

There is a place for staying in shape. People who are fit are able to enjoy more activities—and just feel better. But as with anything else, fitness can become an obsession that takes over a person's life. And that's taking it too far.

It's kind of funny to read about people who have broken all the health rules and end up living to a vigorous 104 years old. Likewise, we read about people who have been so very careful about their diet and supplements and exercise regimen and they die out on the tennis court or on a jog. The fact is, only God determines how long a man or woman will live—no matter how much tofu and bran they may consume.

It is God who sets the date of your birth and the date of your death. You, however, have everything to say about that little dash in between those two dates and what you do with the time it represents.

Paul talked about the balance between physical and spiritual fitness in 1 Timothy 4:8-9 (NLT): "Physical training is good, but training for godliness is much better, promising benefits in this life and in the life to come. This is a trustworthy saying, and everyone should accept it."

2. Worry doesn't make your life longer—just more miserable.

Jesus said, "Which of you by worrying can add one cubit to his stature?" (Matthew 6:27). Another translation reads, "Can any one of you by worrying add a single hour to your life?" (NIV). Psalm 90 says, "We glide along the tides of time as swiftly as a racing river and vanish as quickly as a dream. We are like grass that is green in the morning but mowed down and withered before the evening shadows fall. . . . Teach us to number our days and recognize how few they are; help us to spend them as we should" (verses 5-6,12, TLB).

3. Putting God first is the secret to a worry-free life.

Again, looking at Matthew 6:33 we read, "But seek first the kingdom of God and His righteousness, and all these things shall be added to you." What does that mean? The Greek word translated *first* means "first in the line of more than one option." There are many options I can seek to follow or live for: I can live for my physical appearance; I can live for a successful career; I can live for experiencing pleasures; I can live for many different things. But here is what Jesus was saying: Take that list of options and write God into the number one position. "*Seek first the kingdom of God.*" If you want a life free of worry and anxiety and fear, put God's kingdom before everything else. Seek it first.

"That sounds fine, Greg," you say, "but what does it really mean?"

Let's take your career as an example, whatever business you happen to be in. Ask yourself this question: "Am I bringing glory to God in this career, this line of work?" In other words, "Am I seeking God first in what I am doing?"

"Well, that's easy for you, Greg," you say. "You are a pastor. It's easy for you to seek God first. My job is in the real world dealing every day with real people."

I understand what you are saying. But one thing is the same for both of us: Our goal should be to honor God in everything we do, no matter what our career or job. If you can't honor God in what you do, do something else.

Ask yourself, "As I pursue this occupation, what is my goal?" If your goal is to simply make money no matter what it takes, you have the wrong goal. Your goals should be to honor God, do honest work, and maintain personal integrity and a good testimony in the workplace.

I know Christians who have been successful in business but have a bad reputation because they cut corners or don't do the job right. They may have achieved some financial goals, but their testimony as a believer is in tatters. When the day is done, we want to have a good name and a good reputation. Proverbs 22:1 (NLT) says, "Choose a good reputation over great riches; being held in high esteem is better than silver or gold."

Here's how it works. There are people who cut corners. There are people who cheat on and ace the exam, when you had to study your head off to just squeak by with a pass. There are people who lie on their résumés and get the position you were hoping to get. There are people who flatter the boss and move up the ladder more quickly than you do.

You see all this happening, and you are tempted to think, "Being honest and having integrity just doesn't pay off!"

But hold on a moment. Scripture tells us that if we live godly and honest lives, maintain integrity, and work hard, God will bless us for it. Solomon wrote, "GOD's blessing makes life rich; nothing we do can improve on God" (Proverbs 10:22, MSG). Yes, there will be times when others seem to be doing better than you are, but just wait awhile and see how everything plays out. The Bible assures us that a person will reap what he or she sows.

Seek God first and He will take care of you.

Are you a single person? Seek first the kingdom of God and His righteousness as an unmarried man or woman. What does that mean? It means that you allow God to find that right person for you, if you are supposed to be married. It means you don't rush out and grab someone who might be "available" or fool yourself into thinking you can date a nonbeliever and bring him or her to Christ. I've seen so-called missionary dating on multiple occasions, and I can tell you from experience that it doesn't usually end well. For some reason, it is much easier for the nonbeliever to pull the believer back than for the believer to pull the unbeliever forward.

Don't just look for someone who claims to be a Christian; look for evidence of their faith in the way they live—in the way they do business, in the way they treat their loved ones and their not-so-loved ones, in the way they care for those Jesus called the "least of these." Is the person wise? Loving? Humble? Growing in faith? That's the person you're looking for.

The Bible tells a beautiful story of how the Lord found a bride for Isaac. His father Abraham sent out his servant Eliezer to find a godly woman to bring home to his son. While the servant was gone, Isaac went into the fields every evening to pray and wait on God. One night Isaac looked up from his prayer time and saw two people riding camels toward him. Soon Eliezer and the beautiful Rebekah came into view. What am I saying here? That you should go stand in a field every night and wait for your future husband or wife to show up? No, my point is that Isaac sought God first, and in the Lord's timing He brought the right woman into Isaac's life.

When we seek God and His kingdom first, our lives will be brought into proper perspective. Matthew 6:33 tells us, "all these things shall be added to you." What things? What was Jesus talking about? Food, clothing, and we could expand that to shelter, work, pay, and future plans. God is saying, "I will take care of these things if you will seek Me first in your life."

The Context

Jesus began this portion of the Sermon on the Mount we've been looking at with the word *therefore*. He said, "Therefore I say to you, do not worry. . ." (verse 25).

As you may already know, whenever you read the word *therefore* in the Bible (or anywhere for that matter), it always helps to find out what it is *there for*. So what did Jesus say prior to this section on worry and anxiety? Go back to Matthew 6:19-21:

> Do not lay up for yourselves treasures on earth, where moth and rust destroy and where thieves break in and steal; but lay up for yourselves treasures in heaven, where neither moth nor rust destroys and where thieves do not break in and steal. For where your treasure is, there your heart will be also.

Jesus wasn't saying it's wrong for us to have stuff. Effectively, He was saying it is wrong when stuff has us!

The phrase "do not lay up for yourselves" means to lay something horizontally, as in storing it permanently. He wasn't talking about the man who is saving, but the man who is stockpiling. He's not talking to the woman who merely has possessions, but rather the one who flaunts them to impress people. Jesus said, don't do that. Don't pile up treasures in that way. Seek God's kingdom first.

Many believers struggle financially today because they haven't learned the simple principle of seeking God first in their giving. The Bible, Old Testament and New Testament alike, tells us to bring our tithes and offerings to the Lord. A tithe is 10 percent. We bring this percentage of our income to Him, and our offerings to Him are above and beyond that. People say to me, "Well, Greg, we can't afford to give that much." As far as I'm concerned, I can't afford *not* to give that much! Throughout my life, I have found that when I am faithful in my giving to the Lord, He blesses me in unexpected ways as I seek to keep His kingdom number one in my life.

In Proverbs 3:9-10 (NIV) we read,

Honor the LORD with your wealth,
with the firstfruits of all your crops;
then your barns will be filled to overflowing,
and your vats will brim over with new wine.

Again, God is saying, "If you will trust Me and put Me first in all things, I will take care of you."

There is only one instance in the Bible when God asks us to put Him to the test. It is in the Old Testament book of Malachi. And in that passage God says, "Bring the whole tithe into the storehouse. . . . Test me in this . . . and see if I will not throw open the floodgates of heaven and pour out so much blessing that there will not be room enough to store it" (3:10, NIV).

This verse is not telling us to give to God to obligate Him to give back. This is giving because God has done so much for us, and our gratitude and love overflow to Him.

Do your giving while you are living, and you will be knowing where your money is going. No, you can't take it with you, but you can send it on ahead of you.

In summary, a lot of us go through life just spinning our wheels. Our tombstones could say, "Hurried, Worried, Buried." We rush here and there and find ourselves stressed out. Even in moments of so-called leisure or vacation, when we're supposed to be having fun and "really living," we feel an emptiness. We spend our lives chasing a dream that seems always just out of reach.

Instead of channeling your energies and pouring your years into chasing empty visions of "success," why not chase after God, seek Him, and put Him first?

Those who do will never be disappointed.

CHAPTER SEVENTEEN
THE THREE Cs OF LIFE

Every day of our lives, we are flooded with choices. Little choices. Big choices. Thousands and thousands of them.

Consider a trip to the supermarket. Sometimes, when there is no other viable alternative, my wife will send me to the market to pick something up for her. It hardly ever ends well, because I usually come home with a variety of items she never asked me to get. And if I bought what I thought she asked for, it usually isn't what she wanted. I always get the wrong thing, the wrong brand, or the wrong size.

The choices are overwhelming. She asks me to bring home some cheddar cheese, but then I find myself looking at thirty different kinds, prepared and packaged in thirty different ways. After a while I just grab one and go, because I already know it will be the wrong one before I put it in the basket.

But these sorts of choices, after all, are pretty minor. There are lifestyle choices as well, both small and large. Whom will we marry? What career path will we follow? And, of course, the most important choice of all is what we will do with Jesus Christ.

This brings me to the title of this chapter, "The Three Cs of Life." Yes, I know, there are a lot more than three. But the trio I want to focus on includes *challenges, choices,* and *consequences.* Whether we want them or not, like them or not, or think about them or not, these three elements play a determining role in our lives every day.

First there are the *challenges.* Sometimes these show up as opportunities. Sometimes they slip into our lives as temptations. When a particular challenge comes at me, I have to decide how I will respond.

That brings me to *choices.* If I make right choices, it will result in blessings in my life. If I make wrong choices, it will result in *consequences.*

Think on the choice of young Moses as he stood at a watershed moment of his life. The writer of Hebrews said, "It was by faith that Moses, when he grew up, refused to be called the son of Pharaoh's daughter. He chose to share the oppression of God's people instead of enjoying the fleeting pleasures of sin" (11:24-25, NLT). He could have been a man of great power in Egypt, perhaps even next to the pharaoh himself. Instead, when he saw the plight of his fellow Jews suffering under the tyranny of the Egyptians, he chose to suffer with them. That one choice resulted in all of Israel being delivered from the kingdom of Egypt and finding a home at last in the Promised Land.

In other words, Moses' choice affected *generations* of his people.

Or consider Joseph's choice of obedience when he was tempted by the wife of Potiphar. Or Daniel's decision not to compromise on even the smallest matters as he sat at the king's table in Babylon. These were choices that would end up moving nations.

Then there were those who made wrong choices. Adam's wrong choice cost him paradise. Esau's wrong choice cost him his birthright. Saul's wrong choice cost him his kingdom. Judas lost his apostleship and his very life because of a wrong choice. Pilate, Agrippa, and Felix (as far as we know) all missed eternity with Christ because of their wrong choices.

In the story *Alice in Wonderland*, author Lewis Carroll described Alice coming to a fork in the road.

"Which road do I take?" asked Alice.

"Where do you want to go?" responded the Cheshire Cat.

"I don't know," she answered.

"Then it doesn't matter," said the cat.

The Bible says that in the course of life, every one of us comes to a major, all-important fork in the road. According to Scripture there are two different roads we can take in life. One narrow, the other wide. One hard, the other much easier. Solomon wrote, "There is a way that seems right to a man, but its end is the way of death" (Proverbs 14:12). Ultimately, the Bible tells us there are two places where we can spend eternity.

In His Sermon on the Mount, Jesus made those choices, those destinations, very clear. He described two roads, two foundations, and two gates.

Two Roads

Not everyone who says to Me, "Lord, Lord," shall enter the kingdom of heaven, but he who does the will of My Father in heaven. Many will say to Me in that day, "Lord, Lord, have we not prophesied in Your name, cast out demons in Your name, and done many wonders in Your name?" And then I will declare to them, "I never knew you; depart from Me, you who practice lawlessness!" (Matthew 7:21-23)

The Lord's closing words are a warning to people in churches today. Jesus was saying that His followers will sometimes find themselves sitting alongside those who *seem* to be followers, but really aren't. They will look like followers and sound like followers, but in reality they are *posers*—people pretending to be something they are not. In other words, there are both genuine and imitation believers.

Jesus told a parable about a farmer who sowed a field of wheat. At night, an enemy who wanted to undermine his crop came in and sowed tares among the wheat. Tares are darnel seed, which looks like wheat in its initial growth, but with the passing of time it uproots and destroys the wheat. Jesus told that story to illustrate for us that wherever there is something real there will also be the false. Wherever there is the true, there will also be the imitation. And that's what we see in the Scripture before us.

I would like you to take note of three significant truths.

1. Just saying "Lord, Lord" doesn't make you a true believer.

Let's look at this passage again in another translation. Jesus said,

Not all who sound religious are really godly people. They may refer to me as "Lord," but still won't get to heaven. For the decisive question is whether they obey my Father in heaven. At the Judgment many will tell me, "Lord, Lord, we told others about you and used your name to cast out demons and to do many other great miracles." But I will reply, "You have never been mine. Go away, for your deeds are evil." (Matthew 7:21-23, TLB)

What I find fascinating here is that the people in this story are not your hum-drum, garden-variety believers. These aren't your basic pagans who are biblically illiterate with no knowledge of God or the Bible. These people seem to be deeply religious with more than a passing profession of faith.

Did you notice how respectful they are? They call Jesus "Lord." In the original Greek the word is *kurios*, which implies divinity. So there are even people who affirm the deity of Christ who are not true believers.

Now obviously, real Christians believe that Jesus Christ is God. Jesus even said, "If you do not believe that I am he [the Son of God], you will indeed die in your sins" (John 8:24, NIV). If you think Jesus is just a great prophet or teacher, you are missing the point. He was and is God in human form. That was the whole purpose of His birth, of His becoming a man. It was *God with us* in that manger in Bethlehem.

Let me take it a step further. To be a real Christian, you must believe in the virgin birth of Jesus Christ. Why? Because if Jesus were not supernaturally placed in the womb of Mary by the Holy Spirit, then He was no different from any other man. Therefore, His death did not atone for the sin of the world. It wasn't enough to just die on a cross. Many men died on crosses in the days of Rome. It wasn't enough to rise from the dead, because others, like Lazarus, came back to life. What was significant about Jesus is that He was fully man and fully God. And yet He went to the cross and died for us.

There are any number of ways God might have sent Jesus to this earth. He could have come down in a shaft of light and simply materialized among us, *Star Trek* style, and said, "Hello, everyone. I am Jesus. I am here to save you." But who would relate to someone like that?

Or He could have been born of two human parents. Joseph could have been His biological father and Mary His biological mother. But then we would say, "What's the difference? He's just like us. He was born into sin just like we were."

But Jesus was born of a virgin. He had a physical birth, but a supernatural conception.

Coming back to Jesus' story, however, we realize that *just believing the right things about Jesus isn't enough*. There must also be a personal commitment of our lives to Christ. The Bible says that demons also believe in God—and tremble. If you could interview a demon (and, by the way, I wouldn't recommend it) I think you might be surprised how orthodox demons are in their belief system. They would agree with us that the Bible is the Word of God and that Jesus is the Son of God, born of a virgin. They know these truths all too well. But they also oppose the Bible and Jesus with everything in them.

Returning to the imitation Christians in Matthew 7, these people say, "Lord, Lord," calling Jesus God. And they also seem to be passionate and enthusiastic in this belief, repeating His title. It is possible for nonbelievers to get caught up and really excited in a time of exuberant worship. They can sing louder than anyone and lift their hands higher than everyone. But then they can walk out through the church doors and resume a sinful, God-dishonoring lifestyle. It shocks me that people can worship God one moment, then go out and sleep with their boyfriend or girlfriend, become involved in an adulterous relationship, or tell lies and defraud people the next.

These people Jesus spoke of might have had passion and enthusiasm, and even a willingness to make a public profession of faith, but they were *not* real believers.

2. Even though these people were doing miracles in Jesus' name, they still weren't authentic followers of Christ.

In verse 22 we read, "Have we not prophesied in Your name, cast out demons in Your name, and done many wonders in Your name?"

Did you know that the devil can imitate certain miracles? They're not real miracles, they're only imitation. But they can still seem impressive. The Bible tells us that when Antichrist comes he will be able to perform lying wonders. In 2 Thessalonians 2:9-10 we read, "The coming of the lawless one is according to the working of Satan, with *all power, signs, and lying wonders,* and with all unrighteous deception among those who perish" (emphasis added).

3. Real Christians demonstrate their faith by the way they live.

In Matthew 7:23, Jesus said, "I will declare to them, 'I never knew you; depart from Me, you who practice lawlessness!'" The word *lawlessness* in the Greek language speaks of a continuous, regular action. Jesus was saying, "You profess to believe in Me, but you continually and habitually practice lawlessness and sin." This isn't a growing Christian who trips up once in a while, as we all do; this is a pretender. A fake. A fraud.

There is a difference between someone who stumbles, sins, and is sorry for it and repents and the person who willfully sins without any desire to change from that sinful lifestyle. That is the person Christ is talking about here.

In 1 John 3:6 (NIV) we read these words: "No one who lives in him keeps on sinning. No one who continues to sin has either seen him or known him." The passage doesn't say that if you know Jesus you won't sin. It does say that if you continually and habitually stay in the same sin, that is an indication that you are not a true Christian.

Jesus says to these people, "I never knew you." The term translated "to know" from the original language is a word that speaks of intimacy. In fact, it's the same word that is used of the intimacy between a man and a woman in marriage. Jesus was saying, "You knew about Me, but I never knew you." These people are religious, but they don't have a relationship with God.

Two Foundations

Jesus illustrated this contrast by telling a story of two men who each built a house—one on a foundation of rock, the other on a foundation of sand.

Therefore whoever hears these sayings of Mine, and does them, I will liken him to a wise man who built his house on the rock: and the rain descended, the floods came, and the winds blew and beat on that house; and it did not fall, for it was founded on the rock.

But everyone who hears these sayings of Mine, and does not do them, will be like a foolish man who built his house on the sand: and the rain descended, the floods came, and the winds blew and beat on that house; and it fell. And great was its fall. (Matthew 7:24-27)

Think of a tract neighborhood and two guys who want to build the same house with the same floorplan and landscaping on two different lots. They both decide on the same color scheme, paint, roof, and driveway. Everything about these two houses seems identical. If we took time to walk around and through the houses, we would say, "It's the same house, inside and outside." But here's the difference: One man builds on a solid foundation, and the other builds on a poor, inadequate foundation.

And that makes all the difference.

The most important time of building a house or any kind of structure is the construction of the foundation. You have to pour the slab right. You have to get the electrical and plumbing right. If you don't, you'll eventually have to tear things down and start over.

Building a foundation isn't the most fun or exciting time of constructing a new house. The new owners probably don't show up to video this part of the process. When you watch it being done, it almost seems as if nothing is happening for a long period of time.

For those of us who watch, the action really starts when the walls are framed in, the insulation goes in, and the drywall is hung and, finally, painted.

Wall building may be the fun part, but the foundation is still the most important part. It's the same way for us as believers; the foundation is the most vital aspect of our lives as well.

History tells us about an Italian architect named Pisano, who began work on a famous project in 1172. It was to be a lovely tower built next to a majestic cathedral. Apparently, however, this architect was in a bit of a rush and didn't test the soil underneath the proposed structure. As a result, that tower now leans eighteen feet off center. People come from around the world to see the Leaning Tower of Pisa. Scientists travel yearly to Pisa to measure the tower's angle—which leans a little more each year. The experts say that one day it will simply collapse.

If *building* foundations, then, are so critically important, *life* foundations are even more so. Someone might say, "I've built my foundation on the church." I wouldn't advise that; the church is made up of fallible, sometimes unsteady men and women. Someone else will say, "I built my foundation on my wife or my husband." I wouldn't advise that, either. What happens to your life if he or she leaves— or God suddenly and unexpectedly takes your spouse home to heaven? I wouldn't even counsel you to build your foundation on your beliefs, because our viewpoint and perspectives tend to change with the passing years.

You need to build your foundation on Jesus Christ, and Him alone. The church will let you down, pastors will let you down, even your spouse or family members may let you down. But Jesus is the One who will sustain you. As Paul wrote, "For no one can lay any foundation other than the one already laid, which is Jesus Christ" (1 Corinthians 3:11, NIV). Build your foundation on Christ, because if you don't, you won't be sustained when times of crisis and hardship come.

Storms will come into every life. And as destructive and difficult as storms may be, they do have one positive quality: *They will reveal where our foundation really lies.* Adversity will show the true source of our strength and stability. In His parable of the two houses, Jesus said that "the rain descended, the floods came, and the winds blew and beat on that house." That's the way it will always be. Whether we like it or not, storms will come into every life and will take many different forms. Sometimes it's a tidal wave of temptation. Sometimes a sudden tragedy slams into our world out of nowhere. And these stormy seasons will test our faith.

You might say, "I don't know if I would be able to stand in something like that." But you can decide right now to begin strengthening your foundation by building and centering your life on Jesus Christ. Then you will be able to endure whatever blows into your life.

I have been a pastor for over forty-one years, and in that time I have conducted a number of funeral services for parents who have lost a child. Those are the hardest, especially when the children were young. Over the years I've always done my best to bring what comfort I could, knowing that I couldn't really relate to a tragedy like that. I've tried to pick the right Scriptures, say the right words, and gently help them to turn to the Lord in their grief. On more than one occasion I have walked away from a situation like this and prayed, "Lord, I hope that never happens to me, because if it does—I don't think I could handle it."

But then it did happen to me in 2008, with the sudden passing of my son Christopher. The storm was unbelievably strong and dark and difficult—just as hard and crushing and heartbreaking as you might imagine. But God was with me, and my foundation in Jesus Christ held. It sustained me through the worst of storms.

You don't need to worry about the future or the storms that might lie over the horizon in your life. God will give you what you need when you need it. No one will lead a suffering-free life, but Jesus will be there for you just as He was for me.

In his book *If God is Good*, Randy Alcorn writes these words: "Most of us don't give focused thought to evil and suffering until we experience them. This forces us to formulate perspective on the fly at a time when our thinking is muddled and we are exhausted and consumed by pressing issues. People who have been there will attest it is far better to think through suffering in advance."

Sometimes when people go through hardship they turn away from God. Through the years, I have found that trials, suffering, and adversity have one of two effects: Either our faith is strengthened because we have turned to God for comfort, or our faith is weakened and we have become angry at God—or even walked away from Him.

When you go through hardship, it will show you what you are really made of. Character isn't created in crisis, it is revealed. Proverbs 24:10 (NIV) says, "If you falter in a time of trouble, how small is your strength!"

Sometimes people will say, "This crisis has shaken my faith." My question is, what kind of faith do you have? Because the faith that can't be shaken is the faith that has been shaken. When you have been through deep adversity and survived it, leaning hard on God's faithfulness, your faith gets stronger. But if your faith collapses in every little trial or hardship of life, perhaps you should question what you have built your life upon. Have you really built on a relationship with Jesus Christ Himself? If you have, then you will be able to stand in the storms of life when they come.

Two Gates

After teaching us about two foundations, Jesus went on to tell us about two gates. He said, "Enter by the narrow gate; for wide is the gate and broad is the way that leads to destruction, and there are many who go in by it. Because narrow is the gate and difficult is the way which leads to life, and there are few who find it" (Matthew 7:13-14).

If you want to build your life on the right foundation you have to start by getting on the right road. Jesus called it the narrow road that leads to life. Did anyone ever tell you that this is an easy road? It isn't.

Many people find the word *narrow* offensive. Narrow is not a popular word in the twenty-first century. Usually the word is used in the same sentence along with terms like *bigoted, self-righteous,* and *intolerant.* If someone says to you, "You are so narrow-minded," that is not a compliment. It's meant to be an insult.

What did Jesus say? He said we need narrow minds to walk a narrow road. What does it mean to be narrow-minded? It *doesn't* mean a person is an arrogant, self-righteous know-it-all. All that narrow-minded actually means is that we recognize there is a specific road we must travel in order to reach a specific destination.

If you are in the Los Angeles area as I am, and want to drive from Riverside to the Orange County airport, you get on the 91 freeway and then merge onto the 55, and it will take you there. But maybe someone will say, "I don't want to take the 91 freeway. I want to take a different freeway."

Go ahead, but that won't get you where you want to go. It doesn't matter how convinced or sincere you may be, traveling the wrong route won't get you to the right destination. If you want to arrive at a specific place, you have to get on the right road.

The same is true of getting to heaven. Jesus said that the road that leads to life—to eternal life—is narrow, and only few ever find it. Lots of religious people in the world today will say, "All roads lead to God. Follow whatever road you are on, and it will get you there. After all, aren't all religions teaching pretty much the same thing?"

No, they are not. It's not true that world religions teach the same thing. In fact, we could sum up all the religious systems of the world in a very simple way: One is God's grace, the other is man's works; one is divine accomplishment, the other is human achievement; one leads to life, the other leads to death.

All the religions of the world effectively say, "Do." Do this and you will reach nirvana. Do that and you will achieve inner peace. Do X amount of good and you will be admitted into heaven. Christianity, by contrast, says, "Done." We receive salvation as a gift that we accept from God, and there are no good works involved. It was all done for us by Christ when He died on the cross in our place. So we accept the gift of eternal life, and as a result of receiving that gift, we do good works to bring glory to God. This is the narrow road that leads to life.

But Jesus also spoke of a "broad way." This is the easy road, the popular road, with lots of people traveling on it. But it leads to death instead of life. As Solomon wrote, "There is a way that seems right to a man, but its end is the way of death" (Proverbs 14:12).

In 1846, George and Jacob Donner, James Frasier Reed, and their families—eighty-seven men, women, and children—set out in covered wagons for California, some two thousand miles away.

As you may know, the journey ended in tragedy. The pioneers were forced to camp for the winter at a small lake thirteen miles northwest of Lake Tahoe. Enduring a fierce winter and heavy snows, forty of the party died. Some of the survivors were so desperate they resorted to cannibalism.

How did they end up in such a miserable place? As it turns out, a man named Lansford Hastings had told the Donner party of a shortcut to California. Though it was untried, the leaders of the wagon train decided to take it. And that decision cost many of them their lives.

It is the same way in life. There is a so-called shortcut called the broad road, and there is the narrow way that leads to life. We must decide which road we will travel.

Just because you have made bad choices—perhaps some really bad choices—to this point, doesn't mean you can't make the right choice now. You can get on the narrow road to life today. Right now. And it begins by saying, "Lord Jesus, I have taken wrong road after wrong road, and I have made a mess of my life. I need Your help. I want to surrender my life to You. Please forgive me for my sins and put my feet on the right road, the road to Life."

CHAPTER EIGHTEEN
FOLLOWING JESUS THROUGH THE STORMS OF LIFE

We have a lot more warning about approaching storms than we used to. Now, when a huge storm approaches an area, residents usually get a heads-up from the TV, radio, or Internet. If that storm system builds itself up to monumental proportions, with hurricane strength, they might even give it a name. There are certain hurricanes that are famous now, like Hurricanes Carla, Camille, Isabel, Andrew, and Katrina.

Some hurricanes, of course, don't receive the same level of notoriety. Was it because they weren't as powerful or because they had mild-sounding names? There was actually a Hurricane Fabian at one point. And there was a Hurricane Larry. Really? Could anybody get intimidated by a Hurricane Larry? Or how about Hurricane Teddy? Doesn't that just strike fear into your heart? Probably not. The bottom line, however, is that we give names to certain powerful storms because of their significance and potential for great damage and destruction.

There are storms in life, too.

Sometimes these storms will be expected, and we watch them build and brew with great concern in our hearts. But at other times, storms seem to slam into our world out of nowhere, with no warning at all.

Maybe it's a heart attack, or a rebellious child, or a pink slip at work, or a crumbling marriage. It might even be the death of someone you love very much. These sorts of storms can alter the very landscape of our lives.

Here is what you need to know about life storms in general.

You're going to have them.

There are really two kinds of people in the world: those who are experiencing a crisis and those who are about to experience a crisis. You're either in a storm or you are headed into another. That's not pessimism, that's *life*.

According to the Bible, the rain will fall on both the righteous and the unrighteous (see Matthew 5:45). Jesus Himself said, "In this godless world you will continue to experience difficulties. But take heart! I've conquered the world" (John 16:33, MSG).

The simple fact is that we can't control whether storms will come into our lives; all we can control, if we will, is how we *respond* to them. For the next few pages, let's consider a literal storm that came into the lives of Jesus' disciples.

A Storm That Looked Like Death

Now when He got into a boat, His disciples followed Him. And suddenly a great tempest arose on the sea, so that the boat was covered with the waves. But He was asleep. Then His disciples came to Him and awoke Him, saying, "Lord, save us! We are perishing!"

But He said to them, "Why are you fearful, O you of little faith?" Then He arose and rebuked the winds and the sea, and there was a great calm. So the men marveled, saying, "Who can this be, that even the winds and the sea obey Him?" (Matthew 8:23-27)

In another chapter, we looked at the two words Jesus spoke to Matthew, the tax collector: "Follow Me." In the original language, those words implied both the beginning and the ending of something. In other words, Jesus was effectively saying to Matthew, "I want you to follow Me each and every day." So Matthew followed Jesus. In fact, all of the disciples followed Jesus.

And where did that lead them?

Directly into a storm.

Sometimes when storms or hardships come into our lives, we may think, "This is probably happening because I did something wrong." But that certainly wasn't true in this case. These disciples were in the will of God, men who had committed their very lives to following Jesus. *The storm came even as they were obeying the Lord, not because they had disobeyed Him.*

So what do we learn from this story?

1. Storms will come into our lives.

This was a serious storm, so frightening that these seasoned sailors feared for their lives. In the original language, the word used to describe it is also used to speak of an earthquake. One translation says, "High waves began to break into the boat until it was nearly full of water and about to sink" (Mark 4:37, TLB).

So this was a seismic mega-storm that covered the boat with crashing waves.

Have you ever been in a storm at sea? I've been in a few, but never in a boat like Jesus and the disciples were in that day. Theirs was a very simple, primitive boat, and none of the men was wearing a life jacket.

What was Jesus doing while this terrifying storm swept over them? Amazingly, He was sound asleep in the lower part of the boat.

Does it ever seem to you as though God is asleep or not paying attention to what's going on in your life? It can be rather disheartening when someone falls asleep just at the moment when we really need them.

Some people can sleep through anything. My wife can do that quite well. Once she goes to sleep, she is *asleep*. That's not the case with me; I wake up when a bird chirps and then can't go back to sleep again.

Have you ever been talking with someone and seen the person actually fall asleep while you were talking? It happens to me all the time as a preacher. And don't think we don't notice! People can pretend like they've just been praying after their head lurches forward, but I'm not buying it.

People are people, and they will occasionally fall asleep in your presence or take a nap at the very moment you need them most. But God never does that. Psalm 121:4 (NLT) says, "Indeed, he who watches over Israel never slumbers or sleeps."

In a technical sense, Jesus the man, weary from a hard day's work, was asleep. But in the broader sense, God never sleeps. He is always on watch, always on duty, always paying attention. Jesus was asleep because He rested confidently in the will of the Father. And that is what the disciples should have done, too. They should have realized that God would see them through that storm and that they would be fine. Instead, they were beside themselves with fear.

What should we do when storms come into our lives?

2. We need to cry out to Jesus in the midst of our storms.

They cried out, "Lord, save us!" And by the way, I don't think they whispered those words.

When I say cry out to Jesus, I mean *cry out*. Tell Him whatever is on your heart. You will never offend God by raising your voice. Tell Him just how you're feeling. He already knows!

"God, why?"

"God, what?"

"God, where are You?"

"Lord, I don't get this."

"Lord, I don't like this."

"Lord, this is really hard."

"Jesus, this doesn't make any sense to me."

"Lord, HELP!"

All of those expressions are perfectly legitimate. In fact, you can read prayers of much greater intensity in the book of Psalms.

Sometimes I think we feel as though we need to sanitize our prayers or pretty them up a little. No, God wants to hear us speak from our hearts. He wants honest prayer, even if it's shouted or cried out through tears. Again, read the honesty of David and others in the psalms as they cried out to God, even pouring out their frustration to Him. Even Jesus, hanging on the cross, said, "My God, My God, why have You forsaken Me?"

Talk to God about it. Call out to God. That is what those disciples did when they were slammed by that storm. They cried aloud to the Lord.

Though the shrieking of the storm did not wake Jesus, the cry of His people did. You can be sure they had tried everything possible to get out of that mess on their own. But after doing all they knew to do, they realized Jesus was their only hope. That's the way it is with us sometimes. God will let us get to the very end of our rope, coming to the end of ourselves, so that we might (finally) cry out to Him.

The story is told of a hardened old sea captain who was quite vocal about his atheism. One night during a terrible storm, he was swept overboard. Someone quickly threw him a rope, but as he was thrashing about in the dark ocean, his men heard him yelling and crying out to God for help and mercy. After his crew rescued him and got him dried off, one of his men said to him, "Captain, I thought you didn't believe in God."

The salty old captain replied, "Well, even if there isn't a God, there *ought* to be at times like this."

That is how many people respond. C. S. Lewis said, "Even atheists have moments of doubt." Sometimes, in quiet moments when no one else is around, that individual who seems so confident in his atheism and hatred of Christianity has moments of doubt about his philosophy. When great trials come, he might instinctively turn toward God—or want to.

Will God hear that person when he cries out to Him? Yes, He will. We might imagine God saying something like, "Forget it! You made your bed, and now you can lie in in it." But that's not the kind of God He is. When Jesus walked this earth, He responded to the cries of those in distress and need.

Psalm 91:14-15 (NLT) says, "The LORD says, 'I will rescue those who love me. I will protect those who trust in my name. When they call on me, I will answer; I will be with them in trouble. I will rescue and honor them.'"

It was Thomas Watson who said, "When God lays men on their backs, then they look up to heaven."

Not long ago, I got a letter from a woman who had attended our crusade in Chicago. It was a crisis that got her attention. This is what she wrote:

> Dear Greg,
> My husband and I have been going through a lot. He had a stroke a few weeks ago and we have really been struggling. I became upset with God and all of these things that were hitting me at once. So last week I was told by my mother that I never fit into our family and never would and was not welcome in their home anymore. . . . I was ready to take my own life.

So here was a woman enduring deep hardship—rejected by her own mother and devastated by her husband's stroke—who was read to commit suicide. How did God reach her? It was through her eight-year-old daughter who, in her words, "loved the Lord and wanted to go to the crusade." So reluctantly, the little girl's mom relented and took her.

When the invitation was given, her little girl wanted to go forward. The mom didn't really want to go forward, but she went down to the front with her little girl, who wanted to commit her life to Christ.

But something happened to her once she began to move toward Christ. When she got to the front, she dropped to her knees. "I felt His love," she wrote, "and I knew He loved me and had forgiven me."

I love that story. You see, as soon as this distraught woman began to move toward Jesus, Jesus rushed to help her. She needed help, and He responded to her. And that is the way He responds to all of us when we cry out to Him.

3. God has His purposes in the storms of life.

> He [Jesus] arose and rebuked the winds and the sea, and there was a great calm. (Matthew 8:26)

Maybe you are in a storm right now, and you have cried out for it to stop—but it hasn't. In fact, it has gotten worse. You say, "Why? Why is God allowing this?" There are no easy answers to that question, but know this: Where there are no trials in life, there will be no triumphs. It has been said, "The hammer shatters glass but it forges steel." And strangely enough, God often brings surprise benefits to our lives in the midst of our hardships. It is in the difficult places of life, the dark valleys and the steep paths, where we learn and discover truths we couldn't learn anywhere else.

Everyone loves Psalm 23, and many of us have committed it to memory. Its opening verses paint such a beautiful picture:

The LORD is my shepherd;
I shall not want.
He makes me to lie down in green pastures;
He leads me beside the still waters.
He restores my soul. (verses 1-3)

The scene is very soothing and pastoral, with sheep grazing on green grass and a cool stream winding through the meadow. It was written by a shepherd named David, who went on to become the first great king of Israel. David knew quite a bit about sheep, because he'd cared for them for years. He knew they were one of the dumbest animals on the face of the earth and needed the constant care and protection of the shepherd. And that is why he humbled himself and said, "The Lord Himself is *my* Shepherd."

But then David continued, saying,

Yea, though I walk through the valley of the shadow of death,
I will fear no evil;
For You are with me;
Your rod and Your staff, they comfort me.
You prepare a table before me in the presence of my enemies.
(verses 4-5)

"Hold on!" we say. "I signed up for green pastures and still waters, not for dark valleys. I don't like valleys. I don't do valleys. And what's this business about the presence of enemies?"

Yes, if you are a child of God, if you are one of His sheep, you will do the valleys as well as the green pastures. You'll endure the storms as well as relax in the gentle breezes. But He will be with you when you leave the pleasant pastures and quiet waters, and He will take care of you in the dark valleys. It is in and through those valleys that we will learn our most important lessons. After all, fruit doesn't grow on mountaintops, it grows in valleys.

The secret to making it through all the highs and lows of life is *knowing you are not alone and God will get you through whatever you are facing.*

How could David get through that valley? "Yea, though I walk through the valley of the shadow of death, I will fear no evil; *for You are with me*" (emphasis added). That is both the promise and the hope. God is with you, and He will be with you in your storm, no matter how severe.

Three Kinds of Life Storms

When it comes to the storms we face, I have placed them in three categories: correcting storms, protecting storms, and perfecting storms.

Correcting storms

Jonah faced such a storm when he rejected God's command and tried to run from the presence of the Lord on a ship bound for the edge of civilization. As a result, the Lord sent a great storm that rocked the reluctant prophet's world and put his life back on course. That storm was the result of Jonah's own disobedience to God and the sacred call on his life.

Many times we bring storms upon ourselves. If we deliberately do wrong or hurtful things, we will reap the repercussions of those acts. If you rob a gas station, get caught, and are thrown into jail, there's really no need to pray, "Oh Lord, why did You bring me into this storm?" It's a storm of your own making, and you will face the consequences of your own actions. Maybe you have neglected or mistreated your spouse, and he or she abandons you. You say, "Why is this storm coming on me?" The truth is you brought it on yourself. God is letting you reap what you sowed, so that you will change your actions.

Even in the consequences of your own foolishness or sin, however, God is at work. He will use the painful consequences of those sinful actions to discipline you and train you. The book of Hebrews counsels us to "Endure hardship as discipline; God is treating you as his children" (12:7, NIV). The discipline you face when you go astray is a reminder that you are a son or daughter of God.

> My child, don't make light of the LORD's discipline,
> and don't give up when he corrects you.
> For the LORD disciplines those he loves,
> and he punishes each one he accepts as his child.
> (Hebrews 12:5-6, NLT)

We don't discipline other people's children, do we? But we would *like* to sometimes, wouldn't we? You know what I mean. You're in a market and some child is having a total meltdown. The mom is flustered and simply doesn't know what to do or how to control her child. There are times when you'd like to step in, but you can't, because that's not your role. Disciplining is your legitimate role with your own children but not with someone else's.

When God disciplines us for rebelling against Him and going our own way, it's an indication that we really belong to Him, and that He loves us.

Back in the Twenty-Third Psalm, David wrote, "Yea, though I walk through the valley of the shadow of death, I will fear no evil; for You are with me; Your rod and Your staff, they comfort me" (verse 4).

I can see getting some comfort from the staff, but from the rod?

The staff was a long pole with a crook on the end, and the shepherd used it to pull a wayward sheep back into line. But a rod was basically just a club. How does a club comfort a sheep?

It comforts me to realize that God won't let me go too far astray without reminding me that I'm on the wrong path, that He loves me, and that He wants me to return to Him and remain close to Him. His discipline may hurt, but He knows exactly what it will take to get my attention. Sometimes He will use the staff, and sometimes He will use the rod.

Either way, "the Lord disciplines the one he loves" (Hebrews 12:6, NIV). He doesn't bring pain into your life because He is against you but because He is *for* you.

We can all think of times when we've pushed the envelope and walked right up to the edge of some cliff, wondering, "How far can I go?" That's when the Lord may answer us with His discipline, and say, "Not any further than this."

Did you know that sometimes a shepherd will actually take that rod and break a sheep's leg? We might say, "Oh, poor little sheepy." But it's better to have a broken leg than to become leg of lamb. If a sheep keeps wandering and wandering away from the flock, it will become easy prey for predators in the mood for a little fresh mutton. So the shepherd will have to take drastic measures to keep that wayward sheep from completely destroying itself. He will try to protect that wayward sheep—*and the others that follow it*—from its own foolish actions. This is another crazy thing about sheep; when one goes astray, the others will blindly follow along.

How stupid can one animal (or person) be? Pretty stupid when you're a sheep. That is why the Bible says in Isaiah 53:6, "All we like sheep have gone astray; we have turned, every one, to his own way."

In His love, then, God allows those correcting storms to come into our lives.

Protecting storms

The gospel of John gives an account of Jesus performing His most popular miracle: the feeding of the five thousand. With five loaves and two fish borrowed from a little boy's lunch, Jesus fed a multitude and had twelve baskets left over.

The people loved that miracle. So much so that they were talking about taking Jesus by force and making Him their king. Jesus, however, got His boys out of Dodge as quickly as possible. Why? Because He knew that the hearts of those people were dead wrong. They didn't want Him to be their Lord and Master, they just wanted a free lunch from then on. And knowing His disciples were already caught up in visions of grandeur and speculation about an earthly kingdom (with each of them in some prominent position), He wanted to remove them from that whole scene.

So what did He do? Matthew 14:22 says, "Immediately Jesus made His disciples get into the boat and go before Him to the other side, while He sent the multitudes away." And out in the middle of that lake, they encountered a storm.

It was a protecting storm. Protecting them from what? Themselves.

Sometimes God will bring difficulty to our lives to keep us from something worse! Be thankful God doesn't answer all of your prayers in the affirmative. Think back over some of your spontaneous prayers in unguarded moments:

"Lord, if You really love me You'll convince that girl to marry me."

"Lord, I'm begging You for that promotion at work."

"Lord, please help me to win the lottery, just this once."

The fact is, the Lord may know that answering those prayers with a yes might destroy you. The woman or man you wanted might have ruined your life and brought you great unhappiness. That promotion at work might have given you ulcers and a heart attack. Winning the lottery might have been the worst thing that could have ever happened to you and your family.

Sometimes God says no for our own good. And sometimes He sends a protecting storm to get us back on track.

Perfecting storms

These are probably the most common storms we face, coming to those who truly desire to follow Jesus. God has a work He wants to accomplish in these storms, and He seeks to produce a desired result. In his second letter to the church at Corinth, the apostle Paul wrote, "Our present troubles are small and won't last very long. Yet they produce for us a glory that vastly outweighs them and will last forever! So we don't look at the troubles we can see now; rather, we fix our gaze on things that cannot be seen. For the things we see now will soon be gone, but the things we cannot see will last forever" (2 Corinthians 4:17-18, NLT).

Yes, the storms will come, and God is doing a work in our lives. Sometimes we will be aware of that work and begin to see the results; at other times, we will struggle to see anything good come from those storms. Nevertheless, we can know God's intended outcome right from the get-go. Romans 8:29 (NIV) says, "For those God foreknew he also predestined to be conformed to the image of his Son, that he might be the firstborn among many brothers and sisters."

First and foremost, God's work in our lives is to conform us to the image of His Son, Jesus. When we cross over to the other side, in heaven, we will understand why God allowed certain storms to enter our lives and to last as long as they did.

You and I can't control our universe. I know. I've tried, and it doesn't work. We can't determine when a storm will start or when a storm will stop. All we can do is respond to the storm.

To me, one of the greatest examples of faith today is the life of a woman named Joni Eareckson Tada. She has faced incredible obstacles—more than you or I could imagine—with her faith intact. In fact, she has been a constant source of encouragement to millions of people all over the world. Back in 1967, as a vivacious, active seventeen-year-old, Joni dove from a raft into the shallow waters of Chesapeake Bay and broke her neck. As a result, she suffered a spinal cord fracture that paralyzed her from the neck down. Despite this severe disability, Joni has remained a shining light of hope and faith and encouragement to generations of people, both able-bodied and disabled. Through her books, her movie, her artwork (painted with a brush between her teeth), and her radio program, she has spread a message that says God can sustain us and use us in the midst of the worst storms of life.

Recently, after forty plus years in a wheelchair, Joni found out she has breast cancer. So in addition to being a quadriplegic, Joni now has to deal with surgery and weeks of chemotherapy. If she were to say, "I am really struggling with doubt right now; I don't know where God is," we would understand, wouldn't we? But in an interview she did with WORLD Magazine, she said she sees herself in a battle against powers and principalities that want her to despair, and emotions that take her down dark, grim paths.

Joni quoted Hebrews 10:38 (NIV): "My righteous one will live by faith. And I take no pleasure in the one who shrinks back." In the interview she said, "I don't want to be one of those that shrink back. I will not tarnish His name."

To help maintain her faith and her focus, she memorizes Scripture and spends time ministering to others who are disabled or in pain, weeping with those who weep. She says, "I keep thinking God is up to something big. How can I showcase Him to others?" Joni knows her life is on display, before multitudes of people and before the angels, and that others are learning by the way she responds to the heartbreaks and difficulties in her life. Acknowledging that she's in the middle of a battle, she asks, "How can I glorify God in this?"

Joni is a person just like we are, and she certainly has her moments of struggle, disappointment, and doubts. But for forty plus years, she has made it her goal to use her disability as a platform to glorify God.

You and I can do this, too, in the storms that hammer our lives. We need to say, "How can I bring glory to God through this? How can I point people to the Lord through this?"

Most storms don't last forever

For most of us, a storm will have a beginning, a middle, and an end. A child raised in the way of the Lord rebels against the Lord, then comes back to the Lord. A person faces a serious illness, gets treatment for the illness, and then recovers from the illness. It's beautiful when it happens that way, and we get to tell the story of God's goodness and kindness toward us in keeping us through the storm.

For others (Joni included), life itself can be a storm. In other words, the trial comes and never leaves, and the storm doesn't end until that man or woman steps into heaven. Yes, the storm will end for every child of God, but it may not end on this side of eternity. In heaven, we will see the big picture and begin to understand God's ultimate plan and purpose for our lives.

Sometimes Jesus stops the storm, but He is always with us in the storm

In the frightening storm out on the Sea of Galilee, Jesus chose to stop the storm altogether. First He rebuked the disciples, saying, "Why are you fearful, O you of little faith?" And then He simply stopped the storm in its tracks, and the sea became instantly like glass.

In Mark's version of the same story, we have this interesting detail. At the very beginning of that journey across the sea, Jesus had said to His disciples, "Let us cross over to the other side" (Mark 4:35).

Now if He had said to them, "Let's drown today in the middle of the Sea of Galilee," I don't know if I would have boarded that boat. But He didn't say that. He said, "Let's cross over to the other side." *He didn't promise them smooth sailing, but He did promise them a safe arrival.*

If Jesus says to you, "Let's go together to such and such a place," you will get there. Jesus gets to wherever He's going, and if we're with Him, we will too. In Isaiah 43:2 (NLT), we read, "When you go through deep waters, I will be with you. When you go through rivers of difficulty, you will not drown. When you walk through the fire of oppression, you will not be burned up; the flames will not consume you."

Are you in a storm right now?

Know this: He is walking through it with you.

"Be Muzzled!"

What could be more human than Jesus falling asleep in a boat after a day of hard work? And what could be more divine than rebuking a storm?

"Peace, be still!" (Mark 4:39).

In the original language, the Greek term translated "be still" literally means "be muzzled," as you would muzzle a hostile or unruly dog. But who was Jesus talking to? The storm itself? The clouds and rain? No, He was speaking to the power behind that storm: the devil himself. God did not initiate this storm, but He did allow it. Satan was behind the storm, and it was Satan who needed to be muzzled.

The storm stopped in an instant, and they made it to the other side, just as Jesus had told them they would.

Sometimes the devil will whisper in our ear, "You're never going to make it as a Christian. You're going to fail. You're going to crash and burn. You think you're going to heaven when you die? No, you'll never make it."

These are lies from the father of lies. If you have committed your life to Christ, you will make it to the other side *if you want to*.

In the book of Acts, Paul was on a ship being driven along by a huge storm. One night the Lord revealed to Paul that though the ship would be destroyed, not one soul would be lost. In other words, if they stayed with the ship until God brought it close to land, they would be saved. But if they chose to jump overboard during the middle of the storm, they wouldn't be safe at all.

In the same way, if you exercise your free will to turn against God and abandon your faith, you won't make it to heaven. However, if you want to make it to heaven, you will—not through your own effort, but because God will give you the strength to make it.

In Jude 24 we read, "Now to Him who is able to keep you from stumbling, and to present you faultless before the presence of His glory with exceeding joy." God Himself will keep you from falling!

In Philippians 1:6, Paul wrote, "Being confident of this very thing, that He who has begun a good work in you will complete it until the day of Jesus Christ."

In Hebrews 12:2, the writer described Jesus as "the author and finisher of our faith."

As we have said, storms will come into every life, for the believer and the nonbeliever alike. The rain will fall and the wind will blow. But it is only the child of God who has the promise that God will be with them, and that "in all things God works for the good of those who love him, who have been called according to his purpose" (Romans 8:28, NIV).

You will get through the storm, and you will get to the other side. You might have a rough voyage, but you will get there, because Jesus said you will.

CHAPTER NINETEEN
THINGS TO DO BEFORE THE END OF THE WORLD

et's imagine for a moment that we knew the day and hour Jesus was coming back again.

We don't, of course. Jesus said that no one would know that day or hour. But let's pretend for a moment that we did know. Let's say we had a sure word that Jesus Christ would come for us at 3:00 sharp tomorrow afternoon.

What would you be doing at 2:45?

I'm guessing we would be pretty "saintly" during those final fifteen minutes of waiting. We would be wearing our Sunday morning smiles and our Jesus-come-quickly attitudes. We would make sure we were "right" in our relationships with family and friends and that there was no unconfessed sin in our lives.

In reality, we *don't* know when He will come. It might very well be tomorrow afternoon at three o'clock. But it might not be. There is no way of knowing. But shouldn't we have that same smile and attitude, and live very day as though that were the day Christ could come?

The Bible has a great deal to say about the imminent (any moment) return of Jesus. There are 250 chapters in the New Testament, and Christ's return is mentioned no less than 318 times in those chapters. Statistically 1 in every 25 verses mentions the return of Jesus Christ.

Our Lord Himself spoke often of His return. In Mark 8:38, He said, "Whoever is ashamed of Me and My words in this adulterous and sinful generation, of him the Son of Man also will be ashamed when He comes in the glory of His Father with the holy angels." In John 14:2-3, Jesus said, "I go to prepare a place for you. And if I go and prepare a place for you, I will come again and receive you to Myself; that where I am, there you may be also."

I became a Christian in 1970, when a genuine revival known as "the Jesus Movement" was in full swing and many young people were coming to Christ. Back then, there was a lot of talk about the "soon return of Jesus." It was very popular to see bumper stickers on cars with slogans like "In case of rapture, this car will be unmanned." There were many other bumper stickers that essentially said, "Jesus is coming."

But here we are more than forty-five years later, and He still hasn't come.

There are those who say, "You guys were all wrong. He hasn't come and probably never will."

But here is what the Bible says in response: "The Lord isn't really being slow about his promise, as some people think. No, he is being patient for your sake. He does not want anyone to be destroyed, but wants everyone to repent" (2 Peter 3:9, NLT).

Back in 1970 I was praying that Jesus Christ would come back.

Aren't you glad God didn't answer my prayer? Maybe you or some of your loved ones have come to Christ since 1970. The fact is, the Lord is waiting for that one last person to be saved before He returns. I believe that man or woman—that last person to be redeemed from sin—is walking somewhere on the earth right now. The moment he or she turns to Christ and believes, we will be "outta here" and caught up to meet the Lord in the air.

Peter continued:

But the day of the Lord will come as unexpectedly as a thief. Then the heavens will pass away with a terrible noise, and the very elements themselves will disappear in fire, and the earth and everything on it will be found to deserve judgment.

Since everything around us is going to be destroyed like this, what holy and godly lives you should live, looking forward to the day of God and hurrying it along. (2 Peter 3:10-12, NLT)

If you really believe Jesus is coming, Peter said, it should impact the way you live. If it doesn't impact the way you live, you are completely missing the point.

Whenever a pastor starts a sermon series or writes a book about the last days, some people get very excited. They want to learn about Armageddon, the Antichrist, the Second Coming, the Rapture, and all the rest of it.

It's good to be interested. It's useful to study these things. *But the whole point of studying Bible prophecy is to seek to be ready for His return, prompting us to live godly lives.* If all we are interested in is names and dates and places and world events, as I have said, we've missed the point. As Jesus once told some of his critics, "You guys have strained out a gnat and swallowed a camel."

When the Thief Comes . . .

In Luke 12, Jesus spoke words that I believe were addressed directly to us, because we are living in the last days before His return.

Let your waist be girded and your lamps burning; and you yourselves be like men who wait for their master, when he will return from the wedding, that when he comes and knocks they may open to him immediately. Blessed are those servants whom the master, when he comes, will find watching. Assuredly, I say to you that he will gird himself and have them sit down to eat, and will come and serve them. And if he should come in the second watch, or come in the third watch, and find them so, blessed are those servants. But know this, that if the master of the house had known what hour the thief would come, he would have watched and not allowed his house to be broken into. Therefore you also be ready, for the Son of Man is coming at an hour you do not expect. (verses 35-40)

Do you see the "therefore" in verse 40? Whenever you see the word *therefore*, find out what it is there for. Jesus made a series of statements, and at the conclusion He said, "Therefore be *ready*." That's His whole point.

Peter, however, still felt a little fuzzy about the Lord's point. In verse 41 he said, "Lord, do You speak this parable only to us, or to all people?"

At that question, the Lord launched into another illustration, or parable.

> Who then is that faithful and wise steward, whom his master will make ruler over his household, to give them their portion of food in due season? Blessed is that servant whom his master will find so doing when he comes. Truly, I say to you that he will make him ruler over all that he has. But if that servant says in his heart, "My master is delaying his coming," and begins to beat the male and female servants, and to eat and drink and be drunk, the master of that servant will come on a day when he is not looking for him, and at an hour when he is not aware, and will cut him in two and appoint him his portion with the unbelievers. And that servant who knew his master's will, and did not prepare himself or do according to his will, shall be beaten with many stripes. But he who did not know, yet committed things deserving of stripes, shall be beaten with few. For everyone to whom much is given, from him much will be required; and to whom much has been committed, of him they will ask the more. (verses 42-48)

The idea Jesus was communicating is simply this: These servants did not know when their master was returning. Therefore, they were to be on the watch for him, alert and ready for his return.

Applying this parable to our lives, how should we live as believers in these last days?

How Should We Live as Believers in the Last Days?

We should be shining lights in a dark place.

Luke 12:35 says, "Let your waist be girded and your lamps burning." What does that mean? Back in those days they wore long, flowing robes with a belt cinched at the waist. When a person wanted freedom of movement, he could pull his robe up above his knees and retighten the belt, giving him more mobility. He could answer the door quickly. He could move quickly.

To have "your lamps burning" meant to have sufficient oil in them. In those days they carried a saucer-like device with a floating wick in it that could be lit. Think of it as the first-century equivalent of a flashlight. If we updated this verse for today, we would say, "Have fresh batteries in your flashlight." Or maybe, "Keep your smartphone charged."

I charge my iPhone every night so I will be ready for the day with all its demands and activities. It's become a valuable piece of equipment to me, so I wouldn't want to be in a situation where I needed to communicate with someone and my phone was red-lining. That's the idea in this passage. Be mobile. Be prepared. Be alert. Be ready for whatever. That is how the Lord wants us to live, even if He doesn't return as quickly as we had hoped.

We should be watching for His appearance.

Look at verse 37: "Blessed are those servants whom the master, when he comes, will find watching." Jesus says, "When you see these things begin to happen, look up."

As we look at what is happening in our world, we can have our Bible in one hand and our newspaper or iPad in the other, watching Bible prophecy being fulfilled right before our eyes. The Middle East is a powder keg with a short fuse lying next to a lit match. It could blow up at any time. So many things happening in our world point toward New Testament passages that describe the end times. This would include the nightmarish number of mass shootings that continues to rise in the United States, as well as the proliferation of gang-related violence that has now spread even to suburban areas.

We need to be ready to go.

Before I travel, I always pack my bags the day before. This is especially true if I have an early morning flight, as so many of my flights seem to be. I always have everything ready to go, because I want to be at the gate for my flight on time. In fact, I like to get there well ahead of time. My wife often says I leave for the airport way too early. But the peace of mind I gain from knowing I won't miss my flight is worth the inconvenience of getting up early.

That's the idea behind Jesus' admonition to gird our loins and have our lamps trimmed and shining. In other words, cinch up your belt, get all your stuff together, and make sure you have some extra batteries for your flashlight.

Here's another way to state it: Have your bags packed and your comfortable shoes by the door. Be ready to bolt out of there on a moment's notice.

To be ready for the return of Jesus is to be engaged in activities we would not be ashamed of if Jesus were to come. It's a good thing to ask ourselves periodically, "This place that I'm about to go to, this thing I'm about to do—would I be embarrassed or ashamed to be going there or doing that if Jesus were to come back?"

If the answer is yes or even maybe, then don't do it.

If you can't pray over your plans for the evening and ask God to bless them, then change your plans. If you can't write "Hallowed be Thy name" over your activity, then find another activity.

As I said earlier, believing Jesus is coming should cause us to live godly lives. In 1 John 3:2-3 (TLB), the apostle wrote, "Yes, dear friends, we are already God's children, right now, and we can't even imagine what it is going to be like later on. But we do know this, that when he comes we will be like him, as a result of seeing him as he really is. And everyone who really believes this will try to stay pure because Christ is pure."

We should not only be ready, but anxiously awaiting His return.

Notice Luke 12:36: "You yourselves be like men who wait for their master, when he will return from the wedding, that when he comes and knocks they may open to him immediately."

I used to have a dog who would sleep by the door to our bedroom. We didn't let him sleep in the room with us. One of the reasons for that was that he would sometimes have nightmares and start whimpering in his sleep. What in the world could he have been dreaming about? Cats chasing him? I don't know what his problem was, but his whining in the middle of the night would wake me up, so we made him sleep outside the room.

Because he couldn't be inside, with us, he would lean up against the door all night long. Sometimes I would think someone was knocking on the door because he was scratching. I know he leaned against the door because when I woke up in the morning and opened the door he pretty much rolled into the room. The moment he saw me, he became so excited. He would jump to his feet and start turning in circles. In his mind he was saying (I think), "Happy days are here again. The skies are blue. We're goin' for a walk! I know we are!" (I read a prayer somewhere that said, "Lord, make me the person my dog thinks I am.")

Bottom line? Be anxiously awaiting Jesus' return. Keep an eagerness in your heart whenever you think about it.

Have you ever waited for a visit from close friends? Maybe they were from out of town, and you hadn't seen them for a long time. Finally you got a text that said their plane had just landed. Then you got another text that said they were driving over, and would arrive in fifteen minutes. As the time got close, you started looking out your window, watching for the car. Then when it pulled into the driveway, you were so excited. And then—there they were! Walking up the stairs to your front door. You opened the door and threw your arms around them, because you were so happy to see their familiar faces. You hugged them tightly because you'd missed them.

That is how we should be waiting for the return of the Lord. Not hiding in a corner, dreading it, but looking forward to it with real anticipation. That is the idea being communicated in Luke 12.

We are to be working.

Verse 43 says, "Blessed is that servant whom his master will find so doing when he comes."

The servant is *doing* something. He doesn't just talk a good game, he gets up out of his chair and goes to work. He's willing to get his hands dirty. James 2:20 tells us that "Faith without works is dead." If watching is the evidence of faith, working is the evidence of faith in action. Watching for the Lord's return will help us prepare our own lives, but getting involved in the Lord's work will assure that we bring others with us.

Jesus was saying there is a *blessedness* in living this way. Luke 12:37 says, "Blessed [or happy] are those servants whom the master, when he comes, will find watching." *Happy.* We're not talking about a miserable, repressive, confining way to live when we speak about waiting for the return of the Lord. It is a happy, joyful, purposeful way to live.

C. H. Spurgeon said,

> *It is a very blessed thing to be on the watch for Christ. It is a blessing for us now. How it detaches us from this world. You can be poor without murmuring. You can be rich without worldliness. You can be sick without sorrowing. You can be healthy without presumption. If you are always waiting for Christ's coming, untold blessings are wrapped up in that glorious hope.*

In contrast to the believer who is watching and waiting, we see this portrait of an unprepared servant in verses 45-46: "If that servant says in his heart, 'My master is delaying his coming,' and begins to beat the male and female servants, and to eat and drink and be drunk, the master of that servant will come on a day when he is not looking for him." This servant is a picture of those who think they are believers but are not, because of the way that they live.

The apostle Paul added some very specific instruction about how we ought to live in light of our Lord's soon return:

And do this, knowing the time, that now it is high time to awake out of sleep; for now our salvation is nearer than when we first believed. The night is far spent, the day is at hand. Therefore let us cast off the works of darkness, and let us put on the armor of light. Let us walk properly, as in the day, not in revelry and drunkenness, not in lewdness and lust, not in strife and envy. But put on the Lord Jesus Christ, and make no provision for the flesh, to fulfill its lusts. (Romans 13:11-14)

Verse 11 is interesting; Paul wrote, "knowing the time." The J. B. Phillips paraphrase states it this way: "Why all this stress on behaviour? Because, as I think you have realised, the present time is of the highest importance—it is time to wake up to reality. Every day brings God's salvation nearer." We need to wake up. This phrase is used often in Scripture. In Ephesians 5:14, we read, "Awake, you who sleep, arise from the dead, and Christ will give you light."

Paul wasn't writing to nonbelievers here; these words are for Christians. He was addressing his remarks to genuine believers whose spiritual lethargy and laziness made them appear and act as though they had no life flowing through their spiritual veins. Paul was saying, "Wake up. Open your eyes. Splash some cold water on your face if you need to, but come awake!"

These words have more relevance to an older believer than a younger one. Many young Christians—not unlike young people— are full of energy. New believers are excited and want to win people to Christ and change their world. Older believers—not unlike older people—have a bit less energy and look forward to a "spiritual nap."

Napping to a young person is like a punishment. But to an older person, napping sounds like a pretty good idea. I don't know about you, but I get really sleepy after eating a big meal. After Thanksgiving dinner, I practically slip into a coma. Those of us who have known the Lord for many years may be in more danger of falling asleep spiritually than those who are younger in the faith.

Those who are young in the faith may recognize how vulnerable they are to the attacks of the enemy. They may say, "I have to be careful. I don't know that much, so I have to keep my guard up. I want to do things for the Lord."

The person who is older in the faith may smile indulgently and say, "Yes, yes, I heard all that years ago. I know, I know. Been there, done that." Mature believers, then, are in danger of becoming lazy and lethargic. Maybe we have feasted on the Word of God for years, hearing message after message, reading book after book, without any real outlet for what God has taught us in our lives.

We are actually in danger of falling asleep in the light. Resting on our laurels. Living in our past. To us, Paul would say, "Come awake! Come up out of the mist and fog. Open your eyes and get yourself ready, because the coming of the Lord is much nearer than you imagine!"

Paul continued and told us there are things we must get rid of in our lives, and things we must engage in, things we must put off, and something we must put on: "Cast off the works of darkness," he said, and "put on the armor of light" (Romans 13:12).

Have you ever fallen into a septic tank? Let's imagine for a moment (gross as that thought might be) that you actually did. May I offer a word of advice about those clothes you were wearing? They're over with! Don't wash them; you would only ruin your washing machine. *Just throw them out.* Those clothes are done.

Paul was saying, "Cast off the works of darkness as though you fell into a septic tank. Strip 'em off. Cast them from you. Get rid of them. And then in their place put on the armor of light. Trade in the old for the new. Suit up."

In Romans 13:13, the apostle was very specific about the deeds of darkness—the septic tank articles of clothing—we are to discard: "not in revelry and drunkenness, not in lewdness and lust, not in strife and envy."

We are to avoid drunkenness.

Here is a word for last-days believers. It is so simple, it's a no-brainer. But surprisingly, some people miss it: Don't party and drink.

That is what Paul meant by "revelry and drunkenness." These words used together picture drunken individuals walking—staggering—through the streets, party animals making a lot of noise. When people drink too much, often they get noisy, don't they? They start laughing at things that aren't funny. They start raising their voices. The more they drink, the more stupid they act, though they imagine themselves to be super-cool. They think they're acting sober, when in reality they're acting like drunks, because that is exactly what they are.

It almost seems ridiculous to bring something like this up. Why do I have to say Christians ought not to get drunk? Because there are some Christians who say, "I have the liberty to drink, and I know when to stop." Even so, people under the influence of alcohol do and say things they wouldn't otherwise do or say.

As believers, we want to be under the influence of our God. That is how we are to live as last-days believers—not being filled with spirits, but filled with the Holy Spirit.

We are to avoid immorality.

After telling us not to live in revelry and drunkenness, verse 13 continues, admonishing us to walk "not in lewdness and lust."

Lewdness comes from a Greek word that could simply be translated "bed." It had the same connotation in Paul's day that it does today. When someone says, "They went to bed together," we know that means they had sexual relations.

The word *lust* used here is one of the ugliest words in the Greek language. It describes someone who is not only given over to immorality but is incapable of feeling shame for his or her behavior. It speaks of shameless excess and the complete absence of restraint. This is a person who is not only living immorally but one who is shameless about it. The individual proclaims it and is proud of "sleeping around." This behavior is the very thing Hollywood promotes so aggressively today. They want to make bad things look good, and they want to make good things look bad.

Here's what scares me. I speak to people who profess to be believers and yet admit to having affairs or living with their boyfriend or girlfriend before marriage. Somehow they have managed to rationalize their actions and say they "have grace for it" or that "God is okay with it."

But God is not okay with it.

This is a sin against Him.

These are the things we want to be aware of or steer clear of. In the Pacific Northwest and other parts of the country, there are signs along the road warning of deer or elk crossings. If you're driving along one of those highways about twilight, you really need to keep your eyes open and use your peripheral vision. A deer could dart into the road in the blink of an eye and without warning be right in front of you. In the same way, we need to stay alert and not be sleepy or careless as we move along the highways of our lives. The moment we become spiritually lethargic is the moment we become vulnerable to these sins. Think of King David, a good and brave king of Israel who loved the Lord. He was a wonderful, powerful, and godly man. But after years of walking with the Lord, David allowed his spiritual life to slip into cruise control. Instead of leading his troops into battle, he sent his general, while David himself stayed home to relax.

In the book of 2 Samuel we read, "One late afternoon, David got up from taking his nap and was strolling on the roof of the palace. From his vantage point on the roof he saw a woman bathing. The woman was stunningly beautiful. David sent to ask about her, and was told, 'Isn't this Bathsheba, daughter of Eliam and wife of Uriah the Hittite?' David sent his agents to get her. After she arrived, he went to bed with her" (11:2-4, MSG).

David the warrior-king should have been leading his troops as he always did. Instead he thought, "I'm going to kick back for a while. I've worked so hard, led so many battles. I'm just going to take some time off."

He had no idea that his decision would make him more vulnerable to danger than if he had been on the front lines fighting the enemies of Israel. It reminds me of a kid I met years ago when I was speaking over in Hawaii. I ran into this young man in a mall, and we started talking. I asked him where he went to church.

"I used to go to church," he said.

"Why don't you go anymore?" I asked him.

"I am on a spiritual vacation," he told me.

"What exactly is that?"

"Well," he explained, "I'm just sort of taking some time off from my Christian life."

"That is no vacation, buddy. You can't take a vacation from God."

We had a long talk there in that mall, and he ended up recommitting his life to the Lord. He is still serving the Lord today, I'm happy to say.

The truth is, the moment you back off in the battle with Satan and his demons is the moment you become vulnerable. The moment you let yourself become sleepy and drowsy in your spirit is the moment you become spiritually weak, and the vultures begin circling.

That is why Paul told his young friend Timothy, "Flee the evil desires of youth and pursue righteousness, faith, love and peace, along with those who call on the Lord out of a pure heart" (2 Timothy 2:22, NIV).

Those words aren't directed only to young people. The text says to flee the evil desires of youth, but people can chase after those desires long after their teenage years. Maybe they haven't got the memo that they should have moved past the self-centeredness of youth by this time in their lives.

Also note Paul's use of the word *flee*. He didn't tell us to contemplate or entertain evil desires, but to run away from them! Dwelling on pornographic images, holding grudges, planning revenge—it's like throwing gasoline on a fire. Starve your sinful desires rather than feeding them. Stay away from anything that encourages immoral living.

Some of you may be thinking, "I don't live this way, Greg. I don't get drunk, and I'm not immoral." That's wonderful. God bless you. But here is one additional danger that may hit a little closer to home.

We should not compete or argue with one another.

The last warning Paul gave in Romans 13:13 is to live "not in strife and envy." What does this mean? Strife refers to persistent contention, bickering, petty disagreement, and enmity. This reflects a spirit of antagonistic competitiveness that fights to have its own way regardless of the cost or the effect on others. Really, Paul was talking about the desire to prevail over other people. A person who "strives" wants the highest prestige, the greatest prominence, the most recognition. He or she wants to be top dog and can't tolerate coming in second.

Have you ever played a game with someone who became unreasonably upset or angry over losing? You say, "Hey, it's just a game. Relax."

"I don't care. I'm going home."

Some people live their lives that way. They always have to be number one and can't bear losing. They know how to direct conversations toward themselves and seem to crave constant attention. They always have to be the star and be better than everybody else.

But this isn't right. We're not competing with one another in the body of Christ. Our opponents are not fellow Christians. Rather, our opponents are the world, the flesh, and the devil. Those are our enemies.

After listing "strife" as something to avoid, Paul then mentioned "envy." An envious person is someone who can't stand being surpassed and begrudges others' success and position. Have you ever felt that way?

I remember a Christmas from years ago. I was a little boy living in an apartment complex in Costa Mesa, and my friend and I were showing each other our presents. I was happy with what I got for Christmas until I saw what *he* got. I can remember it to this day. His present was a little plastic scuba diver. Basically, you wound it up and it sank to the bottom of the pool, with little bubbles coming out. This was 1960s technology and pretty lame by today's standards, but I'd never seen anything like it. I thought it was the coolest toy ever. Was it really better than the toy I had? No. But he had it and I didn't. As a result, I was no longer happy with what I had.

It sounds childish, I know. But do we really outgrow that attitude?

My neighbors are building an addition on their house.

My friend got a raise.

That couple I see on Facebook are always going somewhere wonderful.

My fellow pastor's ministry is booming. His church is growing by leaps and bounds.

It's been said that envy shoots at another and wounds itself. The only person you hurt when you allow envy into your heart is yourself. I hate to break it to you, but the person you are envying probably has no idea how you feel and most likely couldn't care less. You're the one who's suffering because of your bad attitude.

I heard about a crab fisherman who would carry the crabs he had caught in an open bucket. Someone said, "Why don't you put a lid on that bucket? Aren't you afraid your crabs will get out?"

"No," he replied. "The moment one of them starts to climb out, the others reach up and pull him back down."

Don't we do that sometimes? *How dare you succeed? How dare you do well? You come back down here with the rest of us where you belong!*

Focus your energies on becoming like Jesus.

After a number of negatives—beware of this, take care with that—Paul gave us something extremely positive to focus on. In Romans 13:14 it says, "Put on the Lord Jesus Christ, and make no provision for the flesh, to fulfill its lusts."

This refers to a practical, day-by-day choice to "put on" Jesus Christ, embracing Him again and again. It's just like in the morning when you put on your clothes and get ready for the day. Most of us pay at least some attention to how we look when we step out the door in the morning. Even the people who look like they don't care probably care more than many people do. (It's a cultivated careless look.)

You care about the way you look, and there's nothing wrong with that. We put our clothes on and expect them to do what we do and go where we go. Most of us like practical clothing—shirts and pants that breathe, move with us, and feel comfortable.

This is the idea of "putting on" the Lord Jesus Christ. It's inviting Him into every area of your life on a daily basis, asking Him to be a part of all you say and do and think. He goes with you where you go and becomes part of your decision-making process. He is Lord of every day of your life. He is Lord when you go to church, when you go to the beach, when you go to the movies, when you go out to dinner, when you head to work in the morning.

He is Lord of *all*. And if He is not Lord of all, He is not Lord at all.

I like the Phillips translation of Romans 13:14: "Let us be Christ's men from head to foot, and give no chances to the flesh to have its fling."

Someone might say, "But what if Jesus doesn't come in your lifetime, Greg? Isn't this chapter about "how to live in the last days" just so much wasted ink?

Let's just say for the sake of an illustration that Jesus doesn't come in my lifetime—or in yours. Does that mean we were wrong to believe He could come back at any moment? Is that a bad thing to live in readiness to meet God? To serve God? To refuse to get drunk? To avoid arguments? To try to walk as close as you possibly can with Jesus Christ?

Are those negative things?

No, they are very positive things.

I want to be ready to meet God. I want to remember that whether Jesus comes for me today or not, I could very easily leave this earth and go to Him. If we are ready to meet God at a moment's notice, we don't have to walk around in doubt and fear. As Paul said, "To live is Christ, and to die is gain" (Philippians 1:21). That doesn't mean a Christian has a death wish. It doesn't mean a Christian gets up in the morning and says, "I hope I die today." What it does mean is that if we do die today or tomorrow, we will meet God and don't have to be afraid.

If He comes for us, we will be ready.

If we go to Him, we will be ready.

Ready is a very happy way to live.

CHAPTER TWENTY
THE PRODIGAL SONS

ears ago we had a dog named Charmaine. My wife named him. I have no idea where she came up with that name.

Charmaine was a Blue Merle Collie, with a gray tint to his fur. He was a very handsome dog, but he was also a wayward dog. He was always finding a way to get loose and run away. How often? Maybe about every other day.

Again and again I would find myself walking up and down the streets of our neighborhood calling out, "Charmaine! Charmaine!" People would look at me as if to say, "What's up with this guy? Who is he calling for?"

Then I would get a call from the pound. "We found your dog." I would pay the fee, pick him up, and take him home. But two days later he would escape again, and I would be back at the pound, paying another fee, again reclaiming the errant dog. It happened about six times, it was getting very expensive, and Charmaine showed no signs of regret or repentance. It was all a game to him.

On maybe the seventh call from the pound, I told them over the phone, "Look, I'm tired of paying this fee. I will make you a deal. I'll come and pick up the dog, but this time I'm not going to pay you."

"I'm very sorry sir," they replied, "but unless you pay we cannot release the dog."

"Okay," I said, "you've just got yourself a new dog."

And that was the end of Charmaine the dog's brief career with the Laurie family. No doubt he was adopted into a loving family and perhaps, in time, he mended his wandering ways.

We got another dog, and this time my son Christopher named him. We had just returned from my grandmother's house where we had feasted on her heavenly homemade biscuits. Suitably inspired, Christopher named the new dog "Biscuit."

But Biscuit got out of the yard, too. And I found myself walking the streets again, calling out, "Biscuit! Biscuit!" The neighbors probably said, "Isn't that the same guy who yells 'Charmaine' all the time? Now it sounds like he's hungry. Throw him some bread."

It's one thing to lose an animal. (I have always loved animals and have no idea why my dogs run away.) But it is another thing altogether to lose a child. Have you ever been in an amusement park and turned around to find your child gone? That sense of awful panic sweeps over you like a cold wave. There is nothing worse.

In Luke 15, Jesus told a story about a father losing an adult son. The story is best known as the parable of the prodigal son. Only Luke records this parable, and through the years it has become one of the best-known stories Jesus told. The celebrated British author Charles Dickens said of this parable: "This particular story was the greatest short story ever written. It is so rich and inexhaustible, yet at the same time a child can grasp its basic truth."

I have preached this story to people all over the world, and it has resonated wherever I have gone. It doesn't matter what language or what culture or whether the people listening are rich or poor, young or old. Everyone gets it. It connects with people everywhere.

A Story in Three Movements

Luke 15 is really one story with three distinct movements to it. A triple play. Jesus portrayed God as a shepherd seeking a lost sheep, a woman looking for a lost coin, and a father waiting for a lost son. It's like looking at three different snapshots of God in quick succession. Each picture shows us something special, yet there is one common theme running through the entire chapter.

God is seeking lost people because God cares deeply about lost people.

That was an alien thought to the Lord's listeners in that day. In fact, it was a highly offensive thought. The Pharisees and teachers of the law were already upset with Jesus because of the people He'd been hanging out with. Luke 15:1-2 says, "Then all the tax collectors and the sinners drew near to Him to hear Him. And the Pharisees and scribes complained, saying, 'This Man receives sinners and eats with them.'"

These religious leaders, who claimed to know their Bible backward and forward, had apparently forgotten about the book of Genesis, where the Lord used to walk in the Garden with Adam and Eve in the cool of the day. Then after the first couple sinned and turned away from God, He called out to the man, "Adam, where are you?" This was God crying out for fellowship with man—seeking him and calling him home.

But the Jewish leaders of that day had forgotten all about that.

It's interesting that the first two stories about the sheep and the coin emphasize God as the seeker and the One who finds and rejoices. In the third movement of Luke 15, where a father loses his son, we see the story from the human point of view. That's the way Jesus chose to tell this three-part story: The first two movements are from the divine side—God coming after us. The third movement is from the human side—us coming to God.

Let's take a moment to read through the first two episodes of this moving story.

Then all the tax collectors and the sinners drew near to Him to hear Him. And the Pharisees and scribes complained, saying, "This Man receives sinners and eats with them." So He spoke this parable to them, saying:

"What man of you, having a hundred sheep, if he loses one of them, does not leave the ninety-nine in the wilderness, and go after the one which is lost until he finds it? And when he has found it, he lays it on his shoulders, rejoicing. And when he comes home, he calls together his friends and neighbors, saying to them, 'Rejoice with me, for I have found my sheep which was lost!' I say to you that likewise there will be more joy in heaven over one sinner who repents than over ninety-nine just persons who need no repentance.

"Or what woman, having ten silver coins, if she loses one coin, does not light a lamp, sweep the house, and search carefully until she finds it? And when she has found it, she calls her friends and neighbors together, saying, 'Rejoice with me, for I have found the piece which I lost!' Likewise, I say to you, there is joy in the presence of the angels of God over one sinner who repents." (Luke 15:1-10)

The lost sheep

In this first movement of the story, Jesus portrayed God as a shepherd seeking a single lost sheep—searching and searching until he finds it. You might think that a shepherd with a hundred sheep would say, "We have one missing? Well, you win a few and you lose a few. It's the cost of doing business." But no, after the shepherd found his count was off, he immediately left the ninety-nine and searched until he found the sheep. He brought back the wanderer draped around his neck, and called his friends to rejoice with him.

We are like that sheep that goes astray. And God does not rest until He finds us.

The lost coin

This coin, a *drachma*, represented a day's wages and was possibly part of the woman's life savings. More likely the coin was part of her wedding headband or garland. When a Jewish girl would marry, she would wear a headband of ten silver coins signifying that she was now a wife. Losing such a coin would be even more devastating than the lost value it represented, which would be bad enough. It would be more like us losing our wedding band—something we treasure with all our hearts.

Thankfully, even though I have always been prone to losing things, it would be humanly impossible for me to lose my wedding band. My finger is now so fat the ring can't budge. You would need the Jaws of Life to pry it off right now. But that's okay, because I don't want to take it off anyway.

So this woman had lost something of great symbolic and sentimental value to her. She didn't just shrug her shoulders and say, "Oh well, it will turn up." No, losing that coin was simply not an option. She searched and searched, turning the house upside down until she found it again.

What's the point of these two stories? *God loves to see lost people found.* Again, verse 10 says, "Likewise, I say to you, there is joy in the presence of the angels of God over one sinner who repents." Do you realize what this means? It means that every time a conversion to Christ takes place on earth it triggers an exultant celebration in heaven. To me, that establishes beyond all doubt the direct connection between heaven and earth.

I have heard it said, "People in heaven don't care what's happening on earth." I beg to differ. I do believe there is some knowledge in heaven of happenings here on earth. I'm not implying that people on the Other Side sit around in lawn chairs and peer through portals, watching all the events unfold on earth. But I do think there is an awareness. And every time a sinner comes to faith a wave of joy rolls across that heavenly landscape.

Notice that the text doesn't say there is joy *among* the angels when one sinner repents. It says, "There is joy *in the presence of* the angels." I think that means both angels and people in heaven. Is it possible, then, that when we are in heaven we might be aware of someone we influenced for Christ finally coming to faith? I like to think so.

I tell the story elsewhere in this book about a ninety-year-old man who accepted Christ in one of our Harvest Crusades. His Christian wife had prayed for him for their entire marriage, but he never came around. Finally, after she died and went to heaven, he gave his life to Jesus. When the victory shout over that conversion reverberated across heaven, do you think she might have been aware that her husband had finally believed? I think it's entirely possible.

This reminds me of something else. If God gets excited about lost people coming to faith, we should get excited, too. Or, to say it another way, if we are not concerned about lost people coming to faith and celebrating when they do, maybe there is something out of balance with us spiritually.

If we are in tune with God's Spirit and in tune with heaven, we will realize the wonder and the enormity of what has happened, and it will move us to joy.

The Lost Son

Then He said: "A certain man had two sons. And the younger of them said to his father, 'Father, give me the portion of goods that falls to me.' So he divided to them his livelihood. And not many days after, the younger son gathered all together, journeyed to a far country, and there wasted his possessions with prodigal living. But when he had spent all, there arose a severe famine in that land, and he began to be in want. Then he went and joined himself to a citizen of that country, and he sent him into his fields to feed swine. And he would gladly have filled his stomach with the pods that the swine ate, and no one gave him anything.

"But when he came to himself, he said, 'How many of my father's hired servants have bread enough and to spare, and I perish with hunger! I will arise and go to my father, and will say to him, "Father, I have sinned against heaven and before you, and I am no longer worthy to be called your son. Make me like one of your hired servants."'

"And he arose and came to his father. But when he was still a great way off, his father saw him and had compassion, and ran and fell on his neck and kissed him. And the son said to him, 'Father, I have sinned against heaven and in your sight, and am no longer worthy to be called your son.'

"But the father said to his servants, 'Bring out the best robe and put it on him, and put a ring on his hand and sandals on his feet. And bring the fatted calf here and kill it, and let us eat and be merry; for this my son was dead and is alive again; he was lost and is found.' And they began to be merry.

"Now his older son was in the field. And as he came and drew near to the house, he heard music and dancing. So he called one of the servants and asked what these things meant. And he said to him, 'Your brother has come, and because he has received him safe and sound, your father has killed the fatted calf.'

"But he was angry and would not go in. Therefore his father came out and pleaded with him. So he answered and said to his father, 'Lo, these many years I have been serving you; I never transgressed your commandment at any time; and yet you never gave me a young goat, that I might make merry with my friends. But as soon as this son of yours came, who has devoured your livelihood with harlots, you killed the fatted calf for him.'

"And he said to him, 'Son, you are always with me, and all that I have is yours. It was right that we should make merry and be glad, for your brother was dead and is alive again, and was lost and is found.'" (Luke 15:11-32)

Here was a young man who wanted independence from his father. In verse 12 he said, "Give me the portion of goods that fall to me." In Jewish law at this time the oldest son would receive two-thirds of the inheritance, with the rest divided among the younger children. There are two sons in this story, and the younger knew his older brother would get most of the estate. This would take place after the father had died and the will was read.

The younger son said to his dad, in effect, "Dad, I'm getting sick of waiting for you to die." In other words, "Dad, I wish you were already dead. I don't care about you. I don't care about your rules and regulations. I want to live! I want my money right now."

If we would have next read, "And the father smacked his son," it would have made perfect sense. Amazingly, however, the father acquiesced to his boy's request. What does this say to us? We are like the son or the daughter, and God is like the father. We say to God, "I'm going to leave." But God doesn't reply, "You aren't going anywhere, buckaroo. I'll put a leash on you if I have to!" No, He says, "I love you, so you are free to go."

That is mind-blowing. He has given us free will. We have a choice when it comes to a relationship with God. God will not force us to stay close to Him in fellowship if we don't want to. In our story, the father granted the son's request. The boy took the money and hit the road—probably without a glance over his shoulder.

Verse 13 says, "the younger son gathered all together." In the Greek that means he turned his inheritance into cash. That can't have been easy. It was very possibly a vast estate with buildings, livestock, hired help, and so much more. How do you liquidate a third that quickly? He probably sold it off at a steep discount because he was so impatient to have the money in his pocket.

What are some of the first things we might consider in this most famous of all our Lord's stories?

This was an inconsiderate and selfish young man.

He had grown up in a stable home with a godly, loving dad. Did he realize what a treasure he had? Obviously, he didn't. In the age and culture in which we live today, stable homes and two-parent households are a rarity. Even in the church today parents divorce and families fall apart at a rate not much different from those outside the church. More and more people in our culture are being raised in fatherless homes. We can take almost every social ill in our country today and directly connect it to the breakdown of the family—and specifically the absence of the father. In this home there was a father. A good father. He wasn't a raging alcoholic and he wasn't an absentee parent. This was a secure home and family with a hands-on dad who loved and cared about his boys.

The father was caring, nurturing, and affectionate.

When the son came dragging back, the father welcomed him— and it wasn't with a half-smile and formal handshake. The dad embraced his boy, and kissed him again and again. In so many homes fathers can be aloof and disconnected. Not this father.

Theirs was an affluent home.

How do we know? For one thing, they had hired servants performing all sorts of tasks on the property. This boy would have lived on a spectacular estate with great food and the finest clothes. He didn't want for anything. He had everything he needed in life and more.

There was faith in this home.

Maybe the father even read the Bible to his two boys and led the family in prayer. But the young son didn't appreciate that. He may have thought, *I'm tired of all this religion. I'm getting out of here the first chance I get. See a little of the world. Spread my wings.* I don't think the boy had really thought through the implications of what he was about to do. He just wanted a ticket to ride.

This is a picture, of course, of a man or woman leaving God. This is a portrait of a backslider. By the way, that word is biblical. In Jeremiah 2:19 (NIV) God says, "Your wickedness will punish you; your backsliding will rebuke you. Consider then and realize how evil and bitter it is for you when you forsake the LORD your God." Then in Jeremiah 3:22 (NIV) God calls out, "Return, faithless people; I will cure you of backsliding."

What is a backslider? We think of a backslider as someone who has pretty much abandoned their faith. Maybe they've stopped attending church, and even say, "I don't follow Christ anymore." I would suggest to you, however, that a person can be a backslider and still be in church.

Someone has said, "The Christian life is like a greased pole. You are either climbing or slipping." In other words, the moment you stop growing as a believer is the moment you potentially begin going backward again. Someone might say, "I still go to church when I can find the time. I still read the Bible. (By the way, where did I leave that Bible? I haven't seen it for a few weeks.) I still obey God—unless, of course it conflicts with what I really want to do."

Backsliding is not something you plan on. It happens when you begin neglecting your spiritual life. You don't call up your buddy some evening and say, "Hey, do you want to backslide tonight? Let's totally turn our backs on God and ruin our lives. I will pick you up at 7:00." That's not the way it happens. It's more like relaxing your grip a bit. Backing off a little. Not moving forward as you ought to. Then the backsliding process begins.

One of the first steps to backsliding is saying, "Not me. I will never backslide." But that is a dangerous attitude. As Scripture says, "Let him who thinks he stands take heed lest he fall" (1 Corinthians 10:12). You have the potential within you to backslide and worse, and so do I. It's like the line from the old hymn, "Prone to wander, Lord, I feel it, prone to leave the God I love."

The alcoholic doesn't set out to become one. It just happens as life rolls along. For whatever reason, someone begins to drink a lot of alcohol. A woman says, "I need a drink in the morning to get started." A man says, "I have a drink with the guys after work. If I don't they'll think I'm stuck up or strange." Then one day, these two individuals find they have a problem with drinking.

In the same way, most married men and women don't plan on having affairs, breaking up their marriages, and destroying their homes. They engage in a little flirting, just for the fun of it. Nothing serious. But one thing leads to another, and suddenly they're involved in a much deeper way than they ever intended.

Every backslide begins with a first step. A shortcut off the main path. A little side road that you never intended to follow very far. But then you wake up and find yourself a long, long way from God.

With his pockets bulging with cash, the younger brother took to the road. And what a popular guy he became as he hit the town! He had his posse. He had his money. He had lots of pals until the money ran out. Then they faded away. As the older brother said when the boy came home, the younger son had spent his money on hookers. And probably on expensive booze. Was it fun while it lasted? Maybe. But it didn't last. And suddenly the ATM was rejecting his debit card everywhere he went.

He discovered the emptiness of life without his father.

In Luke 15:14 we read that there was "a severe famine in that land, and he began to be in want." Was it because he had blown his money? Yes. But that wasn't all of it. He had also lost his support system. His family was gone. His friends were gone. If he'd had a girlfriend, she had packed up and left, too, probably without leaving a note or a forwarding address. Suddenly, this young man had nothing to fall back on. This is why some people who reach this stage take their own lives. They lose hope, and no one can live very long without hope.

Desperate for someone to help him and overcome with hunger—probably for the first time in his life—he hired out to a local farmer. As Scripture puts it in verse 15, "He went and joined himself to a citizen of that country, and he sent him into his fields to feed swine." We don't know anything about this "citizen" except that he didn't want the prodigal hanging out with him. The term "joined himself" could be translated "glued himself." In other words, the kid came to this guy's door and was clinging to this guy for help. Maybe hanging onto his leg, pleading.

This may have been his first real job. Slopping hogs. Can you imagine this? He went from the lap of luxury to a pigpen. And for a good Jewish boy, this wasn't a very kosher thing to be doing.

Sometimes we pray for our friends or even our children to come to know the Lord and get their life straightened around. Then something bad happens to them. They get busted for a sin or even a crime. They get thrown out of school, fired from a job, or run into trouble with the law. We say, "Oh no, what's going on, Lord? Haven't I been praying for this person? Haven't I been asking You to get through to them?"

Could it be that the Lord is actually answering your prayers? Some people will simply never come around until they get the wake-up call—and begin to reap what they have sown. As long as they keep getting away with their rebellious lifestyle, with no ramifications and no penalties, they imagine themselves to be free as a bird. Then one day those chickens come home to roost, and that is the moment when God finally gets their attention.

That is what happened to the prodigal. He suddenly came to his senses. His eyes were opened. Luke 15:17-19 says, "But when he came to himself, he said, 'How many of my father's hired servants have bread enough and to spare, and I perish with hunger! I will arise and go to my father, and will say to him, "Father, I have sinned against heaven and before you, and I am no longer worthy to be called your son. Make me like one of your hired servants.""

Here's an interesting little twist in the story. The young man was talking about the people who worked for his father. These would probably be day laborers, who worked from sunrise to sunset. Most such laborers would be paid a minimum wage, barely enough to survive. But the young man reflected, "My father's hired servants have bread enough and to spare." The father overpaid the day laborers because he was a generous, caring man. He no doubt had a reputation as a good man to work for—and an even better guy to have as your dad.

Now the young man was thinking, *This is insane. Why did I ever leave?* One day he woke up and couldn't wait to get away from his father's home. And then on another day he woke up and couldn't wait to get back!

This is what happens to people. They say, "I hate the church. It's full of hypocrites. Everyone is so judgmental. I want to go out there in the world where people just accept you as you are."

So they leave. But before long they have been chewed up and spit out and betrayed by their new friends. And some of them begin thinking, *I sure miss the church. It was really loving there. People cared about me. It wasn't perfect, but looking back, it was a good place to be.*

By and large, there is nothing like a good church. Yes, every church has its hypocrites. I always like to say, "Don't let that stop you. There's always room for more!" Seriously, anywhere we find people we will find some hypocrisy. But there is nothing out there in today's culture like God's people gathering together. The world can't offer us anything like a genuine worship experience. We won't find truth after truth and insight after penetrating insight like we will in God's Word as it is taught and proclaimed. The church is the only organization Jesus started, and Jesus said that the "gates of hell will not prevail" against it.

As the prodigal was practicing the speech he would give to his dad at the front door, he used the phrase, "I have sinned against heaven and before you." In the Greek, this could be translated, "I have sinned *into* heaven." In other words, his sins stank to high heaven, and he knew it.

So the prodigal retraced his steps. He went to the dogs . . . fed the hogs . . . and homeward he jogs.

Homecoming

Meanwhile, back at the ranch, there's the father in the story. In verse 20 we read, "But when he was still a great way off, his father saw him and had compassion, and ran and fell on his neck and kissed him." This would indicate that the father was watching for the boy. I picture him sitting on the front porch, probably in his old rocking chair, looking off toward the horizon to the end of the road, hoping and praying and longing for the day when he would see his boy again.

Maybe he would walk through his younger son's room at times, looking at mementos of their life together and remembering events from the boy's growing-up years. How they used to play together, learn together, go through hardship together. He longed for the young man's return.

Then someone appeared on that horizon, someone who immediately looked familiar, even at a distance. The old man's heart leaped. He bolted to his feet and began to run—not walk—to the forlorn-looking figure trudging down the road. The word in the Greek translated *ran* is actually the word for "sprint." This old, silver-haired landowner was actually sprinting down the road. What makes this more amazing is that in this culture it was considered undignified for an older man to run. What's more, he would have had to hike up his robe above his knees as he ran, and this was another cultural no-no. It was considered shameful for people of a certain age to expose their legs. But at that moment, this overjoyed dad couldn't have cared less.

They embraced in the middle of the road, and we have to imagine the boy smelled more than a little gamey. Have you ever caught a whiff of someone who hasn't bathed for quite a while—like a month? How about someone who has been hanging out with pigs for weeks on end? You could probably smell this kid a block away. He was covered with sweat and filth, and had a strong stench to him.

It would be easy to imagine the dad stopping about four feet away and saying, "Whoa! I'll tell you what, son. Go take a bath and then I will hug you." But no. The father threw his arms around his son right then and there and gave that young man the biggest bear hug he'd ever had in his life. This is a reminder that when we come to Jesus Christ, He accepts us just as we are, but He doesn't leave us that way.

The son had been practicing his speech all the way home, but when the reunion came, it was the dad who did the speaking: "But the father said to his servants, 'Bring out the best robe and put it on him, and put a ring on his hand and sandals on his feet. And bring the fatted calf here and kill it, and let us eat and be merry'" (verses 22-23).

One modern translation says, "They had a barbeque." That is exactly the picture. It was party time. They put together a makeshift band, the music started flowing, the meat was sizzling on the barbeque, and the celebration really started to roll.

The theme of this chapter, remember, is the joy of God! The shepherd had joy when he found the lost sheep. The woman had joy when she found the lost coin. There is great joy in heaven over one sinner who changes their mind over the way they have been living and turns toward God.

But What's with the Older Brother?

Now we come to a strange twist in the story—and this is the part of the parable that usually gets left out. What happens next is why I titled this chapter "The Prodigal *Sons*." Let's look at Luke 15:25-32 in a different translation:

Meanwhile, the older son was in the fields working. When he returned home, he heard music and dancing in the house, and he asked one of the servants what was going on. "Your brother is back," he was told, "and your father has killed the fattened calf. We are celebrating because of his safe return."

The older brother was angry and wouldn't go in. His father came out and begged him, but he replied, "All these years I've slaved for you and never once refused to do a single thing you told me to. And in all that time you never gave me even one young goat for a feast with my friends. Yet when this son of yours comes back after squandering your money on prostitutes, you celebrate by killing the fattened calf!"

His father said to him, "Look, dear son, you have always stayed by me, and everything I have is yours. We had to celebrate this happy day. For your brother was dead and has come back to life! He was lost, but now he is found!" (NLT)

What part does this angry older brother play in the story? Remember the context of why Jesus told this parable in the first place. The sinners, godless, and riff-raff of society—the broken, destitute, and hurting—had been flocking to Jesus, cheering Him on, and listening to His teaching with delight. He was a big celebrity with the drunks, prostitutes, and hated tax collectors, and they were finding all they needed and craved in a relationship with the living God. Meanwhile, the religious leaders of the day were scandalized that Jesus would have anything to do with such people. How could He be a teacher sent from God when He spent time with sinners? With shocked, angry voices, they were saying to Him, "How dare you!"

In reply Jesus said, "Let me tell you a story . . . and see if you can find yourself in it."

The Pharisees and teachers of the law had a sense of entitlement. Just as the prodigal son in the story is a picture of the sinner coming to Christ, the older brother is a picture of the person who has never left the church, but whose heart has turned away from God.

You can be a faithful church attender and a backslider. You become one of those judgmental people who look down on others who don't dress right, talk right, or behave right (as you define "right").

This could happen very easily to any of us as we grow older. You want the whole world to cater to you. You want everybody to bow to your needs. You want everybody to give you what you want. You resist change. You don't care about reaching lost people or impacting the culture. In fact, you resent all those "new people" and the fact that you can't find a parking place anymore. And when that longwinded preacher begins giving an invitation, that's your cue to slip out the back door and beat the crowds and the traffic.

Guess what? You just became the older brother. If there is a party and joy in the church and in heaven, you want nothing to do with it. And this is a form of backsliding. You become as much of a prodigal as the one who has rebelled and left the church.

If your heart doesn't leap when you see a lost person come to Christ, you need to go to God and say, "God, melt and change my heart! I am in a wrong place right now."

The whole thrust of Luke 15 is to remind us that God is passionate about reaching people outside of Jesus Christ, and He wants us to be passionate, too.

God help us not to fall into the trap of the older brother, more concerned about our comfort, convenience, and reputation than about hurting men and women who need to hear about a God who loves them and a Savior who laid down His life for them.

CHAPTER TWENTY-ONE
A HELLFIRE AND BRIMSTONE MESSAGE

Not long ago on a Christian television show, the interviewer asked me why I speak so much about eternity.

"When I've watched you preach on your TV program or at a crusade," he said, "I've noticed whatever topic you're dealing with, you always come back to eternity."

I'd never really noticed that before. Since my son went to heaven in 2008, I suppose it's truer now than ever.

"So why do you do that?" he asked me. "Why do you always come back to the eternal in your messages?"

After thinking about it for a moment, I answered, "I guess when you get down to it, it's the most important thing there is."

As a pastor, I want to teach the Word of God and help people grow in their faith as followers of Jesus. I want them to learn how to know God's will, resist temptation, build a great marriage, walk in integrity, and all those things we talk about as pastors and teachers. But when it's all said and done, the most important thing to me is intercepting people on their way to hell and pointing them toward heaven instead.

I want people to change their eternal address.

So that is why I do what I do.

Most people believe in some kind of heaven, and most also believe they're going there. Statistics show that for every American who believes he or she is going to hell, there are 120 who believe they'll end up in heaven.

That is a direct contradiction, however, to what Jesus said: "Enter by the narrow gate; for wide is the gate and broad is the way that leads to destruction, and there are many who go in by it. Because narrow is the gate and difficult is the way which leads to life, and there are few who find it" (Matthew 7:13-14).

No matter how fervently we might wish otherwise, Jesus taught that most people are not headed to heaven. If we believe the Bible, we have to accept this simple fact. Most people are actually headed to hell, though none of us likes to hear that.

It's interesting to me that even though many in our culture don't believe in a literal hell, people will use the word to punctuate their sentences. Someone says, "All hell just broke loose." Or maybe, "He really gave me hell." Or even, "You go to hell."

That last phrase is always used as an insult. But at the same time, if someone had a great time somewhere, he or she will say, "Man, we had a hell of a good time together."

I actually had a guy come up to me after a message on a Sunday morning, shake my hand, and say, "That was a hell of a speech, Reverend." I laughed. I didn't know what else to do. I suppose in his own way he was trying to compliment me. I said, "Well, I was hoping it was a heaven of a speech." But I understood what he was saying.

It's funny how people will say to another person, "You can go to hell," but at the same time they will say, "I don't believe a place called hell actually exists." I guess it's not quite as effective to yell at someone, "You can just go to a place that doesn't exist!"

Why do people say, "Go to hell"? Because deep down inside, even if you are a nonbeliever, you know there is a hell.

Hell is a real place, but because we are uncomfortable with that idea we make jokes about it. Did you know there is an actual town in Michigan called Hell? Can you imagine? It was founded in 1841 by a man named George Reeves, who had discovered a low, swampy place in southeast Michigan and didn't know what to name it. Someone said to him, "What do you want to call it?" And he replied, "I don't care. Name it Hell if you want to."

And so they did. Hell, Michigan.

People feel free to joke about the topic of hell. Comedian Woody Allen said, "Hell is the future abode of all people who personally annoy me."[5] Jim Carey said, "Maybe there is no actual place called hell. Maybe hell is just having to listen to our grandparents breathe through their noses when they are eating sandwiches."[6]

But there is a hell. A real hell. And it's no joke.

The fact of the matter is that Jesus Christ spoke more about hell than all of the other prophets and preachers of the Bible put together. Most of the teaching we have on the topic of hell was given to us by Christ Himself.

That fact surprises some people. They say, "Really? Wasn't Jesus the very personification of love and mercy and grace? Why would He talk about hell?"

For that very reason! It's precisely because He was and is the personification of love and grace and mercy that He doesn't want any man or woman uniquely made in His image to spend eternity in this place called hell. And Jesus, being God, knows about it because He has seen it with His own eyes. As a result, He carefully, sternly, and repeatedly warned us about its existence.

It has been estimated that of the forty parables Jesus told, more than half of them deal with God's eternal judgment and hell. Make no mistake about it; there is a real hell for real people.

J. I. Packer said, "An endless hell can no more be removed from the New Testament than an endless heaven can."[7] It is there.

It's interesting to me how the concept of judgment in the afterlife becomes more or less popular, depending on the time in which we are living. I think belief in hell probably went up after 9/11, because when some great evil takes place, people tend to believe in a place of final retribution. But when things aren't going as badly, and the memory of mass murderers fades a little, then belief in hell actually starts to tail off.

Years ago John Lennon famously sang, "Imagine there's no heaven. It's easy if you try. No hell below us. Above us only sky."

Dear John, we can "imagine" all we want, but it won't change eternal realities. There is a heaven. And there is a hell.

The Second Death

The Bible teaches that there are two deaths—one physical and one spiritual. Furthermore, Jesus warned that we are to fear the second death more than the first! In Revelation 20:14 we read, "Then Death and Hades were cast into the lake of fire. This is the second death." In Revelation 21:8 (NLT), the One who sits on the throne says, "But cowards, unbelievers, the corrupt, murderers, the immoral, those who practice witchcraft, idol worshipers, and all liars—their fate is in the fiery lake of burning sulfur. This is the second death."

The second death is hell, which is eternal separation from God. One commentator wrote, "Eternity to the godly is a day that has no sunset. Eternity to the wicked is a night that has no sunrise."

The Bible describes hell in different ways.

Hell is pictured as a garbage dump.

One picture we have of hell in the Bible is that of a garbage dump—but not like any garbage dump we have ever seen. I don't know if you have ever taken your trash to the dump and looked around at all the rubbish and castoff items. You might see an old refrigerator, a television, and maybe even part of a car sticking out of the garbage. You think about how hard people must have worked at one time to obtain those items, and now here they are, moldering in a landfill.

But the dump in New Testament days, also known as Gehenna, was far worse than that. People would not only throw their trash and rubbish there, but it was a place where they could toss in dead bodies as well, and it was constantly smoldering and burning. You can imagine what a horrific place this was.

So Jesus took the picture of Gehenna, the dump if you will, and used it to describe hell.

Hell is pictured as a prison.

One of the clearest pictures Christ gave of hell was that of being incarcerated. He told a parable of a king's servant who was sent to jail for cruel and unforgiving behavior, then the Lord added this warning: "This is how my heavenly Father will treat each of you unless you forgive your brother or sister from your heart" (Matthew 18:35, NIV).

I don't know if you have ever been to prison. I receive letters on occasion from people in prison who listen to our radio broadcast.

When we held a crusade in South Dakota, I had the honor of receiving a special blanket from some Christian Native Americans there. The man who gave me the blanket first heard the gospel on our radio broadcast in prison and came to Christ. Now he is serving the Lord and preaching the gospel. That was an encouraging thing to hear.

In this prison called hell, however, there will be no opportunities to repent or to find release. It will be too late for that.

Hell is pictured as a fire that never stops burning.

The most well-known picture given to us in Scripture is of hell likened to a fire that never stops burning. That brings us to a story in Luke 16, where Jesus spoke of hell as an unquenchable fire.

The Story of Lazarus and the Rich Man

Jesus told many parables or stories to make His points clear, but I don't believe the account in Luke 16 is a parable. I think it's a true account of real people and real events.

Why do I believe that? Because Jesus used actual names in the story, and He didn't do that in His parables. So, we might describe this as a behind-the-scenes look into the invisible world. If you have wondered what happens on the other side when believers and nonbelievers pass into eternity, here is a glimpse into those realms provided by Christ Himself.

There was a certain rich man who was clothed in purple and fine linen and fared sumptuously every day. But there was a certain beggar named Lazarus, full of sores, who was laid at his gate, desiring to be fed with the crumbs which fell from the rich man's table. Moreover the dogs came and licked his sores. So it was that the beggar died, and was carried by the angels to Abraham's bosom. The rich man also died and was buried. And being in torments in Hades, he lifted up his eyes and saw Abraham afar off, and Lazarus in his bosom.

Then he cried and said, "Father Abraham, have mercy on me, and send Lazarus that he may dip the tip of his finger in water and cool my tongue; for I am tormented in this flame." But Abraham said, "Son, remember that in your lifetime you received your good things, and likewise Lazarus evil things; but now he is comforted and you are tormented. And besides all this, between us and you there is a great gulf fixed, so that those who want to pass from here to you cannot, nor can those from there pass to us."

Then he said, "I beg you therefore, father, that you would send him to my father's house, for I have five brothers, that he may testify to them, lest they also come to this place of torment." Abraham said to him, "They have Moses and the prophets; let them hear them." And he said, "No, father Abraham; but if one goes to them from the dead, they will repent." But he said to him, "If they do not hear Moses and the prophets, neither will they be persuaded though one rise from the dead." (verses 19-31)

Jesus mentioned the name of the beggar, Lazarus. The wealthy man in the story is described as "a certain rich man."

One man owned everything, yet possessed nothing.

The other owned nothing, but inherited everything.

One went to comfort, the other went to torment.

The believing man, Lazarus, was ushered by the angels into the presence of God, into a place called Paradise.

By the way, prior to the arrival of Jesus and His death and resurrection, when a person died in faith he or she went to a place called "Paradise," or to "Abraham's bosom," as the King James Version describes it. When Jesus was crucified and the man on the cross next to Him came to his senses and asked the Lord for mercy, Jesus said to him, "I assure you, today you will be with me in paradise" (Luke 23:43, NLT).

So that thief who had been crucified next to Jesus went into a place of waiting, a realm of bliss and comfort called Paradise. That was before Jesus had been raised from the dead. But the Bible says that after His death and resurrection, a believer who dies goes straight to heaven and into the presence of God. The apostle Paul told us that to be absent from the body is to be present with the Lord (see 1 Corinthians 5:6-8).

One other point about that thief on the cross. We might describe what happened to him as a "deathbed conversion," and I hope this encourages you to never stop praying for friends and loved ones who are still outside of Jesus Christ. Time and again, I've heard glorious stories of people who have come to the Lord right before passing into eternity.

On the other hand, sometimes we know of someone who died and who we fear is in hell right now. I've heard people say, "That person is in hell."

The truth is, you and I don't know who is in hell. We're in no position to say. Now I do think we can authoritatively say who is in heaven. If an individual has put his or faith in Christ, we can say, "They're with the Lord now." The Bible assures us of this. But who are we to say what may or may not have happened to an individual in those final seconds before leaving this life? I know this: If a person cries out to Jesus in repentance with their last breath or last fading thought, God will forgive them and accept them into heaven. And remember, no one wants to save a person more than the Lord Jesus Christ.

But what happens if a person truly rejects God's salvation to the very end? We have a picture of that in this story Jesus told in Luke 16.

Tormented

The rich man also died and was buried. And being in torments in Hades [or hell], he lifted up his eyes and saw Abraham afar off, and Lazarus in his bosom. (verses 22-23)

The sin of this man was not his wealth; the sin of this man was that he had no time for God. You might say he was possessed by his possessions. The Bible says he "fared sumptuously" and "was clothed in purple and fine linen" (verse 19).

In that culture, purple was the color of royalty. Clothing makers would crush a special worm and use the dye to produce luxurious garments worn only by the richest of the rich. And this man was clothed in purple and fine linen from head to foot. Again, the account tells us that this man "fared sumptuously every day." That's another way of saying he had a daily, nonstop banquet going on. He was apparently really into food and had unlimited resources to eat whatever he wanted.

It was a different story for the beggar lying out by his front gate. His name was Lazarus, and he was weak, covered with sores, and severely impoverished—to the point of starvation. Apparently, he had been living off the scraps from the rich man's table—when he could get them.

In those days, people didn't eat with a knife and fork. They didn't use utensils at all. They would pick the food up with their hands using bits of bread, and then they would wipe their hands on pieces of bread and throw them on the floor for the dogs to eat.

That was Lazarus's diet. We are also told that he was carried to the rich man's estate and laid at his gate, which would imply that he was either disabled or maybe so weak and sick that he couldn't walk.

Surely, the rich man saw Lazarus's situation. He could have invited him to his table or, at the very least, sent a proper meal out to him. But he cared nothing about Lazarus. His mind was filled with "looking out for number one" and having his nonstop feast of pleasure.

But then death came.

And death is the great equalizer.

When the rich man died, it probably made all the papers. It was a big deal for a few hours. Then the poor man died, and the event didn't even make a ripple. No one really cared about him. But God did! And Lazarus was ushered into Paradise by angels.

It was now time for the rich man to face the repercussions of a life that had no room for God. And he was going to find out that it wasn't so glamorous on the other side.

Malcolm Forbes, one of the world's wealthiest men, said shortly before his death, "The thing I dread most about death is that I know I will not be as comfortable in the next life as I was in this one."[8] I have no idea where Mr. Forbes was at spiritually, but for the sake of a point, if you don't know God, you can be sure it won't be as comfortable on the other side.

What Do We Learn from This Story?

People in hell suffer.

That this man spoke of torment indicates that suffering is a very real thing in the hereafter. In fact, the word *torment* is used four times in the text of this story. People in hell are fully conscious, and they are in pain. It doesn't say this man went to purgatory. There is no such thing as a place called purgatory. Nor was he reincarnated as a higher or a lower life-form. Once you pass from this life, you pass into eternity—into either heaven or hell. This man was in hell.

Once people are in hell, they can't cross over to heaven.

Sometimes people will say, "I've got the gift of gab, and when I stand before God, me and the Man Upstairs will sort this out." But there will be no more sorting it out. It will be too late for that; once we are in eternity there is no changing things.

It's different now. While there is life, it is still possible to change things—including your eternal destination! There are no chances after death, but thousands before.

The Bible says, "It is appointed for men to die once, but after this the judgment" (Hebrews 9:27). Physical death is a separation of the soul from the body and constitutes a transition from the visible world to the invisible world. For the believer, it is entrance into Paradise, into the presence of Jesus. For the nonbeliever, death marks the entrance into Hades. Physical death is not the end of existence, but only a change in the state of existence.

When people are in hell, they are conscious and fully aware of where they are.

They are also aware of where they were. In heaven, as we will discuss later, we will still be ourselves. We will still know what we knew on earth, but far more. We will be aware of where we came from and of where we are. In the same way, in hell people will be cognizant of where they came from and where they are, as the rich man demonstrated when he spoke about his five brothers in Luke 16:28. "I have five brothers," he said, "and someone needs to testify to them so they don't come to this place of torment."

In a way this man was blame-shifting. It's as though he were saying, "Hey, I really didn't know about this. No one warned me!" Abraham, however, corrected him in verse 29: "They have Moses and the prophets; let them hear them." And the man replied, "No, father Abraham; but if one goes to them from the dead, they will repent" (verse 30).

Really?

Well, one man actually did come back from the dead. His name was Lazarus, too. But the Lazarus who came back from the dead was a personal friend of Jesus, and the Lord raised him from the dead after he'd been in the tomb for four days.

But even though the miracle was verified by many people, it only made the religious leaders of the day more determined than ever to kill Jesus—and Lazarus, too, if they could manage it. And they were speaking this way even though they acknowledged "This man certainly performs many miraculous signs" (John 11:47, NLT). So here was a dead man who came back to life. But still the Jewish leaders refused to believe.

Even more to the point, Jesus Christ Himself rose again from the dead, and was seen by as many as five hundred people at one time (see 1 Corinthians 15:6). Did everyone believe? No. Really, only a small percentage of the people did. So the rich man's argument that "someone coming back from the dead" would cause his brothers to believe just wasn't true.

The Great White Throne

After death, the nonbeliever goes to a place of torment, but that isn't the end of it. There is still a judgment yet to come, known as the Great White Throne—a terrible final judgment for nonbelievers only.

Then I saw a great white throne and Him who sat on it, from whose face the earth and the heaven fled away. And there was found no place for them. And I saw the dead, small and great, standing before God, and books were opened. And another book was opened, which is the Book of Life. And the dead were judged according to their works, by the things which were written in the books. The sea gave up the dead who were in it, and Death and Hades delivered up the dead who were in them. And they were judged, each one according to his works. Then Death and Hades were cast into the lake of fire. This is the second death. And anyone not found written in the Book of Life was cast into the lake of fire. (Revelation 20:11-15)

Who will be at the Great White Throne judgment? Everyone who has rejected God's offer of forgiveness through Jesus Christ. Notice that there are no exceptions. Verse 12 reads, "I saw the dead, small and great, standing before God, and the books were opened."

God is no respecter of persons. The fact that a person may have been a king or a queen, an emperor or president, a prime minister or rock star doesn't matter. Everyone standing before that throne will be in the same position, and each person will have to give an account of his or her life.

Actor Robert De Niro was asked, "If there are pearly gates and you stand before God one day, what will you say to Him?" De Niro's response was, "I will say to God, if heaven exists, He has a lot of explaining to do."

No. I don't think so.

At this Great White Throne, all unbelievers will have to give an account of their lives. The big issue in this final judgment, however, won't be a sin issue as much as it will be a Son issue.

The greatest and final question in the last day will be, "What did you do with the offer of salvation in My Son, Jesus Christ?"

The apostle John put it very, very simply: "And this is the testimony: God has given us eternal life, and this life is in his Son. Whoever has the Son has life; whoever does not have the Son of God does not have life" (1 John 5:11-12, NIV).

The fact is, good people don't go to heaven. Forgiven people do. Because apart from the gift of righteousness in Jesus, no one is good enough.

Why Are People at the Great White Throne Judgment?

They will be there because they did not believe in Jesus and receive His offer of forgiveness and salvation.

In John 3:18, Jesus said, "He who believes in Him is not condemned; but he who does not believe is condemned already, because he has not believed in the name of the only begotten Son of God."

If the nonbeliever is already condemned, then what is the purpose of the last judgment? This is a very important question. The purpose of the final confrontation between God and man is to clearly demonstrate to the nonbeliever why he or she is already condemned.

If someone spoke up at that judgment and said, "Wait a second, I never knew about this," their argument would be refuted, because in Revelation 20:12 it says that "books were opened." What are these books? We don't know for certain, but one of them may be a book of God's law. And everyone who has been exposed to the truth of God's law will be held responsible. As Romans 3:19 (NIV) says, "so that every mouth may be silenced and the whole world held accountable to God."

I bring this up because some people say, "I really don't need Jesus Christ. I just live by the Ten Commandments."

No, actually you don't.

Have you ever taken the Lord's name in vain—using it in an empty, insincere, frivolous way? Have you ever taken anything that didn't belong to you? Have you ever lied? Of course you have. The fact is, if you want to live by the law you're in deep trouble, because the Bible says, "For whoever shall keep the whole law, and yet stumble in one point, he is guilty of all" (James 2:10).

The law was never given to make a man or a woman righteous. The law is a moral mirror that shows us our real state before God—and its intent is to drive us into the open arms of Jesus. The law says, "You are not good enough. You need God's help."

Maybe another book opened at the Great White Throne would be a record of everything you have ever said or done. That's not so hard to believe, because in this high-tech world of ours, you're being recorded by some kind of surveillance camera almost everywhere you go. If you run a red light, you might get your picture taken, and there will be no getting out of that ticket. If humankind can do this in an increasingly effective way, can't we imagine that the Creator of the universe might have some pretty tricked out and sophisticated recording equipment?

Actually, we can be sure of it. The Bible tells us that everything that we do, whether good or bad, is recorded, and we will be judged for it.

For God will bring every deed into judgment,
including every hidden thing,
whether it is good or evil. (Ecclesiastes 12:14, NIV)

But I say to you that for every idle word men may speak, they
will give account of it in the day of judgment. (Matthew 12:36)

The most important record of all, however, is the Book of Life. Revelation 20:15 tells us, "And anyone not found written in the Book of Life was cast into the lake of fire."

Some people may say, "That's just not right. How could a God of love create a place called hell?" The truth is, it is because He is a God of love that He created a place called hell. There are terrible injustices and wrongs done that people should never get away with. And though they may escape the long arm of the law, they will never escape the long arm of God.

Justice will be done, and that justice will be final and complete.

Beyond all of that, however, hell was not made for people. Jesus said hell was created for the devil and his angels (see Matthew 25:41). It was never God's intention to send a person to hell, and He does everything He can to keep people out of hell.

But in the final analysis, it's our choice. God has given to you and to me a free will. I have the ability to choose, and God will not violate that. If you want to go to heaven, my friend, you will, if you put your faith in Christ. If you want to go to hell, you will. That is really your choice.

J. I. Packer writes, "Scripture sees hell as self-chosen. Hell appears as God's gesture of respect for human choice. All receive what they actually choose. Either to be with God forever worshipping Him or without God forever worshipping themselves."[9]

C. S. Lewis said, "There are only two kinds of people in the end. Those who say to God, 'Thy will be done' and those to whom God says in the end, 'Thy will be done.' All that are in hell choose it. Without that self-choice there could be no Hell."[10]

Timothy Keller said, "All God does in the end with people is give them what they most want, including freedom from himself. What could be fairer than that?" Indeed, hell is "the trajectory of a soul, living a self-absorbed, self-centered life, going on and on forever." In the end, we get what we most truly want.

It's not enjoyable to preach or write about these things. But if you belong to Jesus Christ, I hope that being reminded of these realities will make you want to redouble your efforts to reach people with the gospel. The Bible tells us to "Rescue others by snatching them from the flames of judgment. Show mercy to still others, but do so with great caution, hating the sins that contaminate their lives" (Jude 23, NLT).

Sometimes we don't warn people about hell because we don't want to offend them. We're willing to talk about the glories of walking with Christ, and how He gives us peace and joy and purpose, but the person just blows us off, and says, "I don't need that. I'm happy enough as I am."

But there is a warning in the gospel, too.

Yes, there is a heaven to gain, but there is also a hell to avoid.

Just a brief warning, but then the message turns positive again. God poured all of His judgment on Jesus two thousand years ago at the cross so you and I would not have to go to a place called hell. And He will forgive you of every wrong you have ever done if you will turn to Him.

And right now would be the best time of all.

CHAPTER TWENTY-TWO
DO YOU WANT TO CHANGE YOUR LIFE?

Without question, God loves you deeply and wants to reveal the personal, custom-made plan He has just for you. He wants to flood your life with peace, joy, and purpose. Ultimately, He wants to spend all eternity with you in a place that exceeds your wildest dreams—a place called heaven.

God says, "For I know the thoughts that I think toward you, . . . thoughts of peace and not of evil, to give you a future and a hope" (Jeremiah 29:11).

But just as surely as there is a loving God who cares for you, there is a hateful devil who wants to destroy you. He is like "a roaring lion, seeking whom he may devour" (1 Peter 5:8). Jesus, in speaking of Satan, said that he comes "to steal, and to kill, and to destroy" (John 10:10).

That pretty much sums up Satan's agenda: *steal, kill,* and *destroy.*

On the other hand, Jesus came "that [we] may have life, and that [we] may have it more abundantly" (John 10:10).

In Scripture we find the story of a man who had been completely taken over by the power of the devil. He was a tortured, suicidal, miserable, lonely shell of a man in an absolutely hopeless situation.

This basically shows us the "package deal" Satan has in store for every person in his grip. First and foremost, he wants to keep you from coming to Jesus Christ. He may entice you with all the glitz and glamour this world has to offer. It may be greed for the acquisition of things. But once he has you where he wants you, he'll chew you up and spit you out.

Judas Iscariot is the classic example. It's hard to believe, but those thirty pieces of silver offered by religious leaders looked pretty appealing to him. Yet once the devil had what he wanted, Judas was cast aside like yesterday's garbage.

The stuff this world offers us can look so cool and so appealing. MTV, for example, has mastered the practice of making bad stuff look good. One of their most popular shows in times past was *The Osbournes*. The head of the clan is the wacky Ozzy Osbourne of Black Sabbath fame. Ozzy is the parent a lot of kids wish they had, because if some kid were to brag, "My dad started his own business!" the kid with Ozzy for a father could say, "Oh yeah? Well, my dad bit the head off a dove *and* a bat!"

Ozzy and his wife, Sharon, have two kids, Kelly and Jack. Ozzy has been a heavy drug user and drinker, but he has told his kids not to follow his example. Unfortunately, Jack entered the drugs and drinking scene and, at age seventeen, entered a rehab facility to get help. Jack explained, "I got caught up in my new lifestyle and got carried away with drugs and alcohol." But do you think MTV was quick to do a really clever show about Jack in rehab? No, because they don't want you to see the reality of what sin does. That might scare you off, you see.

Madonna is someone who has "been there, done that." She has said,

> Take it from me. I went down the road of "be all you can be; realize your dreams," and I'm telling you that fame and fortune are not what they're cracked up to be. I feel I've earned the right to speak my mind in that area. People think, "Easy for you to say," but it's not easy, because in a way I have to say that so much of what I did and fretted over was a waste of time, like worrying about whether I'd be popular or not.[11]

The world's idea of fulfillment is a complete rip-off, and the end result is frightening.

The story before us illustrates these points. And in this story, we see three forces at work in a man's life: Satan, society, and the Savior. We will see what Satan did in his life, what society offered, and then what the Savior did.

Here is how Matthew captures that dramatic story.

The First Force at Work: Satan

When He had come to the other side, to the country of the Gergesenes, there met Him two demon-possessed men, coming out of the tombs, exceedingly fierce, so that no one could pass that way. And suddenly they cried out, saying, "What have we to do with You, Jesus, You Son of God? Have You come here to torment us before the time?"

Now a good way off from them there was a herd of many swine feeding. So the demons begged Him, saying, "If You cast us out, permit us to go away into the herd of swine."

And He said to them, "Go." So when they had come out, they went into the herd of swine. And suddenly the whole herd of swine ran violently down the steep place into the sea, and perished in the water. (Matthew 8:28-32)

As our story begins, we find two pathetic, demented men. In Luke's account of this story, he zeroed in on one of these men in particular. He seems to have been the more extreme of the two: "When He stepped out on the land, there met Him a certain man from the city who had demons for a long time. And he wore no clothes, nor did he live in a house but in the tombs" (Luke 8:27). In addition to this, he would beat and bruise himself, as well as cut himself with sharp rocks. He was so strong that when he was put in chains, he broke them.

So here was quite a creepy scenario: a frightening, evil man with superhuman strength, who hung out at the graveyard. No doubt local people gave this place a wide berth, especially at night. Superstitious people would have said this was a place for ghosts and goblins. This man who lived in the tombs was certainly a dangerous and frightening man, but underneath that dark exterior was a truly tortured soul. And, as I mentioned earlier, he is a picture of Satan's ultimate goal—the finished product.

What steps led to this state we can only imagine. But here we see the "package deal" of sin, Satan, and death all intertwined together. What a dark and depressing situation. Sin truly is a living death, and the unbeliever is spiritually "dead in trespasses and sins" (Ephesians 2:1). The Bible says, "But she who lives in pleasure is dead while she lives" (1 Timothy 5:6).

Nevertheless, this is a story with a happy ending.

Why?

Because Jesus came into this poor, tortured man's life and made him into an altogether different kind of person.

When Jesus showed up at this place seeking out these men, Satan reacted with force: "They began screaming at him, 'Why are you interfering with us, Son of God? Have you come here to torture us before God's appointed time?'" (Matthew 8:29, NLT). The power of Satan was so entwined with this man that most would not have been able to see the hurting person deep inside, but only the crazed, suicidal maniac roaming the graveyard. Yet in this cry, Jesus must have also heard a cry for help.

Perhaps that describes you right now. Underneath all of your talk, all of your arguments against God, you secretly long for His help and for some peace and purpose in your life. Underneath an outward show of confidence, you may be lonely and afraid.

This man may not have been doing many right or wise things, but on that day he did. He realized he did not have power and he was trapped beyond human hope by the enemy.

So he cried out to Jesus.

And Jesus came to him.

The only thing stronger than the power of Satan is the power of Jesus.

The demons possessing this man screamed out a bizarre question: "What do you want with us, Son of God? . . . Have you come here to torture us before the appointed time?" (Matthew 8:29, NIV).

The apostle James told us, "You believe that there is one God. You do well. Even the demons believe—and tremble!" (James 2:19). It may surprise you to know that the demons, and the devil himself, are neither atheists nor agnostics. They believe in the existence of God. They believe in the deity of Jesus Christ. They believe that the Bible is the very Word of God. They believe Jesus is coming back again. In fact, you could say that (in a very limited sense) demons and the devil are quite orthodox in their beliefs. But they are *not* followers of Christ.

I remember as a very young Christian hearing someone say, "Let's pray for Satan's conversion!" It's not going to happen! The point in James' words is simply this: It's not enough to simply believe in God. It's not enough to believe that Jesus is the Son of God. It's not enough to believe that the Bible is the Word of God. *You must personally choose to follow Jesus.*

In Luke's account of this story, we read that Jesus asked, "What is your name?" He answered, "'Legion,' because many demons had entered him" (8:30). This man was so wrapped up in demonic powers that he couldn't even answer for himself. A Roman legion consisted of six thousand soldiers, which means this man was possessed by perhaps hundreds, even thousands, of demons.

Somewhere along the line, these men had opened themselves up to satanic invasion. They played around with sin, and now sin was playing around with them. They had lost everything—their homes, their families, their friends, and even their wills. They were completely under the power of the devil. We must remember this when we start playing games with sin. Satan will dangle what he must in front of us to get us to take the bait.

There are many who open the door to the supernatural through their use of drugs, as there is a definite link between drugs and the occult. The Bible warns of the sin of *sorcery*, and in fact the word sorcery comes from the Greek word *pharmakia*, the same word from which our English word *pharmacy* is derived. The biblical definition of sorcery has to do with the illicit use of drugs. When people begin to use drugs—whether it's marijuana, cocaine, or any other mind-controlling substance—it opens them up to direct demonic influence.

Marijuana may be in widespread use and even legalized in some of our states. But that only means that for those who abuse it, there will be a wider door for the occult to gain a foothold in our communities.

Dabbling in black magic, witchcraft, Ouija boards, or astrology can also open the door. The Bible tells us that "those who practice such things will not inherit the kingdom of God" (Galatians 5:21).

I did drugs for a couple of years. I had already been drinking and into the party scene, and I thought drugs would be the thing that would finally fill some of those big empty places in my life. But drugs only made my problems worse and that void in my heart seem even deeper and wider. That huge emptiness in my life could only be filled by God Himself.

The Second Force at Work: Society

As I pointed out earlier, we see three forces at work in this story: Satan, society, and the Savior. We've already seen what Satan did with these men. So what did society do for them?

Society, represented by the people in the village, chained them up.

In our country, violent crime continues to spread, particularly related to the establishment and growth of gangs in many communities. Law enforcement is often understaffed and underpaid. Many of our courts and judges give out lenient sentences. And sadly, the family is continuing to fall apart at an unprecedented rate. Meanwhile, back in our schools, "situational ethics" are taught, asserting there really is no such thing as absolute values, right or wrong, black or white, but only shades of gray. What is a society to do? Like those in Jesus' day, we just lock people up.

According to an article in the *Washington Post*, America's prison population today stands at more than 2.4 million people. That's more than quadrupled since 1980, and it basically means that one out of every 100 Americans is behind bars today.[12]

Despite all of its wonderful scientific and cultural achievements, society still cannot cope with the problems caused by Satan and sin.

No one could help these demon-possessed men. Their situation was absolutely hopeless. But what the chains could not do, Jesus did with one word.

The Third Force at Work: The Savior

What did Jesus do for these men? He sought them out in their spooky little graveyard and offered them hope. And apparently, these demons preferred inhabiting something instead of nothing, so Jesus conceded to their request and sent them into a herd of pigs. The pigs all ran over the cliff in madness. You might say this was the first recorded mention of "deviled ham."

Luke's account of this story tells us what happened to this man who was delivered: "People rushed out to see what had happened. A crowd soon gathered around Jesus, and they saw the man who had been freed from the demons. He was sitting at Jesus' feet, fully clothed and perfectly sane, and they were all afraid" (8:35, NLT).

What a change!

If you want proof of the existence of God, then just look at the changes He has made in the lives of people you know who have given their lives to Jesus Christ.

I recently saw some statistics that said 95 percent of those who entered secular drug treatment programs went back to using drugs again. However, of those who went through Christian drug and alcohol treatment programs, 67 percent were living drug-free, seven years after they had left the program.

Not long ago, I met a man from the Czech Republic who gave me his firsthand story of how Christ had changed his life.

I grew up in the Czech Republic and in a family where my father was an alcoholic. My first drunkenness occurred when I was three years old, when my father left me in a room with glasses of liquor while he was partying with another guy. They took me to a hospital and found that I had been drunk for fifty hours and had almost died. I grew up in the communist system. It gave me a rough, hard, and angry attitude. Soon I was known as a fist-fighter and an angry man. As I got older, I became even more violent. I went into the military. I spent a short time in prison for violence, alcoholism, and drunkenness.

He then explained that he relocated to the United States and moved in with a girl. He went on to say,

I continued my spiral into alcohol and all the rest of it. On one occasion, my life was spinning down into the bottomless pit. I lost fifty pounds and was ready to commit suicide. I was staring at a gun I was pointing in my mouth. I didn't have any resolve to live. My whole life was one big emptiness, only existing, just a waste of time.

Here is this man, hopeless, alcoholic, violent, and suicidal. And what happened? He continued:

At that time, my neighbor in Mission Viejo and her friends invited me to the Harvest Crusade in 1994. After the music and the message, I knew the Lord was knocking, was on my heart, and wanted me to give up being in control of my life. I got up, walked down to the platform, and asked the Lord to take me out of this garbage and mess, and if He did that, I would do anything He asked. God's Spirit surrounded me and began to melt all of the pain and hurts that I had all of those years, and God's Word started to work in a miraculous way in my life.

He started going to church and learning the Word of God, and now he has gone back to his homeland, started a church, and is preaching the gospel. What this world can't do, Jesus Christ can.

Jesus delivered the suicidal, tormented, demon-possessed man. So how did the people react? Amazingly, they were afraid. The demonstration of the power of God frightened them. They should have been rejoicing and praising God, but instead they became very anxious and uncomfortable. They couldn't understand or process what had just happened, and rather than seeking to learn more about it, they wanted to push it away and hide it from their sight.

You would have thought they would have asked Jesus to stay with them and perhaps heal some more people or teach them about this power that could transform lives. But they did the very opposite: "Then the whole multitude of the surrounding region of the Gadarenes asked Him to depart from them, for they were seized with great fear" (Luke 8:37).

The owners of the swine were angry at Jesus. For some people, after all, Jesus is bad for business. Apparently they felt that something might be required of them. In their case, it was an economic loss. So they decided it would be best for Jesus to go away. Hogs were big business on this side of the lake. Clearly, if Jesus stuck around, it might hurt the economy. Two thousand hogs is a lot of bacon, and they now were at the bottom of the lake.

But the fact that Jesus was bad for business wasn't the only reason these Gadarenes wanted Him to go away. More than that, they wondered, "If He did that for this one man, would He do the same to us?" Sometimes the prospect of change can seem frightening. It's much more "comfortable" to live in the same old rut, doing the same old stuff—even if you're bored or miserable.

Then there was their own guilt. The presence of Jesus Christ always will awaken that. They could see in His eyes that He knew everything about them and read them like an open book. Just as He cast the demons out of the men and into the pigs, so He seemed able to look through them and see their deepest thoughts. They felt themselves withering in His presence, and they were highly nervous about what He might say or do.

What if He wanted to bring change into their lives?

What if He turned things upside down (or right side up)?

The prospect was too unsettling. It would be much easier if He just went away.

It's important to note, however, that before conversion there must first come the conviction of sin. Guilt comes before repentance, because it shows us our desperate need. But remember this: The very One who causes us to experience that guilt can also remove it—forever.

These people told Jesus to go away. And He did.

Really, when you get down to it, this sums up the reaction of all humankind to Jesus Christ. It's either "Away with Him!" or follow Him. In the final analysis, each of us belongs to one of those groups.

You might protest and say, "I admit that I haven't made a commitment to Christ or said, 'I want to be with Him,' but I've never said, 'Away with Him!' either. I simply haven't decided yet."

But to not be for Jesus *is* to be against Him. Either we pray for Him to go away or we pray to ask Him into our lives. Which is it for you?

What are some ways people say, "Away with Him"?

Some reject Jesus out of fear. Perhaps there was a time when they were sitting in church and God began to work on their hearts. They realized this was both true and exactly what they needed. A little bit of hope and a little bit of joy began to bubble up as they edged nearer to God. Yet because of their fear of what their friends would think or say, they resisted and shook off the influence. They vowed not to go back to church. In essence they said, "Away with Jesus!"

Others reject Jesus out of selfishness. God has clearly shown us in His Word what is right and wrong, but they have decided to do what they want to do. They will continue in that sexual relationship with someone they aren't married to. They will continue partying their lives away. They will continue with that drug or alcohol use. Though God has spoken to their hearts through conscience, friends, and of course, His Word, they are in essence saying, "Away with Jesus!"

Others reject Jesus because of busyness. This isn't as blatant as deliberately breaking His commandments. These are just people who get wrapped up with the concerns and activities of life—work, family, responsibilities, and hobbies—so that there isn't any room for Jesus. They don't deliberately push Him away; they're just too preoccupied and busy to care much about Him.

Which is it for you? Is it "Away with Jesus!" or "Lord, come into my heart"?

Do you know what Jesus did when they told Him to go away?

He left.

"The entire town came out to meet Jesus, but they begged him to go away and leave them alone. Jesus climbed into a boat and went back across the lake to his own town" (Matthew 8:34–9:1, NLT).

I can't help wondering what it was like in that neighborhood after they sent Jesus away. Do you suppose people felt a little empty? A little lonely? A little restless? Do you think they might have experienced some regret as they reflected on what had happened in their midst?

The fact is, Jesus is a gentleman. He will not force His way into your life. He says, "Behold, I stand at the door and knock" (Revelation 3:20). He doesn't say, "Open up or I'll jimmy the lock or kick the door in!"

There never has been a better time for you to get right with God than now. The Bible says, "Now is the day of salvation" (2 Corinthians 6:2), and "Seek the LORD while He may be found, call upon Him while He is near" (Isaiah 55:6).

You may never have another opportunity like this one.

CHAPTER TWENTY-THREE
THE WHOLE STORY

H ave you heard a good story lately?

We all like a good story, whether in a book or a movie. For a story to be effective, certain elements are usually present. There is a clear plot, there are characters we can relate to, and there is some kind of conflict that emerges that engages and holds our interest. Ultimately, everything comes to a point of resolution—or perhaps even a surprise ending.

Some Hollywood movies are driven by special effects, to make them visually interesting. But the best movies are those with an engaging story and characters.

On more than one occasion, filmmakers have held a limited screening before a major release to see how people react to the film. If they find that the audiences don't like the ending (the hero dies or the couple never gets together), they'll rewrite those last scenes and shoot those parts again.

They redo the endings.

Wouldn't it be nice if we could do that in real life? We might say, "I didn't like this last week. I've had some hurts, I've had some disappointments, I've been depressed. Let's shoot that one more time."

The fact is, the Bible tells us that our lives are a lot like a story. Psalm 90:9 (KJV) says, "We spend our years as a tale that is told."

Real life, however, isn't a Hollywood story. There are certain things that happen in movies that never happen in real life, and vice versa. Someone took the time to write down some recurring features we see in movies time and time again. Think about this for a moment. In every movie you have seen, you have probably noticed some of these elements in it. For example, if someone walks out of a supermarket with a shopping bag, they always have one loaf of French bread sticking out of it. Also, the ventilation system of any building is a perfect hiding place, and no one will ever think of looking for you in there. And as it turns out, you can travel to any other part of the building you want to without difficulty.

In the movies, if you happen to be in France you will be able to see the Eiffel Tower from every window. If you are being chased by someone, you can always take cover in a passing Saint Patrick's Day parade, no matter what time of year it is. When someone in a movie gets out of a taxi, they never have to pull out their wallet, because they always have exactly the right amount for cab fare randomly in their back pocket.

Also in the movies, all bombs are fitted with electronic timing devices with large red readouts so you know exactly when they are going to detonate. In the movies, you can always park directly outside the building you are visiting even if you are in the middle of New York City. Here is another thing true only in movies: It doesn't matter if you are heavily outnumbered in a fight involving martial arts; your enemies will patiently wait to attack you one by one, dancing around in a threatening manner until you have knocked out their predecessors.

And finally, in the movies bad guys can spray machine-gun fire everywhere and hit everything but the hero. Then the hero pulls out his five-shot revolver, hits all the bad guys, and never has to reload.

That's the movies.

That's not real life.

Real life has twists and turns that don't make sense. Sometimes we find ourselves in the middle of something that doesn't seem to fit, and we wonder why in the world it's happening to us.

Cut! Take Two!

Imagine how the Bible character Joseph felt mid-story. His life had started well, raised as he was in a loving home with a doting father. One night he woke up in the comfort and security of his own bed, and the next night he was in chains, in a caravan headed for Egypt, where he would be sold as a slave—by his own brothers!

Eventually he was bought by a wealthy Egyptian who put Joseph in charge of his whole household. Joseph was so diligent and hardworking that he was elevated to a position of complete control over this man's finances. However, the Egyptian had an attractive, attention-starved wife, who immediately began trying to seduce Joseph. She was far from subtle. She would come right up to him as he was walking through the house and say, "Have sex with me." Joseph resisted, but it couldn't have been easy. He was a red-blooded young man with a normal God-given sex drive. When he continued to resist her advances, she got so mad at him she falsely accused him of rape, and he was sent off to prison.

Imagine how he felt sitting in that prison cell. He'd done nothing wrong in Canaan to have been sold as a slave. He'd done nothing wrong as a slave to have been sent to a dungeon. We might imagine him thinking, *So this is what I get for obeying God? Maybe I should have just given in to that woman.* But as readers of the book of Genesis know so well, the story took an amazing, supernatural twist, and Joseph ended up becoming the second most powerful man in all the world.

Or consider Job's story. He woke up in the morning, had his breakfast, and everything seemed to be blue sky and roses. His large family was happy, the bills were paid, his health was strong, and he had more money than he knew what to do with.

And then . . .

In a matter of moments, everything changed. He lost his children, his wealth, most of his possessions, and eventually his health. Unfortunately, he still had his wife. Why do I say that? Because after all those calamities—one after another—had fallen on Job's head, his wife turned to him and said, "Why don't you just curse God and die?" *Thank you for those encouraging words, dear.*

But you know how the rest of his story turned out: God restored everything to him and more.

In the beginning, however, Job didn't know the ending to his story. He didn't know he'd have more wonderful children. He didn't know his wealth and health and possessions would all be restored. He was still in the middle of the story.

And so are we.

You and I are in a story, and the Author of that story is God Himself. There is a plot, you are the main character, and there will certainly be conflict. But here is the good news: If you belong to Jesus Christ, there will be a happy ending to your story. Why? Because the Author of your story is the almighty God, whom Scripture calls "the author and finisher of our faith" (Hebrews 12:2).

He is the Author of our lives, and He will finish what He has begun.

In his letter to the Philippians, Paul wrote, "There has never been the slightest doubt in my mind that the God who started this great work in you would keep at it and bring it to a flourishing finish on the very day Christ Jesus appears" (1:6, MSG).

In the book of Matthew, chapter 9, Scripture gives us two powerful, interwoven stories—two plot lines that intersect and somehow, for a moment, become one.

Two in Distress

One of these stories is a snapshot of a poor, broken woman on the ragged edge of despair. Her life had been miserable for years, with no end of her misery in sight. She had lost her health and spent all of her money to get well. To no avail. Then she found what she needed in the person of Jesus.

In contrast, the second story's main character was a man of great importance. While she was low, he was high. She was pitiful, he was powerful. She was insignificant, he was in high demand.

But he also had a problem and a crisis. His beloved young daughter was dying, and there was seemingly nothing he could do to save her. This reminds us that tragedy levels social topography. Pain visits every life without exception. So these two suffering, despairing people—though they would have likely never met and didn't know one another—found themselves on the same path in the same village on the same page of the Bible.

Here is how it reads in Scripture:

A ruler came and worshiped Him, saying, "My daughter has just died, but come and lay Your hand on her and she will live." So Jesus arose and followed him, and so did His disciples.

And suddenly, a woman who had a flow of blood for twelve years came from behind and touched the hem of His garment. For she said to herself, "If only I may touch His garment, I shall be made well." But Jesus turned around, and when He saw her He said, "Be of good cheer, daughter; your faith has made you well." And the woman was made well from that hour.

When Jesus came into the ruler's house, and saw the flute players and the noisy crowd wailing, He said to them, "Make room, for the girl is not dead, but sleeping." And they ridiculed Him. But when the crowd was put outside, He went in and took her by the hand, and the girl arose. And the report of this went out into all that land. (Matthew 9:18-26)

Twelve years is a significant period of time in the lives of both of these hurting people. The woman with the hemorrhage had been in hell for twelve years. The young girl, as we will find in another gospel, was sick and near death at the age of twelve. So while this young girl had experienced twelve years of relative happiness, this sick woman had experienced twelve years of pain, rejection, loneliness, and tears. And yet on the same afternoon both were impacted by Jesus.

Where the Story Begins

Jairus is called "the ruler of the synagogue" (Mark 5:36), which means he was a powerful and respected man. And on the day recorded in Scripture, he did something he probably never expected to do: He got down on his knees in the dust before Jesus Christ and begged for help. That wasn't a typical thing for a man of his position and stature to do. He was a leader in the community, a person of great influence, and someone others looked up to.

But he also loved his little girl with all his heart, and he was willing to humble himself before Jesus to ask for help. He was pleading for Jesus to come and touch his daughter so she might live. He was pleading for Jesus to come and touch His daughter before it was too late.

Much to his relief, Jesus heard his request. The account says that "Jesus arose and followed him."

The Plot Thickens

It all started with an interruption and a change in direction.

Jesus had been having a discussion with the disciples of John the Baptist when Jairus fell on his knees before the Lord and begged Him to intervene in his little daughter's illness. But then, even as the crowd began to head for Jairus's house, the woman in the story seems to have come out of nowhere and reached out to touch the hem of Jesus' garment.

This proved to be an interruption of the interruption, as Jesus stopped to confront the despairing woman. In a moment of confusion, she suddenly reached out to Jesus and was made whole.

That's the way God's economy works sometimes: Interruptions can become opportunities. Disappointments can become His appointments. And sometimes when things seem to be going very wrong, they are actually going right. God can use interruptions to intervene in your life for good.

So Jairus's young daughter, the apple of this man's eye, hovered near death. Actually the gospel of Mark tells us that when he initially approached Jesus the girl was still alive, but she apparently died while he was trying to get Christ to his home (see Mark 5:23,35), which adds even more pain to the story.

She was so young. In Jewish culture, a boy becomes a "son of the commandments" (literally, *bar mitzvah*) at age thirteen. He is considered as responsible as any other adult man for obeying God's commands. He has his bar mitzvah and says, "Today I am a man." A girl, however, becomes a "daughter of the commandments" (literally, *bat mitzvah*) at age twelve. At that age, she, too, is considered to be as responsible as any other adult woman for obeying God's laws. (The difference in ages seems to correlate to the ages when boys and girls reach puberty.) So here is a young woman on the cusp of her womanhood, and her life is about to slip away.

As they were on their way, we read in the gospel of Mark that "messengers arrived from Jairus's home with the message, "Your daughter is dead. There's no use troubling the Teacher now" (5:35, NLT).

To hear those words is beyond a father's ability to comprehend them. I have been with fathers on two occasions when they have heard those words from a doctor. Both of their daughters had been in accidents and they were in the emergency room. On both occasions I was with the father, waiting for news, hoping his daughter would survive. And then we got the horrific news.

The pain in that moment is unimaginable. Indescribable. And, of course, I have been in a similar place, too, when I got news about my own son Christopher being killed in a traffic accident. There is just no way to explain what it feels like. It's as though your life has just ended—but it's even worse, because you wish it had ended but realize you have to go on living without your beloved child.

Because of my own experience, I have a sense of what Jairus was going through when he got the message: "Don't bother Jesus anymore, Jairus. It's over. She just died."

I love how the gospel of Mark records what happened in that moment: "As soon as Jesus heard the word that was spoken, He said to the ruler of the synagogue, 'Do not be afraid; only believe'" (5:36). I can imagine Jesus laying a hand on this grieving father's shoulder and looking him straight in the eyes. "Don't be afraid, Jairus. Keep trusting in Me. Even now."

I'm sure Jairus was feeling like a failure for not getting to Jesus more quickly. But Jesus was saying to him, "Just wait and believe and keep believing."

So while this tragedy was unfolding for Jairus, while this distraught dad wanted to get Jesus to his little girl's bedside as quickly as possible, wouldn't you know it—there was an interruption! A woman burst onto the scene, bringing the whole group to a standstill.

How easily Jairus could have said, "Hey. Excuse me? No cuts!"

Don't you hate it when people cut in line? If I'm driving on the freeway and someone tries to cut in to the little space in front of me, I feel like stepping on the gas a little and closing that gap so they can't get in. If they're stuck in a bad position or have their turn signal on, I don't mind letting them in. But when people suddenly cut in, well, I don't like that.

It's the same when you're waiting in a line for a movie. If you've been waiting for a while in a big long line and someone comes along and steps into the line in front of you, that's just a little offensive.

Imagine how Jairus felt! "Excuse me, but I have an emergency here, ma'am. I don't know what your problem is, but you need to wait your turn."

I think this was a test in the life of Jairus. How would he fare? Maybe Jairus had heard how Jesus always had time for the underdogs of the world. Maybe he'd been told the story of how Jesus called the hated tax collector Matthew to be one of His followers. Or perhaps he'd heard about the way Jesus had touched a demon-possessed man and delivered him. Maybe he considered those things in that moment and said to himself, "I don't like this interruption, but I know this is the way Jesus is. He takes time with needy people. I'm not going to create any trouble here. I'll just wait on Him. He knows what He is doing."

If this really was a test, Jairus passed it with flying colors. As anxious and distraught as he was, he waited on the Lord and kept trusting in Him. Sometimes when you and I are being tested, we aren't even aware of it. God usually doesn't tell us when we're being tested. And sometimes "waiting on the Lord" isn't easy.

By nature I am an impatient person, and I hate waiting on anything. If I have to wait, I'm always doing something else—maybe checking my e-mail on my iPhone or fiddling around with something else. When I go to pick up a pizza, it's virtually impossible for me to get the whole pizza home intact. On more than one occasion I have eaten the pizza while I was driving because it smelled so good and I didn't want to wait. I'll grab a piece out of the box, burn my mouth, and get tomato sauce and grease on my shirt. When I get home my wife will say, "What happened to half of the pizza?"

Sometimes we don't like to wait on the Lord, either. We'll complain to Him and say, "Lord, what's going on here? Are You paying any attention to this situation? When are You going to provide me with a husband (or wife)? When are You going to open a door of ministry for me? When are You going to help me find a better job? How long are You going to let that person get away with his sin?"

Or how about this one? "Lord, how long is it going to be until You come back to this earth? Have You noticed how bad things have gotten? How long, Lord?"

In spite of our complaining and fretting, God is certainly aware of our needs and hears our prayers. But He will act according to His timing, not ours.

Difficult and heartbreaking as it must have been, Jairus was willing to wait on the Lord for His timing.

A Desperate Woman

In Matthew 9:20, we read that a woman who'd had a flow of blood for twelve years came up behind Jesus and touched the hem of His garment. She apparently had some kind of chronic hemorrhage that had caused continual bleeding for twelve painful years. Blood simply wouldn't stay in her body, and in that culture, the stigma and humiliation of this condition was second only to leprosy. Her hemorrhage caused her to be declared ceremonially unclean, which meant that she was not allowed to worship in the synagogue with God's people.

The synagogue was the center of both spiritual and social life in the city. Cut off as she was from her neighbors, friends, and family, she had really lost everything. Mark's version of the story tells us that she "had suffered many things from many physicians. She had spent all that she had and was no better, but rather grew worse" (5:26).

The truth is, first-century medicine was very primitive. Among the so-called remedies of the day was an instruction to carry the ashes of an ostrich egg in a linen bag in the summer and a cotton bag in the winter, and you would be healed. Really? Another superstitious remedy involved carrying around a kernel of barley corn that had been found in the dung of a white female donkey. How would you like to take a prescription for *that* to your local pharmacy?

Then the woman heard about Jesus, the rabbi from Nazareth. She'd heard amazing stories of how He could heal any disease with a word or a touch. So she reasoned to herself, "If I could just slip up behind Him and touch His clothing, I could be healed. And maybe no one will even notice!"

In those days, a rabbi's outer garment had a strip of blue at the hem. And that's what she would have been aiming for as she reached out her hand that day.

It might have been a risky maneuver for her, but she had become so desperate she was willing to chance it. What did she have to lose? She was already rejected and shunned by everyone, not to mention financially destitute. So when she saw Jesus walking with Jairus, she slipped up as inconspicuously as she could and touched her finger to His robe. Instantly, the healing power of God was released and her disease was completely cured. She had no doubt. The hateful disease that had dogged her steps for twelve long years was *gone*.

One of the reasons she had thought she could escape unnoticed was because of the large crowd that followed Jesus. There were all kinds of people milling around, trying to get a glimpse of Him, pushing and pulling and creating a commotion.

In the middle of that general chaos, as Jesus made His way through that gaggle of people, He suddenly stopped and said, "Who touched Me?"

Peter must have looked at John and John looked at Andrew, and everyone just shrugged. What kind of question was that? Everyone was touching Him; He was being pushed on from all sides.

Jesus, however, was insistent. "No," He said. "I know that something happened. I know that power has gone out of Me." The crowd parted as the woman, trembling and afraid, pushed her way forward. But when she saw the Lord's face, it must have set her heart at ease. He didn't want to single her out to scold her or humiliate her, but rather to commend her and to acknowledge her faith. I imagine that He smiled at her and spoke gently to her, saying, "Be of good cheer, daughter; your faith has made you well."

In the gospel of Mark's version of the account, we read that "the woman, fearing and trembling, knowing what had happened to her, came and fell down before Him and told Him the whole truth" (5:33).

Another translation says that she "gave him the whole story" (MSG). That's why I have called this chapter "The Whole Story."

It had probably been a long time since someone had actually listened to her story. People had probably avoided her for years, crossing over and walking on the other side of the street when they saw her coming. Their actions said, "You're unclean. Get away from me."

But Jesus said, in effect, "Tell Me your story, dear woman. I'm all ears."

Have you ever tried to talk to someone who was distracted and wouldn't give you their full attention? Let me restate the question: Have you ever had a conversation with *me*? I have to admit that I'm very easily distracted, and it's hard for me to focus on anything for more than a few seconds. I had ADHD before ADHD was cool.

It's frustrating to be pouring your heart out to someone, only to have the person say, "Just a second, I'm getting a text," and start fiddling with his smartphone. You want to say, "Would you put that thing away and pay attention to me for a moment? You are with *me* now."

Jesus was there for this woman at what must have been the greatest moment of her life. He listened to her whole story as she poured out her heart to Him. He cared about her, comforted her, and commended her for her faith.

How to Break Up a Funeral

Jairus, of course, was standing there watching all of this unfold. He had been racing against time to find Jesus and persuade Him to come to his daughter's bedside. And now? Well, there was this woman telling her life story, and Jesus was giving her His full, sympathetic attention.

After what must have seemed like an hour, but was probably only a few moments, Jesus turned His attention back to Jairus and they made their way to his home.

In the gospel of Mark we read,

> And He permitted no one to follow Him except Peter, James, and John the brother of James. Then He came to the house of the ruler of the synagogue, and saw a tumult and those who wept and wailed loudly. When He came in, He said to them, "Why make this commotion and weep? The child is not dead, but sleeping."

> And they ridiculed Him. But when He had put them all outside, He took the father and the mother of the child, and those who were with Him, and entered where the child was lying. Then He took the child by the hand, and said to her, "Talitha, cumi," which is translated, "Little girl, I say to you, arise." Immediately the girl arose and walked, for she was twelve years of age. And they were overcome with great amazement. But He commanded them strictly that no one should know it, and said that something should be given her to eat. (5:37-43)

Arriving at the house, they encountered a scene of noise and great commotion. At that time, grieving and funerals were loud and noisy affairs. People would scream, wail, and shriek. In fact, the family would actually hire professional mourners, which seems strange to us today. These weren't people who necessarily knew the dead person; they were professionals who could work themselves up at the drop of a hat. They would come in with their musical instruments, and they would sing and wail the name of the deceased over and over.

So Jairus and Jesus arrived at a room filled with fifty to one hundred shrieking, screaming people (the wealthier you were, the more mourners you could hire), along with the discordant sounds of multiple musical instruments.

It was chaos, but Jesus was just about to take charge.

Stepping into the middle of it, He raised His voice and said, "Why all this weeping and commotion? . . . The child isn't dead; she is only asleep!" (Mark 5:39, TLB).

At that, everybody started laughing. They went from mourning to laughing, which shows that their "sadness" wasn't real grief at all.

The Bible says Jesus "put them all outside." In other words, He said, "Get these people out of here," and He pushed them right out the door.

I love that.

This was not the kind of environment God wants to work in. The house was full of despair and empty tears and fake grief, but mostly it was filled with unbelief. Elsewhere in the Gospels, we read that Jesus could do no mighty works in His hometown, because the whole atmosphere reeked of skepticism and unbelief (see Matthew 13:54-58).

Sometimes we hinder the work of God in our lives when we are filled with unbelief. We will say things like, "I could never change," or "Jesus would never do that for me," or "This won't work for me."

If you keep saying such things, you may begin to believe them and actually bring them to pass. What you need is a little bit of faith. You don't even have to have a lot. The woman who reached out to Jesus probably said, "What do I have to lose? I'm going to take a chance and reach out to Jesus with what faith I have."

Jesus went into the room where the little girl was lying. She had already passed to the other side; her spirit was in heaven, in the presence of the heavenly Father. And Jesus simply called her back—back to earth, back to her physical body, back to her home and her parents. When you are Jesus, you can do things like that.

Notice that He didn't shout. When He summoned Lazarus from the tomb behind that big stone, He called out, "Lazarus, come forth." And it's a good thing He said, "Lazarus, come forth." If He had just said, "Come forth," every grave in the world would have been instantly emptied.

Here, however, in the now quiet room with the dead little girl, He was very tender and sweet. He simply said, "Little maiden, arise." Her eyelids began to flutter, the color returned to her ashen face, and she opened her eyes and sat up. What incredible joy that must have brought to the hearts of her dad and mom.

I love the fact that He also instructed them to give her something to eat. That was so thoughtful, and the little girl had been on quite a journey. I can imagine that dad saying, "Honey, you can have anything you want. Twinkies. Froot Loops. Whatever your heart desires!"

So what do we learn from this story?

If you have a need, reach out to Jesus.

If Jairus or that afflicted woman hadn't sought out Jesus, the next morning would have been very, very different for them. Jairus and his wife would have opened their eyes to the realization that their little girl was gone. The woman would have faced another day of illness, another day of rejection, loneliness, and depression.

But that's not what happened. Their lives had changed because they sought out Jesus, believing He had the answers to their deepest needs.

I think there are many times, possibly more times than we imagine, when we continue to wrestle with problems and situations simply because we have neglected to cry out to God for help.

Have you prayed about your problem? Have you talked to the Lord about your medical condition? Your finances? Your marriage? Your seemingly mountain-sized concerns?

God is still in the miracle business. He still heals, delivers, helps, and provides. The psalmist said, "The LORD is with me; he is my helper. I look in triumph on my enemies" (Psalm 118:7, NIV).

Is there a decision you need wisdom on? Have you prayed for

wisdom? The Bible says, "You do not have because you do not ask God" (James 4:2, NIV).

Whatever you may be facing, call out to Jesus. Your need isn't too large, nor is it too small or "trivial." And guess what? Jesus is a good listener. He will pay attention. He won't cut you off. He will hear you out.

He may give you what you ask for, He may say, "Not now," or He may say, "No, My child, that wouldn't be good for you now. You have to trust Me to do what's best for you." Then again, He may give you abundantly above and beyond what you ask for.

The important thing is to call out to Him.

In Jeremiah 33:3, God says, "Call to Me, and I will answer you, and show you great and mighty things, which you do not know."

Call out to Jesus.

Your story isn't finished yet.

God finishes what He begins. The day started badly for Jairus, and it got even worse. But what had been the worst day of his life turned out to be the best and most joyous day of his life. It was the same for the woman who touched Jesus' robe. She was at the end of her rope physically, financially, and emotionally. Her story seemed to be coming to a close. But then Jesus intervened and gave her a happy ending.

If we trust in Jesus, our stories will all have happy endings.

You might say, "What are you talking about, Greg? Are you living in the same world I'm living in?"

Yes, as a matter of fact, I am.

And I've experienced my share of suffering and sorrow. So how can I come to the end of this chapter and tell you that your story will have a happy ending?

Because I believe in heaven.

Your story will not be over at the end of your life on earth. In fact, if you belong to Jesus Christ, your story will just be beginning—in eternity, in the presence of God. This is where every follower of Jesus will have a happy ending.

Not so for the nonbeliever. This life is as good as it gets for the non-Christian. It will only get worse—much, much worse—later. But if you are a Christian, life here on earth is as bad as it gets.

When Jairus went looking for Jesus, he realized that he was in a race against time and that death was drawing close. That's a good thing for all of us to remember. We all live on borrowed time, and there will come a day when we step out of this life into eternity. Some of us will live long lives here on earth, but some of us won't. That's up to God. But what we want to do is live in such a way that when our day is done and our number is up, we will be ready to meet Him.

Only those who are prepared to die are really ready to live. I don't mean that in a morbid way. I think no one lives life more fully than a follower of Jesus Christ. No one can appreciate the joys of life more than a Christian. But at the same time, no one has a better perspective than the Christian, because we realize that this life is all temporary and passing away.

Life here on earth, with all its happy moments and tears, all its struggles and blessings, all its setbacks and triumphs, is only a tiny part of our Whole Story.

The best is yet to come.

CHAPTER TWENTY-FOUR

TWELVE MEN WHO SHOOK THE WORLD

*I*f you were God and you wanted to reach this world of ours with the good news of forgiveness and salvation in Jesus Christ, how would you do it?

Remember, you're God, and you can do anything you want. Nothing is impossible for you. You can write in the sky. You can speak from heaven. You can send armies of powerful angels into every city center and town square to tell everyone to believe in Jesus. You could just roll back the clouds and poke Your face through. Of course, that would kill everyone on the spot, so you might not want to do that.

God Himself could have employed any or all of those methods to reach the world. Instead, He chose to use flawed human beings to accomplish the task. While Jesus Christ, God in human form, lived on this earth, He chose twelve men. Twelve men who would shake the world. We recognize some of their names—Peter, James, John, Andrew, and so on—but do we really know them?

Here is what's amazing to me about these apostles Jesus called. They didn't have any of the technology we have. No television networks. No radio. No Internet. No iPads or smartphones. Peter didn't have a Facebook page. Philip didn't tweet. Everything they did was through word of mouth. Person to person. Face to face.

Today we call these guys—or at least most of them—"saints." When we see them depicted in religious literature or paintings or in stained glass windows, they are one-dimensional figures and don't seem real. And they always have their requisite halos over their heads.

Really, what is a saint? I heard about a little girl who was asked in her Sunday school class what a saint was. Thinking of the stained glass windows she saw in the church, she replied, "Those are people that the light shines through." Actually, she was on to something! Jesus said, "Let your light so shine before men, that they may see your good works and glorify your Father in heaven" (Matthew 5:16).

The word *saint* is really just another word for "believer." All men and women who have put their faith in Christ can legitimately call themselves saints. I am a saint (you may call me Saint Gregory if you like), and so are you if you belong to Jesus Christ.

So the twelve men whom Jesus called to be apostles were just regular people. They made mistakes. They had personality flaws. They were hopelessly human and remarkably unremarkable. However, despite these shortcomings, they were obedient to the Lord and available to Him.

This is one of the reasons why I believe the Bible to be the Word of God. It is a completely honest book—sometimes *painfully* so. In other religious books, those who speak for God are presented as flawless or perfect. But the only one presented as flawless in the pages of the Bible is Jesus Christ Himself. Everyone else has shortcomings, inconsistencies, and sometimes devastating faults.

God doesn't airbrush His heroes.

When Britain's Oliver Cromwell had his portrait painted, he is reported to have told the artist, "Paint me warts and all." And that's just what the painter did. Cromwell wasn't what you'd call a handsome man, but he wanted an honest portrait.

The Bible gives us its heroes, warts and all, with all of their flaws and mess-ups recorded. Does that encourage you like it encourages me? I too am a flawed person, and when I see that God can use an inconsistent, imperfect man or woman, it gives me hope that He might be able to use me as well.

Jesus didn't call these men because they were great; their greatness came as a result of the call of Jesus. *The Message* translation captures 1 Corinthians 1:26-28 with these words: "Take a good look, friends, at who you were when you got called into this life. I don't see many of 'the brightest and the best' among you, not many influential, not many from high-society families. Isn't it obvious that God deliberately chose men and women that the culture overlooks and exploits and abuses, chose these 'nobodies' to expose the hollow pretensions of the 'somebodies'?"

When God gets hold of a man or woman and works through that human life, something wonderful happens. In 2 Corinthians 4:7 (PH),

Paul reminds us that "this priceless treasure we hold, so to speak, in a common earthenware jar—to show that the splendid power of it belongs to God and not to us."

Count on it, *God can use you.* I can't imagine a person with less potential than myself at age seventeen, when God called me. I came to Him with so very little. It's not false modesty to say that anything good that has come from my life has been something God has given me or worked through me. It is His blessing and favor on my life. And if God can use someone like Greg Laurie, He can certainly use you.

The Twelve

And when He had called His twelve disciples to Him, He gave them power over unclean spirits, to cast them out, and to heal all kinds of sickness and all kinds of disease. Now the names of the twelve apostles are these: first, Simon, who is called Peter, and Andrew his brother; James the son of Zebedee, and John his brother; Philip and Bartholomew; Thomas and Matthew the tax collector; James the son of Alphaeus, and Lebbaeus, whose surname was Thaddaeus; Simon the Cananite, and Judas Iscariot, who also betrayed Him. (Matthew 10:1-4)

Simon Peter

Simon Peter is probably the most well known of all the apostles. Apart from Jesus Himself, no name is more mentioned in the New Testament than Peter's. He was a central figure of Jesus' three years of ministry and of the first three years of the early church. Jesus spent more time with Peter than with anyone else. At the same time, no other disciple was corrected and reproved as often as Peter.

Peter said what he thought, which isn't always the best idea. Maybe you know people like that. They don't know the difference between inside and outside thoughts; they just verbalize everything.

What's more, Peter wasn't shy about asking Jesus questions. He would often speak the questions everyone had on their minds, but no one was willing to ask. For instance, when the disciples were concerned about the rewards they would get for following Jesus, Peter didn't hesitate to speak his mind. In Matthew 19:27 (NIV) he said to Jesus, "We have left everything to follow you! What then will there be for us?"

Up on the Mount of Transfiguration, Peter, James, and John had the privilege of glimpsing their Lord in shining glory as He spoke with Moses and Elijah about His upcoming death. The three disciples had been asleep, and when they woke up, there was Jesus, shining like the sun. Unaccountably, Peter decided this would be a good time to say a few words. He said, "Sir, it's wonderful that we can be here! If you want me to, I'll make three shelters, one for you and one for Moses and one for Elijah" (Matthew 17:4, TLB).

I love how the gospel writer Mark gives a little commentary about Peter at this point: "He said this just to be talking, for he didn't know what else to say and they were all terribly frightened" (Mark 9:6, TLB).

Have you ever said something when you didn't know what to say? May I offer you a little advice? Don't say anything! As the old proverb tells us, "Better to be silent and thought a fool than to open your mouth and dispel all doubt." Peter, however, always spoke up.

But he also showed great boldness at times. It was Simon Peter who walked on the water to Jesus. On a dark and blustery night, the disciples saw Jesus walking across the waves toward their boat. Peter called out, "Lord, if it's You, tell me to come." And Jesus said, "It is Me. Come." Immediately, Peter put one leg over the side of that boat and pressed down on the water. It held him up. Then he put the other foot down and started walking, doing something no man has ever done apart from Christ Himself. Then, suddenly noticing the wind and waves, his faith faltered and he began to sink. He cried out, "Lord, save me!" And Jesus reached down, pulled him up, and said, "Peter, why did you doubt?" (see Matthew 14:22-33).

We can snicker at Peter and be critical of what he did, but no one else in that boat tried to walk on water!

In many ways, for all his faults, he was a commendable and courageous man. We all know about his denial and how he caved in to fear at a crucial moment. But when all was said and done, Peter had the courage to face the dark hours of martyrdom for his faith in Jesus. Before he was crucified, tradition says that Peter had to watch the crucifixion of his wife. Standing at the foot of his wife's cross, it is said he repeated to her the words, "Remember the Lord." After she died, he pleaded to be crucified upside down, because he felt unworthy to die in the same way his Lord did.

Peter was a hero of the faith.

Andrew

Andrew was Simon Peter's brother and the first disciple Jesus called. Right away, he went out and got his brother. John 1:41-42 (NIV) says, "The first thing Andrew did was to find his brother Simon and tell him, 'We have found the Messiah' (that is, the Christ). And he brought him to Jesus."

After that, of course, Andrew had to go through life being the brother of someone more well known than he was. Does that describe you? Maybe you were always recognized as the son or daughter of a well-known father or mother. Maybe your brother was a successful athlete or your sister got straight As, and that became the point of reference with everyone you met. *Oh, you're John's brother. Oh, you're Barbara's son.*

After Jesus called him, Andrew might have thought, "I'm onto a good thing here. I don't want to tell Peter about this; he gets all the breaks. No, Jesus called me and I want this all to myself." But Andrew didn't do that. He immediately went out, found his brother Simon, and introduced him to Jesus. That's a great description of what Andrew did for the rest of his life; he was always bringing people to Jesus.

Before Jesus miraculously fed five thousand people, the disciples were wondering how in the world they would ever find food for such a crowd. It was Andrew who said, "Here is a little boy with five loaves and two fish." And he brought the boy to Jesus.

Toward the end of the Lord's ministry, when some men from Greece showed up and wanted to see Jesus, Philip went to Andrew and Andrew took them personally to Christ. Andrew was the go-to guy when you wanted to get to Jesus. That would be a great thing to have said about you—that you were always bringing people to Jesus wherever you were. We celebrate the bigger-than-life, outspoken people like Simon Peter but sometimes forget about the Andrews. But if there were no Andrews, there would be no Simon Peters!

We might think of Andrew as the patron saint of the relatively unknown but faithful followers of Jesus Christ. These are people who labor behind the scenes. We don't know their names or much about them, but the Lord knows. God takes note of everything we do for Him, and He will someday reward us. Scripture tells us, "Let's not get tired of doing what is good. At just the right time we will reap a harvest of blessing if we don't give up" (Galatians 6:9, NLT). Even that little, quiet, barely noticeable thing you have done in the name of Jesus, something you would never even mention, has been seen and noted in heaven.

According to church tradition, Andrew ended his life lashed to an X-shaped cross. There he hung for two full days, calling on those who passed by to come to Jesus. In other words, he ended his earthly walk with Christ as he had begun it—leading people to Jesus. He may have been quieter than Simon Peter, but in his own way he shook the world.

James and John

You've got to love these guys—they were so colorful! James and John were known as the "sons of thunder," and you don't get a nickname like that for being quiet and blending in. Those men had a reputation! If those two were around today, I wonder if they would be biker dudes—all tatted up and riding obnoxiously loud choppers, with "Sons of Thunder" written on the backs of their leather jackets.

Obviously, you get a name like that because of a tendency to lose your temper. On one occasion, when Jesus preached to the

Samaritans, James and John were not hospitable toward them. The brothers thought it might be a good idea to roast all of them on the spot. They said, "Lord, do You want us to command fire to come down from heaven and consume them . . . ?" (Luke 9:54).

Jesus might have replied (in a loose paraphrase), "Guys, I did not come to toast people, but to save them."

It's worth noting that three men were in the Lord's inner circle and spent more time with Him than anyone else: Peter, James, and John. Jesus took this trio with Him when He raised Lazarus from the dead, when He was transfigured on the mountain, and when He agonized in prayer at Gethsemane.

Why did He do that? We might be inclined to think they had this privilege because they were elite apostles or just a little more spiritual than the rest. Maybe. But then again, maybe these guys needed extra attention.

When I was in school I used to get in trouble a lot for talking and goofing off. On more than one occasion the teacher would say, "Greg Laurie, you bring your desk right up next to mine where I can keep an eye on you." Was that why the Lord spent so much time with Peter, James, and John? We have no way of knowing, but we do know God used them mightily through the years of their ministry, and they stayed faithful to the Lord to the very end.

Frail, faulty, and imperfect as these men might have been, Jesus changed them and used them. He changed Simon from a man who was impulsive, talked too much, and gave in to fear into a fearless preacher of the gospel. He changed James and John, too. James was the first of the apostles to be martyred, beheaded by Herod. John, once known for his anger, became known as the apostle of love. If you read his New Testament letters, you can't miss how much he talked about the love of God.

As far as we know, John was the only apostle who did not die the death of a martyr. History tells us that his enemies tried to boil him in a cauldron of oil, but for some reason he wouldn't cook. Then they banished him to the lonely, rocky island of Patmos, never expecting to hear from him again. But during his time in that place Jesus gave John the book of Revelation.

Philip

We don't know much about Philip. Matthew, Mark, and Luke give no details about him. Everything we read of Philip is recorded in John's gospel. He was personally called by Jesus. John 1:43 says, "The following day Jesus wanted to go to Galilee, and He found Philip and said to him, 'Follow Me.'"

Jesus Himself found Philip. Most of us came to faith because someone led us to the Lord or brought us to a church service or crusade where we heard and understood the gospel. In my life, I just happened upon the gospel by accident, being attracted to a group of Christians out on the lawn of my high school campus. Of course, it was the Lord who was calling me all along. There are times, however, when the Lord seems to overrule the typical ways He works and just reaches out and gets hold of someone. That's what happened with Saul of Tarsus as well, when the brightness of the Lord's appearing literally knocked him out of the saddle.

Philip, like Andrew, didn't keep the good news to himself. We read,

> Now Philip was from Bethsaida, the city of Andrew and Peter. Philip found Nathanael and said to him, "We have found Him of whom Moses in the law, and also the prophets, wrote—Jesus of Nazareth, the son of Joseph."
>
> And Nathanael said to him, "Can anything good come out of Nazareth?"
>
> Philip said to him, "Come and see." (John 1:44-46)

Philip pops up again in the story of the feeding of the five thousand. The great crowd had been gathering, and Jesus used the occasion to test Philip.

When Jesus looked up and saw a great crowd coming toward him, he said to Philip, "Where shall we buy bread for these people to eat?" He asked this only to test him, for he already had in mind what he was going to do.

Philip answered him, "It would take more than half a year's wages to buy enough bread for each one to have a bite!" (John 6:5-7, NIV)

That's what teachers will do! They will ask you a question, already knowing the answer. But they want to see if you know the answer—and if you have been really listening.

Philip didn't exactly ace that test. Instead of remembering who it was who asked him that question, Philip pulled out his calculator and started working out the numbers. He hadn't learned much yet. He was still looking at life through the eyes of logic instead of the eyes of faith.

Andrew did a little bit better on the exam. He said to Jesus, "Here is a boy with five small barley loaves and two small fish, but how far will they go among so many?" (John 6:9, NIV). If Philip got a D on that quiz, Andrew got a C+ or maybe a B-. He was close but wasn't quite there. Yet both of these men stayed true to their Lord to the very end. Church tradition tells us that Philip reached many people with the gospel and was stoned to death for his faith.

Bartholomew (or Nathanael) and Thomas

Jesus found Nathanael under a fig tree. Philip may have urged his friend Nathanael to meet the Lord, but Jesus already had His eye on this good man.

When Jesus saw Nathanael approaching, he said of him, "Here truly is an Israelite in whom there is no deceit."

"How do you know me?" Nathanael asked.

Jesus answered, "I saw you while you were still under the fig tree before Philip called you."

Then Nathanael declared, "Rabbi, you are the Son of God; you are the king of Israel."

Jesus said, "You believe because I told you I saw you under the fig tree. You will see greater things than that." (John 1:47-50, NIV)

Thomas was another disciple who only appears a few times in Scripture. In contrast to Peter's impetuous ways and the thunder of James and John, Thomas was more of a steady-as-she-goes kind of individual. Peter would have sailed his boat twice across the Sea of Galilee while Thomas was still making up his mind whether the weather was suitable for sailing.

This disciple has been wrongly characterized as a doubter; we call him "Doubting Thomas." I like to think of him more as a skeptical man. By nature, I too am skeptical. In other words, I'm not the first to believe something just because someone says it is true. When Thomas missed the appearance of the resurrected Christ, even though the other disciples insisted it was true, Thomas declared, "I won't believe it unless I see the nail wounds in his hands, put my fingers into them, and place my hand into the wound in his side" (John 20:25, NLT).

We can criticize a response like that, but Thomas was only asking for what the others had seen. But within a little more than a week, Thomas would see for himself, and would then declare, "My Lord and my God!" (John 20:28).

There's nothing wrong with wanting to know something for yourself. Sometimes as Christian parents we freak out a little bit when our kids start pushing back and asking some intelligent questions. We immediately assume the worst: "My son doesn't believe what we've taught him!" But doubt isn't always a sign that a man is wrong; it is also a sign that he is *thinking*. Someone once said, "Skepticism is the first step toward truth." Being a little skeptical of something you've heard isn't a bad thing—as long as you go to Jesus for the answers, which Thomas did.

Just before He went to the cross, Jesus spoke to His apostles about leaving them to go to the cross and later back to heaven. He told them that in His Father's house there are many mansions and that He was going to prepare a place for them. Then He said, "Where I go you know, and the way you know" (John 14:4). I can imagine all the disciples nodding in agreement and saying, "This is so good, so deep," when they didn't have a clue what Jesus meant. Thomas was the only one who actually said what he was thinking: "Lord, we do not know where You are going, and how can we know the way?" (John 14:5).

In other words, "What are You talking about? What do You mean about mansions and Your Father's house? You seem to be talking about going somewhere without us, but I don't get it. How do You expect us to know the way?"

To that Jesus answered, "I am the way, the truth, and the life. No one comes to the Father except through Me" (John 14:6).

He didn't reprove Thomas or smack him down for the question. No, Jesus answered him, and that answer has brought comfort to believers for two thousand years. Church tradition tells us that Thomas died as a martyr, thrust through with a lance.

Matthew (or Levi)

The author of the gospel of Matthew had been a hated tax collector, a Jew collaborating with the Roman overlords. Besides the high taxes Rome already demanded of the Jewish nation, these tax collectors would add more on top of the bill and pocket the difference. No wonder they were so despised! Matthew probably did that as well. He would sit in his little tax booth, elevated above the people so he could keep his eye on everyone. He had a ledger in front of him, where he kept a record of who was current in paying their taxes and who was delinquent.

It must have shocked him deeply to see Jesus Christ striding toward him one day. And then Jesus looked at Matthew. That phrase in the Greek could be translated, "He looked right through him."

Have you ever had anyone look right through you? Moms have a way of doing that, don't they? You come home late at night and she confronts you: "Where have you been?" You reply, "Aw, nowhere, Mom."

Then she says, "Look me in the eyes. Where have you been?"

Jesus looked right through him and then said two words that forever changed Matthew's life: *"Follow Me."* And the amazing thing is, he did! Right then and there, with no hesitation. Matthew got up from the table, left his little tax booth, followed Jesus, and never looked back. In his own gospel, I love the fact that Matthew simply wrote that he "followed Jesus." He didn't talk about what he gave up or left behind that day. In fact, he probably gave up more financially than any of the other apostles. Peter, James, and John were simple fishermen, but Matthew was probably wealthy. He could have stayed in this career trajectory and ended up on easy street in his old age.

But he didn't do that. He saw it as a privilege to follow Jesus, and he left everything behind to do that.

Judas Iscariot

Judas was the one wild card in the middle of the Twelve. He is possibly the most mysterious, paradoxical, and misunderstood individual in all of Scripture. His very name has become synonymous with treachery. If we call someone a "Judas," everyone knows exactly what we mean. We all know that he ended his life in suicide after selling out Jesus for thirty pieces of silver. But was he really as obviously evil as we imagine him to be?

When we visualize Judas, we might picture someone in a black Darth Vader robe with a cunning, evil expression on his face. Not at all. In fact, Judas came off as the ultimate good guy, a man of great compassion. At an intimate dinner party for Jesus shortly before the cross, Judas scolded Mary of Bethany for pouring out a bottle of expensive perfume on the Lord's head. In John's gospel we read,

"Why wasn't this oil sold and the money given to the poor? It would have easily brought three hundred silver pieces." He said this not because he cared two cents about the poor but

because he was a thief. He was in charge of their common
funds, but also embezzled them. (John 12:5-6, MSG)

The other disciples thought Judas was being wise and benevolent. "Oh yes, Judas, that's a good point. You're such a compassionate man!" But in truth, he was a common thief. Sometimes people look good on the outside when they are corrupt on the inside. Judas may have looked like a good and godly guy, but in reality he was as wicked as they come.

Someone might say, "Yes, but didn't he come to his senses later? Didn't he go back to the chief priests and tell them he'd made a terrible mistake? Wasn't he filled with remorse?" Maybe he was. But remorse is not the same as repentance. There's a big difference between repentance and just being sorry for what you did (and sorry you got caught). Peter denied Jesus three times but deeply repented of what he had done. Judas betrayed Jesus for thirty pieces of silver, and he could have repented, too. But he never did.

The truth is, Jesus loved and chose Judas. In the upper room, He washed the feet of all the disciples, including Judas. That was after Judas had already decided to betray Jesus. If you knew someone was going to betray you, would you wash their feet? Not me. I'd *break* their feet—right before I broke their neck. But Jesus washed this man's feet even though He knew what he was up to. Judas had no doubt been toying with the evil idea in his mind for some time, and then at that same dinner in the upper room, Jesus said to him, "Whatever you're planning, Judas, get it done." And Scripture says that Satan entered the man's heart, and he betrayed his Lord (see John 13:27). One thing this incident suggests is this: Don't toy with sinful ideas or fantasies in your mind if you don't want them to become tragic realities in your life. If you let evil hang around long enough, if you refuse to put it to death, it will end up having its way with you (see Colossians 3:5-10).

Right up to the end in the Garden of Gethsemane, Judas could have repented. He could have been forgiven if he had wanted to be. When Judas brought the temple guard, armed to the teeth, to apprehend Jesus, the Lord greeted him with the word *friend*. He said to him, "Friend, why have you come?" (Matthew 26:50).

But Judas did not want to change the direction he was traveling, and in the end, he reaped the consequences of his actions.

He Will Use You, Too

There were others within the Twelve that we don't know very much about: James the son of Alphaeus, Simon the Zealot, and Judas (or Thaddeus) the son of James. Each had their own unique personalities and their own faults, flaws, and shortcomings, but Jesus called each one of them.

Do you relate to any of these guys? Maybe you are skeptical like Thomas, impulsive and impetuous like Peter, or quiet and soft-spoken like Andrew. Maybe you are short tempered and quick to draw conclusions like James and John, or lacking in faith like Philip. It really doesn't matter what personality God gave you or what your track record might be. God can change you and use you, as He changed and used these men.

God can make you into the man or woman He wants you to be, and He can accomplish a great deal with even a little raw material.

The bottom line is that we need to bring who we are and what we have to Jesus. Remember the little boy with his simple lunch of barley loaves and dried fish? It wasn't much of a lunch, really, and yet when he gave it to Jesus, the Lord used it to feed five thousand.

Bring what you have to Christ, and say, "Lord, I know this isn't a lot. You don't have a great catch here. I am not one of the world's most beautiful or intelligent people. But what I have and who I am I give to You. I want You to shake my world."

Then just watch what God will do with you!

CHAPTER TWENTY-FIVE
DEALING WITH DOUBT

swald Chambers once said, "Doubt is not always a sign that a man is wrong. It may be a sign that he is thinking."

Most of us, if we were honest, could admit to times when we doubted God and doubted our faith. Sometimes things happen that seem to make no earthly sense. In the midst of these experiences, we wonder where God is and why He permitted these circumstances. Or perhaps we come to a crucial crossroads where we desperately need an answer from God, but heaven seems silent and unresponsive to our cries.

We wonder, *Is God just sitting on His hands, watching me twist in the wind? Is He paying any attention to me at all?* And in such moments, we may (at least momentarily) entertain a few doubts.

Someone once said, "When the warm moist air of our expectations collides with the icy cold of God's silence, inevitably clouds of doubt begin to form."

And then, of course, we know that Satan loves nothing better than to pile on to those negative thoughts, encouraging us to slip even further into darkness. He will say, "I can't believe you're entertaining thoughts like that! You're such a failure, such a hypocrite. If you have doubts like this, you're probably not even a Christian."

You may be surprised to learn, however, that some of the greatest men and women of God in the Bible and in history had their moments of doubt. This includes the prophet Jesus Himself called the greatest "of all who have ever lived" (Matthew 11:11, NLT).

That's what we're going to talk about in this chapter. We're going to see how Jesus dealt with John the Baptist in his hour of doubt and uncertainty.

It Begins with Confusion

John's doubt began with confusion. From the beginning of his ministry, and perhaps for most of his life, John had cherished an idea of what the Messiah would be and do when He came. But then as John watched Jesus' ministry develop, he became more and more puzzled. Jesus simply wasn't doing what John had expected and anticipated. John had misunderstood what God was intending to do, and his perplexity and confusion pushed him into doubt.

We have that same problem sometimes.

I like to tell the story of the elderly couple celebrating their sixtieth wedding anniversary. The husband wanted to tell everyone how much he loved his wife, who happened to be hard of hearing. Standing and offering a toast, he said, "I just want to say to my dear wife that after sixty years I have found you *tried and true*." A ripple of applause swept through the room, and everyone said, "Oh, that was so sweet."

But his wife said, "What?"

So he offered the toast again, a little louder this time. "My dear wife, after sixty years I have found you tried and true." Frowning, she shot back with the words, "Well, after sixty years I am tired of you, too!"

That's what can happen with a little confusion and misunderstanding!

In the same way, the doubts we may feel can sometimes start with a misunderstanding. Sometimes we are simply confused about what we think God should be doing. In the following pages, let's take a closer look at Scripture and see how Jesus dealt with John's confusion and disappointment.

"More than a Prophet . . ."

Now it came to pass, when Jesus finished commanding His twelve disciples, that He departed from there to teach and to preach in their cities.

And when John had heard in prison about the works of Christ, he sent two of his disciples and said to Him, "Are You the Coming One, or do we look for another?"

Jesus answered and said to them, "Go and tell John the things which you hear and see: The blind see and the lame walk; the lepers are cleansed and the deaf hear; the dead are raised up and the poor have the gospel preached to them. And blessed is he who is not offended because of Me."

As they departed, Jesus began to say to the multitudes concerning John: "What did you go out into the wilderness to see? A reed shaken by the wind? But what did you go out to see? A man clothed in soft garments? Indeed, those who wear soft clothing are in kings' houses. But what did you go out to see? A prophet? Yes, I say to you, and more than a prophet. For this is he of whom it is written:

'Behold, I send My messenger before Your face,
Who will prepare Your way before You.'

"Assuredly, I say to you, among those born of women there has not risen one greater than John the Baptist; but he who is least in the kingdom of heaven is greater than he." (Matthew 11:1-11)

We need to understand who John was. In another translation, Jesus said of him, "No one in history surpasses John the Baptizer" (Matthew 11:11, MSG). At the time Jesus spoke those words, John was super-significant in Israel, a man of national prominence and renown, greatly admired and followed by thousands. You might say John was a first-century rock star. He was someone people looked up to and loved because he was a prophet of God.

This was a big deal? A *very* big deal. Israel hadn't heard from the God of Israel for four hundred years—from the death of the prophet Malachi, last of the Old Testament prophets, to the angelic announcement of John's birth. For four hundred years, heaven had remained silent, without a single prophet, angelic appearance, or miracle. And then suddenly a colorful prophet burst onto the scene out of the wilderness, dressed in the skins of wild animals, subsisting on a diet of locusts and wild honey, and crying out in a loud voice, "The kingdom of heaven is near."

He captured the imagination of the people, and they loved him. So significant was John in his day that the ancient historian Josephus wrote more about him than he did about Jesus Himself. In fact, John was so popular some thought he might be the Messiah himself. But that was never his role; it was his God-given task to prepare the way for the Messiah, to go before the Lord and blaze a trail.

Famous as he may have been, however, his motto as time went on became "He must become greater and greater, and I must become less and less" (John 3:30, TLB).

John the Baptist had no doubt about his job description: It was to point people to the Messiah. In his gospel, John described a day when Jesus was walking toward John and his followers, and John declared, "Behold! The Lamb of God who takes away the sin of the world!" (John 1:29).

Though John had his own followers, he was essentially saying, "My work is done. You guys need to follow Jesus now." Almost overnight, he walked away from a huge national ministry because his mission was completed. The Messiah had now come, and John had done his best to prepare His way.

Herod, Israel's puppet king, had been impressed by John's preaching. John was maybe one of the only men in Herod's life who would stand eyeball to eyeball with him and tell him the truth about life. Herod no doubt found that shocking—but maybe also a bit refreshing as well.

Theirs was something of a strange relationship. We read that Herod imprisoned John, yet he feared and protected him while he was in custody. Mark 6:20 (NIV) tells us that when John spoke to Herod, the king was "greatly puzzled; yet he liked to listen to him."

What Herod didn't appreciate hearing was John's straight-forward rebuke regarding the king's immoral relationship with a woman named Herodias. As it turned out, she was already married—to Herod's brother Phillip. She was also the daughter of Aristobulus, another half-brother of Herod, meaning that Herod had taken up with his own niece and sister-in-law.

John called him on it, and Herod didn't like it one bit.

Herodias liked it even less.

While Herod might have been perturbed, Herodias was coldly furious. She hated John, and wanted him silenced ASAP.

Herodias finally had her chance in the course of a drunken banquet, when she had her daughter Salome perform a seductive dance in front of the leering king and his guests. In the fog of his drunkenness and the excitement of the moment, Herod made an oath to give the girl whatever she wanted, up to half his kingdom. Salome hurried back to her mother, but there was never any real question about what the girl would ask for. Herodias said, "You tell the king I want the head of John the Baptist on a platter *right now*." Because the king had made an oath in front of all of his guests he felt he had to comply, and John was executed.

In Matthew 11, however, John was still alive and in prison. How difficult it must have been for an outdoorsman like John, used to roaming far and wide and sleeping out under the stars every night, to be locked away in a dark, smelly dungeon. How strange it must have been to be a national news story and phenomenon one moment, only to be plunged into total obscurity the next.

For John, however, that wasn't the worst of it.

There in confinement in Herod's jail, he began to wonder if he'd misunderstood the Lord or missed the boat somehow. *Was Jesus Christ really the Messiah?*

Misunderstanding God

The fact was, Jesus simply wasn't doing what John had thought, anticipated, or imagined He would be doing. It didn't make sense to John, and he felt perplexed—and probably disappointed. John's problem was that of many others when Jesus first came on the scene: He thought Jesus would overthrow Rome and establish His kingdom then and there.

After a while, however, it became evident that Jesus wasn't going to do those things (yet). The situation in Israel was as bad as ever, and John had seemingly been left to languish in Herod's dungeon.

Besides those things, John was hearing rumors that Jesus had been hanging out with some pretty unsavory characters. What was that all about? Maybe the reports sounded something like this: "Say, John, did you know your cousin Jesus—the One you said was the Lamb of God—was just at a big party with a bunch of tax collectors and prostitutes? I kid you not!"

John, in his humanity, began to wonder if he'd made a mistake.

"After all," John might have reasoned, "when Messiah comes, isn't He supposed to bring deliverance to the captives, and hope to the brokenhearted? But here I sit in this dungeon. This isn't working out the way I thought it would."

In fact, events were developing exactly as God intended. The Lamb of God was headed toward a cross to give His life as a ransom for all people, for all time. The restored kingdom of Israel, with Jesus on the throne, had to await His Second Coming. This time, He had to suffer and die. Before Jesus would wear a crown of gold, He would first have to wear a crown of thorns. Before He would sit on a throne, He would first be nailed to a cross.

The Scriptures, of course, taught this all along. Passages such as Psalm 22 and Isaiah 53 speak extensively about the suffering of the Messiah. But because John didn't understand this—or possibly because he longed with all his heart to see Rome overthrown and the kingdom of God arrive—he felt confused by the Lord's actions. That's how he ended up sending Jesus a message that said, "Are You the One? Did we misunderstand this?"

This can happen to us as well. Sometimes we misunderstand God and His Word. This might happen when a tragedy hits, when a child goes astray, when a loved one dies, when we receive devastating news from a doctor. A shocking event like this just doesn't fit in with what we had planned for our lives or how we believed things would work out. And perhaps we find ourselves saying, "God, are You really paying attention? Why did You let this happen to me?" Our problem is that we tend to interpret God in the light of the tragedy, instead of the other way around.

I think John in Matthew 11 was essentially crying out to Jesus, saying, "Why haven't You helped me?" And he found himself wrestling with doubt.

The Foyer of Doubt

Doubt is not necessarily a sin.

There is a French proverb that says, "He who knows nothing doubts nothing." Sometimes doubt is not the opposite of faith; it is rather an element of faith. It means you are thinking some things through and grappling with the issues. It means you are trying to process certain events or information, wondering how it all fits in with life as you understand it.

Sometimes you and I have to pass through the foyer of doubt to enter into the sanctuary of certainty. That's something to keep in mind if your kids come to you and say, "Mom, I'm struggling with this. How can you say that God created the world?" Or, "Dad, I'm having a hard time with what the Bible says about living morally." Or, "My teacher says there are lots of contradictions in the Bible." Don't panic. That can be a good sign. It means that they're starting to grow up and think for themselves, and you need to be available to help them through this process of finding their own faith. They can't live off the faith of their parents.

The key, however, in this matter of dealing with doubts is to cry out to God.

British pastor G. Campbell Morgan put it like this: "Men of faith are always the men who have to confront problems." And Warren Wiersbe continues the thought:

For if you believe in God, you will sometimes wonder why He allows certain things to happen. But keep in mind that there's a difference between doubt and unbelief. Like Habakkuk, the doubter questions God and may even debate God, but the doubter doesn't abandon God. But unbelief is rebellion against God, a refusal to accept what He says and does. Unbelief is an act of the will, while doubt is born out of a troubled mind and a broken heart.[13]

Doubt, then, is a matter of the *mind*. Unbelief is a matter of the *will*. Doubt says, "I don't get it. Help me understand this. Work with me through this." Unbelief says, "I do get it, I don't like it, and I refuse to accept it."

John the Baptist, closed up in his lonely prison cell, was simply doubting. But it wasn't unbelief.

Even the great men and women of God have their moments of despair. Moses was ready to quit on one occasion after listening to the Israelites complain for the umpteenth time. He said, "Lord, if this is the way it's going to be, I'd prefer if You just killed me right now."

And Elijah? He said pretty much the same thing after hearing that Queen Jezebel had put out a contract on his life. He said, "Enough of this, Lord. Please take my life. I've had it."

Even the great apostle Paul became discouraged. Listen to this passage from his life journal, recorded in 2 Corinthians 1:8-9 (NLT): "We think you ought to know, dear brothers and sisters, about the trouble we went through in the province of Asia. We were crushed and overwhelmed beyond our ability to endure, and we thought we would never live through it. In fact, we expected to die."

So then, if you find yourself struggling with some doubts right now, take heart. You are in very good company.

When you think about it, John wasn't asking for information as much as confirmation. He was saying, in effect, "Lord, explain this to me again. Did I get this right? Are You the Messiah? Are You the One we've been looking for?"

To allay his doubts, he sent two messengers to Jesus with his honest question: "Are You the Coming One, or do we look for another?" (Matthew 11:3). Notice how Jesus responded:

Jesus answered and said to them, "Go and tell John the things which you hear and see: The blind see and the lame walk; the lepers are cleansed and the deaf hear; the dead are raised up and the poor have the gospel preached to them. And blessed is he who is not offended because of Me." (Matthew 11:4-6)

In His answer, Jesus referred to Old Testament passages that John would have been familiar with, including Isaiah 35 and 61. He was effectively saying something like this: "No, John, I'm not leading a revolt, and I'm not going to overthrow Rome. That's not in the program right now. But I am removing disabilities wherever I encounter them, and I am bringing men and women into a right relationship with God. When that is right, everything else will change as well."

To borrow a current popular expression, Jesus could have thrown John under the bus in that moment. He could have said, "It's disappointing that John is doubting Me. I'm sorry to see him cave under pressure like this." Instead, He stuck up for John, giving him high praise.

Do you do that? When someone criticizes one of your friends in your presence, do you stick up for your friend? Do you defend him or her? Or do you give a listening ear to gossip instead of challenging it? "Wait a second. That's my friend you're talking about. I happen to know that this person is a godly man, a godly woman. Where did you get that stuff?"

Stick up for your friends, as Jesus stuck up for His friends. John the Baptist was a loyal man of God, and the Lord spoke well of him before the people. In verse 6, He used the occasion to make a point about persevering in faith: "Blessed is he who is not offended because of Me." Or literally, "Blessed is the man or woman who is not annoyed or repelled or made to stumble whatever may occur." In essence Jesus was saying, "Look, you may not understand My methods or My ways or My timing. But I am asking you to trust Me, even when you are unable to see why I am doing what I am doing— or why I'm *not* doing what you think I ought to be doing. Just trust Me, hang in there, and hold your course."

Jesus told the people, "What were you looking for when you went searching for John out in the desert? A reed blowing in the wind? Someone unstable with no courage? Listen, John the Baptist is a great man. And even though he's in a tight place right now and wrestling with some doubts, I love him."

Then He made this amazing statement in verse 11: "Assuredly, I say to you, among those born of women there has not risen one greater than John the Baptist; but he who is least in the kingdom of heaven is greater than he."

Why would Jesus say that John was the greatest of all men—or maybe the greatest of all the Old Testament prophets? After all, we have no record of John performing any miracles, as Elijah and Elisha did. John never wrote a prophetic book like Isaiah, Jeremiah, or Ezekiel. So why would John be the greatest of the prophets?

First of all, he was the greatest because he was the last of them. Yes, he was the final prophet of the Old Testament economy or system. But beyond that, John was the greatest because he and he alone was the direct forerunner and herald of the Messiah. His greatness was a direct result of his nearness and connection to Jesus. His story is in the New Testament, but his life and ministry were actually part of the Old Testament system. The New Testament system didn't really begin until Jesus inaugurated it and fulfilled the Old.

John, then, was the greatest of the greatest, the best of the best, and the finest of the prophets. Jesus was saying, "This is My man John. Don't even think about criticizing him!"

What, then, does the last phrase in verse 11 mean? Jesus concluded, "But he who is least in the kingdom of heaven is greater than he."

This speaks to the incredible privilege you and I experience now as believers in Jesus Christ, with Christ actually taking up residence within our very lives. Jesus is saying that the least among us—the most timid, least visible Christian you can imagine—is greater than John the Baptist. John, still living under the Old Testament economy, hadn't experienced Jesus' consistent presence.

But we have.

Jesus said, "Look! I have been standing at the door, and I am constantly knocking. If anyone hears me calling him and opens the door, I will come in and fellowship with him and he with me" (Revelation 3:20, TLB).

We really have no idea what an awesome privilege that is. To have the Son of God actually enter our lives, live inside us, and be our constant Companion and Friend? What an incredible opportunity! John was a herald of the King, you and I get to be friends of the King. John was a friend of the Bridegroom, you and I are the bride of the Bridegroom. You can't find a higher privilege than that.

John the Baptist lived and died on the other side of the crucifixion, resurrection, and ascension of Jesus. We live in the New Covenant with Christ living in our hearts. As great as John was, he didn't have that kind of privilege and closeness to Jesus.

How Did the Lord Deal with John's Doubt?

The Lord dealt with John's season of doubt in the same way He will deal with doubt and uncertainty in our lives.

Jesus refocused John's priorities.

John had some unbiblical and unrealistic expectations of the ministry, purpose, and timing of Jesus. And that was true pretty much of all of His disciples. He didn't rebuke John for his expectations, but He didn't release him from prison, either. Instead, He just corrected his thinking.

All of us need that sort of correction and refocusing in our lives at times, because we tend to lose perspective. An unexpected bill comes due, you can't imagine how you will ever pay it, and you panic. What do you need to do? You need to remember the Word of God, which tells you, "God shall supply all your need according to His riches in glory by Christ Jesus" (Philippians 4:19).

Maybe some crisis slams into your life, and you feel like events are spinning out of control. You need to remember the Word of God, which says, "God is our refuge and strength, a very present help in trouble. Therefore we will not fear, even though the earth be removed, and though the mountains be carried into the midst of the sea" (Psalm 46:1-2).

We have to allow the Word of God and God's Holy Spirit to correct our thinking. It's like being in a car that's run into a curb and knocked itself out of alignment. Unless you get the car's steering realigned, it will pull to the left or pull to the right, and it will be difficult to keep it on the road. In the same way, taking time to meditate on the Scriptures will realign our thoughts and our emotions.

In the interest of full disclosure, I'll tell you I have to do this myself. There are times when unexpected, stressful events can send me into a tailspin. Even though my son Christopher went to heaven back in 2008, the terrible finality of that will sometimes just hit me. *My son is no longer here with me. I will never see him again in this life.* In those moments, I will sometimes feel gripped by a panic, thinking, "No! This can't be true!" Even though several years have gone by, Christopher's death is still hard for me to accept at times, and in those times I have to correct my thinking with biblical truth. I quote Scripture to myself, and I say, "Now, Greg, you listen. The Bible says your son is still alive. He is in heaven, and you're going to see him again. Jesus is the resurrection and the life, and both you and Christopher belong to Him."

I allow God's Word to realign my thinking and refocus my priorities, clearing away the fog and barrage of emotions. God does this for me, and He uses His Word to accomplish it.

Jesus brought him back to the Word of God.

In the message Jesus sent back to John, He quoted prophesies from the book of Isaiah, reminding John what the Word of God says about the ministry of the coming Messiah. It was a firm but kind way of saying, "John, remember the Word of God. I am fulfilling the Scriptures."

When you're going through difficult times, you don't need pious platitudes, empty human wisdom, silly sayings, or greeting card verses. You need the Word of God. That alone gives hope. That alone resonates in our souls. Advice from other sources or humanist philosophies not only fails to help us, it might actually hurt us.

People in crisis need the Word of God. We might try all day to think of something clever or insightful to say to someone in distress or pain, but if it isn't based in God's eternal Word, it might do more harm than good.

Even those of us who have been Christians for years, who have studied the Word and perhaps even preached the Word, still need to be reminded from time to time of what that Word *says*.

The apostle Peter stated right up front that reminding believers of what they already knew was one of the main goals of his New Testament letters. One of the newer translations records Peter's words like this:

> *Because the stakes are so high, even though you're up-to-date on all this truth and practice it inside and out, I'm not going to let up for a minute in calling you to attention before it. This is the post to which I've been assigned—keeping you alert with frequent reminders—and I'm sticking to it as long as I live.* (2 Peter 1:12-13, MSG)

I find that I often forget what I ought to remember, and then I remember what I ought to forget. I have reams of worthless information permanently embedded in my mind that I can call up at a moment's notice, while other things—including some very, very important things—are fuzzy to me at times. How do I overcome this short-term spiritual memory? By constantly going over those things I have read and reread in Scripture, calling to memory those eternal truths that really matter.

Jesus encouraged John to hold his course.

In essence, Jesus was saying to John, "Hold your course! I know it's hard, and I know you don't get it right now. I know it isn't making sense to you. But I am asking you to hold your course."

That is what we need to do in our times of heartache and trial. We can honestly pray, "Lord, I don't understand this at all right now. These things don't make any sense." But the Lord says to us, "I know you can't understand right now. But remember that I am in control, remember that I love you, and remember that I am working all things together for your good. You just stay on course, and don't let this situation throw you. Keep trusting Me, and keep doing what you know to do."

In the book of Hebrews, the author told a group of hurting, under-pressure believers: "Take a new grip with your tired hands, stand firm on your shaky legs, and mark out a straight, smooth path for your feet so that those who follow you, though weak and lame, will not fall and hurt themselves but become strong" (12:12-13, TLB).

One day everything will come into focus when we see the Lord, and we will realize that the Lord wasn't sitting on His hands during our hard times. As a matter of fact, those hands were nailed to a cross. One day we will understand why God did or did not do what we thought He should do. And until that day, Jesus wants us to simply trust and follow Him.

A Reed in the Wind

What did you go out into the wilderness to see? A reed shaken by the wind? (Matthew 11:7)

That wasn't John. He didn't flip-flop or follow the latest fads. John knew who he was, understood his God-given role, and held to his course.

As Christians, we experience many different cross-currents of wind that blow into our lives.

Winds of Adversity

Adversity can feel like a strong, cold wind that cuts through everything and everyone in its path. Where we live, in Southern California, we don't experience those frigid winter winds very much. On the east coast or in the Midwest, however, you'd better wear layers in the winter and make sure you have a scarf, gloves, and something over your ears, because the icy, biting wind will sometimes make you feel like you're not wearing anything at all. The winds of adversity can swoop down upon us unexpectedly, and with great and devastating force. We really can't avoid those winds. John the Baptist faced them, too, but he held to his course in spite of them. He was no spineless reed, bowing before every breeze. John stood strong in his faith, and so should we.

I heard a story about a traveler who was visiting a logging area in the Pacific Northwest. He watched with great interest as a lumberjack walking alongside a mountain stream would periodically jab his sharp hook into a log, pulling it away from the others and separating it. The traveler asked the logger what he was doing, and the man replied, "These logs probably all look alike to you, but I recognize that some of them are quite different. The ones I let pass are from trees that grow in a valley, where they're always protected from the storms. The grain on those logs is rather coarse. But the logs I pull aside come from high up in the mountains, where they're beaten by strong winds from the time they're seedlings. This toughens the trees and gives them a fine grain. We save them for choice work. They're too good to be used for ordinary lumber."

So maybe you are facing the wind of adversity right now and you wonder why. Could it be that God is saving you for a choice work? Could it be that the Lord is allowing this to toughen the grain of your life, letting you go through hardship so you'll be able to do something unique for Him?

Winds of Temptation

Here in coastal Southern California, we have to deal with the hot, dry Santa Ana winds, justly called "devil winds." They come roaring out of the deserts in the east and instantly change the temperature. Any small spark in the dry hills can turn into a raging fire. If an arsonist gets involved to exploit the situation, these winds can create devastating property damage and even loss of life.

Temptation can be like that in our lives. Those hot winds can suddenly blow across our lives, and Satan, the master arsonist, will seek to exploit those temptations to lead us down a destructive path. But we have to stand strong in those winds, not bowing to them or giving way before them. We need to be like John the Baptist and stand our ground.

Winds of Compromise

In contrast to the winds of adversity or the hot blast of temptation, the winds of compromise feel more like a soft summer breeze, lulling us to sleep. Can you picture it? The ukuleles are playing, the soft trade winds are blowing, and the palm trees are gently swaying. You're half asleep and at your ease, and in that state of mind compromises don't seem like such a bad thing.

Temptations to compromise our honesty, our purity, or our integrity will blow our way every day. If Satan can't get us to fall into the "big" sins, he will encourage us to simply cut the corners a little, perhaps dabbling with sins or playing around the edges of immorality or dishonesty.

Jesus said John the Baptist wasn't that kind of man. He wasn't a reed swayed by the wind. He didn't adapt his message to please people or ingratiate himself to those in power. He stood his ground and spoke the truth—even to the enemies who wanted to destroy him.

Whatever You Are Facing . . .

Doubts will come into our lives as surely as the wind will blow. We need to remember, however, that no matter how the wind howls or tries to shake us, God is in control, and He has His purposes in all the struggles, doubts, and trials we face. We need to stand our ground as John did, trusting the Lord and remembering that He will never give us more than we can handle (see 1 Corinthians 10:13).

Remember that amazing statement Jesus made—"He that is least in the kingdom of God is greater than John the Baptist"? As I mentioned, this refers to all of us who have put our faith in Jesus Christ. We who have Jesus Christ actually living at the core of our lives have even greater resources that John the Baptist had available to him. Whatever you may be facing in your life, you don't have to face it alone. There is a God who cares, a God who loves you, a God who will forgive you of your sins and then give you the strength to get through your circumstances and challenges.

The kingdom of heaven doesn't begin for us when we die, it begins the moment we yield our lives to Jesus Christ.

He is with us, and He is in us.

There is no greater privilege than that.

CHAPTER TWENTY-SIX
THE UNFORGIVABLE SIN

A pastor had been talking to his congregation about sin and repentance. He had gone into painstaking detail about how to admit sin and turn from sin. Wanting to make sure they were getting the message, he said, "What do you need to do before you can receive forgiveness from God?"

After a moment of silence, a small boy in the back of the church yelled out, "You have to sin first!"

It's so easy to sin. Have you noticed? It comes so naturally to all of us. My wife and I raised two sons, and now we have five grandchildren. But strangely, we never had to teach any of them to sin. Yes, sometimes it's a little cute when a toddler does something naughty and selfish, and we might even chuckle about it. But it's not so cute when they get older and continue in that pattern of sin.

Here's the good news, and it is really, really good news: Despite the sin we may have committed, we serve a God who forgives sin. Our God has a big eraser, and He loves to use it in our lives. Both the Old and New Testaments overflow with teaching about the forgiveness of God.

In Psalm 130:3-4, the psalmist said,

If You, LORD, should mark iniquities,
O Lord, who could stand?
But there is forgiveness with You,
That You may be feared.

In Psalm 86:5, David wrote,

For You, Lord, are good, and ready to forgive,
And abundant in mercy to all those who call upon You.

In the book of Micah, the prophet reflected,

Where is another God like you,
who pardons the guilt of the remnant,
overlooking the sins of his special people?
You will not stay angry with your people forever,
because you delight in showing unfailing love.
Once again you will have compassion on us.
You will trample our sins under your feet
and throw them into the depths of the ocean!
(7:18-19, NLT)

Don't you love that picture? God takes our sins and throws them into the depths of the ocean. Corrie ten Boom used to say it like this: "When we confess our sins, God casts them into the deepest ocean, gone forever. Then God places a sign out there that says, 'No fishing allowed.'"

Shifting into the New Testament, we see divine forgiveness in action again and again. To the disabled man being lowered through the roof by his friends, Jesus said, "Friend, your sins are forgiven" (Luke 5:20, NIV). To the woman caught in adultery and flung at Jesus' feet, He said, "Neither do I condemn you. . . . Go now and leave your life of sin" (John 8:11, NIV).

That is the essence of the gospel. God assures us in 1 John 1:9, "If we confess our sins, He is faithful and just to forgive us our sins and to cleanse us from all unrighteousness."

No matter how severe the sin, God can forgive it. Consider this: The worst conceivable sin ever was to kill God's only Son. Yet the first words Jesus spoke from the cross were, "Father, forgive them, for they do not know what they do" (Luke 23:34).

Whatever you have done in the course of your life, God can and will forgive it. Lying, cheating, stealing, drunkenness, immorality, whatever it might be. The only sin God will not forgive is the sin we will not confess.

However, there is one exception.

There is one sin that God will not forgive. It is called "blasphemy of the Holy Spirit." Over the years, I have probably been asked about this "unforgivable sin" more than anything else. *What is the unforgivable sin? What does it mean to blaspheme the Holy Spirit?*

Why do we ask this question? Because we did a lot of bad stuff before we were Christians. Stupid stuff. Stuff we're ashamed of. We look back and think, "Wait a second. What if I cursed the Holy Spirit somewhere along the line? Did I commit the unforgivable sin?"

Let's read the words of Jesus and try to find an answer to this troubling question.

Frightening Words

Then a demon-possessed man, who was blind and couldn't speak, was brought to Jesus. He healed the man so that he could both speak and see. The crowd was amazed and asked, "Could it be that Jesus is the Son of David, the Messiah?"

But when the Pharisees heard about the miracle, they said, "No wonder he can cast out demons. He gets his power from Satan, the prince of demons."

Jesus knew their thoughts and replied, "Any kingdom divided by civil war is doomed. A town or family splintered by feuding will fall apart. And if Satan is casting out Satan, he is divided and fighting against himself. His own kingdom will not survive. And if I am empowered by Satan, what about your own exorcists? They cast out demons, too, so they will condemn you for what you have said. But if I am casting out demons by the Spirit of God, then the Kingdom of God has arrived among you. For who is powerful enough to enter the house of a strong man and plunder his goods? Only someone even stronger—someone who could tie him up and then plunder his house.

"Anyone who isn't with me opposes me, and anyone who isn't working with me is actually working against me.

"So I tell you, every sin and blasphemy can be forgiven— except blasphemy against the Holy Spirit, which will never be forgiven. Anyone who speaks against the Son of Man can be forgiven, but anyone who speaks against the Holy Spirit will never be forgiven, either in this world or in the world to come." (Matthew 12:22-32, NLT)

These are heavy-duty words. Words hard to hear: *"Never be forgiven, either in this world or in the world to come."* According to Scripture, there is a point of no return.

First, let's take a moment to understand the context of the Lord's words and what was happening in this situation. Something very dramatic had taken place that prompted Jesus to utter such sobering words. And that something was done by the very ones who should have known better!

The Pharisees.

These religious leaders were boiling with anger toward Christ. Why? Because, quite bluntly, Jesus was bad for business—the religious business. They were envious of Jesus and jealous of His growing popularity. In fact, they ultimately crucified Him because of their jealousy—as Pilate, the Roman governor, knew very well (see Mark 15:10). The people loved Jesus, and the religious leaders hated Him for that. Jesus was loving, approachable, kind, and charismatic. Even children would crawl up into His lap to hear His words. In Mark 12:37 we read that "the common people heard Him gladly." Jesus never spoke over anyone's head. He was a master storyteller and broke the truth down in a way they could grasp.

This is something that every communicator of God's Word should do. Frankly, many preachers are just plain boring. Even the way they read the Bible drives me crazy. It's like they suck all the life out of it and speak as if there were no urgency, power, or authority in it.

The people who crowded up close to Jesus were drawn by what He said.

The leaders should have been drawn to Him too—if only for His miracles alone. It had been four hundred years since Israel had experienced a miracle of God. Four hundred years since a prophet had appeared on the scene. Four hundred years since an angel had appeared. And then, seemingly out of nowhere (but right on God's schedule), John the Baptist stepped onto the scene, introducing Jesus as the long-awaited Messiah. And then when Jesus made Himself known, He began performing miracle after undeniable miracle.

But instead of rejoicing, these leaders were jealous and angry. And when they couldn't think of any other way to explain His miracles, they attributed the work of the Holy Spirit to Satan. They had the sheer audacity to say that this supernatural working of God was the product of hell.

This is where we all need to be very careful, even as Christians. Because sometimes we become very critical of people or ministries that we really know very little about. In my position as a pastor and evangelist, I hear quite a few things about quite a few people. But I do my best not to draw conclusions about anyone or arrive at a judgment until I know the facts. I have found that my perceptions can change a great deal when I talk *to* people instead of *about* people. Why am I sensitive about this? Because people have said things about me and my ministry—things that were believed by some—that simply weren't true.

We can be very quick to believe negative things about others when we haven't even taken the trouble to seek the truth or talk to the individuals involved. As J. Vernon McGee used to say, "The only exercise some Christians get is jumping to conclusions and running down others." You would think this was some people's favorite sport!

To those who are inclined to make quick conclusions about other pastors, Christian leaders, and ministries, even to the point of saying, "This is the work of Satan, not God," I would offer a word of warning. Be very careful. Don't be like these Pharisees in the Gospels who attributed the works of Jesus to Beelzebub. To say such things is an indication of a hard heart, not a spiritually perceptive one.

Here is the problem. These men should have known better. For all you may have heard about the Pharisees, they were devout individuals who had dedicated their lives to prayer and the study of the Scriptures.

If they were truly men of God, shouldn't they have recognized God's Son?

A Pharisee would have been regarded as the theological conservative of his day, in contrast to the Sadducees, who were very liberal and rejected all Scripture and oral law other than the Torah, the first five books of the Bible.

And here were these theologically conservative, orthodox believers in grave danger of committing the unpardonable sin.

In a sense, church is a dangerous place. You say, "Dangerous? I thought church was a safe place." Maybe, maybe not. It is in church that we hear the Word of God, and we have a choice as to what we will do with what we hear. Knowledge, as you know, brings responsibility. And the more we know, the more we will be held accountable for. Jesus said in Luke 12:48 (NIV), "From everyone who has been given much, much will be demanded; and from the one who has been entrusted with much, much more will be asked."

If you come to church and listen to God's Word being proclaimed with no intention of obeying that Word, church might not be a good place for you. If, however, you come to church wanting to hear and respond to God's Word, it is the perfect place for you.

To step through the doors of a Bible-believing church and sit with God's people while you have no desire to respond or to grow spiritually can be detrimental to you. In the very place where your heart should be touched and impacted by God, it can actually grow hard. It can be summed up with this simple statement: *The same sun that softens wax hardens clay.* The same message from the Word of God that touches the heart of one individual and turns him or her toward God causes another to become more hardened in sin.

It all comes down to the way we hear His message. That is why Jesus said, again and again, "He who has ears to hear, let him hear." To put it in modern vernacular, "Listen up. Pay attention."

The hearts of the Pharisees had grown hard, and now they were turning against God Himself, rejecting Him outright. This wasn't a momentary doubt, this was out-and-out unbelief. There is a difference! We've all experienced moments of doubt. We're not human if we don't doubt now and then. The best thing to do in such times is to doubt our doubts and to believe our beliefs, to keep filling our minds and hearts with the living, transformative Word of God.

These men, however, had allowed their doubts to morph into rejection of God's purposes. They refused to believe. They were saying, "We see the evidence right before our eyes, but we refuse to believe in Jesus Christ." Luke 7:30 (NIV) says, "The Pharisees and the experts in the law rejected God's purpose for themselves."

By the way, this is the same reason people reject Jesus today. It's not because they have carefully examined and then rejected the evidence. No, they simply refuse to acknowledge it; they refuse to believe. Someone will say, "The Bible is full of contradictions."

So we reply, "Really? Why don't you show me where. I have a Bible right here."

"Put that thing away."

"Why? It won't attack you."

"Put it away!"

People who have decided to reject Christ don't want to see the Bible or hear from the Bible. They say the Bible is unreliable, but they have never read it. They say it's full of contradictions, but they can't name a single one. They just don't want to hear it, think about it, or talk about it.

These same people don't want to go to church, either. Why don't they? Because they don't want to hear the gospel, and they don't want to change their lifestyle. Jesus Christ is a threat to their cherished sins.

In John 3:19-20 (NIV) we read, "This is the verdict: Light has come into the world, but people loved darkness instead of light because their deeds were evil. Everyone who does evil hates the light, and will not come into the light for fear that their deeds will be exposed."

Because the Pharisees had chosen not to believe and had completely rejected God's Son and the miracles done right before their eyes, Jesus was saying to them, "Be very careful. You guys are right on the edge of committing an unpardonable sin—blasphemy of the Holy Spirit."

To blaspheme is to insult a person, which reminds us that the Holy Spirit, as part of the Trinity, has personality. Did you know there are actual, specific sins that can be committed against the Holy Spirit? It's true. Let's take a moment to consider them.

Specific Sins Against the Holy Spirit

Resisting the Spirit

In Acts 7:51 (NIV), young Stephen was giving what would be his final message on earth before the Sanhedrin, a group of Sadducees and Pharisees that made up the highest legal and religious body in existence in that day. Stephen had given them an amazing overview of Israel's history, leading up to his accusation that these men were now rejecting Jesus, God's Messiah. He concluded with a strong rebuke: "You stiff-necked people! Your hearts and ears are still uncircumcised. You are just like your ancestors: *You always resist the Holy Spirit!*" (emphasis added).

What does that mean? What is the mission of the Holy Spirit? According to John 16:8 (NLT), "And when he comes, he will convict the world of its sin, and of God's righteousness, and of the coming judgment." The Spirit of God is incredibly patient and persistent. But it is possible to deliberately close our ears to His voice and resist all of His pleadings. The idea behind Stephen's message was this: "You guys know this to be true. *You know it!* And yet you continually resist it."

It is the Holy Spirit's task to come to us and convince us of our sin, of our separation from God and our need of a Savior. And if we say, "I don't want to hear that. I don't want to believe that. I reject that," then we are resisting the Spirit. And that is a gravely serious thing to do.

Insulting the Spirit

In Hebrews 10:29 (TLB), we encounter these strong words: "Think how much more terrible the punishment will be for those who have trampled underfoot the Son of God and treated his cleansing blood as though it were common and unhallowed, and insulted and outraged the Holy Spirit who brings God's mercy to his people."

Wow. "Outraged the Holy Spirit." How would we do that? Again, the work of the Spirit is to convince, but He will not convert without our consent. We can reject Him. We can say no to Him. I do not believe in the concept of "irresistible grace," which says there is no way we could say no to God's Spirit. If God has chosen us (according to this view), we will say yes. Again, I don't believe it.

Stephen said to the Sanhedrin, "You always resist the Holy Spirit!" And people continue to do that to this day. God has given each of us a free will, and He will not violate that free will. We do have a choice in the matter.

Remember how Joshua put it to the Israelites before he died? "Choose for yourselves this day whom you will serve. . . . But as for me and my household, we will serve the LORD" (Joshua 24:15, NIV).

Here's the scenario. The Spirit convicts a person of sin and clearly shows him his need for Jesus. But as he hears the message of the cross and the shed blood of Christ, he says, "What do I care about that? So Jesus suffered and died. Who cares? It means nothing to me."

That insults God, and specifically His Holy Spirit, and that person is on the very verge of committing the unpardonable sin.

If You Care, Then You Haven't

Let's review what we've learned. Blasphemy of the Holy Spirit is to reject the work of the Spirit. The work of the Spirit is to convince us of our sin and bring us to Jesus Christ. Therefore, the blasphemy of the Holy Spirit, the only unforgivable sin, is a rejection of Jesus Christ as Savior and Lord. If we reject Jesus as Savior, where will we go? The Bible says, "Salvation is found in no one else, for there is no other name under heaven given to mankind by which we must be saved" (Acts 4:12, NIV). It also asks the question, "How shall we escape if we ignore so great a salvation?" (Hebrews 2:3, NIV).

A person can actually go beyond the point of no return. Where that point is in an individual's life, I have no idea. God knows. But I do believe there is a line out there somewhere, and once someone crosses it, there is no turning back. I believe the Old Testament character Esau crossed that line. He was the fraternal twin of Jacob, and as the firstborn of the two he should have had the birthright and blessing. But he sold his birthright for a bowl of stew and eventually lost the blessing as well.

Afterward, he realized he should have never given that birthright up. In Hebrews 12:16-17 (TLB), the Bible says, "Watch out that no one becomes involved in sexual sin or becomes careless about God as Esau did: he traded his rights as the oldest son for a single meal. And afterwards, when he wanted those rights back again, it was too late, even though he wept bitter tears of repentance. So remember, and be careful."

Esau took something very, very precious for granted, blowing off concern about it again and again—until he went too far. And, yes, a person can go too far.

Nothing is worse than a hard heart. Sometimes we think, "Oh no, my kid is on drugs! Abusing alcohol! It's the worst-case scenario." And yes, those activities may be very bad, illegal, and worrisome, but they are not the worst. *The worst-case scenario is a hard heart.* A young man or woman struggling with drugs may come under the conviction of the Holy Spirit and in their great need seek the Lord. They're just prodigals who need to come home again. On the other hand, there may be a person sitting in church with a smile on her face and an open Bible in her lap whose heart is like stone. This person is actually further away from God than the prodigal.

Coming back to Esau, we read these words about him in a paraphrase of Hebrews 12:15-17 (MSG):

> Keep a sharp eye out for weeds of bitter discontent. A thistle or two gone to seed can ruin a whole garden in no time. Watch out for the Esau syndrome: trading away God's lifelong gift in order to satisfy a short-term appetite. You well know how Esau later regretted that impulsive act and wanted God's blessing— but by then it was too late, tears or no tears.

A bitter heart can lead a person into ruin. Are you bitter toward someone today? The Bible says that if we harbor bitterness in our hearts toward someone else, we are grieving the Holy Spirit. In Paul's letter to the Ephesians, he wrote, "Do not grieve the Holy Spirit of God, with whom you were sealed for the day of redemption. Get rid of all bitterness, rage and anger, brawling and slander, along with every form of malice. Be kind and compassionate to one another, forgiving each other, just as in Christ God forgave you" (4:30-32, NIV).

You might say, "But Greg, someone has hurt me—deeply hurt me—and now I must hurt them." Really? But that's not what the Bible says you should do. First Peter 3:9 (NLT) says, "Don't repay evil for evil. Don't retaliate with insults when people insult you. Instead, pay them back with a blessing. That is what God has called you to do, and he will grant you his blessing."

That's what God calls you to do. Turn the bitterness into a blessing.

"But Greg, you have no idea. They don't deserve that sort of kindness."

Did you?

As Scripture says, "And be kind to one another, tenderhearted, forgiving one another, even as God in Christ forgave you" (Ephesians 4:32). Listen, you did not deserve the kindness and forgiveness of God, and neither did I. For this reason, we must extend this forgiveness to others.

"They don't merit it, Greg."

But did the people crucifying Jesus merit it when Jesus said in Luke 23:34 (NIV), "Father, forgive them, for they do not know what they are doing"?

When we forgive someone, we set a person free. And that person is ourselves! We are the ones who suffer when we hold bitterness and hateful feelings close to our hearts. Scripture tells us to be careful, or we may fall into the Esau syndrome and allow the bitterness in our hearts to consume us.

Get rid of the bitterness. Let go of the anger. God will take it away from you if you ask Him to.

A Final Reminder

Ask God to keep your heart soft and pliable. Sometimes that means He will take you through some trials and difficult passages, but that's okay. You want to stay dependent on Him, waiting on Him, day by day, hour by hour, moment by moment.

What will keep your heart soft? Spend time in His Word, in His presence in prayer, and in the company of His people. Seek His forgiveness and cleansing daily as you let go of your resentments and bitterness toward others.

Instead of resisting the Holy Spirit, be filled with the Holy Spirit, asking Him to keep your conscience responsive and tender. When the Spirit brings something to your mind, seek the Lord's forgiveness immediately. The apostle John put it like this: "But if we are living in the light of God's presence, just as Christ does, then we have wonderful fellowship and joy with each other, and the blood of Jesus his Son cleanses us from every sin" (1 John 1:7, TLB).

The message of this chapter has been that it is possible for individuals to let their hearts become so embittered and hard that they no longer even hear God's voice, and they find themselves in danger of going too far.

But if you desire God at this moment and seek Him with all your heart, that person isn't you.

CHAPTER TWENTY-SEVEN

THE DEATH OF A CONSCIENCE

Sir Arthur Conan Doyle, the author of the famous Sherlock Holmes mysteries, was a bit of a practical joker. One day, as a prank, he decided to write an anonymous note to twelve of his best friends. On a given day, the note arrived at each of their respective houses.

The note read, "Flee at once. All is discovered."

Within twenty-four hours, all twelve of his friends had left the country. That is what is called "having a guilty conscience."

What is a conscience? One person said, "A conscience is the inner voice warning us that someone may be looking." Another said, "Conscience is what hurts when everything else feels so good." Along that same line, someone else said, "Conscience doesn't always keep you from doing wrong, but it does keep you from enjoying it."

As Jiminy Cricket sang to his little wooden friend Pinocchio in the Disney movie by that name, "Take the straight and narrow path and when you start to slide, give a little whistle, give a little whistle, and always let your conscience be your guide."

God has placed a conscience in every individual—man and woman, believer and nonbeliever. We're born with a conscience, that inner sense of right and wrong. We might think of it as a smoke alarm that goes off when it detects trouble. (Or when the battery needs to be changed. If you're like me, mine always goes off at 3:00 a.m.)

What shape is your conscience in? Is it tender and responsive? Is it dull and unresponsive? An old Chinese proverb says, "Clear conscience never fears midnight knocking."

We must be very careful to give attention to our conscience. Be attuned to it. Take care of it, and don't stifle it. The Bible speaks of those who traffic in lies and hypocrisy as "having their own conscience seared with a hot iron" (1 Timothy 4:2).

I heard about a man who went to see a psychiatrist. "Doc," he said, "I've been misbehaving and my conscience is troubling me."

"I see," said the psychiatrist. "And do you want something that will strengthen your willpower?"

"No," the patient replied. "I want something that will weaken my conscience."

That's how many people are. They want to weaken or drown out their conscience. But we really don't want to do that. If we deliberately ignore our conscience or allow it to weaken, it may begin to calcify and die.

In this chapter we will consider the story of a man who allowed his conscience to grow harder and harder—and what became of him after that.

Herod and John

At that time Herod the tetrarch heard the report about Jesus and said to his servants, "This is John the Baptist; he is risen from the dead, and therefore these powers are at work in him." For Herod had laid hold of John and bound him, and put him in prison for the sake of Herodias, his brother Philip's wife. Because John had said to him, "It is not lawful for you to have her." And although he wanted to put him to death, he feared the multitude, because they counted him as a prophet. (Matthew 14:1-5)

At this time Jesus was beginning His public ministry, and His name was on everyone's lips. Lives were being transformed, sick people made well, dead people resurrected, demon-possessed people delivered. Herod heard about this, and something began to disturb him. It was his conscience, which was dying but not quite dead as yet. When he heard about Jesus, he was reminded of someone very significant in his life: the man known as John the Baptist. This evil puppet king began to have the uneasy feeling that Jesus was in fact John, returned from the dead to haunt him.

There are a number of Herods mentioned in the New Testament, and while they're not all the same person, they all came from the same twisted dynasty. The first of the lot was Herod the Great. He was the Herod, or king, who was on the throne when the wise men came from the east, looking for one who was born King of the Jews. He was not called Herod the Great because of his acts of benevolence or because he was such a wonderful ruler. He was called that because he was known for his amazing building projects, including the rebuilt Jewish temple and the great desert fortress Masada.

But Herod the Great was also known for his wickedness and paranoia, as well as how he had members of his own family executed because he thought they might pose a threat to his throne.

His son who followed him was named Herod Antipas, and, clearly, the rotten apple didn't fall very far from the rotten tree. Herod Antipas was also an evil man—cruel, scheming, indecisive, and utterly immoral. But this was also the Herod who had contact and personal counsel from one of the greatest men in the kingdom: John the Baptist. Other Herods followed, and none of them good. But we will focus on Herod Antipas as the central character in this chapter.

When John the Baptist emerged on the scene, he was an instant sensation. Israel had just been through a four-hundred-year dry spell with no word from God at all. No voice of the prophets or seers, no miracles, no angelic appearances. No one, seemingly, speaking for God. Just an icy silence from heaven.

Then, seemingly out of nowhere, but right on God's timetable, John the Baptist stepped out of the shadows. He was powerful, dynamic, and charismatic. And wherever he went, crowds would gather. He was almost like a rock star of his day. He wore a garment of camel's hair and must have seemed to some like the reappearance of Elijah the prophet.

If John were alive today he would probably hang out at Whole Foods, subsisting as he did on a diet of locusts and wild honey. This guy was fearless. He called out the religious elite of the day—

the Pharisees and Sadducees—labeling them as a nest of snakes who would face the judgment of almighty God. No one had ever spoken that way before, and it was an instant sensation. People swarmed to wherever John was to see and hear more.

Contrast John with Herod. They were opposites. While Herod was unsure of himself, torn, proud, and excessively worried about his image and the opinions of others, John was sure of his calling and mission, humble, and concerned only with the opinion of God. John was a man of immense moral courage, and Herod was a man of spineless weakness. John was a man who kept his conscience and lost his head. Herod was a man who took John's head but lost his own conscience.

In his own insecure, twisted way, Herod respected John and even liked him. In Mark 6:20 (NLT) we read, "Herod respected John; and knowing that he was a good and holy man, he protected him. Herod was greatly disturbed whenever he talked with John, but even so, he liked to listen to him."

Herod may have found John interesting, but his wife Herodias hated John. This royal couple, Herod and Herodias, had a bizarre relationship. The Bible notes that she had been the wife of Philip, Herod's brother. While she was still married to Philip, Herod seduced her and took her as his own wife. But it gets worse. Herodias was also the daughter of Herod's half-brother, making her his niece (as well as sister-in-law). This would have been a great episode for the Jerry Springer or Maury Povich TV shows ("kings who marry their sisters-in-law who are also their nieces").

If all of that wasn't enough, lecherous old Herod was also lusting after Herodias's daughter, Salome, and Herodias was fully aware of this.

John, however, called him out on it. He told the king, in effect, "This is crazy. This is really messed up. You people need to repent." Believe it or not, Herod respected John for saying so. He admired the courage it had taken for John to speak up like that. If John had retained some PR people, which he didn't, they would have told him, "Hey, ease up a little, John. Relax a bit. You have to be more diplomatic. You have to change your tone and think through what you're saying. You can keep Herod as a friend if you play your cards right. He could really help you advance your ministry, so just pull your punches a little."

But John didn't care. He just told the truth and let the chips fall where they may.

We need more people like John in our world today. More men and women who will simply tell the truth. We need them in culture, in politics, in universities, and in pulpits.

John was honest with Herod, and was probably the only man in this wicked king's entire experience who had ever spoken plain truth to him. Really, John was Herod's truest friend because he told the king the truth. Do you have a friend like that? If you have a friend who tells you the truth (instead of what you want to hear), hang on to that friend.

David once wrote, "Let a righteous man strike me—that is a kindness; let him rebuke me—that is oil on my head. My head will not refuse it" (Psalm 141:5, NIV). In other words, a friend who tells me the truth, even if it hurts, is a friend who truly loves me.

That's the kind of friend we want and need. We want to have someone we can call up and say, "I've got to run something by you. You have to be honest with me." We don't want someone who flatters us and says, "Go for it," when we really shouldn't go for it. We want someone who will say, "That is a bad idea, and here's why."

Solomon wrote, "Faithful are the wounds of a friend, but the kisses of an enemy are deceitful" (Proverbs 27:6). A true friend will occasionally wound you—not to deliberately hurt you, but to help you. It has been said that a true friend stabs you in the front, not in the back.

That was John. He told Herod the truth, and it ultimately cost him his head.

Herod was so impressed by John that he even made a few changes in his life. We earlier quoted Mark 6:20 in the New Living Translation, where it says, "Herod was greatly disturbed whenever he talked with John." But the New King James Version says, "When he heard him, he did many things, and heard him gladly."

"He did many things"? We don't know what those things were.

Clearly he didn't repent of his sins and his immoral relationship with Herodias. But maybe he didn't torture as many people for a while, or maybe he gave his slaves a day off, or contributed a little money to the poor. Who knows? But even if he did many things, he did not do the most important thing—and the thing that might have saved his soul. He didn't repent of his sin.

There are people like Herod today who think, "I need to check out Christianity, get a little religion in my life. That would be good."

No, you don't need a little religion. You need a whole lot of Jesus. That is the only answer. A little religion isn't going to help you. "Why not?" you say. "At least I'd be better off than the outright atheist who doesn't believe anything."

Yes, but you might be fooled into believing that a little bit of religion would be enough to save you, when it is not. In fact, "a little religion" will keep you from God! Even if you say you are a "seeker," until you put your faith in Jesus Christ you are still separated from God by your sin. In reality, you are as far from God as any nonbeliever out there.

You are either in or out. Or as Jesus said, "You are either for Me or against Me."

The Revenge of Herodias

Herod may have liked John and admired the man's courage and chutzpah, but Herodias didn't feel that way at all. She despised John. Mark 6:19 says, "Herodias held it against him and wanted to kill him, but she could not." Another translation says, "Herodias, smoldering with hate, wanted to kill him, but didn't dare" (MSG).

What a family! How would you like to attend one of their family reunions?

Herodias was as serious as a heart attack. Enraged at John, she wanted him silenced. She lay awake at night plotting and scheming his doom.

As it happened, this sister-in-law-niece-wife of Herod knew her brother-in-law-uncle-husband pretty well. She knew he liked to get drunk, and that he would be very foolish in his drunken state.

That's when she had a brainstorm. She said to herself, *I will get the old fool drunk and then bring in my daughter, Salome, to do a seductive dance for him. Then, when he gets all worked up and offers her half his kingdom, I will have her ask for the head of John the Baptist.*

And that is exactly what happened. Herod threw a party, Herodias made sure he had too much to drink, and she did not hesitate to pimp out (for lack of a better term) her daughter. The whole scene began to unfold as Herodias got her daughter to dance in front of the lustful king.

Here is the way the gospel of Matthew lays out the scene:

> *But when Herod's birthday was celebrated, the daughter of Herodias danced before them and pleased Herod. Therefore he promised with an oath to give her whatever she might ask.*
>
> *So she, having been prompted by her mother, said, "Give me John the Baptist's head here on a platter."*
>
> *And the king was sorry; nevertheless, because of the oaths and because of those who sat with him, he commanded it to be given to her. So he sent and had John beheaded in prison. And his head was brought on a platter and given to the girl, and she brought it to her mother. (14:6-11)*

Why would Herod do such a horrible thing? He murdered his only real friend in the world, John the Baptist.

Two things prompted him: sexual lust and a desire to impress and please others. When Salome danced, the Bible says that Herod was "pleased." He was pleased, all right. That's a euphemism for being sexually aroused. The wicked old king got all worked up watching the young woman dance and ended up making a foolish commitment.

Someone might say, "I don't understand how he could do that."

Really? Haven't you seen what people will do when they are driven by lust? Haven't you seen the irrational, self-destructive decisions people will make in those situations? A husband will walk away from his faithful wife and loving children because he says he is "having a midlife crisis"—or whatever else he wants to blame it on. We see it the other way around, too—wives walking out on their husbands and abandoning their children because they are under the control of lust.

Lust is powerful. That is why we never want to feed it. On the contrary, we want to *starve* it. When we feed it and play with it, looking at pornography or engaging in inappropriate and flirtatious conversations, we make it stronger.

We need to deny it. Put it to death.

Herod was also concerned about his image in this incident, and impressing others. The text says, "The king was sorry . . . because of the oaths and because of those who sat with him." How stupid. He could have—and should have—retracted the ridiculous offer. He could have said, "There's no way. I don't know what I was thinking. I was drunk. Forget it."

But no, Herod was afraid he would lose face if he went back on his word. He said to himself, *I'm trapped by my own words. People are watching me, to see what I will do. I can't look weak here.*

Herod had probably spent a lot of time talking to John. Maybe he would be restless in his palace or unable to sleep at night. So he would go down to the dungeon and talk to John. How John must have hated being locked up in that miserable place! John was a great outdoorsman as well as a powerful preacher. He loved to be under the blue sky out in the elements with sun on his face and the wind in his hair.

But Herod had him locked up in a little hellhole. Almost like a pet rat for the king. But after that dreadful night of lust and drinking, he had killed his only friend in the world. There would be no more late-night talks.

And the deed tormented Herod. Night and day. He deeply regretted his decision. What was left of his conscience wouldn't let him rest or sleep. Herodias might have said to him, "Now, honey, just forget about that nasty old John. He's gone. He won't bother you anymore. Don't trouble yourself."

But Herod was troubled.

Unbeknownst to him, his conscience was dying.

And then he started hearing reports about someone named Jesus—a Messiah figure who was allegedly healing people, raising the dead, and preaching amazing things. And because Herod's conscience was so guilty, he said to himself, *It's John! I know it is! He's come back from the dead to haunt me.*

In Mark 6:16, Herod said, "This is John, whom I beheaded; he has been raised from the dead!" The words "whom I beheaded" are interesting. In the Greek language, the phrase could be translated, "I am the one." He could have blamed it on Herodias, Salome, the booze, or the dinner guests. But he didn't. He was saying to himself, *I did it. I gave the command. I had him executed. I had him beheaded. This is on me.*

Herod was flooded with guilt. It almost seemed as though the king heard from John when he was gone more than when he was alive. This was a sick and guilty conscience.

The story is a good reminder of the truth in Numbers 32:23 (NIV): "You may be sure that your sin will find you out." Sometimes we may commit what we regard as a little sin, but instead of repenting of it or dealing with it, we just move on. We don't think about the fact that sometimes the repercussions of sin don't hit us until later. Sometimes we may not even fully understand what we did until later on in life. The devil loves to torment us with such things! He will hit the play button. Then rewind. Then play. Then rewind. Something triggers an old memory, and we recall that thing we did, remembering that we have never really dealt with it.

Maybe a young woman finds herself pregnant and goes to Planned Parenthood for an abortion. While she is there, she is told that it's okay, that it's not a big deal, and that she is simply terminating an unwanted pregnancy. She thinks nothing of it. She just moves on in life.

But then down the road ten years or so, she sees a ten-year-old girl or boy, and it dawns on her: *That is the age my child would have been if I had brought it to term.* Suddenly it comes crashing down on her like a landslide, and she is hit by the enormity of what she has done. I have talked to girls and young women in situations such as this, and they are devastated. But where are those counselors who made the access to abortion so easy, and failed to explain to them what they were really doing and what the aftermath might be? The Planned Parenthood counselors are long gone, having moved on to their next victims.

Two studies show that women who have had abortions are six to seven times more likely to commit suicide than women who have not had abortions. One study revealed that depression is often triggered *years* later—perhaps when the woman sees an ultrasound picture or holds a friend's baby. Regret comes flooding in.

A quick aside here. If you have had an abortion or encouraged some girl to have an abortion, what you have done is a sin. But God will forgive you of that sin if you call it what it is, refuse to justify it, and ask for His forgiveness. Furthermore, I believe that every one of those unborn children killed in the womb is taken immediately into the presence of God, and they are alive in heaven right now. That's a bit of consolation, but still doesn't lessen the impact of how horrible this really is.

Herod, too, was filled with regret. It hit him later, perhaps months or years later. He kept saying to himself, *What have I done? I can't believe I did it.* As the reports about this new teacher kept surfacing, this Jesus of Nazareth, Herod's uneasy conscience immediately jumped to the conclusion that this must be John, somehow raised from the dead. Was it? He had to know! So he sent out some of the religious leaders to find Jesus and summon Him to the palace.

Jesus replied, "Tell that fox that I've no time for him right now. Today and tomorrow I'm busy clearing out the demons and healing the sick; the third day I'm wrapping things up" (Luke 13:32, MSG).

What kind of message was that to send to the king? When Herod received that reply, he probably thought, "Now I *know* this is John. Only John would say something that crazy to me." But it wasn't John at all; it was Jesus.

Not long after that incident, however, Jesus stood face to face with Herod, beaten and bloodied and in Roman chains. But if Herod thought he could banter back and forth with Jesus as he had done with John, he was mistaken. Jesus wouldn't say a single word to the corrupt king.

It's interesting to me that *Herod never heard the voice of Christ.* Many others had and had even engaged Him in conversation: the Pharisees, the Sadducees, the guards who arrested him, the high priest, the Roman governor. Jesus had even conversed with Satan as He was being tempted and tested in the wilderness. But to Herod, Jesus never uttered a single word.

Here is Luke's account of Christ's encounter with Herod.

Now when Herod saw Jesus, he was exceedingly glad; for he had desired for a long time to see Him, because he had heard many things about Him, and he hoped to see some miracle done by Him. Then he questioned Him with many words, but He answered him nothing. And the chief priests and scribes stood and vehemently accused Him. Then Herod, with his men of war, treated Him with contempt and mocked Him, arrayed Him in a gorgeous robe, and sent Him back to Pilate. (Luke 23:8-11)

What an incredible scene. There was Herod in the throne room of his palace—a twisted king with a dying conscience on his regal throne. And there before him, just feet away, stood Jesus Christ. This wasn't a man of God, like John the Baptist, this was God the Man. So Herod had already met the greatest prophet in human history, and now he was sitting in the proximity of the living Son of God, the very Creator and Sustainer of the universe.

Herod was excited, thinking he might get to see a miracle. Why did he want to witness Jesus performing a supernatural act? Was it because he wanted to believe in God? No, he just wanted to be entertained with a parlor trick. Like David Copperfield pulling a rabbit out of a hat. *Entertain me,* he was saying. *Dazzle me. Impress me. Go ahead. This is Your chance.*

But Jesus didn't utter a single word. Why didn't He?

Because He knew it was too late for Herod's heart. It had become irreparably hardened. Herod had danced right up to the line of no return, and now he was past help. He had blasphemed the Holy Spirit, and Jesus would not engage him.

Belief . . . or Shallow Interest?

The last three verses in John 2 give us a thought-provoking statement on what it means to believe in Jesus.

Now when He was in Jerusalem at the Passover, during the feast, many believed in His name when they saw the signs which He did. But Jesus did not commit Himself to them, because He knew all men, and had no need that anyone should testify of man, for He knew what was in man. (verses 23-25)

Someone might say, "That doesn't make sense! I thought if people believe in Jesus, He forgives and accepts them."

Yes, He does—if they come with the right motive in their hearts! But Jesus is God and can read the human heart like a book. He knows when a commitment is genuine and when it is fake. And He knew that these people really weren't believing in Him; they were simply enamored of Him and entertained by Him. He was the celebrity-of-the-moment, but they weren't ready to follow Him or commit their lives to Him. Knowing this, Jesus didn't commit Himself to them, either. And it was the same when He was in the presence of Herod.

I've noticed a similar dynamic at church, after I've preached a message. Sometimes I will stay around for a while after the service, making myself available to talk to people. Occasionally someone approaches me and says, "I have a few things I would like to ask you."

"Okay."

Then they start firing their questions, most of which really have nothing to do with the sermon. As I answer a question, it's obvious the person isn't even listening to me; he's just teeing up the next challenge, checking off all the talking points. It's obvious what's going on in this situation. The person has a certain theological persuasion and wants to convince me he is right and I am wrong.

"Look," I eventually say, "you see this differently than I do. I don't want to stand here and argue with you." But this person *wants* to argue. He wants to keep pressing his positions. Finally, I will say (politely, I hope), "I don't really see any reason to continue this conversation." And that makes him angry!

Why do I want to move on? Because maybe I can see someone standing right behind that individual who really *needs* to talk—a woman with tears in her eyes or a teenager with the weight of the world on his shoulders. I want to talk to the person with the real spiritual need, not to the person who only wants to push a personal agenda.

That's the way it was with Herod. He had an agenda, but it had nothing to do with repentance or seeking God. By keeping silent, then, Jesus was saying in effect, "We have nothing to say to one another. There is no need for conversation here."

What happened next proved that very point: "Then Herod, with his men of war, treated Him with contempt and mocked Him, arrayed Him in a gorgeous robe, and sent Him back to Pilate" (Luke 23:11). Herod rejected Christ and Christ rejected Herod. For fear of his reputation, for fear of his throne, and for a lack of fear of God, Herod damned his own soul forever.

He could have repented at the preaching of John, but he closed his heart to it. He could have and should have fallen at the feet of Jesus Christ, worshiped Him as God, and cried out for mercy; but his heart was no longer capable of responding. He mocked Jesus instead, and dismissed Him with a wave of his hand.

How to Re-sensitize Your Conscience

How does a conscience die? It starts with small things, which invariably become larger things.

You do something you know to be wrong, and your conscience lets you know it. But you continue on. You don't repent or acknowledge it as sin. You cover it up instead. As a result your conscience begins to grow hard, calloused, and resistant. You need to come to God and say, "Lord, soften my heart and help me get my conscience clean. Help me to get it working again. I want to please You, but I have forgotten how!"

In 1 Timothy 1:19 (NLT), Paul told his young friend, "Cling to your faith in Christ, and keep your conscience clear. For some people have deliberately violated their consciences; as a result, their faith has been shipwrecked."

But we don't have to shipwreck. We can get back on course again in the Christian life. It starts by simply going to Jesus. Hebrews 10:22 (NLT) urges us, "Let us go right into the presence of God with sincere hearts fully trusting him. For our guilty consciences have been sprinkled with Christ's blood to make us clean, and our bodies have been washed with pure water."

Jesus Christ can forgive sin and re-sensitize your conscience.

I love going outside after the rain. The air feels cool and smells clean. Even people who drive dirty cars get a little carwash. Birds seem to want to sing for joy. If I look up, I might catch a glimpse of a rainbow. It's a wonderful moment.

That's what Jesus can do for us.

In the book of Acts, Peter spoke about "times of refreshing" that come from the Lord. That freshness, that new surge of gladness and hope, can be yours today. Open the doors and windows of your heart and mind to Jesus, and let the sweet, fresh air blow through.

CHAPTER TWENTY-EIGHT
LOST IN TRANSLATION

I read an interesting article about American companies trying to sell their products overseas—and running right into something called the language barrier. In other words, American English, with its expressions and colloquialisms, doesn't always translate very well.

Schweppes Tonic Water wanted to market their product in Italy, but accidentally used the wrong Italian word in their promotions. What they ended up with was, "Schweppes Toilet Water." Not surprisingly, it didn't sell very well.

Years ago in Taiwan, Pepsi sought to translate their slogan, "Come alive with the Pepsi generation." Translated into their language, however, the slogan read, "Pepsi will bring your ancestors back from the dead." That's quite a promise for Pepsi to live up to.

The Parker Pen Company was expanding their ballpoint pen company to Mexico. Their slogan was, "It won't leak in your pocket and embarrass you." But they used the wrong Spanish word for "embarrass" and the phrase translated as "It won't leak in your pocket and impregnate you."

Clairol marketed their curling iron in Germany. It was called "The Mist Stick." What they didn't understand was that the word "mist" in German means manure. And not that many ladies wanted to buy a manure stick for their hair.

In China, Kentucky Fried Chicken took their slogan "Finger lickin' good" and translated it into Chinese. At least, they tried to. But instead of "Finger licking good," it translated to "Eat your fingers off."

But translation difficulties work both ways, don't they? The Scandinavian vacuum manufacturer Electrolux used the following phrase in an American ad campaign: "Nothing Sucks Like Electrolux." It didn't go over so well, because their message was lost in translation. The words just weren't connecting in the way the company intended.

In the sixteenth chapter of Matthew, we see Jesus speaking to His disciples about some heavy events that were just around the corner. It was important for these men to hear and understand their Lord's words, but their minds were in other places. They weren't really paying attention to what He was saying. It was as though Jesus' words were lost in translation.

The disciples believed Jesus was the Messiah, and their minds quickly leaped to grand and glorious conclusions. They thought He would establish His kingdom then and there, overthrowing Rome and the corrupt Jewish leadership. They were eagerly waiting for the rule and reign of Christ on earth, believing they would share that reign with Him. That's why they kept arguing about who was the greatest and who would get to sit at Jesus' right hand. The idea was, "When Jesus comes into power, what role will I play?"

They were listening to their own expectations and listening to each other, but they had only been listening with half an ear to Jesus. What they hadn't heard (and really didn't want to hear) was that He had not come to establish a physical kingdom on earth quite yet. Before the crown, there would first be a cross. Before He sat on a throne, He would first suffer and die for the sins of the whole world.

In Matthew 16, He was seeking to prepare them for what lay ahead. In the process, He posed a question and a challenge to them. It's a question and a challenge He still poses today to you and me. It is a question every one of us must answer.

Who is Jesus Christ to you?

The Question and the Challenge

When Jesus came into the region of Caesarea Philippi, He asked His disciples, saying, "Who do men say that I, the Son of Man, am?"

So they said, "Some say John the Baptist, some Elijah, and others Jeremiah or one of the prophets."

He said to them, "But who do you say that I am?"

Simon Peter answered and said, "You are the Christ, the Son of the living God."

Jesus answered and said to him, "Blessed are you, Simon Bar-Jonah, for flesh and blood has not revealed this to you, but My Father who is in heaven. And I also say to you that you are Peter, and on this rock I will build My church, and the gates of Hades shall not prevail against it." (verses 13-18)

Jesus asked this question: "Who do you say that I am?" And it is a question every man and woman must answer. There will come a day, of course, when every person who has ever lived on earth will declare, "Jesus Christ is Lord." This will include every Christian and every non-Christian. It will also include every atheist, agnostic, Jew, Hindu, Muslim, and every practitioner of every religion on earth—past, present, and future. It will include every Republican, Democrat, and Independent. Vladimir Putin will say those words. So will Benjamin Netanyahu, Justin Trudeau, and Barak Obama. Lady Gaga will declare it, as will Taylor Swift, Tom Cruise, Bradley Cooper, Jack Nicholson, and Matthew McConaughey. Bill Maher will cry out, "Jesus is Lord!" And so will Howard Stern.

The apostle Paul put it like this: "Therefore God exalted him to the highest place and gave him the name that is above every name, that at the name of Jesus every knee should bow, in heaven and on earth and under the earth, and every tongue acknowledge that Jesus Christ is Lord, to the glory of God the Father" (Philippians 2:9-11, NIV).

Really, when it comes to the identity of Jesus Christ and what we think about who He is, there are four options:

1. Jesus was a legend and never existed at all.
2. Jesus was a liar and lied about His identity as the Son of God.

3. Jesus was a lunatic, out of His mind, and didn't really know what He was doing.
4. Jesus is the Lord, just as He said.

If you are looking for another alternative, you won't find any. You have to choose one of these.

Was He a legend? It would be difficult to make a case for this, because there is so much historical evidence for the life and ministry of Jesus. *Something* happened back in first-century Israel, and we still feel the shockwaves to this very moment.

Was He a liar? You might say such a thing, but you would also have to deal with the fact that His claims have changed countless lives in radical, inexplicable ways through the centuries.

Was He a lunatic? You can hardly read the actual words of Jesus—the greatest, most revolutionary words ever spoken—and conclude such a thing.

That leaves us with one option: Jesus is Lord. Someone might say, "I don't want to call Him that. How about, 'Jesus was a super good guy,' or, 'Jesus was a great prophet'?" But the words and claims of Jesus don't allow for those lesser titles. That's not what He said about Himself or who He claimed to be. Jesus presented Himself as far more than just a "super good guy."

Where did Jesus ask this important question of His disciples? It was in Caesarea Philippi. That may not mean much to us, but people of that day would have recognized it as a place named for the Greek god Pan. It was at this very place, a location known for worship of false gods, a place of paganism and unbelief, where Jesus asked this question about His identity.

It's possible that even as they were having this discussion, they could look around and see people bowing down before images and offering their prayers to nonexistent gods. In this place of paganism and confusion, Jesus looked His men in the eyes and said, "Okay guys, who do *you* say I am?"

It's one thing to say that Jesus Christ is Lord in the church, among people of like minds. But it is another thing to say it outside of the church. It's another thing to say, "Jesus in Lord" in your workplace, on your campus, or in our hostile, anti-Christian culture. Sometimes we may be willing to say it among believers, but not in front of nonbelievers. Yet Jesus said in Luke 9:26 (NLT), "If anyone is ashamed of me and my message, the Son of Man will be ashamed of that person when he returns in his glory and in the glory of the Father and the holy angels."

Are you willing to declare your allegiance to Him in front of your friends and family and coworkers? Are you willing to say, "Jesus is Lord of my life"?

"Who do men say that I am?" our Lord asked. He was effectively asking them, "What's the word on the street? As you rub shoulders with people, what are they saying about Me?" Back in those days, of course, there was no social media—and no phoning, texting, or e-mailing. Nobody was tweeting about Jesus: "Love the Sermon on the Mount #beatitudes." There were no selfies of Jesus and the boys posing together. No Facebook posts. But there was still conversation, and Jesus was asking, "What are people saying about Me right now?"

Why did He ask this? Was it because He didn't know? Was He ignorant of what people thought? No, not at all. He knew what people thought. But He was leading up to asking the men who were with Him the same question. Did His disciples know who He was? You can see by their answers that they really didn't have this totally dialed in yet.

"Well, we hear lots of stuff. Some say You're John the Baptist, back from the dead. Some say You are Jeremiah, or maybe Elijah or some other prophet."

"Okay. But what about you guys. Right now. Who do *you* say I am?"

He had turned a speculative conversation into a direct, one-question final exam. And Simon Peter didn't even hesitate. He stepped up and said, "I think You are the Christ, the Son of the living God. That's what I think." Peter was pointing out that Jesus was not just a good teacher, prophet, or godly Man. No, Jesus was and is the God-man.

It was an amazing moment, and Jesus replied with strong words: "God bless you, Simon, son of Jonah! You didn't get that answer out of books or from teachers. My Father in heaven, God himself, let you in on this secret of who I really am" (Matthew 16:17, MSG).

The birth of Jesus was the most momentous event that has ever occurred. It was when the eternal, all-powerful, everywhere-present God of the universe confined Himself to a single cell, and grew in the womb of a woman, in order to be born the Savior of the world. God became a fetus. It is the most earth-shaking event this world has ever seen. And old Simon Peter, inspired by the Father, got it right.

Can you imagine how he felt in that moment? I already mentioned that these guys were competitive and had been arguing about who would be top dog under the new power structure. So when Jesus spoke and singled out Peter, saying that the Father had whispered this answer into his ear, Peter was no doubt congratulating himself. And the other guys were quietly saying, "Grrrr."

Peter the Rock?

Jesus, who had already praised Peter for listening to the Father, went on to make this amazing statement: "And I also say to you that you are Peter, and on this rock I will build My church, and the gates of Hades shall not prevail against it" (Matthew 16:18).

This statement has been much misunderstood through the centuries. Some people claim that Jesus was making Peter the first pope—the first leader of the church—and that the church was to be built on Simon Peter.

But that's not what Jesus was saying. The original language clears this up immediately. If Jesus were indeed building His church on Simon Peter, He would have said, "You are Peter, and upon you I will build My church." But that is not what He said.

The word Jesus used for *Peter* in Matthew 16:18 could be translated to mean "a rock" or "a stone." It is the Greek word *petros* and means "a little stone." But then He went on to say, "On this rock I will build My church." In this phrase He used a different word; it is the Greek word *petra*, which means "a big stone." We're talking about something massive here, like the Rock of Gibraltar.

The church is not built on Simon Peter. The church is built on what Simon Peter *said:* that Jesus is the Christ, the Son of the living God. *That* is the foundation of the church. And *that* is the foundation of our lives. The apostle Paul declared, "For no other foundation can anyone lay than that which is laid, which is Jesus Christ" (1 Corinthians 3:11).

Build your foundation on Christ. Don't ever build it on a person.

You might build your foundation of faith on the faith of your parents. But your parents may falter, have problems, or maybe split up. And it will shake you! You will say, "Christianity is all a sham. I don't believe it anymore." Or you could build the foundation of your life on your spouse, on the church you attend, on some pastor or spiritual leader.

Don't do it. People are imperfect, and will eventually let you down. We are all human beings with foibles and flaws and weaknesses. No, build your life on Christ. He will never fail you or forsake you. He will sustain you through the worst storms of life, I can guarantee you that.

In the same way, Christ's church is built on Christ, and no one else.

"The Gates of Hell Shall Not Prevail . . ."

What was Jesus talking about when He said, "On this rock I will build My church, and the gates of Hades shall not prevail against it"? The gates of hell, or Hades, represent the organized power of Satan and his demonic forces. As you may know, Satan was once a high-ranking angel, but turned against God and became a fallen angel. When he fell, he took multitudes of angels with him, who also became fallen angels, or demons.

Jesus was saying that these gates of hell, the organized armies of Satan, will not prevail against His church. This pictures hell as a fortress with gates, with the church of Jesus Christ marching against that fortress and those gates. But the gates of hell will not be able to withstand or prevail over the church.

How do we as believers prevail over the gates of hell?

Primarily through evangelism—proclaiming the gospel of Jesus Christ. As we win people from Satan's kingdom of darkness and bring them into the kingdom of light in Jesus, we are attacking and prevailing over the enemy's fortress.

As His church, we don't want to just hold ground, we want to *take* ground. Will Satan take this lying down? Of course not. He will dispute every inch of his territory. He will always bitterly oppose the advance of God's kingdom. But Jesus reminded us that the gates of hell shall not prevail against His church.

Sometimes the devil will draw a circle around a certain person and make it really hard to reach that individual. In effect, he says to us, "Back off. This one is mine. He or she is too far gone for you to rescue." But he can't say that. No one is "his," in that sense.

Sometimes people say, "I think I sold my soul to the devil."

Here's a newsflash: You can't sell your soul to the devil. It doesn't belong to you, so it's not yours to sell. God says, "Every soul—man, woman, child—belongs to me, parent and child alike" (Ezekiel 18:4, MSG). No one, no matter how far they have fallen into sin, is beyond the reach of God.

The Bombshell

From that time Jesus began to show to His disciples that He must go to Jerusalem, and suffer many things from the elders and chief priests and scribes, and be killed, and be raised the third day. (Matthew 16:21)

Notice the detail in this verse. Jesus knew what was coming. It wasn't a guess or a vague perception; He *knew*. And He was spelling it out for the twelve men who followed Him.

Can you imagine how this would have sounded to these guys? Don't forget, they thought He was about to establish His earthly kingdom—within days, perhaps. And then He says, "Boys, you'd better get ready for this. I'm going to be murdered in cold blood."

Having missed the part about "rising from the dead," the disciples were stunned. It's as though they were saying, "What are You talking about? Killed? No way! We've left everything to follow You. We've turned our backs on our careers, our jobs, and our homes. We've left our families. And You tell us You're about to be *murdered*?"

That's when Simon Peter stepped up to save the day. He thought he would straighten Jesus out a little. Verse 22 says, "Then Peter took Him aside and began to rebuke Him, saying, 'Far be it from You, Lord; this shall not happen to You!'" Peter, as you remember, had been on a roll. The Father had spoken through him. Jesus had called him "a rock." So after Jesus made His statement, Peter called Him to one side to "talk sense" into Him.

Can't you just hear him? "Jesus, Jesus, Jesus. No, this will not happen to You. How can You say such things? Of course it won't turn out this way!" Can you see him poking his finger in Jesus' face, rebuking Him? The Greek language here implies that Peter did it over and over, assuming an authoritarian position over Jesus. *"You are not going to do this! This is crazy talk!"*

Peter had suddenly become too big for his first-century britches, and Jesus had to put him in his place. And He did it in a most startling way.

> But He turned and said to Peter, "Get behind Me, Satan! You are an offense to Me, for you are not mindful of the things of God, but the things of men." (Matthew 16:23)

What a comedown! One moment Peter was speaking under the inspiration of the Father, and the next moment he was speaking under the inspiration of the devil. Why did Jesus repel Peter here? Why was He so forceful with him? Because Jesus knew very well that Satan wanted to stop Him from going to the cross.

In the very beginning of the Lord's ministry, the devil took Jesus into the wilderness and tempted Him. On one occasion he showed Him all the kingdoms of the world in a moment of time. Satan said,

"All this I will give you . . . if you will bow down and worship me" (Matthew 4:9, NIV).

Effectively, the devil was saying, "Jesus, we both know why You are here. We both know You are here to purchase back that which was lost in the Garden of Eden. I will give the glories of this world back to You if You will give me the momentary satisfaction of seeing You worshiping me."

And Jesus said (to paraphrase), "No way. Not a chance. The Word says to worship the Lord God and Him only."

Jesus knew from the very beginning why He had come and that He had to go to the cross to die for the sins of the world. So Satan hit Jesus at the beginning of His ministry, and then again (through Peter!) at the end of His ministry as He was headed toward Calvary. And then remember the great pressure Jesus was under in the Garden of Gethsemane. Dr. Luke told us that He was sweating, as it were, great drops of blood during that time. Why? Because Satan was there trying to stop Him. Trying to talk Him out of the cross.

In the same way, Satan will come to us at the beginning, middle, and end of our lives. When we are brand-new believers he will come and challenge our commitment. He will say, "Do you really think you are a Christian? After all you've done? Do you really think God could forgive someone like you?"

One of the first things we tell new believers is this: "You are not saved because you feel like you are; you are saved because the Bible *says* you are." And then we quote the wonderful words of 1 John 5:13: "These things I have written to you who believe in the name of the Son of God, that you may know that you have eternal life." We assure them with solid, comforting, reassuring verses like these. Why? Because young Christians get attacked. I remember! I had some really heavy-duty temptations come my way soon after my profession of faith.

But Satan will hit us at the end, too. In the last lap. His aim will be to trip us up toward the end of our lives, making a mockery of all we have stood for and lived for. In the book of Hebrews, the author pleaded with believers who have walked for years with Jesus not to abandon their faith because of increased trials and the attacks of Satan: "So don't throw it all away now. You were sure of yourselves then. It's *still* a sure thing! But you need to stick it out, staying with God's plan so you'll be there for the promised completion" (10:35-36, MSG). This is why we need to pray for both a good start, and to finish well in our Christian lives.

Jesus was laying it out for them; He was going to die, but He would rise again! He was saying, "Boys, trust Me here. I am in control. No one takes My life from Me. I will lay it down of My own accord and I will raise it up again. That's where we're headed."

But the disciples didn't like it. Not one bit. How could the murder of their wonderful Lord and Friend fit into any kind of plan that made sense? It certainly didn't make sense to them! Peter just couldn't wrap his mind around the Crucifixion. How could something so horrible ever be a part of God's purpose? (Remember, these men had seen crucifixions. Probably lots of them!) How could that suffering and sacrifice and degradation have any possible value?

Some still have a problem with that today. The cross is frightening to them. Repellant. But listen to this. Jesus was now saying, "I am not the only one who will carry a cross. I want you to carry a cross, too."

Making It Personal

The Lord personalized this for them and us in Matthew 16:24-26—with words that could literally change our lives. If we would take these words to heart and start living them, it would transform our world. This is the Christian life as it is meant to be lived.

Then Jesus said to His disciples, "If anyone desires to come after Me, let him deny himself, and take up his cross, and follow Me. For whoever desires to save his life will lose it, but whoever loses his life for My sake will find it. For what profit is it to a man if he gains the whole world, and loses his own soul? Or what will a man give in exchange for his soul?"

"If anyone desires to come after Me . . ." We could take out "anyone" and put our own names in the blank, making it personal:

"If Greg will come after Me . . ."

"If Megan will come after Me . . ."

"If Juan will come after Me . . ."

"If Abigail will come after Me and deny herself . . ."

What does it even mean to deny yourself? Here's a simple translation: "Say no to." *Say no to yourself.* We don't like that, do we? But even more, *Say no to yourself and say yes to God.* That's what it means to deny yourself. Selfish people will find this outrageous. Even offensive. And narcissists need not apply.

What is this cross Christ calls us to carry? The cross is still a controversial symbol and icon today. We adorn our churches with massive crosses. We get into lawsuits over where crosses can or cannot be displayed. We wear the cross as a fashion accessory. We have it stitched on our clothing. We have it tattooed on our arms or legs. But we need to understand that though it is a recognized symbol of Christianity today, that was not what it meant in the first century. When a person spoke about the cross, he or she was talking about a horrible, barbaric death.

The Romans didn't invent crucifixion. It was probably the Carthaginians. But the Romans embraced the practice and (shall we say) "perfected" it. It was a horrific form of torture, a way to execute a man so he would experience the maximum amount of pain possible. It wasn't simply an execution device; beheading was far more efficient. It was designed to bring pain and misery, with the victims dying slowly by suffocation.

If you were living in a city occupied by Rome and saw a man carrying a cross down the road, you would know that man was about to die a terrible, degrading death. And *that* is what the cross meant to people. It was a symbol of shame and horror. Nobody in that day would wear a little gold cross around their neck. It would be like wearing a hangman's noose or a little electric chair. The cross was a symbol of execution.

When Jesus spoke about the cross, then, and "taking it up," the disciples must have felt shocked. They needed to understand what He was saying about a cross, and so do we. People today often use the word casually: "I have my cross to bear." Someone with a physical affliction of some kind might say, "Yes, well, my arthritis [or whatever] is my cross to bear."

But that is not what it means to bear a cross.

To take up your cross means that you die to yourself and identify yourself as a follower of Jesus Christ.

This flies in the face of conventional wisdom and polite conversation. We rarely hear messages like this in church. When we go to church we want to hear a series about how to lose weight, how to be more successful in business, or how to have a happier family. And there's nothing wrong with any of those things.

But what about a message on taking up the cross? What about a message on dying to yourself? That's not very popular, is it?

I've been a Christian for well over forty years. Right after my conversion I remember being impressed by certain things that don't impress me as much today. I was very impressed with gifted people—a gifted preacher, a gifted evangelist, a gifted singer. And though I still appreciate such people today, I am *more* impressed by other things.

- I am impressed by people who live faithful lives, day in and day out, as followers of Jesus Christ.

- I am impressed by a husband who keeps his vows to his wife all the way to the end.

- I am impressed by a wife who stands by her husband through thick and thin.

- I am impressed by a Christian who maintains her faith through sunny days and stormy nights.

- I am impressed by a believer who weathers the storms and grows stronger in his faith.

That's what following Jesus is all about. It is "a long obedience in the same direction." It's about getting up every morning and breathing a word of praise to Jesus Christ, no matter what's on your plate or what your circumstances might be. In another gospel, Jesus said, "Take up [your] cross daily, and follow Me" (Luke 9:23).

Someone reading this might think, *That certainly sounds like a grim life. Denying myself? Does this mean I can never go to Disneyland again? I can never have a great meal and laugh with friends? What in the world does this mean?*

I think Jesus answered these concerns in Matthew 16:25, when He said, "For whoever desires to save his life will lose it, but whoever loses his life for My sake will find it." Jesus was saying that we find our lives by losing our lives. We've all heard the expression, "Finders keepers, losers weepers." But Jesus has a different version of that. He says losers are keepers. If you lose yourself, you will find yourself as never before. *The Message* translation puts it like this: "Self-help is no help at all. Self-sacrifice is the way, my way, to finding yourself, your true self."

This is not a popular message in our culture. Not at all. We had the baby-boomer generation, who were pretty much self-absorbed. Then came their children. And now we have the millennials, who are known as the "me generation." Now the millennials are having their own children and they have been dubbed the "me-me-me generation."

There is so much focus on ourselves. What is the most popular kind of photograph you can take today? That's right—*a selfie*. We even have something called a "selfie stick," so we can hold the smartphone away from us a bit and get a better picture of ourselves.

Jesus says, "Hey, Selfie Generation, do you want to find yourself? Lose yourself for My sake. You who chase after fulfillment, you will never find it by chasing it! You will find it by following Me."

What does it mean to deny yourself? Let me suggest some specifics. It means that you're not embarrassed to bow your head and pray over a meal in a public place. It means that you look for opportunities to share the gospel with people. It means you resist the allure and temptation of this world to live for self and decide instead to serve others. To deny yourself in marriage means to put the needs of your spouse above your own. To deny yourself as a single person means that you control yourself and wait until you are married to have sexual relations. To deny yourself means you take time each day to open the Word of God and read it, to set aside time to talk to God, and to be involved in church. It means you give faithfully of your finances to the Lord.

The word *deny* means disdain, disown, forfeit, disregard. That may sound morbid at first hearing, and yet it is through this self-denial that you will find self-fulfillment beyond what you have ever experienced.

In Galatians 2:20 (NIV), the apostle wrote, "I have been crucified with Christ and I no longer live, but Christ lives in me. The life I now live in the body, I live by faith in the Son of God, who loved me and gave himself for me."

A seventeenth-century pastor named Samuel Rutherford put it this way: "The cross of Christ is the sweetest burden I ever bore. It is a burden to me like wings are a burden to a bird or sails are to a ship. It carries me forward to my harbor."

Here is the positive outcome Jesus speaks of in Matthew 16:25: If we try to live seeking after happiness, we will never be happy. But if instead we focus on seeking after God, happiness will come into our lives as a byproduct. In other words, if we live a holy life we will have a happy life.

What does that mean? That we walk around with our hands folded, staring up into heaven and saying hallelujah all the time? No, not at all. Consider this: We would come closer to the main concept if we change H-O-L-Y to W-H-O-L-L-Y. If you live a life wholly committed to Christ (a holy life), you will be living a happy life.

When you finally stop looking for happiness so desperately and choose to follow Jesus instead, the joy you could never seem to find will slip into your life unexpectedly, like a sweet cool breeze through an open window.

CHAPTER TWENTY-NINE
ONLY JESUS

Have you ever experienced one of those special moments when you felt the presence of God?

Maybe it was in a time of personal Bible study. A verse of Scripture seemed to jump off the page, grab you, and shake you. It became the personal word of the Lord to you, and you sensed His nearness and presence. Maybe you were out on a walk under the stars or watching a magnificent sunrise. Maybe it was in a worship service. For a moment or two as you raised your hands and voice to God in praise, it was almost as though you and Jesus were alone in a room. You sensed the glory of God. You could feel it.

Most of us who have walked with Jesus have experienced memorable, perhaps even life-changing, moments like those.

Just imagine, then, how Peter, James, and John felt when they were given the privilege of seeing Jesus transformed and transfigured before their very eyes up on a mountaintop in Galilee. It was a moment when Christ shone like the sun—with Moses on one side and Elijah on the other. It was such an amazing event for the disciples that they even wanted to set up camp and never leave that place.

But they had to leave, of course. They had to go back to the mundane things in life waiting for them at the foot of the mountain. The disciples learned that while we can't always live on the mountaintops, those experiences can help prepare us for the valleys.

When I speak of mountaintops, I'm using that as a metaphor for times of great blessing, exhilarating emotional experiences, and moments of sensing God's nearness and love. Mountaintops are great, and they're worth remembering and celebrating. But the fact is, we live most of our lives in the valleys.

On the Mountaintop

Now after six days Jesus took Peter, James, and John his brother, led them up on a high mountain by themselves; and He was transfigured before them. His face shone like the sun, and His clothes became as white as the light. And behold, Moses and Elijah appeared to them, talking with Him. Then Peter answered and said to Jesus, "Lord, it is good for us to be here; if You wish, let us make here three tabernacles: one for You, one for Moses, and one for Elijah."

While he was still speaking, behold, a bright cloud overshadowed them; and suddenly a voice came out of the cloud, saying, "This is My beloved Son, in whom I am well pleased. Hear Him!" And when the disciples heard it, they fell on their faces and were greatly afraid. But Jesus came and touched them and said, "Arise, and do not be afraid." When they had lifted up their eyes, they saw no one but Jesus only. (Matthew 17:1-8)

The transfiguration of Jesus Christ came at a significant point in our Lord's life and ministry. It was the halfway point on a very difficult journey between the manger and the cross. At Caesarea Philippi, a place known for false gods, Jesus had asked His disciples this essential question: "Who do men say that I am?"

The disciples looked at each other, possibly shrugged their shoulders, and ventured some tentative answers, but none of them seemed to really grasp who He was at that point. Then Peter, under the inspiration of the Father, declared, "I believe You are the Christ, the Son of the living God."

Jesus affirmed that statement and told Peter that the Father Himself had given Peter that insight. Then He went on to describe what was going to happen to Him. In Matthew 16:21, we read, "From that time Jesus began to show to His disciples that He must go to

Jerusalem, and suffer many things from the elders and chief priests and scribes, and be killed, and be raised the third day."

Jesus felt that the time was right to give three of His closest disciples a glimpse of His glory—and to see Him for who He really was and is. This would fulfill the words He spoke to them earlier: "I tell you the truth, some standing here right now will not die before they see the Son of Man coming in his Kingdom" (Matthew 16:28, NLT). This moment of transformation on the mountaintop was going to be a preview of coming attractions.

What coming attractions?

The Second Coming of Christ in His glory to earth.

You know how it is when you go to the movies. If you arrive on time, you have to sit through several previews of coming movies. Sometimes I will see one of those trailers and say, "Well, that's a big help, because I will never see *that* movie." But at other times my interest has been piqued and I've said, "I have to see that. That looks good." Sometimes the trailers, stringing together the best parts of the movie, are better than the movie itself.

But that is not true of the "preview" these three disciples witnessed on the mountain with Jesus. Though that little keyhole glimpse was awesome, what's going to follow will be far greater.

"Shone Like the Sun . . ."

Again, in Matthew 17:2 (NLT) we read that, "as the men watched, Jesus' appearance was transformed so that his face shone like the sun, and his clothes became as white as light." Can you imagine that? Have you ever glanced at the sun? I hope not, because you could seriously damage your eyes—even with dark glasses on. That is how Jesus appeared at that moment. Who wouldn't be dazzled by such a display of glory? Then on top of that blinding radiance, to have Moses and Elijah appear, one on each side of Jesus? *What a scene. What a moment.*

Was it a miracle, then, that Jesus suddenly blazed out in white radiance like the sun? Not at all. The real miracle was what happened on all the other days when He *didn't* shine like this.

When Jesus called Himself "the light of the world," He meant it. But while He walked among people in a human body, He cloaked or hid that magnificent glory—except for that brief moment on the top of that mountain. I wonder if people watching that mountain from a distance thought they saw a bolt of lightning.

While Jesus never voided His deity, He did veil it. As the old Christmas carol says, "Veiled in flesh the Godhead see; hail, the incarnate deity." Jesus was and is God, and He gave His three friends a sneak peek of the glory they would one day see—along with us—in full measure.

Why were Moses and Elijah in on that brief conversation on the mountain? (How I would have loved to hear that exchange!) We associate Moses with the giving of the Law, remembering that God gave him the Ten Commandments on another mountain, Mount Sinai. We think of Elijah as the greatest of the prophets, and a man who worked powerful miracles. So here were the best representatives of the Law and the Prophets having a conversation with Jesus prior to the cross.

Maybe it's just me, but I can't help wondering how the disciples seemed to know right away who those men were. How did that happen? Was Moses still carrying around the stone tablets with the Ten Commandments on them? Did Elijah call down fire from heaven a couple of times just to identify himself? Did they have nametags? (HI. MY NAME IS MOSES.)

I don't think so. But I do think this is evidence that when we are in heaven we will have no difficulty recognizing one another, and even those we have never met before. We will have that ability, and how good that will be!

Was this Moses' first visit to the Promised Land? You'll remember from the book of Deuteronomy that he was kept out while he was alive on earth; God gave him only a glimpse of the Promised Land, but he wasn't allowed admittance. But there he was on the mountain with Jesus and Elijah, so he got in after all!

Moses had been dead at that point about fourteen hundred years, and Elijah for about nine hundred years. And we do know at least the basics of what they discussed on the mountain in that blaze of glory. In Luke 9:31 (TLB) we read, "They were speaking of his death at Jerusalem, to be carried out in accordance with God's plan."

Even though the disciples didn't understand at that point why Jesus had to suffer and die, apparently Moses and Elijah understood that fact very well. Were they encouraging Him in what He was about to do, and perhaps thanking Him for it? Were they saying, "Lord, thank You on behalf of all humanity for what You are about to do."

And what were the disciples doing while this amazing conversation was taking place? Sleeping, of course. Luke described the scene like this: "Meanwhile, Peter and those with him were slumped over in sleep. When they came to, rubbing their eyes, they saw Jesus in his glory and the two men standing with him" (verse 32, MSG).

These were the same guys who fell asleep while Jesus was praying in Gethsemane, just before the betrayal and crucifixion. They were pathetic!

But maybe we shouldn't be so hard on them. We have all probably fallen asleep at inappropriate times. I read a newspaper account of a man who was burglarizing a house at night, when a police car cruised by on the street. Seeing the patrol car, the robber took cover on the floor with the stolen items still in his hands. But lying there on the floor like that, he fell asleep. When the homeowner came down the stairs in the morning, there was the thief, still sound asleep. The homeowner slipped back upstairs and called the police, who showed up to arrest the intruder. The officer actually had to wake the man up, and said to him, "Sir, this is your wake-up call."

When Peter suddenly woke up in the middle of the transfiguration, he felt he ought to make a statement. The Bible says, "Peter answered and said . . ." He answered, but nobody had spoken to him! And he said, "Lord, it is good for us to be here" (Matthew 17:4).

We have all said things we regret or sent e-mails we'd like to have back. But Peter had the excuse of still being groggy from sleep. Luke says Peter was "all confused and not even knowing what he was saying" (9:33, TLB).

Peter's off-the-top-of-the-head idea was that he, James, and John could get busy and build three tabernacles or shelters on the mountaintop—one for Jesus, one for Moses, and one for Elijah. In essence, he was saying, "Lord this is wonderful. Let's stay here. This is where You belong, in glory, shining like the sun, standing with Moses and Elijah on a mountaintop. Please, Jesus, can't You just forget this idea of going to Jerusalem and suffering and dying? Let's just stay up here on the mountaintop forever!"

But that isn't possible, is it? God never lets us stay on mountaintops. Sooner or later, we have to go back to the valleys. As one commentator put it, "God never allows His people to build their tabernacles in the palace of glory while the world is still in flames." Sometimes as Christians we would like to remain cozy and secure in a Christian bubble and have minimal contact with the messy, unhappy, outside world.

But that's not what Jesus wants. Not at all. Jesus sends us out *into* the world. He says, "Go into all the world and preach the gospel, and make disciples of all nations." Our objective as Christians is not to isolate, it is to infiltrate. It is to permeate our culture with the message of Jesus Christ and with good works, bringing glory to God the Father. And that won't happen on top of a mountain.

The truth is, we really don't need more emotional highs and mountaintop experiences in the Christian life. What we need is more day-to-day obedience, walking by faith and not by feelings. Oswald Chamber once wrote, "We are not built for the mountains and the dawns and aesthetic affinities, those are for moments of inspiration, that is all. We are built for the valley, for the ordinary stuff we are in, and that is where we have to prove our mettle."[14]

In a glorious moment when Peter ought to have been respectfully listening instead of mindlessly blurting out his opinion, the Father suddenly stepped into the story. Matthew 17:5 says, "While he was still speaking, behold, a bright cloud overshadowed them; and suddenly a voice came out of the cloud, saying, 'This is My beloved Son, in whom I am well pleased. Hear Him!'"

It was almost as though the Father was saying, "Listen, Peter. If My Son says He must go to Jerusalem to suffer and die, you had better believe Him! And if My Son says you should take up your cross and follow Him, you should do that. Do what He says!"

As we might expect, Peter remembered this day to the very end of his life, and I'm sure John must have as well. In 2 Peter 1:16-18 (NIV), Peter wrote,

> For we did not follow cleverly devised stories when we told you about the coming of our Lord Jesus Christ in power, but we were eyewitnesses of his majesty. He received honor and glory from God the Father when the voice came to him from the Majestic Glory, saying, "This is my Son, whom I love; with him I am well pleased." We ourselves heard this voice that came from heaven when we were with him on the sacred mountain.

The disciples were terrified by what they had seen and heard. The cloud. The blinding light. The voice. The appearance of Moses and Elijah. It was all so overwhelming. But then the vision faded away, the two heavenly visitors disappeared from the scene, and only Jesus was left.

Why Jesus alone? Because He had come to fulfill all that the Law and the Prophets pointed to. As wonderful as the Law may have been, its purpose was to show us that we are sinners in desperate need of a Savior. The Law opened our eyes to truth, but it also shut our mouths from making any self-righteous claims. The Law drives us into the arms of a merciful Savior.

The Old Testament sacrifices were there to point to the ultimate fulfillment in Christ Himself, who would be the Lamb of God, taking away the sins of the world. When all is said and done, there is only Jesus. He stands alone. Our salvation doesn't derive from Jesus *and* church sacraments, or from Jesus *and* good works.

It is Jesus alone.

It is Jesus and nothing or no one else. He is the only One who can save and keep us.

And what is true of salvation is also true of life in general. When we go through difficult times, He is the answer. Jesus only. Yes, friends and family will help, but they will also disappoint us and let us down at times—as we will do for them. But Jesus will never disappoint. It says in Proverbs 18:24 (NIV), "There is a friend who sticks closer than a brother."

Only Jesus can meet the deepest needs of your life.

Only Jesus can heal your broken heart.

Only Jesus can give you the strength to go on.

Down from the Mountain

And when they had come to the multitude, a man came to Him, kneeling down to Him and saying, "Lord, have mercy on my son, for he is an epileptic and suffers severely; for he often falls into the fire and often into the water. So I brought him to Your disciples, but they could not cure him."

Then Jesus answered and said, "O faithless and perverse generation, how long shall I be with you? How long shall I bear with you? Bring him here to Me." And Jesus rebuked the demon, and it came out of him; and the child was cured from that very hour. (Matthew 17:14-18)

We will all have mountaintop experiences in life. But when the experience is over, at the bottom of the mountain we will experience a valley, a test. The bad news is that mountaintops don't last forever; the good news is that valleys don't either.

Maybe you are on a mountaintop right now, with everything going great in your life. Your health is good, your finances better than ever, your family blessed. Enjoy that time! Savor those golden days and thank God for them. Don't feel guilty that you are on a mountaintop because, trust me, a valley is coming.

Then again, maybe you are in the valley right now. But it is so deep and dark that it feels more like a narrow canyon, and you wonder if you will ever get out of it. The answer is yes, you will. Even the deepest valleys don't last forever in a believer's life. That is why the psalmist David wrote, "Yea, though I walk through the valley of the shadow of death, I will fear no evil; for You are with me" (Psalm 23:4). He didn't say, "Yea, though I collapse and give up in the valley of the shadow," or "Yea, though I curl up and die in the valley of the shadow."

No, he said, "Yea, though I *walk* . . ."

Keep walking. Keep moving. Keep trusting. Keep putting one foot in front of the other and you will get through this.

After their glorious experience, Peter, James, and John found a problem waiting for them at the bottom of the mountain: a man with a demon-possessed child. Just minutes before, they had seen the glory of God, witnessed Jesus transfigured before their eyes, and heard the voice of Father God Himself.

And then they came face to face with the work of Satan.

This will be true for us as well. After Jesus was baptized in the Jordan and heard His Father's blessing, the devil immediately came to tempt Him in the wilderness. First came the dove, lighting on His shoulder, and then came the devil! For Elijah, his great victory on Mount Carmel was quickly followed by the death threats of Jezebel—and a severe depression. It is often true that trials follow soon after blessings.

You might say, "Well, Greg, I really don't go through trials. I don't go through valleys. I can't remember the last time I was even severely tempted."

Then you must be either dead or worthless.

It was Spurgeon who said, "You don't kick a dead horse." If you are not a threat to the kingdom of darkness, why should the devil waste his time on you? But if you begin to be a threat to him and his activities, he will do everything he can to try to stop you.

Don't feel discouraged if you go through times of testing. Don't feel bad if you go through temptation. Those experiences could be an indication that you are heading in the right direction. The devil attacks those who are a threat to his domain.

I heard an interview on a Christian radio station with a man who had committed adultery. He told the host, "I used to tell my friends that if there was one sin that I would never fall into, it would be adultery."

And of course that is the very thing that happened to him. He fell into adultery. As Scripture says, "Let him who thinks he stands take heed lest he fall" (1 Corinthians 10:12). Then the man being interviewed offered this quote from Oswald Chambers: "An unguarded strength is actually a double weakness, because that is where the least likely temptations will be effective in sapping strength."[15]

If I recognize that I have a weak or vulnerable area in my life, I will tell myself, "I have to be careful here. I need some extra prayer and accountability to keep from falling in this temptation." But if I say, "I will never have to worry about this. I have this wired. I'll be okay," then I may find that Satan will come after me in that very area.

The father at the bottom of the mountain who brought his son to the nine disciples is a representative of all those Christian parents who want to see their kids set free from the power of the devil. These are young men and women who may be held by Satan through immorality, drugs, alcohol, or peer pressure. The parents have tried everything to help untangle their son or daughter, but nothing has worked. That was this distraught dad's story. He took his boy to the disciples, but they couldn't do anything. So he brought him at last to Jesus.

Have you brought your kids to Jesus?

You ask, "How do I bring them to Jesus?"

You start by taking them to church. *Taking* them. Not sending them to church, not dropping them off at church. Not saying, as a husband and father to your wife and kids, "Hey, have a good time at church. I'm going to stay home and watch the game. We can meet for lunch when you get out."

No. Dads and moms, you go, too. You say, "Kids, we're going to church."

Your spouse may say, "I don't want to go."

"That's interesting," you reply. "Get in the car. We're going. As a family."

The father in this gospel account may have been at his wits' end, but he did the best thing he could have done. He brought his child to Jesus.

As soon as the dad brought his boy before the Lord, however, the lad had one of his demonic episodes. Luke 9:42 (NLT) says, "As the boy came forward, the demon knocked him to the ground and threw him into a violent convulsion."

The dad may have been embarrassed, thinking, *No, son, not now! Don't do this in front of Jesus.* But Jesus knew what was going on; He knew this was the devil just being the devil.

Here is something to remember. Whenever a person takes a step toward God, the devil will try to stop him. If we try to reach our neighbor, friend, coworker, or family member for the Lord, perhaps inviting them to church, Satan will oppose it. We can anticipate that, and put on our spiritual armor when we share our faith.

It wasn't as comfortable or glorious for Peter, James, and John down in the valley as it was up on the mountaintop with heaven breaking through. But they got to see Jesus in action, and they were being trained to take on Satan in their own deep valleys, as they would have to do after Jesus was taken into heaven.

Here's the good news about mountaintops and valleys: A day is coming when we will stay on that mountaintop, so to speak, and never have to go down. We will be in the presence of the Father and Jesus, Moses and Elijah, the angels, and all the friends and loved ones who have died in Christ and gone on before us. There will be no more temptation, no more sin waiting to trip us up, no more physical limitations.

The transfiguration was a sneak peek, a short trailer and preview of things to come. One day Jesus will come for us all. And looking at this world and all that is happening right now, that may be sooner rather than later.

Yes, we will get to rejoice with the Lord up on heaven's mountaintop.

But for now, we get to work with Him and for Him in the valley.

CHAPTER THIRTY
CHILDLIKE FAITH

"Greg Laurie, will you just grow up?"

It was a statement I heard more than once as a child. Adults would usually say that to me because I was goofing off or pulling a prank or acting crazy.

The truth is, "growing up" is something we all want to do—until we actually grow up! When you're a kid, you look forward to growing up. And then after you grow up, you wish you were a kid again! It's funny how that works. When you're a child, you can hardly wait until you're old enough to hang out with the big kids and do the things they do. And then as you get older, you find yourself looking back wistfully on those days of childhood as "the good old days."

Jesus, however, told us we are to have the faith of a child. So how does that work? How can we grow up on one hand and still maintain a childlike faith on the other?

That's what we'll consider in this chapter.

Jesus and Children

Jesus loved kids during His time on earth—and loves them still.

Some people get irritated when children are being children and start making a lot of noise. But Jesus got irritated when people tried to keep the kids away. Remember how the moms wanted to bring their little ones to Jesus so He could bless them? The disciples shooed them away, saying, "Don't bother Him right now." That's when Jesus made that well-known statement: "Let the little children come to Me, and do not forbid them; for of such is the kingdom of heaven" (Matthew 19:14).

He always had time for kids. When He fed the five thousand— the only miracle recorded in all four Gospels—He found a little boy and used his small lunch of bread and fish to bless the multitudes. And when He went to the bedside of Jairus's daughter, He said to her, "Little maiden, arise," calling her back from the dead.

In Matthew 18, He used a child as an example of what faith ought to look like.

At that time the disciples came to Jesus, saying, "Who then is greatest in the kingdom of heaven?"

Then Jesus called a little child to Him, set him in the midst of them, and said, "Assuredly, I say to you, unless you are converted and become as little children, you will by no means enter the kingdom of heaven. Therefore whoever humbles himself as this little child is the greatest in the kingdom of heaven. Whoever receives one little child like this in My name receives Me.

"Whoever causes one of these little ones who believe in Me to sin, it would be better for him if a millstone were hung around his neck, and he were drowned in the depth of the sea." (verses 1-6)

At a place called Caesarea Philippi, Jesus had revealed to His disciples that He, the Son of Man, would soon be betrayed, tortured, and crucified, and would rise from the dead on the third day.

Yet even though the disciples had heard those sobering words and had a chance to think about them for a while, they fell back into their old argument of "Who is going to be top dog in the new kingdom?"

Does that strike you as just a little bit insensitive?

Jesus told them He would soon have to die, and they started arguing about who was the number one disciple. That would be like telling your friend, "I just came from my doctor's office; he told me I'm going to die in one month." And your friend replies, "Seriously? Could I have your car?"

On more than one occasion, the disciples tuned out what they ought to have been thinking about and became preoccupied with who was the best, who was the brightest, who was the most successful among them.

It's happening to this day. People still want to know how to be number one, how to climb the ladder of success, or how to come out on top, even at the expense of everyone else.

That was the discussion among the disciples. And when they couldn't come to any firm conclusion, they decided to take the question to Jesus to let Him settle it. So they asked Him, "Who is greatest in the Kingdom of Heaven?" (Matthew 18:1, NLT).

Jesus, however, bypassed their question and did something completely unexpected. Seeing a small child nearby, He called the little one over to Him and put him in their midst.

Can't you just see it? There was that little one, staring around wide-eyed at all those serious-looking men with beards. I imagine Jesus gave the child a hug and then said these words: "I tell you the truth, unless you turn from your sins and become like little children, you will never get into the Kingdom of Heaven. So anyone who becomes as humble as this little child is the greatest in the Kingdom of Heaven" (Matthew 18:3-4, NLT).

Jesus was saying, "You need to be childlike."

But what does that mean?

Awe and Wonder

Children, especially when they are small and before they have learned to look bored, have a sense of awe and wonder. That's why I recommend that you always go to Disneyland with a child rather than with adults. Adults are cynical, gripe about the cost of everything, complain about the food, comment on how things look fake, and remark that it was better in the old days.

Little children, however, take it all in. To borrow the title of a Disney song, it's a whole new world to them. And when they see Mickey Mouse or Donald Duck, they think they're the genuine article.

It's really fun to see the Magic Kingdom through the eyes of a child.

For that matter, it's fun to be around a child who tastes ice cream for the first time or plays in the snow or wades in the ocean. It gives you the opportunity to rediscover the wonder in some really wonderful things that you've possibly taken for granted for years.

I think that's part of what Jesus was communicating here when He said we should become like little children. He wasn't saying we should be childish, but rather childlike—and there is a big difference between the two.

Being childlike doesn't mean we are immature. No, we need to grow up spiritually. In Ephesians 4:14 (NLT) we are told, "Then we will no longer be immature like children. We won't be tossed and blown about by every wind of new teaching. We will not be influenced when people try to trick us with lies so clever they sound like the truth."

So we have to grow up, yet at the same time we still want to be childlike. How does that work?

The Humility of a Child

Therefore whoever humbles himself as this little child is the greatest in the kingdom of heaven. (Matthew 18:4)

The twelve disciples were arguing about greatness and who would be the best. So Jesus brought a little child into their midst to illustrate humility. He was saying, "You need to have the humility of a child."

Little children know they need help. They know they need you to pick them up when they get tired of walking on those little legs. They know you will be the one who takes them out of the car seat and puts them back in the car seat. They know they need you to change their diaper, cut up their food, help them get into their clothes, or comfort them when they're scared in the middle of the night. They depend on you. They understand that and they're fine with that.

So Jesus was saying, "Just as a little child is happily dependent upon their parent, so you should be dependent upon Me." Referring to their argument, He told them that the way to be strong was to recognize their innate weakness, and that the way to greatness is along the path of humility.

So which would you rather have happen? Would you rather humble yourself or have God humble you? I don't know about you, but I definitely prefer Option A. The apostle Peter wrote,

"Therefore humble yourselves under the mighty hand of God, that He may exalt you in due time" (1 Peter 5:6). Jesus said, "Whoever exalts himself will be humbled, and he who humbles himself will be exalted" (Matthew 23:12).

That sounds like a really good plan to me. I would much rather get down on my knees before the Lord in real humility than in my pride have the Lord force me to my knees (or flat on my face). In other words, don't wait for God to relieve you of your pride or arrogance, perhaps allowing circumstances in your life that will reveal to you and everyone else how weak you really are.

Jesus summed it up clearly when He said in essence, "Fall on the Rock and be broken, or the Rock will grind you to powder" (see Matthew 21:44).

The first, best step on the road to greatness is to humble yourself like a little child before the Lord.

Don't Ever Cause a Child to Stumble

Whoever causes one of these little ones who believe in Me to sin, it would be better for him if a millstone were hung around his neck, and he were drowned in the depth of the sea. (Matthew 18:6)

People who have set out to undermine the faith of Christians, especially young ones, will be in for a terrible day of reckoning. God takes these matters very, very seriously. Those who would go out of their way to try to challenge, damage, or destroy someone's spiritual life will come into severe judgment. Jesus said it would be better for them if a millstone were tied around their necks and they were thrown into the sea.

We all need to remember that we are being watched by young believers every single day. Paul told Timothy, "Be an example to all believers in what you say, in the way you live, in your love, your faith, and your purity" (1 Timothy 4:12, NLT). In another passage he said, in essence, "Follow me as I follow Christ" (see 1 Corinthians 11:1).

This is what every Christian should be able to say! *Follow me as I follow Jesus.* You might say, "Oh no, Greg. I would never say that. Follow me? No way. I've messed up too many times and made too many mistakes."

I understand that response, because I'm flawed, too. And I would never say to anyone, "I am a perfect example, and you need to do everything I do." No, I couldn't say that. But I think I could say, "Follow me as I follow the Lord." You and I should be living in such a way that a younger believer could look to our example and find something in us that they would want to emulate. Why? Because we are living as examples of what it means to be a genuine follower of Christ.

Is your life a stepping stone or a stumbling block? Are you helping people to come to Jesus through your example or are you driving them away? The truth is, everyone is an example. The only question is, are you a good one or a bad one?

Jesus said, "If your hand or foot causes you to sin, cut it off and cast it from you. It is better for you to enter into life lame or maimed, rather than having two hands or two feet, to be cast into the everlasting fire" (Matthew 18:8). In other words, if anything in your life causes you to stumble, then deal with it. Because if it can cause you to stumble, it can cause someone else to stumble as well.

How do we cause others to stumble? By not caring about them. In Matthew 18:10 we read, "Take heed that you do not despise one of these little ones, for I say to you that in heaven their angels always see the face of My Father who is in heaven." Don't cause these little ones to stumble! Be a good example for your children.

I think of couples with children who decide to divorce. They will say, "Oh, don't worry about the kids. They're resilient."

Yes, we've heard that before, haven't we?

People can say that all they want, but divorce *does* hurt the children. It hurts them profoundly. I know from personal experience what it's like, as I saw my own mom married and divorced seven times. Jesus was definitely saying, "Think about the young ones before you make life-changing decisions. Don't put stumbling stones in their path just as they're learning how to navigate life."

It's true with younger believers, too. Sometimes we will take our so-called liberties and flaunt them in the face of young Christians, causing them to stumble in their faith. Paul told us in Romans 14:21 (NIV), "It is better not to eat meat or drink wine or to do anything else that will cause your brother or sister to fall."

You might say, "Well, that's *their* problem."

No, it is your problem and our problem. Because the Bible teaches that we don't live and die to ourselves. What we do affects other people.

After wrapping up His discussion about being humble like little children in Matthew 18:10, Jesus switched the metaphor and began to talk to the disciples about something even more humble and lowly than a child: a sheep. And a lost one, at that.

The Shepherd Calls a Search Party

For the Son of Man has come to save that which was lost.

What do you think? If a man has a hundred sheep, and one of them goes astray, does he not leave the ninety-nine and go to the mountains to seek the one that is straying? And if he should find it, assuredly, I say to you, he rejoices more over that sheep than over the ninety-nine that did not go astray. Even so it is not the will of your Father who is in heaven that one of these little ones should perish. (Matthew 18:11-14)

So what do we learn from these words?

God cares for us as individuals.

Jesus used the picture of a shepherd looking for a wayward sheep, a familiar metaphor that is used throughout the Bible. Isaiah 40:11 says of God, "He will feed His flock like a shepherd; He will gather the lambs with His arm, and carry them in His bosom, and gently lead those who are with young." In 1 Peter 2:25 we read, "For you were like sheep going astray, but have now returned to the Shepherd and Overseer of your souls."

We love that image of God as a shepherd and us as His sheep.

But we need to understand that the picture is as revealing as it is beautiful. If you know anything about caring for sheep, you know that they are among the dumbest animals on the face of the earth.

As sheep, we have a natural tendency to go astray.

Isaiah 53:6 says, "All we like sheep have gone astray; we have turned, every one, to his own way." Why do we stray? Simple answer: We're stupid, just like sheep.

Not long ago, I read an article about 450 sheep that fell to their deaths in Turkey. The article said that one sheep jumped off a cliff, and 449 others followed him. How stupid is that? It's like the lead sheep said, "Okay, guys. We're all going off the cliff now. Single file. Let's go. It's not that baaaad."

Do you know how sheep are slaughtered? They follow a goat, known as a Judas goat, that leads them up a ramp to where the slaughterers are doing their job. Those sheep just get in line and follow the goat to their deaths.

We say, "Man, that is one stupid animal."

But don't we do the same thing? Don't we go astray? Don't we do things that are outright foolish? Don't we try at times to run from God, disobey the Word of God, and resist His will in our lives? Of course we do. We go astray and we turn to our own way, even though it hurts us and will eventually destroy us. That's just the way we are.

And by the way, there are plenty of Judas goats out there ready to lead us to destruction.

What we need to do is follow the Good Shepherd. In John 10:27-28, Jesus said, "My sheep hear My voice, and I know them, and they follow Me. And I give them eternal life, and they shall never perish; neither shall anyone snatch them out of My hand." The word Jesus used in this verse for "follow" means to deliberately decide to comply with instructions.

We come to realize that God's plan for us is better than our plan for ourselves and that when He leads us to a different place, it is for our ultimate good. It might not be for our *temporary* good, and it might not make much sense to us at the time. But He has a plan, and if we follow Him and comply with His directions, we will always be the better for it.

Psalm 23 is the classic passage that deals with us being sheep and God being the shepherd.

The LORD is my shepherd;
I shall not want.
He makes me to lie down in green pastures;
He leads me beside the still waters.
He restores my soul;
He leads me in the paths of righteousness
For His name's sake.
Yea, though I walk through the valley of the shadow of death,
I will fear no evil;
For You are with me;
Your rod and Your staff, they comfort me. (verses 1-4)

He *makes* me to lie down in green pastures. Sheep are so dumb sometimes they have to be made to do things that will keep them alive. A shepherd will lead them to a green pasture, but if he doesn't guide them on, they'll stay in that one place forever. Even after the grass is long gone they will huddle in the dirt, continuing to nose around for one last blade of grass. The shepherd has to lead them on to new pastures, whether they want to go or not. He also has to take them to still waters, and *then* they will drink.

The shepherd carries a rod and staff, as it says in Psalm 23, to help him deal with a wayward flock. The rod is just a club, and the staff is a long, crooked instrument designed to pull foolish sheep out of trouble. If a predator threatens the flock, the shepherd will use his rod to protect them. But he will also use the rod to discipline his sheep, so that, foolish as they are, they won't end up dead somewhere.

Despite our wandering, God never gives up on us.

Even though God loves us and has our best interests in mind, we will sometimes go astray anyway. What does the Lord do in those circumstances? Does He say something like this? "Oh well, you win a few and lose a few. That's life." No, that's not what He does. He sends out a search party! He looks for you, longs for you, and waits for you.

In Luke 15, a parallel passage to Matthew 18, Jesus described how a shepherd will leave the ninety-nine sheep in the fold and go searching for the one that went astray. And he keeps looking for it until he's found it and brought it home to safety. That is something you need to know about God: If you wander away from Him, He will keep seeking you, trying to bring you back.

Have you ever lost something of value? I don't know why, but I always lose valuable things. I hardly ever lose things I don't care about. If I have a pair of junky sunglasses that are all scratched up, I can't seem to lose them even if I *try*. But if I get a really nice pair that I want to take care of, I'll lose them within three days.

Maybe you've lost a pet. You put up little posters for it or drove up and down the street looking for it. It's one thing to lose a parakeet or a puppy, but it's something else entirely to lose a child.

In one of our out-of-town crusades years ago, our family was staying in a hotel. Jonathan was about five years old at the time. I was walking with him when he spied the elevator and ran ahead of me, because he loved to push the buttons. "Wait for me!" I called to him. "Don't get in the elevator until Dad gets there."

But just as I came around the corner I saw Jonathan standing in the elevator and the doors sliding shut. I thought I would have a heart attack on the spot! I pushed every button I could see and waited for the elevator to come back.

Have you ever noticed that repeatedly pushing the button on an elevator doesn't bring it to you any faster? Finally the elevator arrived, but when the door opened, there was no Jonathan.

I took the elevator down to the lobby and ran up to the front desk, where the employee was on the phone. "Excuse me, ma'am," I said. "My little son just got off the elevator—somewhere? Can you call security?" I wanted security, the police, a SWAT team, the Navy Seals—whoever could help me find our little boy.

But she wouldn't even get off the phone! In fact, she turned her back on me.

I kept saying, "Ma'am, excuse me, excuse me," but I was being ignored. I thought, *Okay, I've got to find him myself.* So I went back to the elevator and pushed every button for every floor. Each time the door opened, I yelled his name as loud as I could.

I would have torn that hotel apart room by room to find him. Losing him was not an option. Well, I did find him. I don't know what floor he was on, but he was just standing there, and I swept him up into my arms.

That is the picture—with all its emotional intensity—that we have here. God will not give up on you. He will seek you out, no matter how far you run. You will never escape His presence.

It's a thought that really gripped David in Psalm 139 (NLT).

I can never escape from your Spirit!
I can never get away from your presence!
If I go up to heaven, you are there;
if I go down to the grave, you are there.
If I ride the wings of the morning,
if I dwell by the farthest oceans,
even there your hand will guide me,
and your strength will support me.
I could ask the darkness to hide me
and the light around me to become night—
but even in darkness I cannot hide from you.
To you the night shines as bright as day.
Darkness and light are the same to you. (verses 7-12)

I have a friend who has some military hardware, including a pair of night-vision goggles. Have you ever looked through a pair of those? You can go into a pitch-black place, slip on those goggles, and literally see in the dark.

God, however, doesn't need night-vision goggles. He sees you wherever you go. Closing a door won't keep Him out, turning off the lights won't remove you from view, and speaking in hushed tones under your breath won't keep Him from hearing you. He sees everything, He hears everything, He knows everything, and He will never stop searching for you, because He loves you.

I love the picture God gives us in the book of Isaiah, when He says, "I have stretched out My hands all day long to a rebellious people, who walk in a way that is not good, according to their own thoughts" (65:2). That's quite an image, isn't it? The Father stands with His arms open, His hands outstretched, waiting for His people to come home to Him.

As our Shepherd seeks us, so we should seek others.

If he should find it, . . . he rejoices more over that sheep than over the ninety-nine that did not go astray. (Matthew 18:13)

In Luke's version of this teaching, we read, "When he has found it, he lays it on his shoulders, rejoicing. And when he comes home, he calls together his friends and neighbors, saying to them, 'Rejoice with me, for I have found my sheep which was lost!'" (Luke 15:5-6).

This is a beautiful picture of God carrying us when we have wandered away or fallen. The shepherd wraps the wandering sheep around his neck and brings it back home again.

We read in Isaiah 46:4, "Even to your old age, I am He, and even to gray hairs I will carry you! I have made, and I will bear; even I will carry, and will deliver you."

My grandkids like me to carry them. They will say to me, "Uppy, Papa," which means "pick me up so I don't have to walk anymore." Sometimes, I have to switch them back and forth in my arms because they get a little bit heavy. But they want to be carried, and I love carrying them.

This is the idea: God carries you right through life, even to your gray hairs—or when there is no hair to turn gray!

I have been preaching for forty years and have pastored a church for thirty-eight of those years. God has carried me right through it all, the good times and hard times, the setbacks and the victories. I can say with Jacob, "God . . . has been my shepherd all my life to this day" (Genesis 48:15, NIV).

In Luke 15:7 (NLT), Jesus declared, "There is more joy in heaven over one lost sinner who repents and returns to God than over ninety-nine others who are righteous and haven't strayed away!" Don't ever doubt it! Whenever there is a conversion on earth, there is a party in heaven. As C. S. Lewis once said, "Joy is the serious business of heaven."

By the way, I do believe people in heaven are aware of what happens on earth. No, I don't think of our loved ones sitting up there in grandstands with binoculars, watching everything we do. But I do believe there is a measure of awareness. This much I know clearly: When someone comes to faith in Christ and repents of his or her sins, the Bible tells us that the news somehow gets all over heaven, and there is joy.

God gets excited when lost people come to repentance, and so should we.

If the residents of heaven want to party over the conversion of one person on earth, we should reflect that same excitement when we hear that someone has come to the Lord.

Sometimes I think we become so absorbed in ourselves and in our own thoughts and plans that we become nonchalant about men and women finding salvation in Christ. We shrug and say, "That's great, but I'm already saved. I'm already going to heaven."

I think Jesus was taking that attitude on in this passage. He was saying, in effect, "Quit being so preoccupied with yourselves. Think about all of those lost sheep out there. Think about the little children I care for."

Sometimes, because I preach in a large Southern California church, some people will slip out of the service early to get to their cars and get a head start on the traffic. Most people know I always give an invitation for people to receive Christ at the end of my messages, so when they hear me begin to speak of that, they head for the back door.

But that's not a good time to slip out of church.

That's a time to be praying with all your heart that people outside of Christ will have their eyes opened and that they will yield to the voice of the Holy Spirit and give their hearts to Jesus.

Again, in Luke 15:5 we read, "And when he has found it, he lays it on his shoulders, rejoicing."

I believe that is what kept Jesus going, even to the cross. Because He was God, He knew what was ahead: the suffering, the rejection, the agonizing death, the sins of the world falling on His shoulders. But He refused to turn back. He set His face like flint (see Isaiah 50:7) and kept going.

How could He do it? How could He press on in spite of what waited for Him? What was it that motivated Him to keep going? Pause just for a moment to consider these amazing words in Hebrews 12:1-2:

> *Therefore we also, since we are surrounded by so great a cloud of witnesses, let us lay aside every weight, and the sin which so easily ensnares us, and let us run with endurance the race that is set before us, looking unto Jesus, the author and finisher of our faith, who for the joy that was set before Him endured the cross, despising the shame, and has sat down at the right hand of the throne of God. (emphasis added)*

It was joy that drove Him on, the joy that was "set before Him." What was that joy? It was you. It was me. It was all those who would receive His forgiveness and the promise of heaven through the ages to come. We were the joy. We were the prize. We were the treasure.

And He gave up all He had to obtain it.

How to Stay Childlike

One of the things I love most about being a grandfather is the chance to get down on the floor, play games with my grandkids, and just be silly for a while. They laugh, I laugh, and people watching us probably laugh, too.

Being around children is a great way to stay young at heart.

In the same way, it's a good thing to be around young believers, too. They need you and you need them. Young believers need your stability, your experience of walking with Christ through the years, and your knowledge of the Word of God. But you need them, too. You need to share that sense of excitement and freshness that they experience as they discover the truths of God for the first time.

We need each other. In His great commission, Jesus commanded us to go into all the world and make disciples, teaching them to observe all things He has commanded us. Our job description as followers of Jesus is to go after lost sheep, try to win them to Christ, take them under our wing, help them get up on their feet spiritually, and then go out and repeat the process again and again and again.

Yes, we all have our shortcomings, and no mature believer wants to be a stumbling block to younger Christians. *So don't be!*

Live your life alongside young Christians, and if you mess up, tell them so and apologize. Then keep going.

You really can say, "Follow me as I follow Christ." Just make sure that you are really following Him.

CHAPTER THIRTY-ONE
WHAT'S YOUR EXCUSE?

*D*eception starts very early in life.

Before a six-month-old child can even say one word, he learns how to engage in fake crying. Even though there's nothing really wrong with him, he understands that Mommy will come running if he cranks up the volume and starts screaming.

It's all downhill from there. In our natural state, all of us are well versed in deceit. In Jeremiah 17:9, the Lord set it down in plain language when He said, "The heart is deceitful above all things, and desperately wicked; who can know it?"

One of the most subtle outgrowths of that tendency to deceive is the fine art of excuse making.

What's the difference between a lie and an excuse?

Frankly, not all that much.

An excuse has been defined as the skin of a reason stuffed with a lie. Or put another way, an excuse is a lie all dressed up for dinner. But it's still a lie. A fancy lie, if you will, but a lie nonetheless.

Why Do We Offer Excuses?

Why do we do it? Why do we rely on excuses rather than reasons?

A reason is what we offer when we are unable to do something. An excuse is what we offer when we don't *want* to do something and hope to get out of it. It has been said that he who excuses himself accuses himself.

We all know an excuse when we hear one, don't we?

We may smile and nod at the person making the excuse, or even try to look sympathetic. But we're thinking, "I'm not really buying this. This is just an excuse."

There is one person in my life who is always late to our appointments and meetings. Every time he shows up, it's always with the same excuse: "There was a lot of traffic."

This is LA, and he's right: There *is* a lot of traffic. But why does everyone else always make it to the meetings on time?

Or someone might say, "I'm sorry I didn't turn the assignment in. My dog ate my homework." I would like to know if a dog anywhere on earth ever in human history literally ate someone's homework. It sounds pretty sketchy to me.

Or how about this one? "Sorry I'm late. My alarm didn't go off." I never used to believe that one until it happened to me last Easter Sunday. We had a very, very early sunrise service, and the pastor was just a little bit late. I didn't even have the heart to tell everyone the reason, because it's the oldest excuse in the book!

Lying, deception, and phony excuses have become far too common in our culture. Studies show that most résumés are full of misrepresentations. Seventy-one percent of applicants increase the tenure of their previous jobs. Sixty-four percent exaggerate their accomplishments. Sixty percent overstate the size of the department they managed. Fifty-three percent cite partial degrees as full. And forty-eight percent inflate their salary history. Studies also show that one-quarter to one-third of all workers tell lies to explain their tardiness or absence.

USA Today published an article not long ago on lying and excuse making. The article stated, "Every one of us fibs at least 50 times a day. We lie about our age, our income, our accomplishments, or we use lies to escape embarrassment." According to the article the most commonly used excuses are the following:

- "I wasn't feeling well."

- "I didn't want to hurt your feelings."

- "The check is in the mail."

- "I was just kidding."

- "I was only trying to help."

In a book called *Excuses and Lies*, the author lists his take on the top lies:

- "I'll be ready in a minute."

- "I'll do it in a minute."

- "Of course I'm listening!"

- "You look great, honey."

- "We can still be friends." (That is usually said in the context of breaking up with someone and means essentially nothing.)

Do you see how easy it is to stretch a truth a little?

When it comes to lame, deceptive excuses, we have all heard them—and probably used them. George Washington (the same guy who supposedly said, "I cannot tell a lie") once said, "It is better to offer no excuse than a bad one."

One of my all-time favorite excuses in the pages of the Bible is what Aaron said once to his brother, Moses. God had called Moses to climb up Mount Sinai to receive the Ten Commandments, and Aaron was left in charge of the Israelites. When Moses had been gone a long time, the people became restless and frustrated. They told Aaron, "We don't know where Moses is. We want gods to worship." Instead of standing strong and discouraging this, Aaron immediately caved and said, "Bring all of your gold earrings to me." He melted those thousands of gold earrings into the shape of a calf, put it up on a pedestal, and told everyone that this was a feast to the Lord.

Meanwhile up on Mount Sinai, Moses had been bathing in the glory of God and watching the finger of the Lord write His commandments on tablets of stone. On his way back down, he met up with Joshua, who had been waiting for Moses partway down the mountain. Soon they heard a noise in the camp. Was it a battle? Had a war started? No, it was an *orgy*—the biggest party of all time.

When Moses and Joshua came in view of the camp, they saw the Israelites dancing naked before a golden calf.

When Moses demanded an explanation from his brother, Aaron's story went like this: "Don't get so upset, my lord. . . . You yourself know how evil these people are. They said to me, 'Make us gods who will lead us. We don't know what happened to this fellow Moses, who brought us here from the land of Egypt.' So I told them, 'Whoever has gold jewelry, take it off.' When they brought it to me, I simply threw it into the fire—and out came this calf!" (Exodus 32:22-24, NLT).

It's as though he were saying, "So what else could we do but strip off our clothes and worship it?"

Apparently animals can offer excuses, too. I read recently about Koko, a gorilla that uses sign language to communicate. Koko must have had a bad morning not long ago, because she tore the sink off the wall in her pen. When the trainers came to see what happened, Koko used sign language to indicate that her pet kitten had done the damage. "Cat did it," she signed. (I like that story so much, I almost titled this chapter "Cat Did It.")

In Matthew 22, Jesus told a parable that featured the great generosity of a king—and the flimsy excuses of those who rejected and misused his kindness.

The Great Banquet

And Jesus answered and spoke to them again by parables and said: "The kingdom of heaven is like a certain king who arranged a marriage for his son, and sent out his servants to call those who were invited to the wedding; and they were not willing to come. Again, he sent out other servants, saying, 'Tell those who are invited, "See, I have prepared my dinner; my oxen and fatted cattle are killed, and all things are ready. Come to the wedding."' But they made light of it and went their ways, one to his own farm, another to his business. And the rest seized his servants, treated them spitefully, and killed them. But when the king heard about it, he was furious. And he sent out his armies, destroyed those murderers, and burned up their city. Then he said to his servants, 'The wedding is ready, but those who were invited were not worthy. Therefore go into the highways, and as many as you find, invite to the wedding.' So those servants went out into the highways and gathered together all whom they found, both bad and good. And the wedding hall was filled with guests." (Matthew 22:1-10)

The parable begins with a king who wanted to throw a great banquet in honor of his son's wedding. This wasn't just any wedding, it was a royal wedding and a magnificent feast of feasts. To be a pre-invited guest to a wedding of this importance and magnitude would have been the greatest of honors.

In those days, the banquet would have been more than just a meal; it was a celebration that went on for weeks, with people actually invited to stay in the king's palace. No expense would be spared, the tables would be elaborately decorated, the finest chefs would work overtime, and the musicians and entertainers would all be top-notch and well rehearsed. It was just an amazing thing to be invited to.

Now the protocol at this time was to extend two invitations, one following the other. In the first invitation the guest would be asked to RSVP, just as people do with weddings today. If the guest received the invitation and couldn't come, this would be the time to decline so the host could know how many places to set at the table, how much food to buy, and so forth. If the guest accepted the first invitation, it was a really big deal to accept the second invitation as well, which essentially said, "Everything is ready. Please come now."

As Jesus unfolded the story, we see people—one after another—rejecting the second invitation after they had already indicated they would come.

It would have been far, far better for those invitees to have never accepted the king's invitation than to accept and then at the last minute impulsively decide to not show up.

But that is exactly what these people in Jesus' parable did. In fact, they treated the whole thing as a joke. They made light of it and went on their way. In the original language, the phrase "made light of it" in verse 5 is linked to the idea of being "careless" or "neglectful." These people the king had so extraordinarily honored couldn't have cared less about showing up at his son's wedding. They were laughing it off and tossing out lame excuses.

In Luke's account of the same story, we get more details on what those actual excuses were.

> The first said to him, "I have bought a piece of ground, and I must go and see it. I ask you to have me excused." And another said, "I have bought five yoke of oxen, and I am going to test them. I ask you to have me excused." Still another said, "I have married a wife, and therefore I cannot come." (Luke 14:18-21)

These aren't even good lies. A guy bought a field without even looking at it? Really? Another man bought ten oxen without testing them first? I doubt it! The third excuse-maker was classic: "Hey, count me out. I got married."

These guys would have known how much money had already been spent, and they had already accepted the king's gracious invitation and sent back their RSVP. To turn the king down at that point was downright insulting. They were deliberately dishonoring this king, and they didn't really care. Why? Because they were thinking of themselves. Matthew 22:5 words their conduct like this: "But they made light of it and went their ways, one to his own farm, another to his business."

The first two excuses, checking out a piece of property and testing oxen, have to do with material possessions. The third excuse, a recent marriage, has to do with affections. The fact is, possessions and affections cover virtually every reason why people say no to God. Every excuse you have ever heard as to why people won't follow Christ will probably fit under one of these two headings.

Excuses for Not Following Christ

Excuse #1: Possessions are more important than God.

*I have bought a piece of ground, and I must go and see it. I
ask you to have me excused. (Luke 14:18)*

Was this guy a complete idiot? He bought a field without looking
at it? Have you ever bought something without seeing it first?

I remember when I was a kid I would sometimes order things
from the ad pages of my favorite comic books. I remember one ad
that promised two hundred World War II soldiers for $1.98. Now
that was impressive. They would send you one hundred American
army guys, and one hundred German soldiers. I remember thinking,
"That's a lot of soldiers. I could have fun with those." So I scraped
together $1.98 and ordered them.

When they finally arrived, however, what a disappointment!
They were smaller than ants! Yes, there were two hundred of them,
but they were microscopic.

Have you ever read the descriptions of homes that realtors
give? They're very creative in their wording, aren't they?

Retirement haven. (A thirty-year-old Sunbeam trailer.)

Ocean view. (Never mind that you have to get up on the roof
with a high-powered telescope to catch a glimpse of the ocean.)

Steps from the beach. (Yes, that's right. About 250,000 of them.)

Cute fixer-upper. (This is a house with no roof but excellent
ventilation.)

Great starter home. (That's a pile of lumber with plans thrown
in for good measure.)

The reality is that in Jesus' day, a buyer would have had many
opportunities to examine the piece of land he was purchasing
before putting his money on the line. So to say, "I bought a piece
of land and have to go see it" was an outright lie. The man simply
didn't want to go to the wedding, so he threw up a threadbare
excuse.

It's not that he was particularly nasty about it. In the original
language, there was a surface politeness about the excuse. The

man was saying, in effect, "Oh, please excuse me. I'm so sorry about this, but I bought a piece of land and I simply must go see it. I hope you understand."

But a no is still a no. And he was rejecting the second invitation after he had already accepted the first. He had an "excuse," but it was really no excuse at all.

Excuse #2: Career is more important than God.

In Luke 14:19, the second excuse-maker said, "I have bought five yoke of oxen, and I am going to test them. I ask you to have me excused."

This man was either a complete fool or a blatant liar. Who would buy ten oxen without looking at them or trying them out? What if they were diseased or maimed?

Would you purchase a car without test-driving it? Imagine you are looking at a used car and say to the salesman, "I'm interested in this car. Can I take this out for a spin?"

What would you think if he said, "No, I'm afraid I can't let you do that"?

"Is the car in good working order?" you ask.

"Yes, it is."

"Well then, let me drive it."

"Sorry, I can't allow that."

Wouldn't that make you just a little suspicious? Of course it would. Yet this man was claiming to have made this significant purchase of ten oxen without even looking at them or testing them. Jesus' audience would have immediately recognized how ridiculous that was—and what a feeble excuse he was throwing out there.

Why would you need ten oxen? To plow your field and make a living by farming. So you might say that this man's career kept him back from God. Of course, there's nothing wrong with a career. I think believers should be the most diligent, trustworthy, hardest-working men and women of all, no matter what their profession. It doesn't matter if you run a corporation or flip burgers, type letters or close big sales deals. Whatever you do, you are to do it for the glory of God, do it well, and work hard at it.

But that's not the issue here.

The issue is when your job or your career becomes more important to you than your relationship with God. If advancing our career assumes greater importance in our lives than advancing our walk with the Lord, then something is out of its proper order.

Excuse #3: Relationships are more important than God.

In Luke 14:20 the third man said, "I have married a wife, and therefore I cannot come."

In contrast to the first two men who offered excuses, this guy wasn't even polite about it. In the original language there is a raw edge and a bluntness in his reply. In contrast to the first man who said, "I'm so sorry, but I can't come," this third guy said in effect, "Nope, not coming. Get lost. Can't you see I'm married?"

What? Don't you think your wife might enjoy taking a break from cooking and the opportunity to attend a royal feast? It would be like getting an invitation to go to a White House dinner or a banquet with the queen in Buckingham Palace. What woman wouldn't love that? The whole excuse about being married was nothing more than a thinly veiled insult—and would have been highly offensive to the generous king who had issued the invitation.

The first man to make an excuse was possessed by his possessions. The second man was preoccupied with his career. This third individual allowed human affection to keep him away from God's best for his life.

On one hand, there is nothing more virtuous or commendable than the love of a husband for a wife and a wife for a husband. Certainly Jesus wasn't putting down the marriage relationship. After all, He is the One who created man and woman, brings us together in marriage, and blesses us in that union. But this man was using his marriage as an excuse to keep him from God.

Phony Excuses of Today

We still make excuses, even as Christians. We offer excuses for why we can't go to church or why we can't make it to our small group or Bible study.

"Oh, I can't go to church today. I was up too late last night."

"I'm going to skip Bible study this time. It's just too hot [or too cold] out there."

"I think it might rain. I don't want to be out there on those slick roads."

We have plenty of excuses, and very few of them are actual *reasons*.

In contrast, look at the commitment sports fans demonstrate, and how they support their team no matter what the weather conditions or circumstances. They dress in team colors, paint their faces, and maybe even camp overnight outside the ticket window in sub-freezing weather to get a good seat at the big game. When their team scores a touchdown, goal, or homerun, they go wild with excitement, yelling and screaming and pounding on both friends and complete strangers. What's more, they can remember their team's scores and major players going back twenty years.

What if people were like that about church—never missing a service, never losing an opportunity to worship the Lord?

I've tried to imagine what it would be like if people offered the same excuses for not going to football games that they offer for not going to church.

"Hey, I heard you quit going to the games. I can't believe it! You were such a fan!"

"Yeah, I don't go to games anymore."

"But why?"

"Well, to tell you the truth, the people who sit around me don't seem all that friendly. Besides that, there are just too many people, the games last too long, the seats are kind of hard, and it isn't all that easy to find a parking place."

"Really?"

"Yes, and what's more, the coach never personally came and visited me. Not once."

"What?"

"And besides that, I read a book on football and think I know more than the coach. Anyway, my parents took me to a lot of football games when I was growing up, so now that I'm old enough to decide for myself I just don't want to go anymore."

Those are the kinds of things people will say about church, but we don't ever see the same excuses applied to a sporting event.

And then we offer up excuses for why we can't read the Bible:

"I'm just so busy these days. Life is so full. I just can't find the time."

"The Bible is so big; I don't know where to start."

"I tried to read it, but there are some parts I don't understand."

"We read the Bible in church on Sunday. Doesn't that count?"

Those are excuses. Not reasons.

Let's imagine you got a call this week from your doctor, who said, "You need to make an appointment with me. I've reviewed the results of your tests, and we need to talk."

Then further imagine that you learned you had only weeks to live. If you found yourself looking eternity in the face, do you think your schedule might flex a little, allowing you to time to open the Bible? Of course it would! You would realize that the afterlife was almost upon you, and you would need God's perspective, God's comfort, and God's peace to face the days ahead.

Our perspective determines our priorities; *we make time for what is important to us*. We find time to read the newspaper, watch our favorite TV program, or go online and spend hours looking at virtually nothing of value. And yet we don't have time to open up God's Word and let Him speak to us?

We need to be honest—with others and with ourselves. Instead of offering excuses, we need to make time for the things that matter most. So what's the antidote to offering up weak, self-serving excuses?

Putting It in Stark Terms

In Luke's version of this story, Jesus gave a strong challenge to the crowds who had been listening to Him and following Him. Immediately on the heels of this parable, Jesus turned to the people and said, "If anyone comes to Me and does not hate his father and mother, wife and children, brothers and sisters, yes, and his own life also, he cannot be My disciple. And whoever does not bear his cross and come after Me cannot be My disciple" (Luke 14:26-27).

This is what you might call a hardcore statement. Many feel that these are some of the most controversial words Jesus ever spoke. *Hate* your father and mother? Really? *Hate* your brother, sister, and kids? What's that all about? Was Jesus actually telling us to hate our loved ones?

This is a passage that cries out to be put in context. After all, God Himself tells us to honor our father and mother, so it may go well with us. And in Ephesians 5, husbands are commanded to love their wives as Christ loves the church. In Titus 2:4 young women are instructed to "love their husbands, to love their children." We're even told to love our enemies. So what did Jesus mean when He used the word "hate"?

A better translation might read like this: You must love God *more* than your husband, more than your wife, more than your children, more than your mom or dad. In fact, compared to your love for God, all of these other loves should seem like hatred by comparison.

The fact is, if you really love God as you ought to, you will have *more* love for your spouse and family, *more* love for your children and parents. But let's get our priorities in order: love of God is the most important love of all. That's the idea being communicated here.

The word *disciple* comes from the root word *discipline*, which certainly includes the idea of making time for what is truly important. In contrast to the people in this story who offered see-through excuses for not attending the king's banquet, true disciples prioritize God in their lives. They make time for God's Word, time for prayer, time for being with God's people.

The answer to weak, deceptive excuses is to keep Jesus at the very center of our lives.

The Wedding Garment

There is a final, fascinating movement in the Lord's parable in Matthew 22: "When the king came in to see the guests, he saw a man there who did not have on a wedding garment. So he said to him, 'Friend, how did you come in here without a wedding garment?' And he was speechless" (verses 11-12).

It seems to me that one of the biggest challenges of being invited to a royal event would be choosing what to wear. What's the right apparel? What's the dress code? It could be very important.

Have you ever dressed inappropriately for some event because you didn't know what to wear? Maybe it was more formal than you thought, and you felt really out of place in a T-shirt, shorts, and flip-flops.

I have a "friend" (I use the word loosely) who had a party for one of his daughters and invited me to come. "It's kind of a costume party with a theme," he explained. "We're all dressing up like cowboys and cowgirls."

I don't own a cowboy hat, but I did put on my western shirt, jeans, big cowboy belt buckle, and cowboy boots.

Then when I walked through the door I knew I'd been had. Everyone else was dressed normally, and I came in looking like John Wayne. My friend's one desire had been to make me look stupid, and he had completely succeeded.

At the wedding feast in Jesus' story, the appropriate garments were apparently handed out at the door at no cost to the guests. People arriving for the celebration didn't have to worry about what to wear because it was provided by the king. Everyone had appropriate attire—except one.

Was he a gatecrasher or just a man who refused to play by the rules? Apparently, when offered the wedding garment at the door, he blew it off and said, "I don't want that."

The answer might have been, "Sir, you are required to wear it."

"I don't care if I am."

"But, sir, you need to do this. It's very important. Just slip it on and everything will be fine."

"Get out of my way. I wear what I want to wear when I want to wear it. I don't need your provision. Let me through."

So he pushed the gatekeeper aside and strolled into the party on his own terms. Of course he stuck out like the proverbial sore thumb and was an offense to the king. The man had ignored all protocol, rejected the free gift the king had offered him, and broken all the rules. By doing so, he had gravely insulted and offended the king.

This is a picture of what happens to people who say they will get to God or enter heaven on their own terms or through their own good works without receiving God's provision of grace in Christ. When you claim that your good life or your good works or your sincerity will get you to heaven, you are effectively saying that the death of Jesus was a waste.

If living a good life could get you to heaven, why did Jesus have to suffer, shed His blood, and die? When you reject Christ, you are in effect saying no to the wedding garment and that you'll elbow your way into God's presence without accepting His free provision for our salvation.

When we become believers in Jesus, we are clothed in the righteousness of Christ. The Bible says we are actually "hidden with Christ in God" (Colossians 3:3).

In the Lord's story, He was speaking of a person who rejects God's provision, rejects God's forgiveness, and says, "I'm betting that God will let me into heaven based on my own strength, my own ability, my own track record, and my own merit."

When the king finally confronted this would-be gatecrasher in Matthew 22:12, the man was speechless. He had no smug remarks, no clever comebacks, and no reason at all for having forced His way into the king's party without wearing the king's provided garment.

In other words, he had no excuse.

In the same way, the only way any of us will ever be admitted into heaven will be because we received God's precious gift of grace and forgiveness and salvation in Jesus Christ.

Don't even think about approaching the door of heaven without it.

CHAPTER THIRTY-TWO
GOD OF THE LIVING

heard a story about a guy who had just died and arrived at the pearly gates. Of course he was met by Peter, who, with a furrowed brow, began searching through the Book of Life for this man's name.

Finally Peter said, "Buddy, I can't find your name in here. It's not that you did that many bad things, but I can't find any *good* things you did, either. If you can show me one good thing you did on earth, I will let you into heaven."

(Clearly this is not a true story, nor is it theologically correct.)

The man looked concerned for a moment, and then said, "Okay, I just thought of one good thing."

"That's great," Peter replied. "What is it?"

"Well, I was driving down the highway and saw that a woman's car was broken down by the side of the road and that she was surrounded by a group of outlaw bikers. Clearly, she was in danger. So I pulled my car over, jumped out, grabbed a tire iron out of my trunk, and ran over to stand between the woman and the bikers. I said to all of them, 'If you want to get to this woman, you'll have to come through me first.'"

Peter was impressed. "Wow," he said. "We don't have any record of this at all. When did it happen?"

The man replied, "Like, three minutes ago."

You get the idea! We're all just one heartbeat away from eternity. We have no idea how thin the curtain is between this life and the next. Generations ago, Christians used to think a lot more about dying and going to heaven. They often referred to heaven and being with Jesus in sermons, hymns, and choruses. That isn't as true today; followers of Jesus seem more wrapped up and preoccupied with the affairs of this life rather than the next one.

Yet in Colossians 3:1-2 (NIV) we read, "Since, then, you have been raised with Christ, set your hearts on things above, where Christ is, seated at the right hand of God. Set your minds on things above, not on earthly things." Turning our thoughts toward heaven and our eternal destiny is a very productive thing to do. It's good to think, now and then, about the afterlife and what we can expect when we get there.

Think of one of your greatest moments in life. Maybe it was with your wife or your husband or your children. Maybe it was with some close friends. It was one of those times when you said to yourself, "This is a sweet moment. I wish life could always be this way." When I experience times like those, I'm reminded that even the best of them are only glimpses of greater things to come.

Deep down inside we want our lives to be fulfilling and happy. We want our lives to have meaning and purpose. Why is that? It's because our Creator wired us this way. We were meant for something more.

C. S. Lewis, in his sermon titled "The Weight of Glory," made this statement:

> If we consider the unblushing promises of reward and the staggering nature of the rewards promised in the Gospels, it would seem that Our Lord finds our desires, not too strong, but too weak. We are half-hearted creatures, fooling about with drink and sex and ambition when infinite joy is offered to us, like an ignorant child who wants to go on making mud pies in a slum because he cannot imagine what is meant by the offer of a holiday at the sea. We are far too easily pleased.[16]

In other words, we settle for too little. Much too little. Yet God has so much waiting for us on the other side.

Misconceptions

Most people, though not everyone, believe in some kind of afterlife. A fascinating study was recently done across twenty-three countries, revealing that 51 percent of the people polled believe in an afterlife. When only Americans are polled, the numbers go much higher. Sixty-six percent of Americans believe in heaven, and 71 percent believe it is an actual place. Looking back through time, we will consistently find that people all over the world believed in something beyond this life.

The pages of the ancient Egyptian *Book of the Dead* are filled with stories about life after death. For instance, in the tomb of one of the pharaohs who died five thousand years ago, archaeologists discovered a solar boat intended to provide him with transportation so he could sail to the heavens. The ancient Greeks often put a coin in the mouth of a corpse to pay his fare across what they called the mystic river of death and send him on his way to the land of immortal life. Some Native American cultures buried their warriors with a pony and a bow, so the dead man could ride well-equipped into the great hunting grounds. Norsemen would be buried with their horse, so they could ride proudly in the afterlife. Romans believed they would "ride in the Elysian Fields." The Inuit (Eskimos) of Greenland were customarily entombed with their dogs to guide them through the cold wasteland of death.

(It interests me to see how animals play a part in these ceremonies. Horses for the Native Americans, Romans, and Norsemen, and dogs for the Inuit. Notice that no one is buried with a cat! Why? Because a cat would never lead you into the afterlife. A cat would abandon you and walk away, just like they do in this life.)

All of these examples, of course, are misconceptions about life beyond the grave. Nevertheless, there is a common belief that something really does exist for us on the other side of life.

In Jesus' day, a group called the Sadducees bucked that common trend and insisted that there was no heaven or afterlife at all. Usually, the Sadducees and the Pharisees ganged up on Jesus, trying to trip Him up and cause Him to stumble. But even though they were united in their hatred of Christ, they could not have been more different in their theologies. As I said, the Sadducees denied any kind of resurrection of the dead—as well as miracles and the existence of angels.

That's a pretty bleak outlook, wouldn't you say? No afterlife. No miracles. No bodily resurrection. No hope of heaven. No angels.

That's probably where they got their name. They were Sadducees because they were so sad, you see.

People still hold such sad views today. Actress Natalie Portman was asked about her view on the afterlife. "I don't believe in that," she said. "I believe this is it. This is the best way to live." Actor George Clooney made this pessimistic statement about life: "I don't believe in happy endings. But I do believe in happy travels, because ultimately you die at a very young age or you live long enough to watch your friends die. It's a mean thing, life."

William Shatner, the captain of the *Enterprise* on TV's *Star Trek*, is now in his mid-eighties and was asked about his life and what follows.

> *There is a sense of not being fulfilled. I don't know what it is. It bothers me because I am approaching the end of my life and I'm trying to do better and better at whatever it is I am doing. I am not ready to die. It petrifies me. I go alone. I go to a place I don't know. It might be the end. My thought is, it is the end. I became nameless when I spent a lifetime being known.*

What a sad outlook. I would love to have the opportunity to share the gospel with Mr. Shatner!

The fact is, if we're going to talk about these things, we need to find an expert—someone who genuinely knows what he or she is talking about. What we really need is someone who has been to the other side and returned.

I'm not talking about people who have "died," come back to life, and then written books and gone on speaking tours. Someone might say, "Greg, don't be so cynical. Have faith." Well, I do have faith in God and in His Word—but not always in people who are motivated to sell lots of books about their experiences. In fact, one of the authors of those visit-to-heaven books recently admitted to making the whole thing up.[17]

I have a much more credible source than these authors with their sensational stories. Allow me to restate that: I have the *only* credible source. The only One who has been in heaven and returned to describe it to us is Jesus Christ Himself. In John 6:38 (NIV) He said, "For I have come down from heaven not to do my will but to do the will of him who sent me." Then in John 3:13 (NIV), Jesus said, "No one has ever gone into heaven except the one who came from heaven—the Son of Man."

I want to know what Jesus said about the afterlife—and in a broader sense, what the Word of God says about the afterlife—because all Scripture is given by inspiration of God.

The Sadducees confronted Jesus in Matthew 22, thinking they would ensnare Him with their clever verbal traps. They presented Him with a phony scenario about marriage and death, imagining that this would somehow punch holes in His teachings on the resurrection and life beyond the grave.

The same day the Sadducees, who say there is no resurrection, came to Him and asked Him, saying: "Teacher, Moses said that if a man dies, having no children, his brother shall marry his wife and raise up offspring for his brother. Now there were with us seven brothers. The first died after he had married, and having no offspring, left his wife to his brother. Likewise the second also, and the third, even to the seventh. Last of all the woman died also. Therefore, in the resurrection, whose wife of the seven will she be? For they all had her."

Jesus answered and said to them, "You are mistaken, not knowing the Scriptures nor the power of God. For in the resurrection they neither marry nor are given in marriage, but are like angels of God in heaven. But concerning the resurrection of the dead, have you not read what was spoken to you by God, saying, 'I am the God of Abraham, the God of Isaac, and the God of Jacob'? God is not the God of the dead, but of the living." And when the multitudes heard this, they were astonished at His teaching. (verses 23-33)

Let's highlight three truths from this amazing portion of Scripture.

1. A believer who is a follower of Christ never dies.

Look again at verse 32: "God is not the God of the dead, but of the living." Notice He said He is the God of Abraham, Isaac, and Jacob; He didn't say, "I *was* the God," past tense. The three patriarchs He mentioned in these words still live in eternity. They are as alive today as they ever were. And so it is with your loved ones who have died in the Lord. Right now, at this moment, they are more alive than when you knew them on this earth. A Christian never dies.

Someone might say, "Greg, are you delusional? Have you ever been to a cemetery?" Yes, I have. And as a pastor, I have been up close and personal with death again and again. I understand that the discarded body goes into the ground. What I am telling you is that the soul lives on forever. According to Scripture death for the Christian is not the end. It is merely a transition.

Maybe you've heard that famous statement made by General Douglas MacArthur in his final speech. "Old soldiers never die," he said, "they just fade away." But I would add a statement of my own: "Old Christians ever die. They just move away." We move on to a different place, a better place. Yes, the body dies and returns to dust, but the soul lives on.

Jesus said to His grieving friend Martha, "I am the resurrection and the life. He who believes in Me, though he may die, he shall live. And whoever lives and believes in Me shall never die. Do you believe this?" (John 11:25-26).

This is the great hope we possess as believers in Jesus. But it's only natural that we would have a lot of questions about life on the other side. Whenever I cohost the radio call-in program "Pastor's Perspective" with Don Stewart, at least 75 percent of the questions deal with life beyond the grave.

2. There is a bodily resurrection.

Again, in Matthew 22:29-30 Jesus said, "You are mistaken, not knowing the Scriptures nor the power of God. For in the resurrection . . . "

These bodies we live in right now will one day live again in a perfected state. Even Job, in the oldest book of the Bible, understood this when he wrote in Job 19:26-27 (NIV), "And after my skin has been destroyed, *yet in my flesh I will see God;* I myself will see him with my own eyes—I, and not another" (emphasis added).

To say it another way, you will still be you in heaven. But you will be a radically upgraded version of you.

I bring this up because sometimes people get confused about these things. For instance, some people believe that when we die we become angels, but that is not true. In the passage we're looking at, Jesus didn't say we would become angels; He said we would be *like* the angels (see Matthew 22:30). Angels are a separate creation from human beings, and in their number there are both good angels and fallen angels, also known as demons. But no angel can become a man or a woman, and no man or woman can ever become an angel. Angels can't give up their immortality and live as mere mortals, as has been portrayed in various movies and TV shows.

On the other hand, Jesus did note a similarity to the angels, and He elaborated on that in Luke 20:34-36 (NLT): "Marriage is for people here on earth. But in the age to come, those worthy of being raised from the dead will neither marry nor be given in marriage. And they will never die again. In this respect they will be like angels. They are children of God and children of the resurrection."

What a fantastic Scripture. Don't ever doubt that if you belong to Jesus Christ, you are a "child of the resurrection." That is who you are!

What happens to a Christian when he or she dies? There are many inaccurate (and depressing) views out there. Some faith traditions teach that when we die we go to purgatory—a place of waiting, suffering, and cleansing—until we are ready for heaven. But there is no such thing. The Bible never once speaks of a purgatory. Others say that Christians who have passed away enter into soul sleep—like a really long nap. This prospect may sound appealing to some, but that doesn't happen, either. What happens to Christians who die? They immediately go into the presence of

God. The Bible is very clear on this: *To be absent from the body is to be present with the Lord* (see 2 Corinthians 5:8).

Paul told the church at Philippi, "If I am to go on living in the body, this will mean fruitful labor for me. Yet what shall I choose? I do not know! I am torn between the two: I desire to depart and be with Christ, which is better by far; but it is more necessary for you that I remain in the body" (Philippians 1:22-24, NIV).

Notice Paul's use of the word *depart*. He expressed his desire to take his leave from earth and be with Christ. The moment you take your last breath on earth you then take your first breath in heaven. It is that fast. Later, your body will be resurrected. But at the moment of death you—the real you—enter the presence of the Lord.

Our new body, our resurrection body, will be similar to that of the Lord Jesus Christ. Remember that after He died and rose again from the dead He walked among His disciples. He could appear in a room without using a door. He ate some fish with them. He invited them to touch His living flesh. He could fly, in the sense that He ascended through the air into heaven. Our bodies will be similar to that!

In 1 John 3:2 (NIV), we read, "Dear friends, now we are children of God, and what we will be has not yet been made known. But we know that when Christ appears, we shall be like him, for we shall see him as he is."

The Bible promises that though our souls go into God's presence, where we will await our resurrection body, there will also be those who have the privilege of experiencing a resurrected body immediately. That will happen for those who are still alive and on earth at the time of the Rapture of the church. At that time, in less than a heartbeat, believers on earth will be caught up into the clouds to meet the Lord in the air. Paul wrote in 1 Corinthians 15:51-52 (NIV), "Listen, I tell you a mystery: We will not all sleep, but we will all be changed—in a flash, in the twinkling of an eye, at the last trumpet. For the trumpet will sound, the dead will be raised imperishable, and we will be changed."

It will all happen so quickly. Scientists tell us that the winking of an eye is one of the quickest movements of the human body.

In the Greek language, however, the "twinkling of an eye" implies half a wink! That is how fast it will happen when God gives us this new body.

Again, here's how it works. When Christians die, our bodies go into the ground, but our souls go immediately into the presence of God (unless we are on earth when the Rapture happens), where we will wait in heaven for our new bodies.

I love to think that you and I could be part of the generation that will be walking the earth when Jesus comes in the clouds for His church. Those who are caught up in the Rapture will never have to go through the process of death; they will be brought immediately into God's presence.

3. Heaven will have differences and similarities to life on earth.

We often wonder what our relationships will be with one another on the other side. Will we recognize our loved ones in heaven? I have been asked that question so many times! My answer goes something like this: "Do you think you will be less aware in heaven than you are on earth?" Do you recognize your loved ones now? Then you will certainly recognize them then. You will know more in heaven, not less.

Remember when Moses and Elijah were brought back from heaven to stand with Christ on the mount of transfiguration in Matthew 17:3-4? They were immediately recognized. And in the same way, you will instantly know those whom you have known and loved on earth.

I love to think about the great reunions we will experience in heaven. The absence we feel from our loved ones who have died in faith as Christians is a comma, not a period. We will see them again.

I am especially looking forward to seeing my son Christopher, who abruptly left for heaven in 2008. I am also anticipating a reunion with my mom, the father who adopted me, my grandparents, and friends who have gone on before me. I'm excited about meeting people in heaven that I have never known on earth, but have admired from the pages of Scripture and from Christian history. But of course, the focus will be on the Lord Himself.

Even in describing the Rapture, Paul wrote about being "caught up together" to meet the Lord in the clouds (1 Thessalonians 4:17). Then the apostle wrapped it up by urging us to "comfort one another" with those words (verse 18). There is such comfort in knowing that those of us who long to see our loved ones will be with them again.

Some will ask, "Yes, but what about the marriage thing Jesus spoke of in Matthew 22? It sounds like we won't be married in heaven." Here is the answer. When we are in heaven, God will be our glorious, joyous focus. Worship will be as common as breathing. We will find that He is sufficient and meets all our needs.

In Randy Alcorn's excellent book *Heaven*, he writes that "Earthly marriage is a shadow of the true and ultimate marriage. The purpose of marriage is not to replace heaven, but to prepare us for it."

The human institution of marriage culminates in heaven. It will change, but in ways we can't even comprehend now. It will change for the better—because everything in heaven is incomparably better. Again, to quote Randy Alcorn, "God's plan doesn't stop in heaven and the new earth. It continues. God doesn't abandon His purposes. He fulfills them. Friendships and relationships begun on earth will continue in heaven, richer than ever."

In heaven everything is perfected—better than it has ever been before. In heaven I will know more than I have ever known before. It won't be a place where memories are eliminated or erased, but rather where our memory is perfected. I bring this up because sometimes people will say, "In heaven we won't remember certain things that happened on earth. We won't recall the bad, hurtful things. We won't remember loved ones who didn't believe in Jesus, because if we remembered them it wouldn't be heaven any longer."

I don't see where the Bible teaches that.

For instance, when God metes out rewards for our faithfulness at the judgment seat of Christ, we will certainly remember our past life. In 2 Corinthians 5:10 (NIV) we read, "For we must all appear before the judgment seat of Christ, so that each of us may receive what is due us for the things done while in the body, whether good or bad." So there will be specific recognition for specific actions on earth that are recalled and rewarded.

Sometimes it is said that we will forget the hardships and pain of earth because Revelation 21:4 says, "God will wipe away every tear from their eyes; there shall be no more death, nor sorrow, nor crying. There shall be no more pain, for the former things have passed away." But this passage doesn't say that our memories will be erased. The difference will be in a changed *perspective*. We will see things from God's point of view.

Think of the difference between the way you viewed things at age twenty-one and the way you viewed the world at age ten. Or how different the world looked to you at forty than how it looked in your twenties. You see life through different eyes, don't you? You see a bigger, more complete picture. You understand more about what really matters and realize what doesn't matter as much.

When you were a child, you lived in the moment. When something bad happened, you didn't understand how it could get better, and you started to cry. I have grandchildren who get upset because a toy breaks. Maybe the doll's head comes off, and they start sobbing. Now, I know I'm about to load those kids up in the car, drive to the toy store, and buy them a new doll—and some ice cream on the way as well. But they don't know those things in the moment, and their little hearts are broken.

So here I am on earth, and something hard, hurtful, and inexplicable happens to me. I don't understand, and I have no idea how this could ever fit into any kind of plan or purpose or pattern for good, as Paul spoke of in Romans 8:28. But when I get to heaven, I will see things from God's perspective. I will have a mind and a heart that have grown in knowledge and understanding that will enable me to see events in the proper way. I will see the broad and large plan that God had in mind all along.

Some go as far as to say that in heaven we won't remember anything on earth. But that is just absurd—and unbiblical, too. In the book of Revelation we read about people in heaven who were martyred on earth. And Scripture records them saying to the Lord, "How long, Sovereign Lord, holy and true, until you judge the inhabitants of the earth and avenge our blood?" (Revelation 6:10, NIV). In other words, they are saying, "Lord, how long will it be until You make this wrong right?"

This incident teaches us several things: We will be aware in heaven of events on earth; we will be aware in heaven of injustices on earth; and we will be aware of the passage of time.

The idea of endless eternity scares some people. They have fears of one long, never-ending church service.

Will heaven, then, be boring?

Never! Not once. Yes, there will be worship. There will also be learning, feasting, adventure, and—dare I say it?—lots of fun and joy.

With these things in mind, we should be preparing ourselves for heaven, because heaven is a prepared place for prepared people. Jesus said, "My Father's house has many rooms . . . I am going there to prepare a place for you" (John 14:2, NIV). That means He's been at that job for the last two thousand plus years.

He has prepared a place for you.

Have you prepared yourself to meet Him?

Someone once asked the great evangelist D. L. Moody, "How would you spend the rest of your day if you knew the Lord was returning tonight?" Moody answered without hesitation, "I wouldn't do anything different than I do every day."

That is how the Christian should live—always ready for that moment when earth will be in the rearview mirror and real life will begin at last.

CHAPTER THIRTY-THREE
WHAT JESUS TAUGHT ABOUT ISRAEL IN THE END TIMES

The Bible is the one book that dares to predict the future. It's plain as day that God wants His people to know about upcoming events, because He has dedicated over 30 percent of the Bible to prophecies!

The Old Testament, for example, features more than one hundred prophecies of the coming of Christ. Through these prophecies we can know for sure that Jesus truly was the promised Messiah. Why? Because He fulfilled every one of those specific prophecies. Believers can be confident that Christ will come again to this earth and set up His kingdom. He promised He would, and He will! In fact, He promised that He would come again the second time five times more frequently than He promised to come the first time.

Some people say Bible prophecy is "confusing" and that they "can't sort it out." That's all the more reason to keep on studying. The book of Revelation contains a specific blessing promised to those who read and hear and keep that book in their hearts: "Blessed is the one who reads aloud the words of this prophecy, and blessed are those who hear it and take to heart what is written in it, because the time is near" (1:3, NIV).

Surely that same blessing must apply to *all* the biblical teachings on end-times events. I think it only stands to reason that the more we know about the next world, the better we will live in this one.

We could discuss many, many clear and present signs of the times that indicate we truly are in this world's last days. But there is one sign, I believe, that is more significant, obvious, and undeniable than all the others: the miracle of the nation Israel, the regathering of the Jewish people back in their ancient homeland. The Bible clearly says this would happen and that it would be a sign of the end drawing near.

As we see prophetic events about the nation of Israel being fulfilled before our eyes, we know the time of His coming isn't far away. Here is the word picture Jesus used with His disciples in Matthew 24:32-33 (NIV): "Now learn this lesson from the fig tree: As soon as its twigs get tender and its leaves come out, you know that summer is near. Even so, when you see all these things, you know that it is near, right at the door."

As events in the Middle East unfold in our newspapers and newscasts, we can clearly see that the fig tree Jesus spoke of already has some new leaves. The times He spoke of are drawing very close.

In Ezekiel 37, God is very specific about the return of the Jewish people to Israel. He said He would take His people from among the nations where they had scattered. He said He would gather them from every side in their own land and that He would make one nation in that land.

These are very pointed and definite prophecies:

- God promised that the Jewish people, scattered across the world in countless lands, would be regathered. *That has happened.*

- He promised they would return to the land of Israel, the ancient homeland of Abraham, Isaac, and Jacob. *That has happened.*

- He promised they would become a nation once again. *That has happened.*

- He promised that Jerusalem, the City of David, would be their capital once again, and *that too has happened.*

The rebirth and regathering of Israel is a sure sign of the end. But it is not just a sign. It is a *super* sign God has given.

The Super Sign

Among the many strange things God asked the prophet Ezekiel to say and do, He once asked him to go to a graveyard. As Ezekiel stood there, wondering what would happen next, countless human skeletons suddenly burst out of the graves. While the stunned prophet watched, bones came together. Muscle attached to bone. Flesh attached to muscle. Then all the re-formed bodies came to life and stood up in front of him, like a great army. After that, God told him what it all meant.

Then he said to me, "Son of man, these bones represent the people of Israel. They are saying, 'We have become old, dry bones—all hope is gone. Our nation is finished.' Therefore, prophesy to them and say, 'This is what the Sovereign LORD says: O my people, I will open your graves of exile and cause you to rise again. Then I will bring you back to the land of Israel. When this happens, O my people, you will know that I am the LORD. I will put my Spirit in you, and you will live again and return home to your own land. Then you will know that I, the LORD, have spoken, and I have done what I said. Yes, the LORD has spoken!'" (Ezekiel 37:11-14, NLT)

Honestly, could God have been any more specific?

Who would have thought such a thing possible during the darkest days of the Second World War? If you were a Jew living in the Warsaw ghetto, fearing every moment that the Nazi invaders would come pound on your door and arrest you, could you even imagine the rebirth of Israel? If you were a Jew in a Nazi concentration camp like Auschwitz or Treblinka or Ravensbruck, would you have ever thought that within a handful of years there would be a homeland for the Jewish people, with the star of David waving from every flagpole?

To return to the homeland! It must have seemed impossible. Unthinkable. A hopeless fantasy. But God said it would happen, and against all odds, it did. On May 14, 1948, a modern-day miracle took place. Israel became a nation once again.

David Ben-Gurion, who might be considered the George Washington of modern Israel, made this remarkable statement on that historic day: "Ezekiel 37 has been fulfilled and the nation of Israel is hearing the footsteps of the Messiah."

On Holocaust Remembrance Day on January 27, 2010, at Auschwitz in Poland, Israel's prime minister Benjamin Netanyahu declared, "We have returned to our homeland from every corner of the earth. The Jewish people rose from ashes. Dry bones became covered with flesh. A spirit filled them and they lived and stood on their own feet as Ezekiel prophesied."

Israel is truly a nation once again, occupying a very tiny strip of land in the Middle East. And why is it so often in the news? Why do we hear about it and read about it so often? Do you realize that Israel at its widest point is just seventy-one miles across? And at its narrowest point, it's only nine miles across! The entire country is about the size of New Jersey. Thirty-two states of Israel would fit into the state of Texas. It's a very, very small nation. And yet, we can hardly pick up a newspaper or go to a news website or turn on the television without hearing some mention of the conflict in the Middle East, and specifically in Israel. Why is this?

The answer is quite simple. Israel stands in the eye of the hurricane of great events in the end times. It occupies center stage in God's drama of the ages, and the curtains are about to open on the final act.

Those who have sought to eradicate or destroy the Jewish people through the centuries have paid a very heavy price. God made a promise to Abraham and his descendants back when the world was still young. The Lord said, "I will bless those who bless you, and I will curse those who curse you."

How true that has been! Look at the nations that have tried to destroy Israel. They lie on the ash heap of history today: Egypt. Assyria. Babylon. Rome, and in more modern times Spain and Germany. Perhaps very soon Russia will be added to that list.

One of the reasons God has blessed the United States of America in such profound ways through our two-hundred-plus-year history is because we have stood by the Jewish people and the state of Israel.

Now let me make a provocative statement: America needs Israel more than Israel needs America. We have been a solid ally for them through the years, providing them with money and arms and technology, and God has blessed us. Because we have blessed them! And the fact is, we need the friendship and goodwill of Israel, because we need the blessing of God. That is why I have great concern over some of the estrangement and tensions I see building up between our two governments today. I hope that changes soon.

The city of Jerusalem also stands in the eye of the storm, which is exactly what God said would happen in the last days. *Jerusalem.* Not Washington, DC. Not Moscow. Not Beijing. Not New York City or Los Angeles. In Zechariah 12:2-3 (NIV), God says, "I am going to make Jerusalem a cup that sends all the surrounding peoples reeling. Judah will be besieged as well as Jerusalem. On that day, when all the nations of the earth are gathered against her, I will make Jerusalem an immovable rock for all the nations. All who try to move it will injure themselves."

In Luke 21:20 (NLT), Jesus said, "When you see Jerusalem surrounded by armies, then you will know that the time of its destruction has arrived." One of Iran's leaders recently stated publicly, "We must spare no effort in liberating holy Jerusalem and cutting off the hands of the infidels from this holy site."

Attack from the North

Ezekiel 37, then, speaks of the Jews regathering in their old homeland, with Jerusalem as their capital. And so it is today.

In the very next chapter, Ezekiel 38, we read about a large force from the north of Israel attacking her. This force is identified as "Gog," from the land of Magog. Is Russia Gog? It very well could be.

But here is where it gets interesting. The Bible identifies one of the allies that will march with Gog against Israel as Persia. And who is Persia? It is modern Iran. There are Iranians today who still identify themselves as Persians. In fact, Iran took on that name as recently as 1935. Up to that point, they were known to all the world as Persia.

This is fascinating, because if Russia is Gog, there has been no close alliance between Russia and Iran—*until very recently.* The two nations have pulled much closer together. I read recently that the Russians are building two nuclear facilities in Iran with six more on the drawing board.

This is why Prime Minister Netanyahu recently stated, "To win the war with [the terrorist army] ISIS and to not disarm Iran is to win the battle and lose the war." Iran makes no secret of their desire to utterly destroy the Jewish nation. Just recently, the Iranians test-fired several missiles believed to have the long-range capability to strike Israel. And at least one of the rockets included a message written in Hebrew that read, "Israel must be wiped out." Iran's supreme leader Ayatollah Khamenei recently tweeted, "Israel must be annihilated." Another Iranian leader declared, "The destruction of Israel is the idea of the Islamic revolution in Iran and it is one of the pillars of the Iranian Islamic Regime. We cannot claim we have no intention of going to war with Israel."

While the Bible says that Iran will be one of the allies to march with Gog against Israel, it also says that God will intervene on behalf of Israel and in a great miracle, turn back these hostile armies. After this divine intervention that destroys much of the invading forces, a great spiritual awakening will break out in the nation of Israel among the Jewish people. And they will begin to turn to Jesus as their Messiah.

How, then, do these events affect you and me right now?

What Comes First

At this moment, God is working primarily outside the nation of Israel.

Chances are, many of you reading this book are not Jewish by birth, but rather Gentile, as I am. As Gentile believers in Christ, we have been grafted into the promises of Abraham, Isaac, and Jacob. God gave us the Scriptures through Jewish people and primarily through Jewish writers. God gave us our Messiah and Savior through the Jewish people. But right now most Jews do not believe in *Yeshua* as *Hamashiach*—Jesus as Messiah. But after the great miracle of God saving Israel and shattering the attacking armies from the north, many of them will turn to God.

But I believe another event has to happen first, what we might call the "full gathering of the Gentiles." Read Paul's words in the book of Romans:

> I want you to understand this mystery, dear brothers and sisters, so that you will not feel proud about yourselves. Some of the people of Israel have hard hearts, but this will last only until the full number of Gentiles comes to Christ. (11:25, NLT)

When the complete number of Gentiles comes to salvation in Christ, mighty events will begin in heaven and on earth. When that last individual God is waiting for finally receives Christ as Savior, I believe all the living Christians on earth will be caught up to meet the Lord in the air at the event we call the Rapture (see 1 Thessalonians 4:14-18). And soon thereafter, the brief war begins against Israel from the north, God delivers the Jewish nation, and revival breaks out among the Jews.

As we have established, these events are beginning to unfold right before our eyes. Knowing this, what are we supposed to do? How are we supposed to live as followers of Jesus? How should this impact our day-to-day living? Bible prophecy, I believe, was not given to *scare* us, but rather to *prepare* us. How then should we prepare?

In the book of 1 Thessalonians, the apostle Paul gave us excellent counsel.

How Are We to Live?

Paul wrote,

> But you, brothers and sisters, are not in darkness so that this day should surprise you like a thief. You are all children of the

light and children of the day. We do not belong to the night or to the darkness. So then, let us not be like others, who are asleep, but let us be awake and sober. For those who sleep, sleep at night, and those who get drunk, get drunk at night. But since we belong to the day, let us be sober, putting on faith and love as a breastplate, and the hope of salvation as a helmet. (5:4-8, NIV)

The teaching of Christ's imminent return is a real litmus test of where we are spiritually. If we are truly walking with God and our lives are right with Him, when we hear that Jesus could return at any moment, we feel a sense of anticipation, of motivation. If, however, we are not right with God, hearing that Christ might come back at any moment frightens and alarms us. If we are living as we ought to live, we welcome His coming. We can say with the apostle John, "Even so, come, Lord Jesus." That is the heart cry of the man or woman who is in fellowship with God.

According to these verses in 1 Thessalonians, there are three things we need to do as believers. We need to wake up, sober up, and suit up.

We need to wake up.

Verse 6 says, "Let us not sleep, as others do."

I read a pretty good definition of sleep in the *Encyclopedia Britannica*. Many of you reading this won't remember these books, but it's how we looked up information on all sorts of things before Google and Siri. (Yes, there was life before Google.) The article described sleep as "a state of inactivity with a loss of consciousness and a decrease in responsiveness to events taking place."

That's a pretty good definition—and it also describes the condition of some believers in the church today: *a state of inactivity with a loss of consciousness . . . a decrease in responsiveness to events taking place.* This is just another way of saying that some people in the church have gone to sleep. Slipped into a spiritual coma. Don't forget that Paul's words are directed not to unbelievers but to Christians. God is saying to you and me, "Wake up!" Be alert.

Be clear-headed. But some of us aren't. For some, there is a state of lethargy, passiveness, even laziness. Some of us are sleepwalking instead of walking in the Spirit.

After I've had a good, satisfying meal, I get sleepy. Sometimes if I eat a delicious Mexican meal I go into what I like to describe as a "food coma." I'm just out of it and groggy for a while.

But there is a spiritual analogy here. If you are in a good, Bible-teaching church and hear the Word of God taught over and over again, you can become spiritually sleepy—unless you find ways to think through and actually *apply* those truths to your life. You take it in and take it in, and if you don't put those good biblical principles to work, you might find yourself becoming lethargic or passive. The fact is, the truths we learn in church or Bible studies should change the way we live and the way we respond to all sorts of situations and circumstances in our lives.

We need to wake up and smell the coffee. Jesus is coming soon!

We need to sober up.

First Thessalonians 5:8 (NIV) says, "Since we belong to the day, let us be sober."

Having spent the first seventeen years of my life around alcoholic people, I have a pretty good working knowledge of what drunk people are like. As a child and teenager, I watched adults drink themselves insensible nearly every night. As I observed, I couldn't help but notice that different people react to alcohol in different ways. We might describe some as "happy drunk." They laugh all the time (really loud sometimes) and think everything is funny. They imagine that they are funny and witty, too, when they're not funny at all. Other drinkers just get tired. Before long they are asleep and snoring. Still others are "mean drunks." No one wants to be around someone like that. They get angry for seemingly no reason at all, start screaming, and sometimes turn violent. I've had more of those mean drunks around me than I care to remember, and suffered for it.

The problem with people who are drinking is that they don't realize they are coming "under the influence." They think they are maintaining themselves well and acting perfectly normal, when they're not.

In 1 Thessalonians 5, God is saying don't be drunk. This could be taken quite literally: Don't get intoxicated on alcohol. As Paul wrote in Ephesians 5:18 (TLB), "Don't drink too much wine, for many evils lie along that path; be filled instead with the Holy Spirit and controlled by him."

Here is an amazing thought: If you drink, you can get drunk. If you don't drink, you won't get drunk. It's really as simple as that. I made a decision a long time ago that I wouldn't drink at all. Some have said, "Greg, you're really missing out!" Am I? I don't think so. I have seen the devastating effects of alcohol on far, far too many lives, and I don't have any desire to go down that road. I don't want to be under the control of anything or anyone but Jesus Christ. I'm happy with that, and don't think I've missed a thing.

But the apostle Paul was talking about more than being intoxicated by alcohol or drugs. Have you ever bought something new and felt a kind of rush? You buy it and endorphins are released. But then, after you get it home, or after UPS brings it to your front door, it doesn't seem like such a big deal anymore. You look at it, shrug your shoulders, and say, "Yeah, whatever." And then you move on to something else.

Some people obsess on hobbies, sports teams, computer games, food, movies, or a thousand other things. In Luke 21:34, Jesus said, "Take heed to yourselves, lest your hearts be weighed down with carousing, drunkenness, and the cares of this life, and that Day come on you unexpectedly."

The cares of life. It's not always the bad or negative things that mess us up. Sometimes the good things become the most important things. Jesus was warning us to not become so wrapped up and concerned about the affairs of this life that we no longer think about the next life, to avoid becoming overly concerned with things we can hold in our hands without stopping to consider those eternal things we can't see.

To be "sober" doesn't mean to be miserable or wound up tight. Some Christians are just downers, take themselves way too seriously, and are no fun to be with. They don't know how to laugh at jokes or just relax and have a good time with others. What sober really means is *clear-headed*. When you are sober you are thinking clearly—seeing things as they truly are.

We need to suit up.

First Thessalonians 5:8 concludes, "Put on the breastplate of faith and love, and as a helmet the hope of salvation." Here's the bottom line: The moment you became a follower of Jesus Christ you entered into a spiritual battle. The devil, of course, never wanted you to believe in the first place. And now he is your active adversary, and will do everything he can do to stop you from moving forward spiritually. Ephesians 6:12-13 (NLT) reminds us,

> *We are not fighting against flesh-and-blood enemies, but against evil rulers and authorities of the unseen world, against mighty powers in this dark world, and against evil spirits in the heavenly places.*

> *Therefore, put on every piece of God's armor so you will be able to resist the enemy in the time of evil. Then after the battle you will still be standing firm.*

Another translation says, "This is for keeps, a life-or-death fight to the finish against the Devil and all his angels" (verse 12, MSG).

You might say, "I don't like to fight."

Maybe not. But if you don't fight and resist the devil and his demons, you will soon get beaten down by these enemies. You *are* in this battle whether you want to be or not. And you have to make a choice: You're either going to win or lose, experience victory or defeat, gain ground or lose ground, progress or regress. It's up to you. God tells us, "Suit up. Be ready to fight and stand your ground. Put on the armor I have provided for you."

What do you put on? Paul picked out two pieces of armor in particular. By the way, this was a man who knew a great deal about Roman armor. Why? Because he spent a lot of time being chained to Roman soldiers. When you're sitting chained to someone for days on end, you start talking. And somewhere along the line Paul probably said to a soldier, "Tell me about your armor. How does it work?"

One very important piece of armor the soldier wore into battle was the breastplate—vital because it protected the vital organs. And using that piece of equipment as a metaphor, the apostle said, "Put on the breastplate of faith and love." This isn't a breastplate of *feelings*. No, our lives as followers of Christ are lived by faith, not emotion. Emotions come and go. If we allow feelings to control us, we will soon crash and burn. We've got to stand on the Word of God, leaning hard on His promises, and putting our faith in spiritual realities we can't see. Put on that breastplate and keep it on every day.

Then Paul spoke of the helmet of salvation. What does a helmet do? It protects the head. The brain. In the same way, we put on this helmet God has provided to protect our minds. Why? Because if we stop and think about it, we will realize that almost every temptation we have ever dealt with started as a thought.

You're going about your business some afternoon and you sense a little thought knocking at the door, asking for admittance. Maybe it's an impure thought. A fantasy. A doubt. An unkind, jealous, or judgmental thought about someone. You say to yourself, "I know this thought isn't true and I know that it really doesn't belong. But I think I'll just try it out for a while. I'll let it come in a little bit."

Before you know it, however, that thought has taken root in your heart, and it has become an issue in your life. You find yourself way down a road you never intended to travel. We've all heard the progression described like this: "Sow a thought, reap an act. Sow an act, reap a habit. Sow a habit, reap a character. Sow a character, and reap a destiny."

The answer, of course, is to not let those thoughts enter our minds in the first place. As someone once said, "You can't stop a bird from flying over your head, but you can stop it from making a nest in your hair." (In my case, that bird better bring his own building materials, because there isn't any hair up there on my head.) In other words, we can't stop the thought from coming our way or even knocking on the door of our imagination. But at the same time, we don't have to open the door and invite it in. That's why the Bible says we should bring every thought into captivity to the obedience of Christ (see 2 Corinthians 10:5).

Sometimes on my computer, when I go to save a picture or a document, a notice comes up on my screen that says, "memory full." That means I have to delete some stuff, empty the trash, eliminate files to make room. Wouldn't it be great if the devil came to us with all of his impure, rotten thoughts, knocked on the door of our minds, and immediately saw the message, "memory full"? In other words, there's no room for you, Satan. My mind is filled with the Word of God. Filled with Scripture. Filled with the promises of God. Filled with songs of praise and worship, and there's no room for your evil suggestions.

We need to put on the helmet of salvation to protect our thoughts from invasions and intrusions of the dark side.

I love the way J. B. Phillips paraphrased Romans 13:11-14:

Why all this stress on behaviour? Because, as I think you have realised, the present time is of the highest importance—it is time to wake up to reality. Every day brings God's salvation nearer. The night is nearly over, the day has almost dawned. Let us therefore fling away the things that men do in the dark, let us arm ourselves for the fight of the day! Let us live cleanly, as in the daylight, not in the "delights" of getting drunk or playing with sex, nor yet in quarrelling or jealousies. Let us be Christ's men from head to foot, and give no chances to the flesh to have its fling.

Are you Christ's man, Christ's woman? Are you prepared for His return? Are you ready to meet Him face to face? Or do you feel uncomfortable, even frightened at that prospect?

Whatever it is that's keeping you from God, it's time to let go of those things. It's time to wake up and sober up, because Jesus is coming soon.

Maybe today. Maybe tonight.

CHAPTER THIRTY-FOUR
TILL HE COMES

Newspapers have a certain size of type they save for truly mega events in our world.

It's called Second Coming type.

They use it only for big, weighty, perhaps cataclysmic events. When the Japanese bombed Pearl Harbor they used Second Coming type. They also used it after President Kennedy was assassinated and after the World Trade Center attack.

Why don't they just call it "mega event type," or "big news type"? Because everyone understands that there is no bigger event than the Second Coming of Jesus Christ.

A recent Gallup poll revealed that 66 percent of the American people believe that Jesus Christ will return to earth in the future. What makes this especially interesting is that this figure is 25 percent more than those who claim to be born again Christians—which means that non-Christians as well as Christians believe in this event.

Why is He coming back again? He is returning to earth to judge His enemies, set up His kingdom, and begin His one-thousand-year reign over the earth. The Bible speaks of this great event many, many times over. Over three hundred Bible passages deal with the return of Jesus Christ. Jesus spoke of it at least twenty-one times when He walked this earth. One of the most well-known statements about the Lord's return occurs in what is known as the Olivet Discourse in Matthew 24.

"The Sign of the Son of Man"

The discussion began as Jesus and the disciples were leaving the temple, and several of the company began pointing out the wonders of the temple's construction.

Jesus said, "Do you not see all these things? Assuredly, I say to you, not one stone shall be left here upon another, that shall not be thrown down" (Matthew 24:2).

I imagine that stopped conversation for a few minutes as the disciples were stunned into silence. *The temple? Thrown down? Not one stone left on top of another? How could it be?*

Later, when they sat down together on the Mount of Olives, someone got the courage to pick up the topic again. "Tell us, when will these things be? And what will be the sign of Your coming, and of the end of the age?" (verse 3).

As the teaching time went on, Jesus began speaking about the physical signs that would accompany His return.

Immediately after the tribulation of those days the sun will be darkened, and the moon will not give its light; the stars will fall from heaven, and the powers of the heavens will be shaken. Then the sign of the Son of Man will appear in heaven, and then all the tribes of the earth will mourn, and they will see the Son of Man coming on the clouds of heaven with power and great glory. (verses 29-30)

Sometimes people will ask, "Is the Second Coming of Jesus an actual, physical event, or is just something *spiritual?*"

Jesus answered that question clearly. He will return physically to earth. His first coming was physical, and His second coming will be physical as well. Though it is true that Jesus indwells every believer who has put his or her faith in Christ, and takes up residence in the human heart, it is also true that He is bodily in heaven.

When Stephen was being martyred he had a vision of the glory of heaven, and said, "Look! I see the heavens opened and the Son of Man standing at the right hand of God!" (Acts 7:56). He saw Jesus in heaven in a physical form, and Jesus will also return bodily to earth. In Acts 1:11 (NLT) two angels told the apostles, "Men of Galilee, . . . why are you standing here staring into heaven? Jesus has been taken from you into heaven, *but someday he will return from heaven in the same way you saw him go!*" (emphasis added).

Why is Jesus returning to earth? Again, to judge the world in righteousness. There are so many injustices and horrific cruelties in this world, aren't there? Criminals seem to get away with their crimes. Terrorists commit brutal, inhuman acts. And sometimes we wonder, "Will all these terrible wrongs ever be righted?"

Yes, they will. When Christ comes back He will right the wrongs and bring justice to a world of injustice.

But First . . . Armageddon

Before the Second Coming, however, another mighty, world-shaking event must transpire. We know it as Armageddon, the final battle of humankind. The very word sounds ominous, threatening, and final. And so it is.

Usually when the word *Armageddon* is invoked, the speaker is making reference to something dark and ominous. For instance, when General Douglas MacArthur stood on the deck of the *USS Missouri* in Tokyo Harbor, signing a peace treaty with Japan and bringing World War II to a close, he made this statement: "We have had our last chance. If we do not devise some great and more equitable system, Armageddon will be at the door."

Soon after he was inaugurated as the fortieth president of the United States, President Ronald Reagan was overwhelmed with the complexities of the Middle East. On Friday, May 15, 1981, he scribbled in his diary, "Sometimes I wonder if we are going to witness Armageddon."

A few weeks later on Sunday, June 7, President Reagan heard that Israel had bombed the Iraqi nuclear reactor. He wrote in his diary, "Got word of Israel bombing the Iraqi nuclear reactor. I swear, I believe Armageddon is near."

What we need to understand is that Armageddon is the actual name of a physical place on earth. It is the valley of Megiddo in Israel. Many battles have been fought on that massive piece of real estate already. Gideon defeated the Midianites in the valley of Megiddo. Deborah and Barak defeated the Canaanites there. King Saul was killed by the Philistines in the same valley.

Why is the valley of Megiddo the location of the final conflict? No less an expert than the military leader Napoleon stood there in 1799 and made this statement: "All the armies of the world can maneuver their forces on this vast plain. There is no place in the world more suited for war than this. It is the most natural battleground on the whole earth."

Yes, Armageddon will be the ultimate, final battle. But the whole history of earth has been written in the blood of ceaseless wars and battles. Here is what we need to know: Satan himself is behind the wars and struggles on this troubled planet of ours. When Christ was born as a Baby in Bethlehem, the angels said, "Peace on earth to those with whom God is pleased" (Luke 2:14, NLT). Jesus came to bring peace on earth. From the very beginning, however, Satan has sought to take peace away from the earth, to set men and women against one another. It happens in times of war; sadly, it even happens in churches when people become angry and embittered toward one another and refuse to forgive others as Christ forgave them.

Sometimes people are perplexed when they see another barbaric act of terrorism from militant Islamic groups like ISIS or Boko Haram. An innocent child tortured. A person beheaded. Someone else crucified or put in a cage and set on fire. The pundits in the press try to explain it but really can't. They say, "We don't know why people do these horrible things. "

I will tell you why.

Because there is a devil. The devil loves carnage, violence, war, death, and all the sorrow and disruption these things bring. Satan and his army of demons stir up mistrust, greed, anger, hatred, sadism, and the thirst for vengeance.

World War I was called "the war to end all wars." At the close of that great tragedy, where ten million people lost their lives, it was said there would never be another war. But it took only twenty years for another conflict to develop. World War II was far worse, and took the lives of fifty million people.

The worst wars, however, are still to come. Jesus said that in the last days there would be "wars and rumors of wars" (Matthew 24:6). These will take place during the period known as the Great Tribulation.

Consider this: Humankind has stored up approximately 15,000 nuclear weapons, each with unthinkable capacity to kill and destroy.

Combined, these weapons could blow up our planet many times over.

When will it all end?

How will it all end?

It will end when a glorious Rider on a white horse suddenly appears in the sky.

The White Rider

Now I saw heaven opened, and behold, a white horse. And He who sat on him was called Faithful and True, and in righteousness He judges and makes war. His eyes were like a flame of fire, and on His head were many crowns. He had a name written that no one knew except Himself. He was clothed with a robe dipped in blood, and His name is called The Word of God. And the armies in heaven, clothed in fine linen, white and clean, followed Him on white horses. (Revelation 19:11-14)

There are some important points we need to see in these verses about Jesus' Second Coming.

It will be public and seen by all.

There won't be any question at all about what is taking place when Jesus returns. No one will say, "Was that just a really bad storm we had, or did Jesus come back?" People will know it is Him. Jesus said, "For as the lightning comes from the east and flashes to the west, so also will the coming of the Son of Man be" (Matthew 24:27).

His return will be accompanied by sadness and weeping.

Israel will mourn as they finally realize that Jesus was and is their Messiah. Zechariah 12:10 (NIV) says, "And I will pour out on the house of David and the inhabitants of Jerusalem a spirit of grace and supplication. They will look on me, the one they have pierced, and they will mourn for him as one mourns for an only child, and grieve bitterly for him as one grieves for a firstborn son."

This event, and this event only, will bring an end to the senseless wars of humankind. We will never be able to wipe out terrorism and violence with military or political solutions. This will only happen when Christ comes back and establishes His kingdom.

Please don't confuse the Second Coming with the Rapture. These are two separate events, occurring at two different times. The Rapture happens before the tribulation period. The Second Coming effectively brings the tribulation period to a conclusion. In the Rapture Jesus comes before judgment. In the Second Coming He returns with judgment. In the Rapture He comes for His people. In the Second Coming He returns with His people. In the Rapture He comes as a thief in the night. In the Second Coming, everyone will see Him.

I love to try to visualize Jesus riding His white horse (think of it as Air Horse One), charging out of the heavenly glory with an army of believers behind Him, all clothed in white. Revelation 19:11 says, "I saw heaven opened, and behold, a white horse. And He who sat on him was called Faithful and True, and in righteousness He judges and makes war."

Jesus was and is and will always be the "Faithful and True Witness." Our God is faithful and true. He will keep every promise He has made to you. Sometimes in this life we live here on earth we feel despondent or even despairing. Sometimes we are frightened and feel all alone. But read the words of the Faithful and True Witness to you: "Surely I am with you always, to the very end of the age. . . . Never will I leave you; never will I forsake you" (Matthew 28:20, NIV; Hebrews 13:5, NIV).

Maybe you are frightened of death, and find yourself facing a devastating medical report. Jesus said in Revelation 1:17-18 (NLT), "Don't be afraid! I am the First and the Last. I am the living one. I died, but look—I am alive forever and ever! And I hold the keys of death and the grave."

I'm so glad Christ has those keys in His possession! If He gave them to me, I would have lost them by now. (I'm always losing keys.) But those keys to death and the grave are in His keeping. And He tells us, "Don't be afraid. I've been there. I've experienced death, and I came back again. I've got you covered."

Of course, in the gospel of John Jesus said, "Do not let your hearts be troubled. You believe in God; believe also in me. My Father's house has many rooms; if that were not so, would I have told you that I am going there to prepare a place for you? And if I go and prepare a place for you, I will come back and take you to be with me that you also may be where I am" (14:1-3, NIV).

Maybe you are living under a load of guilt because of wrongs you have done in the past. You can't escape the memories, and you don't know how to put them behind you. Here are the words of the Faithful and True Witness for you: "If we confess our sins, He is faithful and just to forgive us our sins and to cleanse us from all unrighteousness" (1 John 1:9). Our God is faithful.

His appearance will be striking.

Sometimes people try to speculate on what Jesus looked like. Has it ever struck you as curious that there isn't one physical description of Christ in the Bible? Couldn't one of those guys who spent years with Him have taken two or three minutes to write down just a few details? But they didn't. Or if they did, it never made it into the Scriptures.

In Revelation 19:11-13, however, we do have a description—although it is more spiritual than physical: "Behold, a white horse. And He who sat on him was called Faithful and True, and in righteousness He judges and makes war. His eyes were like a flame of fire, and on His head were many crowns. He had a name written that no one knew except Himself. He was clothed with a robe dipped in blood, and His name is called The Word of God."

Three aspects of this description stand out: His eyes, His head, and His robe.

"His eyes were like a flame of fire." When we meet someone and shake their hand for the first time, we usually look them in the eyes. It has been said that the eyes are the window of the soul. If a person won't make eye contact with us and quickly looks away, that isn't a good sign. Then there are others who make eye contact and just keep staring. That isn't much fun, either. We want to say to them, "Could you look away for a second or two? You're making me uncomfortable."

Can you imagine looking into the eyes of Jesus Christ? Back in the first century, a number of people had that very opportunity. The Bible describes the moment when Jesus called Matthew, or Levi, to be His disciple. We read, "After this, Jesus went out and saw a tax collector by the name of Levi sitting at his tax booth. 'Follow me,' Jesus said to him" (Luke 5:27, NIV).

There must have been something in that look Jesus gave him, because Matthew got up from his table and left everything, just as it was, and followed Jesus for the rest of his life. Jesus looked at him—or maybe we should say He looked right through him. Have you ever had someone look right through you? Did you ever try to cheat on a test in school and have the teacher call you out on it after class? Mrs. Nobody-Gets-Away-with-That-in-My-Class said, "Did you cheat on that test? Look me in the eyes when you answer!" You gulp and try to meet her steely gaze, and pretty soon you're confessing things you hadn't even done! Some teachers have a way of looking right through you, and so did Jesus.

Talk about a penetrating gaze, John wrote that Christ's eyes were like flames! His gaze cuts through every lie and every mask of hypocrisy. He sees the heart. Hebrews 4:13 says that "there is no creature hidden from His sight, but all things are naked and open to the eyes of Him to whom we must give account."

"On His head were many crowns." He wears many crowns because He rules many kingdoms. In Revelation 11:15, an angel cries out, "The kingdoms of this world have become the kingdoms of our Lord and of His Christ, and He shall reign forever and ever!" The idea that there was ever a "United Nations" in our world has been a myth from day one. What's more, nations will never be united until there is one King, King Jesus, ruling over all.

"He was clothed with a robe dipped in blood, and His name is called The Word of God." The phrase "dipped in blood" could be better translated "spattered in blood." It isn't just a drop or two—there is quite a bit of blood here. Why does the Lord have a bloody robe in His Second Coming? It is to remind us of what He came to do in the first place. He died on the cross for our sins, shedding His blood for us, and in the future He will come back as our conquering King.

Compare His first coming with His second:

- In His first coming He was wrapped in rags, or strips of swaddling cloth. In His Second Coming He will be clothed royally with a robe dipped in blood.

- In His first coming He was surrounded by animals and shepherds. In His Second coming He will be accompanied by saints and angels.

- In His first coming the door of the inn was closed to Him. In His Second Coming the door of heaven will be opened to Him.

- In His first coming He was the Lamb of God, who takes away the sin of the world. In His Second Coming He will return as the ferocious Lion of the tribe of Judah to bring justice to the earth.

Think of all the times you have seen His name dishonored in books and magazines and in television and movies. Think of all the times you have heard people take the name of Jesus and drag it through the mud. When He returns, His name will finally be vindicated before all humanity. The Bible says, "At the name of Jesus every knee should bow, in heaven and on earth and under the earth, and every tongue acknowledge that Jesus Christ is Lord, to the glory of God the Father" (Philippians 2:10-11, NIV).

"Armies . . . followed Him."

In Revelation 19:14 we read how "the armies in heaven, clothed in fine linen, white and clean, followed Him on white horses." Who are these armies? Your first guess might be that these are angels. After all, there are untold millions of angels who would be ready to go to war for God's Son at the drop of a hat. But no, these are not angels. In fact, Enoch is quoted in Jude 14-15 as having said,

"Behold, the Lord comes with ten thousands of His saints, to execute judgment."

Someone might say, "Well, that sounds exciting, Greg, but it kind of lets me out. I am certainly not a saint." On the contrary! If you have put your faith in Jesus Christ you *are* a saint. "Saint" is just an interchangeable word with *believer*. Every Christian is a saint.

So who are the saints who ride on horses behind the conquering Christ? Colossians 3:4 gives us a clear answer: "When Christ who is our life appears, then you also will appear with Him in glory." That means you and I will be there! You and I will come back with Jesus in the Second Coming.

"But Greg, I've never ridden a horse in my life!" I'm with you on that. I like horsepower, not horses! I like brakes that work and turning the engine off. But on *that* day, it will be the greatest thrill and most incredible privilege we could possibly imagine to ride with Jesus and see His name vindicated in all the earth. When the horses gather and the saints in heaven mount up, you wouldn't want to be anywhere else!

What Do We Do Until He Comes?

Yes, Jesus is coming back to earth. The newspapers of the world should keep their "Second Coming type" at the ready. But until He does return, what are we supposed to do? How should we be living?

Just in case you were wondering, the Bible says nothing about stockpiling gold, food, water, and weapons, or building underground shelters. Even so, Scripture does give us some specific things we should be doing as Christians as we await His return.

In Luke 19:11-27, Jesus told a parable about a man of great wealth who was preparing to leave on a long trip. Before he left, he called his servants together and gave each of them the same amount of money. He told them, "I've got a long trip ahead of me. I'm leaving each of you with some money to do business with until I get back. Invest it well and wisely."

How does this apply to us? What one thing has been given to every follower of Jesus Christ without exception? *The message of the gospel.* The Great Commission is given to every follower of Jesus in every age and every corner of the world. No, not everyone is called to be an evangelist, but everyone is called to evangelize. Paul mentioned in his letter to young Timothy how the "glorious gospel" was committed to Paul's trust (1 Timothy 1:11). But that same glorious gospel has been committed to your trust, as well.

If we could paraphrase what Jesus was saying in the Luke 19 parable, it might sound like this: "Look, I'm leaving now, but I'll be coming back soon. Take this message I have entrusted to you and get it out to others. Do God's business until I return."

There is nothing wrong with having a career. There is nothing wrong with finding that right man or that right woman, getting married, and having a happy family. There is nothing wrong with enjoying the material blessings the Lord has given you. He wants us to enjoy and be thankful for the things He has provided for us.

But here is the question that each of us needs to ask ourselves: *How am I personally taking care to get the gospel out?* "But Greg," someone might say, "that's your job. You're the preacher. You're the evangelist." You are right; it is my job. And I am doing what I can, though I am sure I could do more. But it is also *your* job to pursue this same goal.

Isn't giving our money to the church or good Christian organizations accomplishing that? Isn't that helping to get the Word out? Yes, it is. But we must also be looking for those opportunities God places directly in our path.

Jesus made this clear in another parable, found in Luke 16:1-9. He told a fascinating story that at first reading might seem a little difficult for us to apply. In this parable, a manager was about to be fired for his poor management practices. Realizing his days were numbered, he set out to ingratiate himself with a number of his boss's most prominent creditors. Meeting with one he said in effect, "Hey, you owe our firm $10,000. Write me a check right now for $5,000 and we will consider it settled." He did this with a number of people.

But here's the surprising part. Instead of reproving this rascal, the boss commends him for his shrewdness. To wrap it up, Jesus said in Luke 16:9 (NIV): "I tell you, use worldly wealth to gain friends for yourselves, so that when it is gone, you will be welcomed into eternal dwellings."

This dishonest manager, for all his character flaws, was shrewd. He used his position to advance himself in a clever (if dishonest) way. In the same way, Jesus was saying, we need to use our money and our resources to gain friends that will last into eternity. Someone might say, "What are you talking about, Greg? Bribing people to become Christians?"

No, I'm talking about using your money, your resources, your time, and your energies for the work of the gospel and advancing the kingdom of God.

God has given to every one of us three things to use for His glory while we live out our days on earth: *time, talent,* and *treasure.* We all have each of these in varying degrees. We have our time every day that we can dedicate to Him. We have our talents—our skills, gifts, and abilities. Finally, we have our treasure to give to Him to advance His work in our world.

In his first letter to the Thessalonians Paul wrote, "For what is our hope, or joy, or crown of rejoicing? Is it not even you in the presence of our Lord Jesus Christ at His coming? For you are our glory and joy" (2:19-20). Paul seems to have been implying that when we leave this world and are caught up into God's presence, we will find ourselves surrounded by those whom we helped bring to Christ in our lifetimes.

"Well, Greg," you may say, "I guess I'll have a pretty lonely homecoming, because I haven't led many people to Christ." Haven't you? Maybe you have accomplished more than you imagine. God doesn't hold you responsible for success, He holds you responsible for faithfulness. In that final day, Jesus is not going to say, "Well done, good and successful servant." No, He will say, "Well done, good and *faithful* servant." All He asks you to do is to take what He has given you and do the best you can with it.

Make up your mind to sow as many seeds as you can, beginning today. How do you sow a seed? Live a godly life, for starters. Love your wife. Love your husband. Seek to do the best you can, with

God's help. Be a caring friend and a loving neighbor. Be a good example of Jesus Christ. Mention your faith in Christ whenever you can, or water a seed that someone else has sown. And if God gives you the opportunity to close the deal and reap a harvest from what others have sown through the years, be alert and ready to do that.

Paul wrote, "Each of us did the work the Lord gave us. I planted the seed in your hearts, and Apollos watered it, but it was God who made it grow. It's not important who does the planting, or who does the watering. What's important is that God makes the seed grow. The one who plants and the one who waters work together with the same purpose. And both will be rewarded for their own hard work" (1 Corinthians 3:5-8, NLT).

There might be seeds you sowed in years past that won't break ground until much later—perhaps seeds you sowed in your children, grandchildren, or even great-grandchildren. Maybe you spoke to someone about your faith, and that individual won't come to Christ until three years after you die. That person in turn leads four people to Christ, who also go out to lead others to the Lord. Then one of those people reaches someone who will be the next Billy Graham, and he reaches a whole generation.

Guess what? All of that fruit is credited to your account. It all comes back to you because you did your part, and we are all interconnected.

Here's the bottom line: Just do what you can for God's glory. Sow those seeds, water those seeds, and then stand ready to reap a harvest when the Lord opens the door.

Occupy yourself with these things until He comes.

CHAPTER THIRTY-FIVE
DO WHAT YOU CAN WHILE YOU CAN

Most of us are thankful for our smartphones, tablets, and laptops, and you can include me in that number. We're convinced that these devices make our lives more efficient and save us time, and I suppose they do. (Have you ever had to look through an airport for a phone booth or look up a piece of information in a card catalog in the library?)

But if we are honest, we also must admit we waste a lot of time on these electronic companions. We check Facebook or Instagram, text our friends, watch a video on YouTube, take selfies, or play endless games on those bright little screens. Yes, we can waste too much time that way. But there is something much worse than wasting time.

Wasting a life. Throwing away a life filled with God-given talent and giftedness. The Bible is replete with stories of people who had amazing, seemingly limitless potential, and squandered it.

Samson comes to mind. A mighty man with godly parents and wide-open opportunities before him. Saul, the first king of Israel, comes to mind. Solomon, son of David, a king with incomparable wisdom and vast wealth, comes to mind.

In the New Testament we read the story of a woman who was accused of a terrible, sinful waste.

But things aren't always as they appear, are they?

Changes in Perspective

When I think of this story in the gospel of Matthew, I am reminded that we will see life differently when we get to heaven. Some of the things we so treasured and prioritized on earth won't look so wonderful and worthwhile on the other side. And some of the things we thought of in a negative light may take on a value beyond anything we could have imagined.

Here on earth, our definition of "good" is prosperity. In other words, life is "good" when we're making a lot of money, enjoying good health, living in a happy relationship, and feeling fulfilled in our careers. Honestly, there's nothing wrong with those things. God can certainly bless us in those ways. We can even take those gifts from heaven and use them for His glory and for furthering His kingdom. But for some people, that kind of prosperity can become a hindrance and distraction, turning them away from things that are infinitely more important. On the other hand, we may look at difficulties in life—sickness or disability or failure—as "bad" things. I suggest that when we get to heaven, we may look back on those hard times and realize those were the *best* times, because those were the times that made us more and more like Christ.

As I said, life isn't always as it appears to be. The critics of the woman we will read about in Matthew 26 judged her for her actions and accused her of great waste. In contrast, Jesus Christ saw her heart and commended her. In fact, He singled her out to acknowledge what she did.

Here's the central question: What do you want more in your life—the approval of God or the applause of man? Bear in mind that much of the time you will have to choose between those two; you can't always have them both. In fact, sometimes if you have God's approval you will have man's opposition and even hatred. Our culture will not applaud the man or woman who totally follows Jesus Christ.

So when it's all said and done, which means most to you—God's opinion or someone else's opinion? Paul said it like this in Galatians 1:10 (TLB): "You can see that I am not trying to please you by sweet talk and flattery; no, I am trying to please God. If I were still trying to please men I could not be Christ's servant."

Let's zero in now on the story of a woman who brought a special gift to Jesus—and was both trashed and praised for what she did.

The Alabaster Flask

And when Jesus was in Bethany at the house of Simon the leper, a woman came to Him having an alabaster flask of very costly fragrant oil, and she poured it on His head as He sat at the table. But when His disciples saw it, they were indignant, saying, "Why this waste? For this fragrant oil might have been sold for much and given to the poor."

But when Jesus was aware of it, He said to them, "Why do you trouble the woman? For she has done a good work for Me. For you have the poor with you always, but Me you do not have always. For in pouring this fragrant oil on My body, she did it for My burial. Assuredly, I say to you, wherever this gospel is preached in the whole world, what this woman has done will also be told as a memorial to her." (Matthew 26:6-13)

When you think about it, this last prophecy of Jesus has just been fulfilled again, today, as you read and consider these words. The fact that we are taking time right now to consider this woman's impulsive act of love is part of the memorial Jesus promised her.

At this point in Jesus' life, He was on the road to Calvary, preparing to die on the cross for our sins. The chain of events that began to unfold in Matthew 26 would ultimately lead to His crucifixion, resurrection, and ascension. By this point in Matthew's narrative, Jesus had already engaged in a number of sharp confrontations with Israel's religious leaders. They were very angry at Him. Plain and simple, they wanted Him dead. But they couldn't engineer His capture and execution at this exact moment because so many people were gathered in Jerusalem for the Passover. And while there were those who hated Jesus, many people admired Him and could take His side. So the leaders had to wait for the "right moment" to carry out their murderous plans.

Meanwhile, Jesus, who knew exactly what was happening around Him, decided to spend an evening with close friends in Bethany. He went to the home of a man known as Simon the leper, and I can imagine some lively discussions taking place that evening. Christ had just delivered what we know as the Olivet Discourse

(Matthew 24–25), where He discussed the end of the world and the coming judgment. There must have been plenty of questions about those things. (And wouldn't you have loved to have been there in that room to hear His explanations?)

To make matters even more interesting, the resurrected Lazarus was in the party that night. Can you imagine talking to a man who had actually been dead for four days and then came back to life again? I can hear people asking, "What was it like, Lazarus? What did you see on the other side?" All of this conversation filled the room and fueled the energy and excitement in the room.

A woman among them that evening became deeply moved by the whole setting. Sitting in the presence of Jesus as she was, and perhaps intuitively understanding what the Lord was facing in the coming hours, she longed to do something extravagant for Him. Something that would somehow communicate her absolute devotion. So we read in verse 7 that she "came to Him having an alabaster flask of very costly fragrant oil, and she poured it on His head as He sat at the table."

Can you imagine? You're sitting at a table and a woman walks up and pours perfume on your head! But this was no mere perfume. It was *very* expensive, imported fragrant oil, possibly from India.

Another gospel tells us that this woman was Mary of Bethany, the sister of Martha and Lazarus. There are a number of Marys in the Gospels, but this was the Mary who could always be found sitting at Jesus' feet.

On this particular night, however, she seems to have been perceiving something no one else has really grasped: Jesus wasn't long for this world. It was one of His last nights on earth. He was headed, very soon, to the cross.

You might ask, "Hadn't He told His followers over and over again about what was planned for Him? Didn't everyone know?" And the answer to those questions is yes He did, and no they didn't. Even at this late date, His followers still imagined He was going to overthrow Rome and set up some kind of earthly kingdom. That's why the disciples argued over who would have the top spots in the new order of things. All of the Lord's teaching about His upcoming betrayal, rejection, death, and resurrection went right over their heads. That wasn't at all what they wanted to hear, so they closed their ears.

But Mary understood.

Mary knew.

Maybe it was intuition or spiritual insight, but whatever it was, Mary suddenly understood that Jesus had been saying what He meant and meaning what He said. He was about to die, and it broke her heart. Filled with love, she wanted to do something really special for Him.

What can I do? she asked herself. *What can I give? What's the most valuable thing I possess? I know! It's that family heirloom of mine—the fragrant anointing oil in the alabaster flask. I will break the flask and pour out the oil—all of it—on Jesus to show how much I love Him.*

One thing I've always loved about my wife is how she thinks of bringing little gifts to friends. That's not something I think of very often (okay, never). We will be heading over to someone's house for dinner, and my wife, Cathe, will say, "Let's stop and get a little gift."

I'm thinking, *A gift? Why? What's the purpose? It's not Christmas.*

So we stop at one of those gifty stores I like to describe as "stores of nothingness." This is where they sell candles and plants and little figurines—and more candles. Sometimes the air in those stores is so heavy with scents and perfumes that I want to make a quick exit. I will tell Cathe, "I'll just wait outside."

So she gives the candle or the little plaque to the hostess when we get to the house, and the woman is just blown away. "Oh my goodness, thank you! That was so sweet!" And I'm thinking, *Wow, no guy I know would ever do that.* When I'm on the way over to see one of my friends I never say to myself, "Maybe I should stop and pick up a little gift." But that's how my wife and other women I know express affection, and I really admire them for it.

Mary understood something none of the others realized that night. She had never had the privilege of spending great blocks of time in the presence of Jesus, as Peter, James, John, and Andrew had. She didn't get to be with Him walking through the vineyards, in the fishing boat on the lake, or out under the stars at night. The only time she saw Him was when He showed up in town. But even so, she picked up on something the twelve disciples couldn't seem to process.

Jesus had returned to Jerusalem one last time, to die, and knowing His death was approaching deeply moved Mary's heart. So she did what she could and brought Him the most precious thing she possessed.

By the way, what's the most important thing in your life right now? If a wind-whipped wildfire was bearing down on your house with flames twenty feet high, and you had only five minutes to retrieve your most valuable possessions from the house, what would you grab?

"Well," you say, "I'd take my husband."

That's a good start. But what else? Maybe you have a special photo album or some irreplaceable data on your computer or some very meaningful gift from someone dear. Think about it. What truly is the most precious thing in your life right now? Your children? Your spouse? Your home? Your physical appearance? Your reputation? Your ministry?

What is more important to you than anything else?

Here is my suggestion: Follow the example of Mary and give it to Jesus.

Giving to the Savior what is most precious is not so much about Him taking it from you as it is about you dedicating it to Him. And so we say, "Lord, I dedicate my marriage to You. I dedicate my children to You. I dedicate my talents and gifts to You. I dedicate my career to You."

Mary brought the most valuable, most treasured thing in her life to Christ and gave it utterly to Him. And Judas was watching. With a first-century calculator in hand, a man who knew the price of everything (and the value of nothing) instantly calculated the retail value of what she had just given away. This special fragrant oil had a street value of $25,000 to $35,000. And she had just poured out the whole contents on Jesus.

Judas said, "What a waste!"

But he wasn't alone. Surprisingly, others joined him in harshly criticizing Mary's act of devotion.

The Least—or Most—You Can Do

Judas is typical of so many today. Many, like dutiful Pharisees, only want to give that which is absolutely required by God. They want to give the bare minimum. In other words, "What is the least I can do and still technically be a Christian?" Or, as I have actually heard it said, "How much can I get away with and still be saved? How far can I go before I'm in danger of jeopardizing my relationship with God?"

That's not a good question to ask. Would you ask that about your children? "How little can I do for them and still be a 'good' parent?" Or about your spouse? "How little can I love my wife and still be a 'good' husband?"

Of course not! And even less should we be asking this about our Lord. Instead, we need to ask, "How much more can I do for the One who has done so much for me?"

Many of us just "paint by the numbers" in our Christian walk. We want to "do the basics" and get on with our lives. We will go to church once a week—or maybe twice a month. We will read the Bible if it's convenient and fits into our busy schedule. We will pray briefly before meals and maybe before we fall asleep at night. We may put something in the offering at church, but in many cases people will give more to a waitress than to the Lord.

We will ask questions like, "Do Christians still need to tithe?" But tithing is really just the entry level, isn't it? We should be saying, "Of course I will give that to the Lord. No problem. How much more can I give?"

The Bible says to bring your tithes *and offerings* to the Lord. If you don't think that way, if giving to the Lord becomes some sort of grim duty you're only doing because you have to, then you're missing the point.

The phrase "all things in moderation" might be a good guideline for some activities, but it's not good for your relationship with God. Don't follow Jesus in moderation; follow Him with all your heart and soul.

Maybe this is why the world was changed by the men and women of the early church, as modeled by Mary of Bethany. They felt a sense of abandon in their love for Jesus. They didn't play it safe. They took risks. God told Philip to leave what he was doing and head toward an unknown destination in the desert, and Philip went. God told Peter to take the hand of a crippled man and pull him to his feet, and Peter did it without hesitation. The early Christians were willing to risk everything—life, wealth, freedom, and reputation—for the kingdom of God.

We are told in Acts 4:13 that many of the Sanhedrin were amazed when they saw the boldness of Peter and John, for they could see that they were ordinary men who had no special training. What's more, they recognized them as men who had been with Jesus.

Can people tell when you have been with Jesus? When you leave church, can people see that you have been in company with Jesus—or that you were just at church? I have actually been told by servers in restaurants that some of the most difficult people they will deal with all week are Christians after church on Sunday. Sometimes they are rude. Usually they are cheap and don't leave a tip. To make matters worse, they will sometimes leave an evangelistic book on the table for the server instead of a tip.

Sometimes when we have been with Jesus "in theory" at church—but not in reality—we're not the best witnesses. We will say, "Wasn't that a great sermon?" And then immediately afterward we'll climb into the car, get up close on someone's bumper, and yell, "Get out of my way, you idiot!" (What's really bad is that we're still in the church parking lot!)

Let me ask you this: When was the last time you took a risk for your faith? When was the last time you left your comfort zone and engaged someone with the gospel? When was the last time you said or did something bold or extravagant for the kingdom? You might say, "But, Greg, what if I fail?" You might fail. But then again, what if you succeed? What if God blesses and gives you great favor? Won't you take that step of faith?

What is it that brought this sense of abandon and sacrifice for

Mary? It was Jesus. Nothing was too good for Him. No sacrifice was too great. She said, "I'm going to give Him my very best. I want to show my love for Him in a way that all will see." And she brought a gift to Him that we're still talking about after twenty centuries.

Do It Now

Sometimes people we deeply love are suddenly taken from us by an illness or accident. It might be a grandparent or parent. It might be a spouse, a son, a daughter, a teacher, a pastor. And after they're gone, we realize we never really told them how much we loved and appreciated them. We groan and say to ourselves, *I wish I would have told her how important she was to me; I wish I would have told him how he changed the path of my life. Why didn't I?*

Here is my suggestion for you: Say it now.

Don't wait to send flowers to your loved one's funeral. Take your flowers now. If someone you love has invested in you and made an impact on your life, tell the person so. Do it today. Write a card. Send an e-mail. At the very least (and it *is* the very least) send a text. Say something about who this person is to you and how he or she has helped you to become who you are. If you're so inclined, post it on social media. Tell the world what this person means to you. Don't wait until later. Don't delay until it's too late.

That's what Mary was doing for Jesus. She knew there would probably not be another opportunity. If she was going to demonstrate her love, it had to be then. And as far as she was concerned, it had to be her very best.

But not everybody appreciated Mary's sacrifice.

The Opposition

Not everyone saw the value in Mary's selfless act of love.

In fact, people in the room that night turned on her.

In Matthew 26:8-9 (NIV) we read, "When the disciples saw this, they were indignant. 'Why this waste?' they asked. 'This perfume could have been sold at a high price and the money given to the poor.'" By the way, the word *indignant* here could be translated, "to feel pain, to grieve, or to growl with displeasure." Another translation of these verses says the disciples "were furious," and said, "That's criminal!" (MSG).

On the surface, at least, we can see a certain legitimacy to this complaint and criticism. Was it really "good stewardship" to pour out thirty-five grand on Jesus in one spontaneous gesture?

In one sense, no. In another sense, absolutely.

John's gospel gives us a significant, behind-the-scenes detail on this story.

> But Judas Iscariot, the disciple who would soon betray him, said, "That perfume was worth a year's wages. It should have been sold and the money given to the poor." Not that he cared for the poor—he was a thief, and since he was in charge of the disciples' money, he often stole some for himself. (12:4-6, NLT)

As treasurer, Judas held the money for the disciples. Don't forget that this was the same greedy man who later sold out Christ for thirty pieces of silver. And isn't it interesting how he acted so concerned about Mary's "stewardship" when he was completely corrupt in that very area? Sometimes we become very critical of others for the very things we struggle with ourselves. But as the old saying goes, as I point one finger of guilt at someone else, I have three pointed back at me. It often comes out that the one who is so critical of what others say and do ends up being guilty of something far worse.

Judas had said, "This is a waste." Ironically, in John 17:12, Jesus says in His prayer to His Father that none of the disciples have been lost except the "son of perdition" or "son of waste," a reference to Judas. Was Jesus thinking of Judas's comment about Mary's sacrificial gift? Possibly. We can't know for certain. We can, however, see Judas trying to project his own guilt onto someone who wasn't guilty at all.

He accused Mary of waste, and yet think of what *he* was about to waste! He was about to sell out his Lord for a handful of silver.

As he did so, he was wasting one of the greatest opportunities and privileges ever given to anyone: to be a close confidant and friend of the Son of God while He walked on earth in human form. Judas threw that privilege away and then had the audacity to accuse a loving, good-hearted woman of wasting a gift she gave to Jesus.

This is so typical of hypercritical people. They are quick to jump down the throat of someone else, questioning the person's motivation and impugning his or her motives. They will say, "You do so-and-so because you are full of pride! What you're doing is just an ego trip."

People have said that to me at different points in my ministry. And I want to say back to them, "Excuse me, but can you really see my heart? How do you know why I do what I do? Yes, you can evaluate my actions, but you cannot tell me why I do what I do, because you have no idea of what's in my heart. Only God can see that."

I have found that those who complain the most do the least, and those who complain the least do the most. The complainers may think they have the "gift of criticism" from God, but often they are insecure, fearful, and full of shame about their own motives and actions. They use their bluster as a way to turn attention away from themselves.

Taking this story at face value someone might conclude that Judas was being virtuous and thrifty, while Mary was impulsive, frivolous, and wasteful. But just the opposite was true. Judas was selfish, greedy, and wicked, and Mary was full of love and devotion for Jesus, wanting to honor Him in the best way she knew.

Giving All

Sometimes people outside of Christ will say to Christians, "*What a waste!* You're just wasting your life going to church and doing your Bible studies. You're missing out on all the fun and parties and joy in life."

Here is my response: Let's get together at the end of life, if we have that opportunity, and compare notes. And even if you're right, even if I've given up some experiences and excitement and events, you're still the one who loses. You had all the fun and frenzy and "freedom" a person could have, but you still have to face a day of judgment. Jesus said, "For what profit is it to a man if he gains the whole world, and loses his own soul? Or what will a man give in exchange for his soul?" (Matthew 16:26).

In reality, however, the so-called freedom and fun envisioned by those who have determined to live for themselves doesn't work out that way. The people who chase after that lifestyle often find themselves into their second, third, or fourth marriages, estranged from their children, lonely, miserable, and empty. Often, the substances they have abused through the years have taken a toll on their bodies.

In contrast, a person who follows Jesus Christ hasn't really given up or wasted anything.

I love the fact that Jesus commended Mary for what she did. Listen to His words: "Why are you bothering this woman? She has done a beautiful thing to me. The poor you will always have with you, but you will not always have me. When she poured this perfume on my body, she did it to prepare me for burial. Truly I tell you, wherever this gospel is preached throughout the world, what she has done will also be told, in memory of her" (Matthew 26:10-13, NIV).

We need to do what we can while we can.

One person said it this way: "I am only one, but I am one. I cannot do everything, but I can do something. What I can do, I ought to do. What I ought to do, by the grace of God, I will do."

Do all that you can while you can to the very end of your life and beyond, and you will never regret it. What you do today impacts you, your children, your children's children, and many generations to come. That's what it means to pass on a godly legacy.

One day each of us will stand before God and give an account of our lives. What will you see as you look back? Will you regret having used your gifts and talents for the glory of God? As you enter eternity, will you be asking yourself, "Why did I share the gospel with those people? Why did I give my resources to God? Why did I go to all those church services?"

No, I don't think you will say that. But you may say, "Why didn't

I do more? I could have reached one more. I could have gone the extra mile. Why didn't I?"

Christians, too, will face a judgment. Sometimes people get a little stressed out when they hear that, but it's true. This won't have anything to do with our eternal salvation or our entrance into heaven. This will be an event that takes place after the Rapture of the church and before the Second Coming. It's called the judgment seat of Christ, and we might think of it as an awards ceremony. We read in 1 Corinthians 3:13-15 (NIV), "[A Christian's life work] will be revealed with fire, and the fire will test the quality of each person's work. If what has been built survives, the builder will receive a reward. If it is burned up, the builder will suffer loss but yet will be saved—even though only as one escaping through the flames." Commenting on this reality again in 2 Corinthians 5:10 (NIV), Paul said, "For we must all appear before the judgment seat of Christ, so that each of us may receive what is due us for the things done while in the body, whether good or bad."

If you have been faithful and used your opportunities, resources, and time for God, you will be rewarded. The Bible speaks about crowns being given out at that time, including the crown of life, promised to those who love the Lord, and the crown of rejoicing, given to those who faithfully serve Him (see James 1:12 and 1 Thessalonians 2:19).

None of us would want to appear empty-handed before the One whose hands were pierced for us on the cross of Calvary—and who wears those scars to this day. Instead, we desire to enter into the everlasting kingdom, as Peter said, "abundantly" (2 Peter 1:11).

John Wesley summed it up in this way: "Do all the good you can by all the means you can and all the ways you can in all the places you can at all the times you can to all the people you can as long as you can." That is a good goal for all of us because, as Jesus said, "the night is coming when no one can work" (John 9:4).

Bring your best to Jesus while you're still able.

CHAPTER THIRTY-SIX
FALLEN BUT FORGIVEN

don't know where your heart might be as you begin this chapter.

Maybe you feel "beaten up" spiritually, or have failed in some way, shape, or form. Perhaps you feel defeated and that when it comes to the Christian life, you're a loser.

"Why," you ask yourself, "did God even call me to begin with? If He has foreknowledge of everything that will happen, why would He pick a loser like me?"

Here is what we need to realize: God doesn't just see you in your weakness. *He sees you for what you can become.*

My little granddaughter Stella and I were hanging out recently, and she was looking at my face, peering into my eyes. Then she got really close to me, pressed her nose against my nose, and said, "Papa, I can see myself in your eyes." She could see her own reflection in my eyes.

Well, I looked into those pretty little blue-green eyes of hers and said, "Stella, you are always in my eyes and in my heart, too."

What would we see if we got really close to the Lord and looked into His eyes? Would we see ourselves? Would we say, "Lord, I can see myself in Your eyes. I can see that You love me and care about me"?

Over in Hawaii they have an expression they use if you look at someone askance or with a mean expression. They call it "stink eye." They will say, "Hey, bra. You no be giving me stink eye." Sometimes, I think we may feel that God is collectively giving stink eye to all of us.

But that isn't true.

If you look closely—and you have to be very close—you will see yourself in His eyes. God sees you for what you can become. When the psalmist David realized this truth it filled him with wonder. He wrote, "How precious it is, Lord, to realize that you are thinking about me constantly! I can't even count how many times a day your thoughts turn toward me. And when I waken in the morning, you are still thinking of me!" (Psalm 139:17-18, TLB).

Jesus looks at you and sees you for what you could be.

Remember when the Lord gave a new name to Simon? He was plain old "Simon, son of Jonas." But Jesus said to him, "You are Peter," a word that means *a rock*.

I wonder if the other disciples laughed up their sleeves a little when Jesus said that. "Simon? A rock? He's joking, isn't He? If there is anything Simon is *not*, it's a rock. He's impetuous. Impulsive. Hotheaded. Shooting off his mouth when he should keep quiet. He's not a rock!"

But that was the reflection of Simon in Jesus' eyes. The Lord saw a rock. He saw Simon for what he would become. And that is the way He sees you, too.

In the same way, we might see a lump of clay, but God sees a beautiful vase. We see a blank canvas, God sees a finished painting. We see a piece of coal, God sees a refined diamond. We see problems, God sees solutions. We see failure, God sees potential. We see a dead end, God sees a new beginning.

You might say, "Greg, you have no idea. I have a horrible failure in my past." Yet I am here to tell you that God can not only forgive you, He can also recommission you. We will see that played out beautifully in the story before us in Matthew 26.

Betrayal and Denial

We pick up the story in a moment of great intensity. We're in the Upper Room with Jesus and the disciples, and Jesus has just revealed that one of them was about to betray Him.

Have you ever heard the cliché, "You could have cut the tension with a knife"? That expression fits this moment to a T. The disciples were staggered by this revelation and couldn't seem to comprehend it. *One of them? Betray Jesus? How could it be?*

That's when Jesus turned to Judas Iscariot and said, "What you are about to do, do quickly." And Judas left the room and went out into the night. Even then, the disciples didn't make the connection. They simply couldn't conceive of their fellow disciple ever doing such a thing. After Judas left, Jesus celebrated the Last Supper with the remaining eleven. They broke the bread, and they drank the cup together.

That was when Jesus hit them with another bomb:

"All of you will be made to stumble because of Me this night, for it is written:

I will strike the Shepherd,
And the sheep of the flock will be scattered.'

But after I have been raised, I will go before you to Galilee."

Peter answered and said to Him, "Even if all are made to stumble because of You, I will never be made to stumble."

Jesus said to him, "Assuredly, I say to you that this night, before the rooster crows, you will deny Me three times."

Peter said to Him, "Even if I have to die with You, I will not deny You!"

And so said all the disciples. (Matthew 26:31-35)

Luke's version of this same story adds a detail we don't find here in Matthew. According to Luke 22:31-32, Jesus went on to say, "Simon, Simon! Indeed, Satan has asked for you, that he may sift you as wheat. But I have prayed for you, that your faith should not fail; and when you have returned to Me, strengthen your brethren."

So let's put it all together, this series of shocking pronouncements the Lord made to that little body of men that night in the Upper Room. Not only was one of their number about to betray Jesus to the authorities, they would all desert Him in the moment of crisis, leaving Him alone.

Peter, however, just wasn't buying it. He said, "Not me, Lord. These other guys, maybe. But not me. I wouldn't desert You if my life depended on it."

That's when the Lord had to give Peter a jolt of reality therapy. He looked him right in the eyes and said, "Simon, let Me say this plainly. Before the rooster crows you will deny three times that you ever knew Me. And you need to know this, too. Satan has been asking, over and over again, that you would be taken out of the care and protection of God."

Now that is a terrifying thought.

Can you imagine Jesus saying that to you? "Oh, by the way, Satan himself has been asking for you by name, so he can destroy you."

The devil is a created being and is not the equal of God. While God is all-powerful and everywhere present, Satan's knowledge is limited, and though he has many demons serving him, he can't be in more than one place at one time.

According to Matthew 26, the devil himself has to actually request to harass someone. And why would he request Peter? Perhaps because he saw Peter as a potential leader and a future threat.

God isn't the only one who recognizes leadership. Satan does, too. And the evil one often sets his sights on those he supposes to be the greatest threats to his kingdom. He isn't going to waste his energy flogging a dead horse, but he (or his demons) will harass and attack those whom God might use.

So if you have been tempted or spiritually beaten up lately, that could be very good news and an indication that God is using you. The reason the devil is after you is because he sees you as a potential threat.

But Jesus went on and told Peter, "But I have prayed for you, that your faith should not fail; and when you have returned to Me, strengthen your brethren."

In other words, "Yes, Peter, you are going to have a lapse, wander away from Me, and even deny that you know Me. But you will learn from this. And when you return to Me, you will be a better man for it, and you will be able to bring words of encouragement to others."

Crushed as he may have been to get that news, Peter should have been encouraged by one thing: Jesus specifically told him, "I am praying for you."

You know what an encouragement it is when someone you know and love says to you, "I have been praying for you night and day." How much more if that Someone is Jesus Himself?

And He is praying for you, too.

Listen to these incredible words from Romans 8:33-35 (NLT):

Who dares accuse us whom God has chosen for his own? No one—for God himself has given us right standing with himself. Who then will condemn us? No one—for Christ Jesus died for us and was raised to life for us, and he is sitting in the place of honor at God's right hand, pleading for us.

Can anything ever separate us from Christ's love? Does it mean he no longer loves us if we have trouble or calamity, or are persecuted, or hungry, or destitute, or in danger, or threatened with death?

In other words, Christ is in your corner. Jesus Himself is praying for you, pleading with His heavenly Father on your behalf. And because of that, you will never be separated from God. Were it not for the prayers of Jesus, I wouldn't stand a chance. Nor would you.

Scottish preacher Robert Murray M'Cheyne once made this statement: "If I could hear Christ praying for me in the next room I would not fear a million enemies. Yet distance makes no difference. He is praying for me."

And He was praying for Peter in those dangerous, critical moments of Peter's life.

I don't believe that anyone "suddenly" falls. I think there were distinct steps that led to this worst stumble in Peter's life.

The Anatomy of a Backslide

First step down: too much self-confidence

Again, looking at Matthew 26:33, Peter declared, "Even if all are made to stumble because of You, I will never be made to stumble."

Peter was saying, in effect, "I don't know about James and John, and I'm not sure about Matthew or Philip or all the rest of them. But I will tell You this, Lord. I will never stumble. It will never happen to me. You can take that to the bank."

Be careful of making statements like that.

Be careful of saying, "Oh, I would never do that. I'm really strong in that area. I would never commit that sin in a million years." Yet that may be the very area where you will fall.

Don't ever put confidence in yourself, in your own strength of character, in your own values system, in your own sense of dignity, in your own common sense.

That's what Peter did.

The Lord told His prophet, "The heart is hopelessly dark and deceitful, a puzzle that no one can figure out" (Jeremiah 17:9, MSG).

When you and I point an accusing finger at someone, we have three more pointing right back at us. We all have the propensity for doing great wrongs, and the moment we think we don't, we're in great peril. It's like the old hymn says: "Prone to wander, Lord, I feel it, prone to leave the God I love."

So don't put confidence in yourself. Cling to the Lord and walk in His protection. The simple fact is, an unguarded strength is a double weakness.

Second step down: neglecting to pray

A little bit further in Matthew 26, when Jesus and His men were in the Garden of Gethsemane, we read the following incident:

[Jesus] went a little farther and fell on His face, and prayed, saying, "O My Father, if it is possible, let this cup pass from Me; nevertheless, not as I will, but as You will."

Then He came to the disciples and found them sleeping, and said to Peter, "What! Could you not watch with Me one hour? Watch and pray, lest you enter into temptation. The spirit indeed is willing, but the flesh is weak." (verses 39-41)

It was surely the lowest moment of Jesus' life to that point. He was in utter anguish as He contemplated the horrors of the cross. All He wanted from His disciples in that moment was for them to be present and praying.

Instead, they were slumbering and sleeping.

This was a direct result of the first sin of self-confidence. Why? Because pride and prayerlessness go hand in hand. We must never forget that prayer is not only for petition, but also for protection and for preparation. Prayer not only gives us what we want, it prepares us and protects us from what we don't want.

Most of us pray when we are faced with a specific need. A crisis hits. We get bad news from the doctor. We're having trouble with our marriage. We just got let go from our job. The prodigal son is acting up. "Oh man," we say, "we'd better start praying. We need to bring these things to the Lord."

And that is exactly what we should do.

But what about when things are going well? We're feeling healthy, the bills are paid, the job is looking good, and there seems to be good news all around. Do we pray as much then?

Jesus said, "Watch and pray, lest you enter into temptation" (Matthew 26:41).

We need to pray for daily protection from the attacks of the evil one and all his minions.

Jesus knew very well what He was about to face: not only the physical torture of dying on a cross, but the righteous wrath of His Father as Jesus took upon Himself all of your sin, all of my sin, and all of the world's sin, past, present, and future.

He recoiled from that. Of course He did! He prayed, "Father, if it is possible, let this cup pass from Me." All He asked for was some companionship in those darkest of all moments. He didn't need a sermon, He needed some friends. But His friends had totally checked out and were fast asleep.

Their defense in one of the Gospels was that they slept from sorrow. Have you ever cried yourself to sleep, where you literally fell asleep because you were so exhausted from weeping? I've been there. I know what that is like. And these disciples just didn't know what to think. Their whole world was unraveling. There was Jesus, their Lord, sweating blood in the garden and crying out to His Father in the darkness over and over again. They didn't know how to react. They didn't know what to do. They stayed awake for a little while, but finally just fell asleep in their sorrow.

Jesus had told them to watch and pray, but instead, they slept.

In Ephesians 5:14 (NIV), the apostle Paul used sleep as a metaphor for spiritual lethargy and apathy. He wrote, "Wake up, sleeper, rise from the dead, and Christ will shine on you."

When we're really sleepy, we can act just a little bit delirious. Have you ever noticed that when someone wakes you up with a phone call, you always deny it?

It may be 3:00 a.m., and they say, "Did I wake you?"

Well, of course they did! But you answer, "Umm, no, I was awake. I'm up." Yes, you may be "up," but you're still half asleep.

Years ago I went to speak in Australia to a group of Christian broadcasters. I had decided I wanted to make it a quick trip, just jetting in and jetting out. So I told them, "I'll tell you what. I will speak on the same night that I arrive."

Normally, when I go to Australia or New Zealand I'll get there a few days ahead of time to acclimate myself to the huge time change. But this time, I decided to dispense with all that. Big mistake!

While we were driving to the venue where we were going to have the event, I was doing radio interviews in the car on the cell phone. We finally got to the venue with an hour to spare before my message, and my brain was scrambled like an omelet. I was so tired and so jetlagged that I couldn't even put a sentence together, let alone an hour-long message.

I grabbed one of my friends and said, "Okay, here is what you need to do. Go get me a triple espresso, and I'll drink it five minutes before I go out." So he brought it to me just as they told me, "You're on in five minutes."

Gulping down the coffee I walked out in front of the audience and began to speak. It was almost like having an out-of-body experience. I felt a strange sort of detachment, as if I were listening to myself speak at the same time I was speaking. But what was I saying? Between the surge of caffeine and the extreme jetlag, I couldn't be sure. It didn't seem to be making much sense.

I finally told myself, "Just read your notes, Greg. When you wrote those you were in your right mind, but right now, you're delirious."

But that's what being half asleep is like. You don't think clearly. Your thoughts are foggy. You don't make good decisions. And spiritual sleep is something we can all enter into, as the disciples did in Gethsemane. If ever those followers of Jesus needed to focus and to pray with all their hearts, it was right then.

Peter had no idea that a storm was brewing. He never realized that his whole world was going to change within just minutes. At one point he flailed around with a sword, but then he just ran away along with the rest of them.

Did you know that failure to pray can actually be a sin? Sin isn't just about breaking commandments, though that's one type of sin. There are also sins of *omission*. In James 4:17 we read, "To him who knows to do good and does not do it, to him it is sin." And what does the Bible say about prayer?

Men always ought to pray and not lose heart. (Luke 18:1)

Pray continually, give thanks in all circumstances; for this is God's will for you in Christ Jesus. (1 Thessalonians 5:17-18, NIV)

So Peter was self-confident and neglected to pray.

Third step down: trusting human effort instead of God's power

Matthew 26:51 says, "Suddenly, one of those who were with Jesus stretched out his hand and drew his sword, struck the servant of the high priest, and cut off his ear." The one with the sword was Peter, of course.

Matthew goes on to record Jesus' response:

Jesus said to him, "Put your sword in its place, for all who take the sword will perish by the sword. Or do you think that I cannot now pray to My Father, and He will provide Me with more than twelve legions of angels?" (verses 52-53)

Poor Peter got everything turned around. He was boasting when he should have been listening. Sleeping when he should have been praying. Now he was fighting when he should have been surrendering.

Fourth step down: following at a distance

Verse 58 tells us, "Peter followed Him at a distance to the high priest's courtyard. And he went in and sat with the servants to see the end."

Distance from closeness and fellowship with the Lord is at the heart of every person's fall.

We could illustrate with a marriage that's falling apart. People will cite all the usual reasons: money problems, child problems, arguments, sexual intimacy, and on and on.

Yes, those are important elements in a happy marriage. But those aren't the places where the marriage broke down. It broke down in *communication*. Something happened to the friendship and companionship on which the marriage was built. The closeness and warmth turned cool, and, as a result, all of those other "issues" found their way into an already fractured marriage.

The same is true of our relationship with God. Our communication with Him breaks down. It's not that He ceases communicating with us, it's because we stop listening to Him. We get too busy to open the day with Bible study and prayer. We allow unconfessed sins to linger. We actually begin closing our ears to the voice of the Holy Spirit. Then, before we know it, we find ourselves following at a distance.

That is what happened to Peter.

I heard the story of a little boy who fell out of bed in the middle of the night. When his mom asked him what happened, he replied, "I think I stayed too close to the place where I got in."

That is why we fall away. We try to walk the edge between our new life and our old life; we stay "too close to the place where we got in." In Peter's case, look where he ended up. At the enemy's fire.

Fifth step down: standing at the enemy's fire

Now Peter sat outside in the courtyard. And a servant girl came to him, saying, "You also were with Jesus of Galilee."

But he denied it before them all, saying, "I do not know what you are saying."

And when he had gone out to the gateway, another girl saw him and said to those who were there, "This fellow also was with Jesus of Nazareth."

But again he denied with an oath, "I do not know the Man!"

And a little later those who stood by came up and said to Peter, "Surely you also are one of them, for your speech betrays you."

Then he began to curse and swear, saying, "I do not know the Man!"

Immediately a rooster crowed. And Peter remembered the word of Jesus who had said to him, "Before the rooster crows, you will deny Me three times." So he went out and wept bitterly. (Matthew 26:69-75)

Peter was trying to go undercover, keeping tabs on events without really committing himself one way or another. He thought he could just blend into the woodwork. Have you ever tried to be an undercover Christian? I heard a story about a man who only went to church on Christmas and Easter. So after the service one Christmas the pastor stopped him at the door and said, "My friend, I only see you like twice a year. You need to join the Lord's army." At that, the man whispered into the pastor's ear, "I'm in the secret service."

Is that you? Are you a secret service Christian?

Following at a distance, Peter had become cold and was attracted to the warmth of a fire in the high priest's courtyard.

The enemy's fire.

At this point, Peter was worn down, defeated, weak, and vulnerable. Yes he was following Jesus, but at a distance.

Why was he even there? Matthew gives the answer in verse 58: "He went in and sat with the servants to see the end."

How sad. Peter had evidently forgotten all Jesus had said about rising from the dead. Now he was just waiting for the end: the end of Jesus' life, the end of his hopes and dreams, the end of everything he held dear.

But it wasn't the end at all. It was very, very near to a new beginning.

Here was Peter's problem: He was in the wrong place with the wrong people about to do the wrong thing. That's what happens when we fall into sin: We're in the wrong places hanging out with the wrong crowd. Before we know it, we're swept along and begin doing the wrong thing.

Some girl says, "Oh man, I really made a big mistake. My boyfriend and I had sex. How did this happen to us?"

"Where did this happen?"

"In a hotel room."

"How did you happen to be in a hotel room with your boyfriend?"

"Well, we just went and booked it. And then, well, we were tempted."

"No, you had already given in to temptation by being in the wrong place with the wrong person at the wrong time for the wrong reasons. What happened after that was just an expected outcome."

Or maybe a man with a drinking problem is crestfallen because he's gone back to the bottle. "I fell off the wagon," he says so mournfully. "I have been clean and sober for almost a year and then I went out and got totally drunk. How could this happen?"

"So where were you?"

"In a bar."

"Why in the world were you in a bar?"

"They've got all those huge TVs, and I wanted to watch the game."

Seriously?

It really isn't rocket science. When you hang out with the wrong people at the wrong place at the wrong time, it's only a matter of time until you do the wrong thing.

Psalm 1 says it so well:

Blessed is the man
Who walks not in the counsel of the ungodly,
Nor stands in the path of sinners,
Nor sits in the seat of the scornful;
But his delight is in the law of the LORD,
And in His law he meditates day and night. (verses 1-2)

What a picture of backsliding! Have you ever noticed the regression in these verses? In verse 1 the man is *walking* in the counsel of the ungodly. Then he is *standing* in the path of sinners. Finally, he is *sitting* in the seat of the scornful.

The fact is, if he had refused to walk anywhere near the counsel of the ungodly, he would have never found himself standing in the path of sinners, or finally, sitting around with those who were utterly scornful of God and His people.

It's like telling yourself one night that you have to lose weight. The next morning, something tells you it would be a good idea to take a different route to work, avoiding going past the Krispy Kreme doughnut shop.

But then you say to yourself, "That's ridiculous. What could it hurt to walk by the place? I don't have to go in."

So you walk by, and the scent of freshly baked doughnuts (is there any sweeter fragrance than that?) wafts under your nose. You glance at the store and see the open sign on. Then you look through the window and happen to see those beautiful glazed doughnuts coming down the little conveyor belt, glistening in the light. You were walking, then you were standing with your face pressed up against the glass, looking and salivating. And the next thing you know you're sitting inside with a doughnut in each hand. That's how it always happens.

The fire wasn't Peter's problem, it was the people around that fire and the subsequent conversation that got him into trouble. So it is with us. When the passion and fire we had for Jesus begins to tail off and grow cold, we begin to look elsewhere for warmth.

That brings us to the final step down for the apostle.

Sixth step down: the denial

Luke's gospel reveals that there was plenty of time between each of Peter's three denials. First some girl said, "Hey, wait a second. I know you. You're one of those followers of Jesus!"

Peter, still in his undercover mode, tried to brush her off. "No. You got the wrong guy. Not me." Another one said, "I know you. You were with Jesus of Nazareth. Right? Come on! You were one of them." Peter got more gruff. "No. It's not me. You've got the wrong guy. *I don't even know this Jesus.*"

Why didn't he just leave? Why didn't he walk away from that fire at the very first challenge? He wouldn't have had to say a word.

We could ask ourselves the same question, couldn't we?

The last time you were tempted, why didn't you just get up and leave? Why didn't you walk out of the theater when that scene came on the screen? You knew you shouldn't have gone to that movie in the first place. And then there it is, right in your face. Why didn't you walk out the door?

Or maybe it was a time when you were in a group of people and somebody started making fun of the Christian faith and even mocking God. Why didn't you speak up?

Sometimes it's not so easy to "just walk away." You just get worn down and you stop fighting. That's where Peter was. He was worn down, emotionally exhausted, and spiritually numb. He allowed himself to become weak and *vulnerable to the attack from Satan he knew was coming.* As a result, he got caught in a miserable web of cowardice and compromise.

Even after he had denied the Lord twice, there was still time for Peter to get out of there. So why did he stay at the fire? It might have been cold, but it wasn't *that* cold.

Nevertheless, in Matthew 26:73 we read, "And a little later those who stood by came up and said to Peter, 'Surely you also are one of them, for your speech betrays you.'"

What does that mean? For one thing, it meant that Peter had been talking with people around the fire. And at least one person had picked up on the fact that he had a Galilean accent.

Busted! At that moment, he could have come clean and said, "Okay, you're right. I am a Galilean, and I am a disciple of that innocent Man being unfairly tried in that house right there."

Instead, he dug himself in deeper. Verse 74 says, "Then he began to curse and swear, saying, 'I do not know the Man!' Immediately a rooster crowed."

This doesn't mean that Peter swore like a sailor, even though he was one. The word *cursed* here is a strong term that means you pronounce death on yourself at the hand of God if you are lying. It's the worst case of taking the Lord's name in vain imaginable. Peter was in essence saying, "May God kill and damn me if I'm not speaking the truth." Or to state it another way, "I swear to God. I take an oath I don't know Jesus."

And then the rooster crowed. Luke adds the heartbreaking detail that in that moment "the Lord turned and looked straight at Peter. Then Peter remembered the word the Lord had spoken to him: 'Before the rooster crows today, you will disown me three times.' And he went outside and wept bitterly" (Luke 22:61-62, NIV).

What was in that look? Hurt? Reproach? Was the Lord giving Peter a stink eye?

We don't know, of course. But I think that if Peter could have managed to get very, very close to Jesus in that moment, he would have seen himself in Jesus' eyes, just like little Stella could see herself in my eyes.

He would have seen that Jesus loved him. He would have remembered that Jesus had predicted this very specifically, but He had also predicted Peter's strong return and restoration. "When you have returned to Me, strengthen your brethren."

As Peter thought about it, he would have remembered Jesus' words. He would have recalled how the Lord said to him, "Peter, you're going to fail badly. But then you're going to repent and turn back to Me. And when you do, you'll be a better man for it. You will learn from your mistakes, and you will help many people turn to Me for salvation."

The repentance began as Peter finally left the fire of his enemies and went out and wept bitterly for his sin.

Three days later, Jesus rose from the dead, and the angels gave Mary a very specific message to deliver to the apostles. And what was that message? "Go, tell his disciples and Peter, 'He is going ahead of you into Galilee. There you will see him, just as he told you'" (Mark 16:7, NIV).

You have to love that! The angels didn't say, "Go tell the disciples and James and John." Nor did they say, "Go tell the disciples and Mary, Jesus' mother." No, it was go tell the disciples and *Peter*.

Why Peter?

Because Peter desperately needed some encouragement.

As far as he was concerned, life was pretty much over for him. He had failed his Lord at the most crucial moment, after bragging in front of everyone about how brave and loyal and fearless he would be. He had denied his Lord in his Lord's own hearing, swearing that he didn't even know anyone named Jesus. So how could he go on pretending he was a follower? There was no hope or future for him.

And yet through that message, Jesus was saying, "I remember you, Peter, and I want you to know I am risen."

Peter had backslidden and done things and said things he was ashamed of. But Jesus was calling him back. Jesus wanted to forgive him, restore him, and fill his life with hope and purpose once again.

I saw a commercial on TV a few years ago for a little device that senior citizens can wear around their necks. If they fall, they can push a button on the electronic pendant and it will call emergency medical help. In the commercial, the elderly person who has fallen is shouting into the pendant: "I've fallen and I can't get up."

That's the way Peter probably felt. And perhaps that's the way you feel, too. You know you're far away from the Lord, but the road back seems difficult or even impossible to you.

But it's not.

Just change your mind about the direction you've been heading and turn toward Jesus, calling on Him to rescue you, forgive you, and restore you.

You don't even have to push a button. Just speak His name.

CHAPTER THIRTY-SEVEN
INDECISION

In a rare moment of personal reflection, songwriter Jimmy Buffet once stated, "Indecision may or may not be my problem."

Make up your mind, Jimmy!

For the most part, I think of myself as a decisive person. I generally know what I want to do, where I want to go, and what I want to say. It's not that difficult for me to make up my mind and just go with it.

When Cathe and I go out to eat at one of our favorite restaurants, I don't even need a menu. I already know what I want when I walk in the door. I'm usually hungry, so I just want to sit down, order the food, and get things moving along.

But then Cathe says to the server, "I'd like to see a menu, please."

A menu?

"Why do you want to look at the menu?" I ask her. "You order the same thing every time."

"Yes," she says, "but I'd still like to look at the menu."

When the server comes back, she asks a dozen questions—all the details about this dish or that dish. And then she orders what she always orders.

I don't really understand it. It's evidently a ritual she feels she needs to go through. I just want to order the food, because I've known what I wanted since we left the house.

Even so, ordering from a menu isn't what you'd call a life-altering decision. We make many other decisions and choices, however, that are truly weighty, and we want to be very sure about our direction before we make them.

Deciding whom you will marry, for instance, is a decision that could shape your destiny and literally impact generations to come. It's never something to take casually or rush into. Someone has wisely said, "Keep your eyes wide open before marriage and half shut thereafter." Too many couples, however, do the opposite. They go into marriage with their eyes half shut, and then somewhere down the road find themselves in an eye-opening moment when they say, "Oh no. What have I done?"

The most important decision we will ever make is what we will do with Jesus Christ. That's a question that will not only touch every part of our lives, it will also determine our eternal destiny.

In this chapter, we will consider an indecisive man who ended up letting others do his thinking for him. He was a man who tried to appease a fickle, bloodthirsty mob and then somehow reconcile that decision with his own troubled conscience.

His name was Pontius Pilate, the Roman governor of Judea.

Decision Time

Back in those days, they didn't elect their governors as we do. Governors were appointed by Rome, and the position was a very important one.

In the account we'll be considering in this chapter, Pilate found himself in Jerusalem at a critical time. Normally, he would have been relaxing in his beautiful palace in Caesarea, on the Mediterranean coast. But on this occasion his duties required him to be in Jerusalem at a time when thousands of Jewish pilgrims filled the city for Passover. During his time there, the well-ordered life of the Roman governor collided with the radically righteous life of Jesus Christ.

Once that happened, there was no escaping the situation in which Pilate found himself. He tried everything he could to get out of or get around the circumstances, but nothing worked.

Pilate had to make up his mind about Jesus of Nazareth.

The last thing the Roman governor wanted at that moment was some kind of conflict with the Jews. He'd had a number of run-ins already with the people, and he certainly didn't need to have negative reports getting back to Caesar in Rome.

History tells us Pilate was a brutal man and an anti-Semite; he hated the Jewish people under his supervision. Nevertheless, he'd been appointed governor of Judea and had to somehow make the best of it.

In a well-preserved document from that era—a letter from Herod Agrippa to Caligula, the Roman emperor—Agrippa described the governor in unflattering terms: "Pilate is unbending and recklessly hard. He is a man of notorious reputation, severe brutality, prejudice, savage violence, and murder."

If even hard cases like Agrippa and Caligula thought Pilate was over-the-top ruthless, he must have been a cruel man indeed. That's one reason why the otherwise unbending, prejudiced Pilate appears to have been so indecisive in this account. Normally he was a guy who could dish out death penalties with ease. "Okay, you're going to get executed. Now, get out of my court. Next!"

But when Pilate was confronted with Jesus, he found himself strangely torn. For political reasons, he didn't want to offend the religious leaders who had hauled Jesus into his court. But on the other hand, he *knew*—way down in his heart of hearts—that Jesus was an innocent man who didn't deserve to die.

There were, of course, other forces at play in this story. God Himself was involved in these events, as were Satan and the powers of darkness. And while the objectives of God and the devil were not the same, their desired outcome was the same: the death of Jesus Christ on a Roman cross. Satan wanted to stop and silence Jesus; God the Father wanted Jesus to die in our place, absorb the wrath of God for us, and allow us to be forgiven of our sins. So both heaven and hell were bending events toward Calvary, and Pilate was caught at the crossroads.

Even so, Pilate had a choice in the matter, and we can't let him off the hook for what he did. As with Judas Iscariot, he became a willing accomplice in the devil's plan. He was about to find out that everybody has to make a decision about Jesus Christ.

Some people have a difficult time deciding what they want to do. I remember hearing about the man back in the days of the Civil War who couldn't make up his mind whether to fight for the North or the South. He finally chose to wear the coat of the North and the trousers of the South. When he stepped onto the battlefield, both sides shot at him.

That's pretty much what happened to Pilate. What was he going to do with Jesus Christ? He had to decide, even though he didn't want to decide. Nevertheless, it's a question every one of us must face. It's not so much the *sin* question as much as it is the *Son* question. We will have to give an account of what we decide about Jesus Christ.

Sometimes we call this event in Scripture "Jesus before Pilate." But we could just as easily call it "Pilate before Jesus." Which man was really in the place of judgment? Pilate may have thought he was giving a ruling determining Jesus' fate, but in another sense he was about to decide his own eternal destiny, based on what he would do with Jesus.

The Horns of a Dilemma

Pilate found himself on the proverbial horns of a dilemma—never a very comfortable place to be.

The Jewish leadership had cross-examined Jesus, deciding He had to die because He'd claimed to be the Messiah. They had also managed to win over many in the large, teeming crowd of Jewish pilgrims, persuading them to also cry out for Jesus' blood.

They sent Him to Pontius Pilate, placing the governor in a quandary. If he didn't go along with the Jewish leaders, they could incite the crowds to riot—and Rome wouldn't like that at all. But on the other hand, he immediately recognized that Jesus was completely innocent of the charges they had made.

Pilate might have wished he was back in Caesarea, on a terrace, in a hammock, sipping a lemonade. But wishing wouldn't do any good.

He had to make a decision.

Now Jesus stood before the governor. And the governor asked Him, saying, "Are You the King of the Jews?"

Jesus said to him, "It is as you say." And while He was being accused by the chief priests and elders, He answered nothing.

Then Pilate said to Him, "Do You not hear how many things
they testify against You?" But He answered him not one word,
so that the governor marveled greatly. (Matthew 27:11-14)

The gospel of John fills in some key gaps in Matthew's account. The Jewish leaders didn't want to execute Jesus themselves, and Pilate didn't want to have to deal with the situation at all. "Judge Him according to your law," he told them. In other words, he was effectively saying, "You want to execute Jesus? So execute Him. Don't bother me with this. I don't want to deal with this. Take this out of my courtroom."

"Oh no," they reminded him. "We're not allowed to put people to death."

But that really wasn't true, as in the case of Stephen in the book of Acts, whom they stoned to death. This time, however, they wanted Pilate to do their dirty work for them, so they demanded a Roman execution.

What they didn't realize, of course, was that their actions would bring about the fulfillment of Bible prophecy. The Scriptures not only say the Messiah would die but also specified how He would die, painting a very clear picture of crucifixion—hundreds of years before that horrific means of execution had even been dreamed up by evil minds.

Passages in the Old Testament give graphic details of what would happen to the Messiah, including these verses in Psalm 22:

They pierced My hands and My feet;
I can count all My bones.
They look and stare at Me.
They divide My garments among them,
And for My clothing they cast lots.
(verses 16-18)

Fulfilling prophecy, however, was the furthest thing from the Jewish leaders' minds. They just wanted Jesus dead and out of the way, and they wanted Pilate to do it.

Pilate didn't want any part of it. But there was Jesus, beaten and bloodied, standing before him, so what could he do?

In verse 11, Pilate asked him, "Are You the King of the Jews?"

Did he ask it sarcastically or with sincerity? We don't really know.

Jesus answered, "It is as you say."

In his years as governor, Pilate thought he had seen everything. All criminal penalties in Judea were subject to his ultimate approval or veto, either directly or indirectly through courts that operated under his oversight. He had presided over hundreds, perhaps even thousands, of criminal proceedings. And usually at this point when someone was brought before him, the person was either protesting his innocence or groveling on the tiles, pleading for mercy.

Jesus was doing neither.

Pilate had never seen anyone like Jesus.

This reminds me of a story I read about Frederick the Great, King of Prussia, who was visiting one of his country's prisons. As the king spoke with each of the inmates, he heard endless tales of innocence, misunderstood motives, and exploitation. Finally, the king stopped at the cell of a convict who remained silent.

"Well," said the king, "I suppose you are innocent, too."

"Oh, no sir," the man replied. "I am guilty of the crime that I committed, and I deserve the punishment they're going to give me." Hearing that, the king said to the warden, "Quick, release this rascal before he corrupts all of these fine innocent people in here!"

It's pretty rare for someone to simply admit to wrongdoing. Most people insist on their innocence or describe all the extenuating circumstances. Police officers hear this all the time: "I didn't do it, officer. I swear, I'm innocent."

That was what Pilate had been expecting. But that's not what he heard from this quiet Man standing before him. He didn't say He was innocent and He didn't admit to being guilty. He just stood there serenely, regally, calmly, and faced the situation head on. That really bothered Pilate, because he'd never seen anything like it. The more he saw of Jesus, the less he wanted to condemn Him.

"I Don't Want to Talk About It"

Again, this wasn't Jesus before Pilate; it was Pilate before Jesus. In that moment, Pilate didn't know what the outcome would be, but Jesus knew the outcome very well.

According to John's gospel, the Lord at this point said to Pilate, "You say rightly that I am a king. For this cause I was born, and for this cause I have come into the world, that I should bear witness to the truth. Everyone who is of the truth hears My voice" (John 18:37).

The governor replied, "What is truth?" (verse 38).

Pilate was your classic pagan, with no core beliefs beyond that of self-preservation. His descendants today would be moral relativists or post-modernists, those who believe that all truth is relative, and up to the individual. You've no doubt heard people express that view, saying things like, "Your truth may not be my truth." It's a shocking statistic, but a recent poll in our country revealed that 67 percent of Americans do not believe in absolute truth.

Pilate, however, wasn't just facing an opinion or a philosophy about truth; he was in the presence of Truth incarnate. In John 14:6, Jesus said, "I am the way, the truth, and the life."

To Pilate He said, "Everyone who is of the truth hears My voice" (John 18:37).

In other words, "You want to know truth, Pilate. Well, you're looking at it. *I am Truth.*"

If only this tired, cynical man could have opened his eyes and opened his heart for a moment. Pilate could have asked Him any question and received an answer. Pilate could have brought any need, any burden, before Jesus and He could have resolved it. If Pilate had repented of his sin, Jesus could have forgiven him then and there. He could have made Pontius Pilate brand new.

What an opportunity! What a lost opportunity.

Pilate could have found everlasting life in that moment. And a million years from that tense day in Jerusalem, if he had given his heart to Christ, he might have been looking back on that encounter with overwhelming joy.

But he couldn't be bothered. He just wanted out of the situation.

Pilate did what many do when confronted with the gospel: They change the subject. They say, "I don't want to hear about it." It's as though they put their fingers in their ears and start yelling, "La-la-la-la. I can't hear you."

Writing these words, I can't help but think of my mom. Though she had been raised in a Christian home, she rebelled against the Lord for most of her life. Whenever I would try to bring up the topic of my faith in Christ, her default response would be, "I don't want to talk about it." Whenever we edged closer to any kind of a serious discussion about the meaning of life, the afterlife, or God, she would say again, "I don't want to talk about it."

One day when she was very ill, just a month before she died, I felt strongly impressed to go to my mother and have a conversation with her.

I remember telling Cathe, "I have to go see my mom today."

"I'll be praying for you," she said.

So I went over, walked into her room, and sat down. I looked at her and said, "Mom, I want to talk to you about your soul. I want to talk to you about the meaning of life and what happens after we die."

Mom said, "I don't want to talk about it."

But this time I said to her, "Today, we *are* going to talk about it."

And we talked. As a result of our conversation that day, my mom made a recommitment of her life to the Lord and went into His presence just a month later. I'm so glad we had that conversation, even though it wasn't an easy one to have.

Mom at that time was married to a man named Bill. Bill had told me he had a belief in Christ, but I never saw any real evidence of it in his life. One day I was getting ready to leave on a ministry trip and got word that Bill was very ill and wanted to see me.

I remember thinking, *I really don't have time for this. I have to pack. I've got a plane to catch. I just can't do it today. I'll go see him tomorrow.*

But then I felt really impressed by the Lord: "You go see him right now." So I went over to where he was staying and sat down at his bedside. He was very, very ill. We had a very candid discussion, and I once again presented the gospel to him. Bill responded that he wanted to put his faith in Christ. We prayed together, and he committed his life to Jesus.

Driving back home I thought, *Thank God I did that. Thank God I went ahead and had that meeting with him.* I still managed to catch my plane, and when I landed at my destination, I had a text that Bill had just died.

As with the conversation with my mom, it hadn't been easy or convenient for me to talk to Bill that day. But I am so glad I responded to the Lord and went to Bill's bedside with the gospel.

I know it's often hard, awkward, and uncomfortable to have these sorts of conversations with people who need the Lord. It's especially difficult to broach these subjects with family members. But difficult or not, we have to step into the gap when the Lord prompts us to speak. It isn't our job to convert anyone; that's God's job. Our job is to simply present the gospel. Someday, we may end up being very happy we swallowed our discomfort and took the plunge.

Pilate's Brief Reprieve

Pilate wanted off the hot seat but didn't know what to do. He didn't want to condemn an innocent man, but he also had his career to think about. He'd had a taste of power and didn't want to let go of it. Even so, he kept on telling himself, *There just has to be a way out of this.*

Luke's gospel tells us at this point Pilate said, "I find no basis for a charge against this man" (Luke 23:4, NIV). The Jewish leaders, however, kept insisting, "He stirs up the people all over Judea by his teaching. He started in Galilee and has come all the way here" (verse 5, NIV).

Galilee?

When Pilate heard that word, his eyes must have lit up. He must have thought, *Maybe there is a way out. The gods are smiling on me today. Galilee isn't my jurisdiction. That's the jurisdiction of Herod. I'll just send them to Herod, get them out of my court, and pack my bags for Caesarea.*

Pilate no doubt congratulated himself as they left the hall. "That was a brilliant move, Pontius. Now Jesus is Herod's problem. And anyway, I hate Herod, so it serves him right."

Luke told us that Herod was excited at the opportunity to see Jesus. He'd heard about Him and had been hoping for a long time to see Him perform a miracle.

When Jesus was brought into Herod's presence, however, He didn't say one word to him. Though Herod peppered Jesus with questions, the Lord wouldn't speak to this evil puppet king at all.

In all the New Testament narrative, Herod is the one man to whom Jesus had nothing to say. Throughout His years of ministry, Jesus had had a great deal to say to all manner of people, young and old, rich and poor, male and female, devout people and sinners. He had spoken to the woman caught in adultery, to the rich young ruler, and to Nicodemus who came by night. He even stopped under a sycamore tree to talk to Zacchaeus the tax collector, who was sitting up in the branches to get a better view of the Lord.

Jesus even had words for Pontius Pilate. But with Herod He didn't speak a single word. Why? Because Herod's heart was irreparably hardened. Herod was responsible for the death of John the Baptist, and his father was the Herod who tried to have the child Jesus executed, murdering all of those baby boys in Bethlehem in the process. This was a wicked dynasty.

Besides that, Herod just wanted Jesus to do a trick, as if Jesus were some type of court jester. He wanted Him to give a little entertainment. But Jesus was unwilling to do any such thing. So Herod mocked and ridiculed Him, clothing Him in a royal robe and sending Him back.

Back to Pilate!

And there He was, standing before the governor again. Pilate wasn't off the hook after all, reminding us that there is no escaping Jesus, and no escaping making a decision about Him.

The governor, however, had one more trick up his sleeve.

One Last Try

Now at the feast the governor was accustomed to releasing to the multitude one prisoner whom they wished. And at that time they had a notorious prisoner called Barabbas. Therefore, when they had gathered together, Pilate said to them, "Whom do you want me to release to you? Barabbas, or Jesus who is called Christ?" For he knew that they had handed Him over because of envy. (Matthew 27:15-18)

Pilate may have reasoned to himself something like this: "Maybe there's a way out of this yet! The Jews have this custom of having a prisoner released during Passover. We've got this guy Barabbas, who's a notorious criminal—an insurrectionist, a terrorist—and doesn't have a friend in the world. I'll put this lowlife alongside Jesus, the miracle worker, the One who raises the dead and feeds multitudes. Surely they will choose Jesus over Barabbas!"

But they didn't.

The crowds picked Barabbas for rescue rather than Jesus, and Pilate was still facing the greatest dilemma of his life. Then, to make matters worse, he got a note from his wife. We read in verse 19, "While he was sitting on the judgment seat, his wife sent to him, saying, 'Have nothing to do with that just Man, for I have suffered many things today in a dream because of Him.'"

Can't you just see the governor rolling his eyes when he read that message from Mrs. Pilate? The fact is, we don't know what happened in her dream, or how she happened to suffer many things because of Christ. Had she come face to face with her own sin? Had the Lord revealed to her the enormity of what her governor-husband was about to do? We don't know. But we do know this: Instead of having nothing to do with Jesus, they should have had everything to do with Jesus. Because He would have forgiven them; changed their bored, empty lives; and given them something to live for.

But sadly, once again, the opportunity was lost, as Pilate continued to dither.

He knew Jesus was innocent. He knew He was a "just Man," as his wife had just told him. He knew he should let Jesus go. But he was afraid of the repercussions and afraid of losing his political base.

As a result, he was about to make a decision based on his fear rather than on his convictions. And that sort of decision is wrong from the get-go.

Many times men are defined by what they do in their career. Pilate had worked hard to worm his way through all the layers of Roman politics to get where he was, and he didn't want to lose his position.

So the people said they wanted Barabbas, and Pilate didn't know what to do.

Pilate said to them, "What then shall I do with Jesus who is called Christ?"

They all said to him, "Let Him be crucified!"

Then the governor said, "Why, what evil has He done?"

But they cried out all the more, saying, "Let Him be crucified!"
(verses 22-23)

Even to a man who had seen all the cruelties and injustices that Pilate had seen, this event must have still been shocking to him. Blood chilling. They wanted Jesus put to death, a Man who had lived a good life and helped so many people.

Wasn't it just hours ago that Jesus had ridden into town on a donkey and people had cut down palm branches to spread in the street before Him? Hadn't they cried out, "Hosanna! Hosanna to the Son of David"?

Maybe. But that was then and this was now. Jesus was good to have around if you were hungry or bored or needed a miracle. But after He had served their purposes, they couldn't have cared less about Him.

So now what was Pilate going to do? The answer is in verses 24-25:

When Pilate saw that he could not prevail at all, but rather that a tumult was rising, he took water and washed his hands before the multitude, saying, "I am innocent of the blood of this just Person. You see to it."

And all the people answered and said, "His blood be on us and on our children."

This is typical of so many people today. They want to put off what they don't want to deal with. But the one thing we cannot put off is Jesus Christ.

Someone might protest, "Wasn't Pilate in effect being used by God? Didn't Pilate bring about God's purposes by sending Jesus to the cross?"

Yes, he did. But that doesn't excuse his actions any more than it excused the actions of Judas Iscariot. Pilate heartlessly had Jesus scourged, beaten, and tortured. He listened to the wrong voices, made the wrong decision, and hardened his heart against God.

Sometime later, in the book of Acts, the young church of Jesus Christ raised their voices to God and prayed: "This has happened here in this very city [Jerusalem]! For Herod Antipas, Pontius Pilate the governor, the Gentiles, and the people of Israel were all united against Jesus, your holy servant, whom you anointed" (4:27, NLT).

This Scripture clearly points out that Pilate was responsible for what he did.

So what happened to Pontius Pilate? History tells us that seven years after this cruel, self-serving decision, Pilate was banished to Gaul by the emperor Caligula. Gaul was a distant region to the northwest of Italy beyond the Alps. In that place, the historical records say, he suffered what appears to have been a mental breakdown. And one night Pilate went out into the darkness and hanged himself, just as Judas Iscariot had done.

What a tragic waste of life. He threw his life away because he was more concerned about what others thought about him than what God thought about him. His craving for popularity and power ended up costing him everything.

The saddest fact of all was that for those minutes or hours, however long it was, Pilate had Jesus right in front of him! He was so close to the Truth, the very embodiment of Truth, that he could have reached out and touched Him! He could have believed in Jesus and instantly been forgiven of his sin, just as the thief next to Jesus on an adjacent cross did.

Pilate, however, did what people do every day: He rejected Christ. And why do people do it? There are no good reasons, there are only excuses. For some it may be a concern over their career or the cares of this life. In His parable about the seed and the soils, Jesus talked about seed sown on ground infested with weeds and how those weeds choked the growth of the young plants. He said, "Still others, like seed sown among thorns, hear the word; but the worries of this life, the deceitfulness of wealth and the desires for other things come in and choke the word, making it unfruitful" (Mark 4:18-19, NIV).

If you've ever planted a flower and watched weeds grow around it, you know that the weeds don't suddenly lunge out of the ground and start violently strangling the flower. It's a gradual process—so gradual you wouldn't even be able to see it if you were watching. But if you set up a camera and did time-lapse photography, you would see the weed wrap its vines around the flower and strangle it.

That's how it works in our lives as well. We might say, "I'm not really rejecting the Lord. It's just that I have a full plate right now. I have a mortgage payment, responsibilities, and a living to earn. I'm just too busy to think about it today."

The more we prioritize money, position, fame, and career, however, the less we will be able to make truly wise decisions. Anything that becomes more important than God to us can end up choking the life out of us. For the sake of a lucrative career, some men and women will cast aside their integrity and even their friends and family. They will give up everything to obtain and hold on to a certain position or status in life.

And in the end, what do they have? A handful of ashes.

That was Pilate. It was more important for him to be in power than anything else. Even more important than God.

Others will choose people or certain relationships over Jesus. Peer pressure doesn't end with high school! We still care about what people think, and we want people to like us and approve of us. I have seen people make the worst compromises imaginable simply out of fear of "what other people might think about me."

That was in Pilate's mind, too. He cared about what the crowd thought, what the religious rulers thought, and what Rome thought.

He should have been more concerned about what Jesus thought.

The fact is, if you give up a position or some friends or certain pleasures for the sake of Jesus Christ and out of love for Him, God will more than make it up to you in this life and in the life to come.

Peter once said to Jesus, "We've given up everything to follow you. What will we get?"

Jesus replied, "I assure you that when the world is made new and the Son of Man sits upon his glorious throne, you who have been my followers will also sit on twelve thrones, judging the twelve tribes of Israel. And everyone who has given up houses or brothers or sisters or father or mother or children or property, for my sake, will receive a hundred times as much in return and will inherit eternal life. But many who are the greatest now will be the least important then, and those who seem least important now will be the greatest then." (Matthew 19:27-30, NLT)

You might say, "Okay, Greg, I've given up some things to follow Jesus. Where are the hundreds of houses He promised?"

Whatever you may have given up to follow the Lord, hasn't God made it up to you? Yes, you may have had to let go of a few friends. But hasn't He given you better Christian friends in their place? You've had to let go of a handful of so-called pleasures. But in retrospect, you can see they weren't really pleasures at all but rather destructive addictions.

Reflecting on my own life, I'd rather have one day of walking with Jesus than a thousand days doing what I used to do to try to find fun and fulfillment. As the psalmist said, "A single day in your courts is better than a thousand anywhere else!" (Psalm 84:10, NLT).

But this life is only a microscopic fraction of the whole story. The best is yet to come! In heaven, those who have faithfully followed the Lord Jesus on earth will receive rewards beyond imagination. Ultimately, we will rule and reign with Him on a new earth.

If Pilate had only known. He thought being a Roman governor over the troubled province of Judea for a few years was such a big deal that he had to hold on to it at all costs. But if he had decided to follow Jesus instead of condemning Him, he would have received more than he ever dreamed. In fact, he would be walking with God in heaven at this very moment.

Pilate couldn't make up his mind what to do with Jesus, and as he dithered and procrastinated, heaven slipped through his fingers.

What you and I decide to do with Jesus in this life will determine what He will say to us in the next one.

You will either hear Him say, "Welcome home, child. Enter into life," or you will hear Him say, "Depart from me. I never knew you."

Pilate missed his chance for eternal joy.

But you don't have to.

CHAPTER THIRTY-EIGHT
WHY DID JESUS HAVE TO DIE?

hy did our Lord come to this earth? Why was He born in a manger in Bethlehem? Why did Jesus walk this planet, breathe our air, tread our dusty back roads, and experience life here?

Some would say, "He came to earth to become the greatest Teacher in history." There's no question that Jesus was the greatest Teacher who ever lived. The words He spoke and the stories He told are repeated in every corner of our world, even after two thousand years. But that's not the primary reason He came.

Others would say, "He came to give us an example of how to live life at its highest level." It's true, Jesus certainly was the ultimate example of life at its highest and best. But that is not the primary reason He came.

Someone else might say, "He came to do miracles and heal people." Yes, He did that, touching many, many lives. But again, that is not the primary reason He came.

Jesus came to buy back the title deed of the earth. He came to die on a cross for our sins. The Bible says in Hebrews 2:9, "that He, by the grace of God, might taste death for everyone." As our Lord Himself said, He came "to give his life as a ransom for many" (Mark 10:45, NIV). That word *ransom* conveys the idea of offering oneself in the place of another. Stating it another way, we could say Jesus was born to die that we might live.

The birth of Jesus was for the purpose of the death of Jesus.

One of the wise men had it right when he brought the insightful gift of myrrh to the Christ child. Myrrh is an embalming element. That is why Jesus came. The cross was Jesus' goal and destination from the very beginning. He warned His disciples it was coming, and He described it in detail. Somehow, that whole discussion sailed right over their heads, until it actually happened.

The Day Jesus Died

On the night before He died, in an olive grove in the Garden of Gethsemane, Jesus came under intense, indescribable inner pressure. I don't think any of us can begin to grasp what our Lord endured in those dark hours. Dr. Luke told us that "His sweat became like great drops of blood falling down to the ground" (Luke 22:44).

Some medical experts have suggested that this may have been hematidrosis, a condition characterized by a unique mixture of sweat and blood when someone comes under the greatest imaginable stress.

Entering the garden that night, Jesus said to His three closest disciples, "My soul is exceedingly sorrowful, even to death. Stay here and watch with Me" (Matthew 26:38).

That phrase "exceedingly sorrowful" could be translated, "He was in terrified amazement." In other words, in the face of the dreadful prospect of bearing God's fury against sin, Jesus was in the very grip of terror. Peter, James, and John had often seen their Master pray, of course. But never like this! They watched as He went to His knees and then to His face, crying out, "My Father, if it is possible, let this cup pass from Me; nevertheless, not as I will, but as You will" (verse 39).

He didn't say these words quietly. He cried aloud in prayer. In Hebrews 5:7 (NIV), we are told, "During the days of Jesus' life on earth, he offered up prayers and petitions with fervent cries and tears to the one who could save him from death."

Jesus knew exactly what was coming. He knew Judas Iscariot was at that moment approaching with the temple guard. He knew He would appear before Annas, Caiaphas, Pilate, Herod, and then be sent back again to Pilate. He knew His tormentors would punch Him in the face and tear out His beard. He knew they would rip His back open with a Roman flagellum (which is similar to a cat o' nine tails). He knew they would nail Him to a cross.

But something else loomed ahead that was worse than even these horrors. He knew He would soon have to bear the sin of the entire world for all time. *That* is why He prayed, "Father, if it is possible, let this cup pass from Me."

The Cup of God's Wrath

What cup? The cup of God's white-hot wrath. The cup of God's judgment that rightly belonged to each and every one of us. Isaiah called it the "cup of [His] fury" (Isaiah 51:22), and Jesus had to drink it down to the dregs.

Have you ever eaten something that was so disgusting it turned your stomach? Try, then, to imagine looking into *this* cup and all it represented. Imagine contemplating the horrors of bearing all of that sin.

R. Kent Hughes wrote, "In the greatest display of obedience that will ever be known, Jesus took the full chalice of man's sin and God's wrath, looked, shuddering, deep into its depth, and in a steel act of His will drank it all!"[18]

Interestingly, when Judas approached Him in the garden with a kiss of betrayal, Jesus said, "Friend, why have you come?"

Some friend!

That would have been about the last thing I would have said to Judas. I might have said, "You dog! If I'm going down, you're going down with me. Do you understand what I'm saying to you, you filthy betrayer? And after all the time I spent with you, being your friend!"

But that's not what Jesus said or did. He reached out to him in one last act of mercy. I believe it was an opportunity—even then—for Judas to repent. But his heart was too hard at that point, and he missed his opportunity forever.

So Jesus was taken away and hauled in to appear before Annas, Caiaphas, and ultimately before the Roman governor Pontius Pilate.

Pilate was a powerful man and a hard man. He didn't like to be trifled with. Apparently, he was also a political appointee in quite a bit of hot water. According to some historical accounts, he'd already had a number of run-ins with the Jewish religious leaders and didn't need another major conflict getting back to the authorities in Rome.

Right from the start, it was clear to Pilate what these Jewish leaders wanted: the execution of Jesus Christ. But he didn't want any part of it. He effectively gave them permission to do it themselves, saying, "Go and take care of Him according to your law." That was another way of saying, "If you guys want to go stone Him to death somewhere, have at it. Just take the responsibility away from *me*."

Those leaders, however, wanted a crucifixion—and nothing less.

In one last-ditch effort to appease the bloodthirsty crowds, Pilate had Jesus scourged. As you may know, this wasn't done with a common whip, but rather with a Roman flagellum. This ghastly implement of torture had a wooden base, with three strands of leather embedded with pieces of metal and glass. Every lash of this whip would rip into the skin, opening up blood vessels and even exposing vital organs. Many men did not survive the scourging. Jesus took the full lashing, and then Pilate paraded Him out before the crowd, looking, perhaps, for a little mercy. "Behold the Man!" he said.

The crowd, however, wouldn't be satisfied. They still cried out, "Crucify Him!" So in the end, after going through a futile show of washing his hands and declaring himself innocent, Pilate gave the command for Jesus to be taken away.

Then they crucified Him, and divided His garments, casting lots, that it might be fulfilled which was spoken by the prophet:

"They divided My garments among them, and for My clothing they cast lots."

Sitting down, they kept watch over Him there. And they put up over His head the accusation written against Him:

THIS IS JESUS THE KING OF THE JEWS.

Then two robbers were crucified with Him, one on the right and another on the left.

And those who passed by blasphemed Him, wagging their

heads and saying, "You who destroy the temple and build it in three days, save Yourself! If You are the Son of God, come down from the cross."

Likewise the chief priests also, mocking with the scribes and elders, said, "He saved others; Himself He cannot save. If He is the King of Israel, let Him now come down from the cross, and we will believe Him. He trusted in God; let Him deliver Him now if He will have Him; for He said, 'I am the Son of God.'"

Even the robbers who were crucified with Him reviled Him with the same thing.

Now from the sixth hour until the ninth hour there was darkness over all the land. And about the ninth hour Jesus cried out with a loud voice, saying, "Eli, Eli, lama sabachthani?" that is, "My God, My God, why have You forsaken Me?" (Matthew 27:35-46)

No details or explanation are given about crucifixion, likely because it was so common in that day. The Romans viciously and routinely crucified thousands and thousands of people. It had become their favorite method of execution throughout the empire and especially in Judea. It was usually reserved for rioters and insurrectionists—those who specifically wanted to overthrow Rome.

According to the historian Josephus, after the death of Herod the Great the Roman governor of Syria crucified two thousand men in order to quell an uprising. That same historian also told us that the Roman general Titus crucified so many people when he sacked Jerusalem in AD 70 that the soldiers ran out of wood for crosses— and room to set them up.

Crosses with dead or dying men were a common sight in Israel. When Matthew simply said, "Then they crucified Him" (27:35), his first audiences knew what that meant.

Even so, as Jesus hung there on that instrument of death and shame, He was fulfilling the very plan and purpose of God. Scripture had specifically prophesied that not only would Messiah die, but that He would die on a cross—even though crucifixion hadn't even been invented when the Old Testament prophecies were penned.

Zechariah 13:6 (KJV) says, "One shall say unto him, What are these wounds in thine hands? Then he shall answer, Those with which I was wounded in the house of my friends."

Isaiah 53 is so vivid a description of the crucifixion that we might think the prophet was an eyewitness. Likewise, Psalm 22, written a thousand years before the first crucifixion ever took place, says, "They pierced My hands and My feet" (verse 16).

But this was not just any man being crucified; this was God in human form. This wasn't a man being taken and nailed to a cross against his will; this was the God-man, who willingly went. With one word to the Father, He could have been delivered from that awful death. But if He had done that, if He had chosen to save Himself, He could not have saved you and me. But because He chose to lose Himself, to die in our place, all of us can now be saved from our sins as a result.

Seven Final Words

Death by crucifixion is essentially death by suffocation. It was not the loss of blood that killed the man but the inability to breathe. There was a little base put on the bottom of the cross—a footrest, if you will. By pushing himself up on the footrest with his feet, a crucified person could get air into his lungs.

That's what Jesus had to do in order to make seven statements from the cross. His first statement was "Father, forgive them, for they do not know what they do" (Luke 23:34).

In Matthew's gospel, we read that the two criminals crucified on either side of Jesus joined in the chorus of mockery by the onlookers, until Jesus made that "Father, forgive them" statement.

Right then and there, one of those dying felons placed his faith in Jesus and said, "Lord, remember me when You come into

Your kingdom." In response to that plea, Jesus made His second statement from the cross: "Assuredly, I say to you, today you will be with Me in Paradise" (Luke 23:42-43).

Looking down at the foot of the cross, Jesus saw Mary—the woman who had borne Him, nursed Him, and loved Him—with the apostle John standing next to her. He said to her, "Woman, behold your son." And then no doubt nodding to John, He said, "Behold your mother" (John 19:26-27). With those words, Jesus effectively entrusted the care of His mother to John.

After this, a mysterious darkness fell over the earth for three long hours. Those of us living in Southern California remember the rolling blackouts, when power went off in whole communities. In seconds, it would be pitch dark, which seemed very eerie to those of us used to seeing the glow of the city.

But the blackout at the cross occurred at three in the afternoon, with the sun still in the sky. Suddenly, it became dark as night, with no light anywhere. And then that eerie darkness was pierced by the voice of Jesus, crying from the cross, *"Eli, Eli, lama sabachthani,"* or, "My God, My God, why have You forsaken Me?"

I believe Jesus was at that very moment bearing the sins of the world; He was dying as a substitute for others. The guilt of our sins and the punishment we deserved fell on Him.

In some mysterious way we can never fully comprehend, during those awful hours on the cross the Father was pouring out the full measure of His wrath against sin, and the recipient of that wrath was God's own much-loved Son. God was punishing Jesus as if He had personally committed every wicked deed ever committed by every wicked sinner for all time. Because of what happened in those moments, God can now forgive us and treat us as if we had lived Christ's perfect life of righteousness. This is what we call justification. It's not just merely the removal of sin, amazing as that might be. It is the imputing of the righteousness of Christ into our spiritual bank account.

Scripture clearly teaches that there was a moment when the sin of the world was placed on the Son. Paul wrote in 2 Corinthians 5:21 (NLT), "For God made Christ, who never sinned, to be the offering for our sin, so that we could be made right with God through Christ." Peter wrote, "[He] Himself bore our sins in His own body on the tree" (1 Peter 2:24).

When Jesus cried out, "My God, My God, why have You forsaken Me?" was it a crisis of faith in His life?

No, it was a declaration of fact.

Jesus was forsaken so you and I don't have to be. Jesus entered utter darkness so you and I could walk in the light. Jesus was forsaken so we might be forgiven. When the sin of the world was placed on Christ, the Father—who is holy and cannot look at sin—turned away as Jesus became the recipient of the wrath of God. But because this happened, anyone who cries out to God for mercy in Jesus' name will be received and never forsaken.

Crying Out to God

Jesus cried out, "My God, My God, why have You forsaken Me?" In this cry of desolation and great anguish, Jesus called out to His Father, acknowledging Him as "My God." The emphasis wasn't on the word *forsaken*. The emphasis was on "My God." He called out to His Father as He bore the sin of the world.

Who will you cry out to when a serious crisis hits your life? What will your cry be? What will happen if tragedy comes to your home? Will you call out to God, or will you close Him out of your mind and heart?

It has been said, "Character is not made in crisis. It is revealed." In other words, hardships show who you really are. You can say, "I am so angry at God I will never speak to Him again." Or, you can cry out to Him in your pain and perplexity. You might even say, "Lord, I don't get this. It makes no sense to me at all. I don't like any part of it. Even so, I am looking to You, God—*my* God."

After this we know Jesus said, "I thirst," which was the first mention of His physical condition. Why did He say it at this point? Because His task was almost finished. He had borne the sin of the world, and now, as a man whose body was literally hanging in shreds, He responded to the pain and the raging thirst.

Jesus' statement reminds us that He not only died, but He suffered. Maybe we can understand why Jesus died as a sacrifice for our sins, but why did He have to suffer such agony in the process?

Here's part of the answer: so that we will know beyond all doubt that we serve a God who understands what we're going through here on earth. John R. W. Stott wrote, "Our God is a suffering God." And I think he was right.

Read Isaiah's description of what Jesus, the Son of God, went through at Calvary:

> He was despised and rejected—
> a man of sorrows, acquainted with deepest grief.
> We turned our backs on him and looked the other way.
> He was despised, and we did not care.
> Yet it was our weaknesses he carried;
> it was our sorrows that weighed him down.
> And we thought his troubles were a punishment from God,
> a punishment for his own sins!
> But he was pierced for our rebellion,
> crushed for our sins. (Isaiah 53:3-5, NLT)

He suffered because of us. He suffered for love of us. And if you are suffering today, you need to know that you do not suffer alone.

Maybe you feel like you are the only person who has to endure your pain or sorrow. Jesus, however, was called a "Man of sorrows," and He is "acquainted with grief" (Isaiah 53:3). No matter how great your difficulty or need, know that He understands. As the apostle Peter reminded us, "Cast all your anxiety on him because he cares for you" (1 Peter 5:7, NIV).

Is your body wracked with pain? So was His.

Have you ever been misunderstood, misjudged, or misrepresented? So was He.

Have you ever had those that are nearest and dearest to you turn away? So has He.

So why did Jesus have to suffer and die? In the following paragraphs, I offer four brief answers to that question, though I know that many more reasons could be given.

Why Did He Have to Suffer and Die?

To show God's love for us

Jesus said, "For God so loved the world that He gave His only begotten Son" (John 3:16). Paul said in Ephesians 5:25, "Christ also loved the church and gave Himself for her." Paul also said that He "loved me and gave Himself for me" (Galatians 2:20). Jesus' suffering and death was a demonstration of love.

If you are ever tempted to doubt God's love, take a long look at the cross of Calvary, because that is where you will see God's love on display.

To absorb the wrath of God

I have broken God's commandments and fallen short of God's standards. Because I have offended a holy God, there was a judgment that had to be meted out. The Bible says, "The soul who sins shall die" (Ezekiel 18:20). So who was going to pay that price? Jesus said, "I will. I will absorb the judgment and wrath of God in your place." And that is exactly what happened.

If God were not just, there would be no *demand* for His Son to suffer and die. If God were not loving, there would be no *willingness* for His Son to suffer and die. But God is just and willing. And because God's love was willing to meet the demands of His own justice, Jesus took the full impact of that judgment on Himself, in our place.

To cancel the legal demands against us and to disarm the devil

We have all broken some or all of the Ten Commandments. The Bible tells us that if we offend in one point of the law, we are as guilty as if we had offended in all of it (see James 2:10). This shows the utter absurdity of the claim, "I don't really need Jesus Christ, because

I live by the Ten Commandments." No, you don't! You do not live by the Ten Commandments, and the fact that you have broken them means that you deserve God's judgment. But Jesus died to cancel the legal demands against us and disarm the evil one, the enemy of our soul. Colossians 2:14-15 (NLT) tells us, "He canceled the record of the charges against us and took it away by nailing it to the cross. In this way, he disarmed the spiritual rulers and authorities. He shamed them publicly by his victory over them on the cross."

So here is what it comes down to: Not only did He cancel the legal demands against us, but He disarmed the devil. The devil says, "You are mine. I will do what I want to do in your life, and you will never be free. You will always be bound by these addictions. You will always be trapped in this lifestyle. You will always do the same stupid things over and over again."

Here is what you can say in reply: "Satan, you are a liar. What you are saying is not true, because Jesus died in my place on the cross and dealt you a decisive blow."

Yes, the devil may be powerful.

But Jesus is infinitely more powerful.

As the apostle John put it, "The one who is in you is greater than the one who is in the world" (1 John 4:4, NIV). In other words, the power of Christ cancels out the power of Satan. If you want to be free from that addiction, free from that sin, free from whatever it is that holds you down, you can be if you *choose* to be—if you will take hold of what Jesus purchased for you at the cross of Calvary.

To provide our forgiveness and justification

We are told in Romans 5:9 that we have "been justified by His blood." To be justified means we have been forgiven of the wrongs we have done. But as I pointed out earlier, it also means that God has placed the righteousness of Jesus Christ into our spiritual bank accounts. As a result, we don't ever need to say, "I'm not worthy to pray to God," or "I'm not worthy to attend church."

In one sense, that's true. We *aren't* worthy. But we never were. Sometimes we may think, "I've done pretty well this week. I read the Bible, prayed a little, and didn't sin as much as I usually do."

Well, that's good if we've had that kind of week. But even on our *best* week, our *best* day, we still fall short. Our ability to approach God has never had anything to do with our "worthiness." It has everything to do with what Jesus has done for us.

Because of the cross, we have instant access into His presence. There is nothing, ever, that should keep us from calling on Christ and placing our trust in Him.

CHAPTER THIRTY-NINE
FAMOUS LAST WORDS

For every man and woman on earth, there will come a last meal, a last breath, and of course, a last statement. And in many ways, what we say in the end offers a real insight into what we were in life, what we stood for, and what we lived for. Generally, we die as we have lived.

I read about a man who had been very successful in the restaurant business and had established many restaurants around the United States. When his life was almost over, as he was on his deathbed with his family gathered nearby, he gave his last whisper: "Slice the ham thin!"

On November 30, 1900, the last words of the famous writer Oscar Wilde were, "Either that wallpaper goes, or I do."

Sometimes people know they are giving their last words. Before he was to be hanged for spying on the British, the last words of American patriot Nathan Hale were, "I only regret that I have but one life to lose for my country."

At other times, people have no idea they're speaking their last words. That was true of John F. Kennedy, who, just before the sniper's bullets took his life, said, "That's obvious!" He made the statement in response to Nellie Connally, the wife of Texas Governor John Connally. As they traveled by motorcade through Dallas, cheered by adoring throngs, she had remarked to the president, "Mr. President, you certainly can't say that Dallas doesn't love you."

"That's obvious," he said.

Seconds later, John Kennedy was in eternity.

Then there were the last words of William "Buckey" O'Neil, an Arizona lawyer, miner, cowboy, gambler, newspaperman, sheriff, and congressman. He was also one of the most important members of Teddy Roosevelt's Rough Riders during the Spanish-American War. Just prior to the famous charge up Kettle Hill, O'Neil was standing up, smoking a cigarette, and joking with his troops while under withering fire from the ridge. One of his sergeants shouted to him above the noise, "Captain, a bullet is sure to hit you!"

O'Neil shouted back his reply: "Sergeant, the Spanish bullet isn't made that will kill me!"

No sooner had O'Neil uttered those words then he was hit and killed by a bullet.

Then there were the last words of U.S. tenor Richard Versalle, who was performing one night at the Metropolitan Opera in 1996. Versalle had climbed a ladder for his scene, and after singing the words, "Too bad you can only live so long," he suffered a fatal heart attack and fell ten feet to the stage below.

"Everybody went into shock," said Joseph Volpe, then general manager of the Met. "They thought it was part of the staging." (News accounts added that Mr. Versalle's replacement declined to climb the ladder for his solo in subsequent performances.)

What's more, death is no respecter of persons—even for royalty. On her deathbed, Elizabeth I, Queen of England, said, "All my possessions for a moment of time." And Princess Diana, following that horrific car accident in a Paris tunnel, was heard to say, "My God, what happened?"

Some people are in denial about their impending death, like Frank Sinatra, who, as his end was near, told his wife, Barbara, "It's none of their d**n business! Dying is a sign of weakness. It's for lesser people. You've got to keep my death a secret. I don't want people gloating. Just bury me quietly. If you don't tell 'em I'm gone, nobody will ever know."

History tells the story of the renowned atheist Voltaire, who was one of the most aggressive antagonists of Christianity. He wrote many things to undermine the church, and once said of Jesus Christ, "Curse the wretch. In twenty years, Christianity will be no more. My single hand will destroy the edifice it took twelve apostles to rear."

But it didn't turn out that way, did it?

A nurse who attended Voltaire on his deathbed was reported to have said, "For all the wealth in Europe, I would not see another atheist die."

The physician, waiting up with Voltaire at his death, said that he cried out with utter desperation, "I am abandoned by God and man. I will give you half of what I am worth if you will give me six months of life. Then I shall go to hell and you will go with me, oh, Christ, oh, Jesus Christ!"

What a difference faith makes. The last words of Stephen, who was being stoned to death, were, "Lord Jesus, receive my spirit. . . . Lord, do not charge them with this sin" (Acts 7:59-60).

The great evangelist D. L. Moody, on his deathbed, said, "I see Earth receding and heaven is opening. God is calling me."

The Most Important Last Words Ever

Now let's consider the most famous and important "last words" ever uttered: the words of Jesus as He hung on the cross. I want to focus on one statement in particular, for in it we see what must have been God's most painful moment.

Jesus had been taken to be crucified on the cross, and death by crucifixion was really death by suffocation. It was extremely hard even to breathe, much less speak. Add to this the fact that He had been brutally scourged. The process of scourging was barbaric. The prisoner was tied to a post with his hands over his head, his body taut. The whip had a short, wooden handle with several leather thongs attached, each tipped with sharp pieces of metal or bone. As the whip was brought down on the prisoner, his muscles would be lacerated, veins and arteries would be torn open, and even the kidneys, spleen, or other organs could be exposed and slashed.

Then there was the crucifixion itself, which would cause most people to turn away in revulsion at the sight of it. There has never been a movie or painting I've seen that has even come close to depicting what really happened when Jesus died—that is, until Mel Gibson's *The Passion of the Christ*. But I don't know that any artist or filmmaker could ever capture all that happened on that day. Even Gibson has acknowledged that what actually happened to Jesus in His scourging and crucifixion was probably much worse than was depicted in his movie.

Next to Jesus as He hung on that cross were two criminals who were there for their personal crimes. Jesus, on the other hand, was there for the crimes of all humanity. They were there against their will. Yet Jesus was there because He willingly went. They could not have escaped. But He could have—with just one word to heaven. They were held to their crosses by nails. Jesus was held to His cross by love.

It is fascinating to see how these three men reacted as they looked death squarely in the face. Initially, as Jesus was nailed to the cross, these two men momentarily forgot their personal pain and joined the chorus of the onlookers' voices:

"He saved others; Himself He cannot save. If He is the King of Israel, let Him now come down from the cross, and we will believe Him. He trusted in God; let Him deliver Him now if He will have Him; for He said, 'I am the Son of God.'"

Even the robbers who were crucified with Him reviled Him with the same thing. (Matthew 27:42-44)

How this mockery and unbelief must have pained the tender heart of Jesus. Even there at the cross they persisted, while He was atoning for the very people who were spewing this venom.

In Matthew's account of this event, we read that both thieves joined the crowd in mockery. Luke's gospel, however, reveals a change of heart in one of the felons. Evidently, something significant happened, bringing him to his spiritual senses. Initially, he had joined the chorus of mockery toward Jesus. But then, he watched with amazement as Jesus suffered the same crucifixion as he and the other thief, yet without any complaint, angry protest, or cursing. Then came those unbelievable, unexpected, incomprehensible words of Christ: "Father, forgive them" (Luke 23:34).

How those words must have reverberated through the thief's hardened heart! His rebellion, bitterness, and anger that had no doubt driven him all those years melted away, and his heart softened.

While the first statement Jesus uttered from the cross was a prayer for His enemies, the second was an answer to prayer, an answer addressed to a single individual. Jesus spoke to him as though he were the only person in the world.

Luke's gospel tells us the believing thief then said, "'Lord, remember me when You come into Your kingdom.' And Jesus said to him, 'Assuredly, I say to you, today you will be with Me in Paradise'" (23:42-43).

In the same way, once you believe in Christ, you can know you are going to heaven. John said, "These things I have written to you who believe in the name of the Son of God, that you may know that you have eternal life" (1 John 5:13).

Can you imagine the joy that must have filled this man's heart? Talk about being in the right place at the right time! You, too, are in the right place at the right time. Jesus will forgive you today of all your sins. He is speaking to you right now as though you were the only person in the world.

There is a lot of debate as to who was responsible for the death of Jesus Christ. Was it the Jewish Sanhedrin and the Pharisees? Was it the high priest, Caiaphas? Was it the Romans? Pilate?

I will tell you who was responsible for the crucifixion of Jesus Christ on that cross: I was! And so were you.

It was *our sins* that put Him there. Looking ahead to the death of Jesus, the prophet Isaiah wrote these words:

> Yet it was our grief he bore, our sorrows that weighed him down. And we thought his troubles were a punishment from God, for his own sins! But he was wounded and bruised for our sins. He was beaten that we might have peace; he was lashed—and we were healed! (Isaiah 53:4-5, TLB)

Because there was no other way to satisfy the demands of a holy God, Jesus, who was God, died in our place. The Bible says, "While we were still sinners, Christ died for us" (Romans 5:8). And

Paul wrote, "I live by faith in the Son of God, who loved me and gave Himself for me" (Galatians 2:20).

Next came the moment Jesus had been dreading. It was here that the tragedy of the Crucifixion reached its horrific climax. In fact, it has been described as "the crucifixion in the Crucifixion":

Now from the sixth hour until the ninth hour there was darkness over all the land. And about the ninth hour Jesus cried out with a loud voice, saying, "Eli, Eli, lama sabachthani?" that is, "My God, My God, why have You forsaken Me?"

Some of those who stood there, when they heard that, said, "This Man is calling for Elijah!" Immediately one of them ran and took a sponge, filled it with sour wine and put it on a reed, and offered it to Him to drink.

The rest said, "Let Him alone; let us see if Elijah will come to save Him."

And Jesus cried out again with a loud voice, and yielded up His spirit. (Matthew 27:45-50)

Without explanation, the sky turned dark. From the sixth hour (12:00 noon) to 3:00 P.M., an ominous darkness fell across the land. The Greek word for "land" in this passage could be translated "earth," possibly indicating the entire world. Some extrabiblical sources suggest that such a universal darkness did occur. A Roman historian mentioned such a darkness. Also, there was a supposed report from Pilate to the emperor Tiberius that assumed the emperor's knowledge of a certain widespread darkness, even mentioning that it took place from 12:00 P.M. to 3:00 P.M.

The darkness was then pierced by the voice of Jesus: "My God, My God, why have You forsaken Me?" (verse 46). No fiction writer would have his or her hero say words like these. They surprise us, disarm us, and cause us to wonder what He meant. We are looking at something that, in many ways, is impossible for us as humans to fathom.

Martin Luther, after considering these words for days on end, finally gave up trying to wrap his mind around what happened in those moments on the cross. Throwing his hands up he said, "God forsaken of God! Who can understand it?"

Clearly, we are treading on holy ground when we look into such a subject, yet the impact on our lives is so significant that it certainly bears looking into. If we can gain a better understanding of what Jesus actually went through for us and what horrendous pain He experienced, it only gives us a greater appreciation for Him and all He has done for us.

The Worst Moment of All

When Jesus cried out these words, they were not the delusions of a man in pain. His faith was not failing Him. After all, He cried out, "My God, My God."

As Christ hung there, He was bearing the sins of the world. He was dying as a substitute for others and suffering the punishment for their—and my—sins. The very essence of the punishment was the outpouring of God's wrath against sinners. In some mysterious way we can never fully comprehend, during those awful hours on the cross the Father was pouring out the full measure of His wrath against sin. And the recipient of that wrath was God's own beloved Son! God was punishing Jesus as though He had personally committed every wicked deed of every wicked sinner. And in doing so, He could forgive and treat those redeemed ones as though they had lived Christ's perfect life of righteousness.

Scripture clearly teaches that this did happen: "For He made Him who knew no sin *to be* sin for us, that we might become the righteousness of God in Him" (2 Corinthians 5:21, emphasis added). Speaking of God the Father in Isaiah 53:10, the prophet told us that "It pleased the LORD to bruise Him." We also read that "'He himself bore our sins' in his body on the cross, so that we might die to sins and live for righteousness; 'by his wounds you have been healed'" (1 Peter 2:24, NIV).

Sin, sin, sin was everywhere around Him at this dreaded moment. We can't begin to fathom what He was going through at this time. All our worst fears about the horrors of hell—and more— were realized by Him as He received the due penalty of others' wrongdoing.

But the worst of the worst was to be forsaken of God the Father.

The physical pains of crucifixion, horrible as they were, were nothing compared to the wrath of the Father being poured out upon Him. This is why, in Gethsemane, "His sweat became like great drops of blood falling down to the ground" (Luke 22:44). This is why He looked ahead to the cross with such horror, because never, not for one moment during His entire earthly ministry, did He ever step outside of intimate fellowship with His Father.

Why, then, did this have to happen?

Because of the unscalable wall between God and man.

God, in all His holiness, could not look at sin, because He is "of purer eyes than to behold evil, and cannot look on wickedness" (Habakkuk 1:13). As a result, man, in all his sinfulness, could not look at God. So the holy Father had to turn His face and pour His wrath upon His own Son.

Understand that for Jesus, this was the greatest sacrifice He could have possibly made. His greatest pain occurred at this moment. To have felt forsaken of God was the necessary consequence of sin. For a man to be forsaken of God is the penalty that naturally and inevitably follows his breaking of his relationship with God.

Jesus was forsaken of God so that we don't have to be. Jesus was forsaken of God for a time so that we might enjoy His presence forever. Jesus was forsaken of God so that we might be forgiven. Jesus entered the darkness so that we might walk in the light. His pain resulted in our gain.

"I Thirst"

After this three-hour ordeal, Jesus gave His fifth statement from the cross—and the first words of a personal nature.

"I thirst!" (John 19:28).

First, He prayed for His enemies, then He reassured the thief on the cross, then He remembered His mother and bore the sins of humanity, and then and only then did He speak of His own needs. Imagine, this was the Creator of the universe making this statement—the One who created water! He could have so easily performed a miracle. After all, He brought water out of rocks in the wilderness. His first earthly miracle during His public ministry was to turn water into wine. He could have simply spoken water into existence.

But it's important to note that Jesus never once performed a miracle for His own benefit or comfort. When tempted by Satan to do this, He refused. Scripture tells us that He was hungry, He grew tired, He wept, and He "was in all points tempted as we are, yet without sin" (Hebrews 4:15). Yes, Jesus was one hundred percent God, but He was also a man. He was not a man becoming God (that's impossible), but God who became a man.

Jesus was called "a Man of sorrows" (Isaiah 53:3). What does that mean to you? It means that no matter how great your need, no matter how overwhelming your difficulty, He understands. You can cast "all your care upon Him, for He cares for you" (1 Peter 5:7).

Is your body racked with pain? *So was His.* Have you ever been misunderstood, misjudged, or misrepresented? *So was He.* Have you had your closest friends turn away from you? *So did He.*

Jesus then uttered His sixth statement from the cross: "It is finished!" (John 19:30). The storm had finally passed, the cup had been drained. The devil had done his worst, and God the Father had bruised him.

The phrase "It is finished" is translated many ways: "It is made an end of," "It is paid," "It is performed," or "It is accomplished."

What was made an end of? Our sins and the guilt that accompanied them.

What was paid? The price of redemption.

What was performed? The righteous requirements of the law.

What was accomplished? The work the Father had given Him to do.

Three days later, Jesus Christ came out of His tomb, rising from the dead. He is alive and here right now, wanting to come into your life.

We see three things as we look at the cross.

First, we see that it is a description of the depth of man's sin. It's been said that you can tell the depth of a well by how much rope is lowered. So don't blame the people of that day for putting Jesus on that cross. You and I are just as guilty. It wasn't the Roman soldiers who put Him on that cross; it was your sins and my sins that made it necessary for Him to die this torturous and humiliating death.

Second, in the cross we see the overwhelming love of God. If ever you are tempted to doubt God's love for you, just take a long look at the cross that He hung on for you. Romans 5:8 tells us, "But God demonstrates His own love toward us, in that while we were still sinners, Christ died for us."

Third, in the cross is the only way of salvation. Jesus said, "I am the way, the truth, and the life. No one comes to the Father except through Me" (John 14:6). If there had been any other way to save you, He would have found it. If living a good, moral life would save you, then Jesus never would have died. But He *did* die. Because there was—and is—no other way.

The story is told of a man who operated a drawbridge. At a certain time each afternoon, he had to raise the bridge for a ferry boat, and then lower it quickly for a high-speed passenger train that crossed a few minutes later. One day, the man's young son was visiting him at work and decided to go down below to get a better look at the ferry as it passed. Fascinated by the sight, he didn't watch carefully where he was going and fell into the giant gears of the drawbridge. One foot became caught, and the boy was helpless to free himself.

His father's heart sank when he saw what happened. He was now forced to make the most difficult decision of his entire life. If he ran to free his son, the train would plunge into the river before the bridge could be lowered. But if he lowered the bridge to save the hundreds of passengers and crew members on the train, his son would be crushed to death.

When he heard the train's whistle that indicated it would soon reach the river, he knew he had to face the inevitable. His son was the dearest thing on Earth to him. These people on the train were complete strangers. Yet he knew what he had to do. With tears flowing down his cheeks, he pushed the master switch forward. That great, massive bridge lowered into place, just as the train began to roar across the river. As he looked up and watched the train rumble buy, he saw businessmen casually reading their afternoon papers, finely dressed women sipping coffee in the dining car, and a little boy enjoying a dish of ice cream. No one looked at the control house. And no one looked at the great gear box.

With wrenching agony, he cried out, "I sacrificed my son for you people! Don't you care?"

The train rushed by, but no one heard the father's words.

This is what happened at the cross of Calvary. God sacrificed His Son for you because He loves you.

And because there was no other way.

CHAPTER FORTY

IT IS BEGINNING

If you have ever lost a loved one, especially unexpectedly, you know how it feels.

The shock. The disbelief, then the denial, followed by anger. Then a soul-deep sadness sets in. Your life changes permanently overnight, because you realize you will never see that person again on earth.

That is exactly how the disciples felt on the day Jesus died. Despite the fact that He had repeatedly spoken of His death and resurrection, they had somehow missed it. Failed to comprehend it. And when they heard Him say on the cross, *"Tetelestai . . .* It is finished," that is precisely how they felt. It's finished. The dream is over. The hope is gone. And they were devastated beyond words. One day they were walking with Him, talking with Him, eating with Him, praying with Him, and the next day He was gone. What's more, they watched Him die right before their eyes.

It would not have been an easy thing to witness.

We know from Scripture that the body of Christ was so abused, so traumatized by the beatings, flogging, and crucifixion, that it was barely recognizable. Centuries before it happened, Isaiah prophesied, "They shall see my Servant beaten and bloodied, so disfigured one would scarcely know it was a person standing there" (Isaiah 52:15, TLB). These men who had been His friends and followers were badly traumatized.

They never even got to say goodbye to Him.

He had been everything to them. Lord. Savior. Master. Teacher. Hero. Friend.

And then He was gone.

Two disciples on the Emmaus Road, walking slowly back home from Jerusalem and the scene of the execution, pretty much summed up the way everyone felt. "We had hoped that he was the one who was going to redeem Israel" (Luke 24:21, NIV). *We had hoped.* And now that hope was past tense. They no longer hoped at all.

There had been a great anticipation leading up to this terrible event. In what we call the Triumphal Entry, Christ had come into the city on the back of a donkey, and people had laid palm branches before Him, shouting, "Hosanna!" And in that brief moment of glory, the disciples were probably thinking, "Now everyone understands what we already know. Jesus is the Messiah!"

Almost immediately, however, things began to unravel. It was almost as though Jesus wasn't Himself. In the Upper Room, He spoke about someone denying Him and someone else betraying Him. Following Him to the Garden of Gethsemane, they were unnerved to see Him screaming, "Father, if it is possible, let this cup pass from Me!" Dr. Luke told us that Jesus was under such intense pressure that He was literally sweating blood as He contemplated the horrors immediately before Him.

But everything that seemed like confusion and chaos to the disciples was actually proceeding according to God's plan. In reality, Jesus was doing everything right on schedule. Why? Because Christ's whole reason for coming to earth was to die on a cross and then rise from the dead.

The Incarnation was for the purpose of the atonement. To say it more simply, the birth of Jesus occurred so there would be a death of Jesus. We don't like to think about that as the Christmas season approaches. We don't like to talk about the fact that the sweet Baby born in the manger of Bethlehem came with a mission to go to the cross. But it all took place according to God's plan.

Peter mentioned that in Acts 2:23 (MSG), as he preached to the very men who had crucified Jesus. With great boldness he declared, "This Jesus, following the deliberate and well-thought-out plan of God, was betrayed by men who took the law into their own hands, and was handed over to you. And you pinned him to a cross and killed him."

It seemed to the disciples that the whole world had come unraveled, but everything that happened to Jesus was according to God's "deliberate and well-thought-out plan."

Why did Jesus come to suffer and die?

Jesus suffered and died to show His love for us.

Jesus said in John 3:16, "For God so loved the world that He gave His only begotten Son." In Ephesians 5:25, Paul wrote, "Christ also loved the church and gave Himself for her." The apostle also wrote that He was "the Son of God, who loved me and gave Himself for me" (Galatians 2:20).

If you ever feel yourself unloved, remember *you are loved by God.* Yes, Jesus died for the world. But He also died for you. Again, Paul said, "He loved *me* and gave Himself for *me.*" God's Son was actually thinking of you when He went to the cross. Jesus showed His love for you in a tangible way.

Jesus suffered and died to absorb the wrath of God.

If God were not just, there would be no demand for His Son to suffer and die. But if God were not loving, there would be no willingness for His Son to suffer and die. But God is both just and loving; at the cross God lovingly met His own demands for justice. We might say that God plays by His own rules. In Scripture He declares that "the soul who sins shall die" (Ezekiel 18:20). Christ never sinned, but He carried our sin. He absorbed the wrath of God that should have fallen on us. He took it upon Himself.

Jesus suffered and died to cancel the legal demands against us.

What does that mean? In conventional wisdom, God is like a liberal school teacher who grades on the curve. In other words, if you do more good deeds than bad deeds, then God will let you into heaven. But that is both unbiblical and untrue. If we are saved from the consequences of our sin, it will not be because they somehow "weighed less" than our supposed good deeds. *There is no salvation for us by balancing records; there is only salvation by canceling records.* We had a debt against us that could never be paid. Take the best day of your entire life when you did everything right. Even on that day you didn't have more good deeds than bad deeds.

Thank God, He doesn't deal with us in that way!

The psalmist cried out, "If You, LORD, should mark iniquities, O Lord, who could stand?" (Psalm 130:3). The answer? No one!

In Colossians 2:13-14 (NIV) we read these incredibly beautiful and liberating words: "God made you alive with Christ. He forgave us all our sins, having canceled the charge of our legal indebtedness, which stood against us and condemned us; he has taken it away, nailing it to the cross."

He *canceled* the charges against us.

He *canceled* the legal demands against us.

Jesus suffered and died to provide our forgiveness and justification.

Because of the death of Christ, you can be forgiven of any sin you have ever committed if you will turn from that sin and ask His forgiveness. That alone is wonderful beyond description, but Jesus did even more than that. He not only forgives us, He *justifies* us. The word *forgive* speaks of canceling out our sins—giving us a zero balance, so to speak. But the word *justify* speaks of what God has done for you. He has placed the righteousness of Christ into your spiritual bank account! The word *justify* gives us the sense of "just-as-if-I'd-never-sinned." That is what Jesus was doing on the cross. That is what He meant when He said, "It is finished." It's as though He cried out, *"Paid in full!"*

New Beginning

As that first Easter Sunday dawned, no one thought of it as a new beginning. Not yet. To everyone who loved Jesus, it still felt like a bitter, heartbroken ending.

But all of that would soon change. The worst nightmare of their lives was about to become their greatest, most impossible dream come true.

In the same way, God can take our endings and turn them into new beginnings. Maybe as you read this chapter you feel like your life has ended. Something unforeseen has crashed into your life. The unexpected death of a loved one. The explosion of a marriage. The ending of a career or ministry. Now you feel like life is over, and you don't even want to get out of bed to face a new day. But

God can take what you think is a dead end and open up a way you haven't even considered.

Here is how the gospel writer Matthew described such a situation that unfolded over two thousand years ago.

> Now after the Sabbath, as the first day of the week began to dawn, Mary Magdalene and the other Mary came to see the tomb. And behold, there was a great earthquake; for an angel of the Lord descended from heaven, and came and rolled back the stone from the door, and sat on it. His countenance was like lightning, and his clothing as white as snow. And the guards shook for fear of him, and became like dead men.
>
> But the angel answered and said to the women, "Do not be afraid, for I know that you seek Jesus who was crucified. He is not here; for He is risen, as He said. Come, see the place where the Lord lay. And go quickly and tell His disciples that He is risen from the dead, and indeed He is going before you into Galilee; there you will see Him. Behold, I have told you."
>
> So they went out quickly from the tomb with fear and great joy, and ran to bring His disciples word.
>
> And as they went to tell His disciples, behold, Jesus met them, saying, "Rejoice!" So they came and held Him by the feet and worshiped Him. Then Jesus said to them, "Do not be afraid. Go and tell My brethren to go to Galilee, and there they will see Me."
>
> Now while they were going, behold, some of the guard came into the city and reported to the chief priests all the things that had happened. (Matthew 28:1-11)

An amazing, unprecedented series of events had transpired since Jesus went to the cross. First of all, an unearthly darkness came at midday; from 12:00 noon to 3:00 in the afternoon it was pitch dark—like the middle of the night. It may have even been a global darkness as Christ died and bore the sins of the world. There was a great earthquake. The thick veil in the temple that separated the Holy of Holies from the rest of the building was ripped in two from top to bottom. Dead people came out of their graves and were walking around town.

Three days later, the Roman guards who had been entrusted with the responsibility to make the Lord's tomb secure saw that it had been emptied, and they were understandably terrified by these things. Not to mention that they also found an angel of the Lord staring them down. Let's look at Matthew 28 again.

> There was a great earthquake; for an angel of the Lord descended from heaven, and came and rolled back the stone from the door, and sat on it. His countenance was like lightning, and his clothing as white as snow. And the guards shook for fear of him, and became like dead men. (verses 2-4)

Apparently there were a couple of earthquakes when Christ died and rose again. One shaking the city and the other shaking these men's hearts. The word used for "shook" in describing the reaction of the guards is the same term used for earthquake. It wasn't a very masculine thing for two Roman guards to do; they trembled in fear and then passed out.

What a different response the believing women had when they saw the angel! Certainly they were startled, but unlike the soldiers they received comfort from this bright heavenly messenger. In Matthew 28:5 we read, "But the angel answered and said to the women, 'Do not be afraid, for I know that you seek Jesus who was crucified. He is not here; for He is risen, as He said.'"

These two reactions parallel the responses of believers and nonbelievers to circumstances and events in their lives. When people who have no hope see our world in the state it's in, they shake with fear. Believers see the same scary things, the same gloomy scenarios, and they too experience some fear. But it is mixed with joy. No matter how frightening or depressing world events may seem, believers remember what Jesus said: "When these things begin to take place, stand up and lift up your heads, because your redemption is drawing near" (Luke 21:28, NIV).

Psalm 46:1-2 (NIV) reminds us that "God is our refuge and strength, an ever-present help in trouble. Therefore we will not fear, though the earth give way and the mountains fall into the heart of the sea." No matter what takes place in our world—or *your* world—God is still your refuge and strength, your hiding place and your inner stability.

Don't you love Matthew 28:8? It says that these women "went out quickly from the tomb with fear and great joy, and ran to bring His disciples word." Have you ever experienced fear and joy simultaneously?

Getting on a roller coaster will do that. So will getting married. Or having your first child. Or buying your first house. In those moments, fear and joy run together like two parallel streams.

Bursting with gladness, the women had reason to be even more glad just a moment or two later. "So the women hurried away from the tomb, afraid yet filled with joy, and ran to tell his disciples. Suddenly Jesus met them. 'Greetings,' he said. They came to him, clasped his feet and worshiped him" (Matthew 28:8-9, NIV).

When He met them that morning, He spoke a common, casual greeting to them, something like, "How's it going? It's good to see you." Just as if this were a normal meeting!

We greet each other in different ways in different parts of the country. In the South they say, "Hey! How are you?" Over in Hawaii they will say, "Howzit, brah? Hey, brah, howzit?" In Australia they say, "G' day, mate." In New York, they just ignore you. But when Jesus gave a morning greeting to these overjoyed women, it was more like, "Hello there" or "Good morning."

The passage tells us that the women fell at His feet and worshiped Him. By the way, this is yet one more clear affirmation of His deity. There are people who insist that Jesus never claimed to be God. But individuals who say such things either don't know the New Testament or don't care about it. He did affirm His deity again and again. In the wilderness, Jesus had specifically told Satan, "Worship the LORD your God, and Him only you shall serve" (Matthew 4:10). Yet here were these women bowing before Jesus, holding His feet, and worshiping Him as God—and He made no move to stop them.

I was driving the other day with two of my grandchildren in the backseat—five-year-old Allie and three-year-old Christopher. Allie was preaching a little to her brother, whom she calls "Keefer." She said, "Keefer, now Jesus is God and God is Jesus." She looked up at me and said, "Right, Papa?"

"Yes," I said. "That's right."

"And Jesus lives in our heart, Keefer," she told him, and I'm thinking, *She's on a roll.*

And then she said, "And one day He will live in our stomach."

I wasn't quite getting that point, but Keefer seemed satisfied with it.

"Why Are You Weeping?"

The gospel of John describes another very tender encounter at the empty tomb, early that Sunday morning.

But Mary stood outside by the tomb weeping, and as she wept she stooped down and looked into the tomb. And she saw two angels in white sitting, one at the head and the other at the feet, where the body of Jesus had lain. Then they said to her, "Woman, why are you weeping?"

She said to them, "Because they have taken away my Lord, and I do not know where they have laid Him."

Now when she had said this, she turned around and saw Jesus standing there, and did not know that it was Jesus. Jesus said to her, "Woman, why are you weeping? Whom are you seeking?"

She, supposing Him to be the gardener, said to Him, "Sir, if You have carried Him away, tell me where You have laid Him, and I will take Him away."

Jesus said to her, "Mary!"

She turned and said to Him, "Rabboni!" (which is to say, Teacher).

Jesus said to her, "Do not cling to Me, for I have not yet ascended to My Father; but go to My brethren and say to them, 'I am ascending to My Father and your Father, and to My God and your God.'" (20:11-17)

This is such a beautiful story. Mary's persistence was rewarded as she waited at the tomb and then met her risen Lord.

Why did Jesus say, "Do not cling to Me"? I think what He was effectively saying was this: "Mary, this is a whole new ball game now, a whole new covenant. Don't cling to Me in the old way as you have. I'm not going to be here as I have been up to this point, physically walking and talking with you. But listen, Mary, it will be even better! Because I will take up residence in Your heart, because I'm ascending to My Father and your Father, to My God and your God."

I don't think we begin to feel the impact of those words as Mary Magdalene did. In the first-century Jewish world, people did not address God, the almighty One, as "Father." But Jesus called Him Father, and because of Christ's death and resurrection, we can now call Him "Father," too.

So Jesus was saying, "Mary, He's now your Father, too. Go spread the news!"

More Appearances

Jesus also appeared to many others after His resurrection, and before He ascended to His Father. Acts 1:3 says, "He also presented Himself alive after His suffering by many infallible proofs, being seen by them during forty days and speaking of the things pertaining to the kingdom of God." That phrase *seen by them* literally means to "eyeball." In other words, for forty days the disciples eyeballed Him. Stared at Him. Gazed at Him. Looked Him over.

Whenever they would be looking at Him they must have been saying to themselves, "I just can't believe my eyes. I can't believe it! This is no ghost. He's here. He's eating with us. He's laughing. This is Jesus! But how could it be?" Years later, the apostle Paul wrote, "He was seen by more than 500 of his followers at one time, most of whom are still alive, though some have died" (1 Corinthians 15:6, NLT).

Jesus was appearing and reappearing over and over again for well over a month before He was taken into heaven.

One of my favorite stories about His appearing takes place in Luke 24. Here is how it unfolds in *The Message* translation:

> That same day two of them were walking to the village Emmaus, about seven miles out of Jerusalem. They were deep in conversation, going over all these things that had happened. In the middle of their talk and questions, Jesus came up and walked along with them. But they were not able to recognize who he was.
>
> He asked, "What's this you're discussing so intently as you walk along?"
>
> They just stood there, long-faced, like they had lost their best friend. Then one of them, his name was Cleopas, said, "Are you the only one in Jerusalem who hasn't heard what's happened during the last few days?"
>
> He said, "What has happened?"
>
> They said, "The things that happened to Jesus the Nazarene. He was a man of God, a prophet, dynamic in work and word, blessed by both God and all the people. Then our high priests and leaders betrayed him, got him sentenced to death, and crucified him. And we had our hopes up that he was the One,

the One about to deliver Israel. And it is now the third day since it happened. But now some of our women have completely confused us. Early this morning they were at the tomb and couldn't find his body. They came back with the story that they had seen a vision of angels who said he was alive. Some of our friends went off to the tomb to check and found it empty just as the women said, but they didn't see Jesus."

Then he said to them, "So thick-headed! So slow-hearted! Why can't you simply believe all that the prophets said?" (verses 13-25)

And then Jesus took them on a little tour through the Old Testament, highlighting all the passages that spoke of the Messiah. I would have loved to have been a fly on the wall for that conversation! When I get to heaven, I would love to just say to the Lord, "Would You go over that little talk in Luke 24 just one more time? I want to find out what I missed!"

These two disciples listened intently as the Stranger spoke—maybe smarting a little from being called "thick-headed" or "fools." But as they listened to the Man speak, they had to admit, "Goodness! This guy really knows His Bible." (You would almost think He wrote it!) The men were so moved by the Stranger's words, but they had reached Emmaus, the end of their journey.

"Join us for dinner!" they said, probably in unison. And He did.

But when He sat down at the table and broke the bread, their eyes were suddenly opened and they knew who He was. And He vanished from their sight. They looked at each other with wide, wondering eyes and said, "Did not our heart burn within us while He talked with us on the road, and while He opened the Scriptures to us?" (Luke 24:32). With reignited hearts burning with hope they hurried back to Jerusalem to be with the other disciples.

This passage about "hearts burning" makes me wonder why our hearts grow cold as believers. Maybe as a younger believer, you had more fire and passion for the Lord than you do now. Some of that excitement and joy has ebbed away through the months and years. Why does that happen? Why does passion give way to passivity? Why don't our hearts burn for Him as they once did?

Maybe it's because we have separated ourselves from His people.

When I was a new believer, I remember someone explaining to me how important being a part of a church was. He said, "Christians are a lot like burning coals. They burn brighter and hotter when they're all together. Take one coal away, set it by itself on the hearth, and it will soon grow cold." That made perfect sense to me then, and it still does.

Something special happens when Christians are together around the Lord, seeking Him and worshiping Him. Jesus said, "Where two or three are gathered together in My name, I am there in the midst of them" (Matthew 18:20).

Technically, of course, God is omnipresent. Everywhere simultaneously. But something special happens when God's people gather for worship and prayer. You might find this statement controversial, but I believe not going to church is a proof of something spiritually wrong in your life. How can you say you love God whom you can't see when you don't love His people whom you can see?

The two discouraged disciples in Luke 24 had separated themselves from other believers. In their depression and grief, they had separated themselves from the church. No wonder they were so downhearted! But when their hearts were reignited again, what was the first thing they wanted to do? That's right, run all the way back to Jerusalem to be with the Lord's people and to share their news.

How had Jesus reignited their hearts? He did it by opening the Scriptures to them. It's the same for us. God will reignite your heart as you read and hear the Word of God, acknowledge that it is true, and apply it to your life.

As the two downhearted disciples did that, Jesus took their ending and turned it into a new beginning, and He can do the same for you.

"Abide with Us"

One last thing to consider about Jesus and the two disciples on the road to Emmaus. As they reached their destination, the text says that Jesus "indicated that He would have gone farther. But they constrained Him, saying, 'Abide with us, for it is toward evening, and the day is far spent.' And He went in to stay with them" (Luke 24:28-29).

What does this mean? It means He didn't want to impose.

Have you ever been at someone's house and maybe stayed a little longer than you intended? They start cooking dinner, and the food smells really good. But you don't want to actually say, "Um, can I stay for dinner?" So you say, "Well, I've got to be going." If they run to get your coat, then you have a clue they don't want you to stay for dinner. But if you say, "I'll catch you guys later," and they say, "No, stay for dinner," then you know it's okay.

Jesus acted as if He would keep walking down that road into the evening. He was not going to push His way into the lives of these two. But when they said, "Stay with us," He came under their roof, sat at their table, broke bread with them, and made Himself known to them.

A similar scenario plays out in our lives as well. Some of us are walking down the road of life without Jesus, trying to make sense of this crazy, frightening world. Trying to make sense of life. Maybe we've made mistakes we regret, and we don't know how to repair the damage. In fact, everything we try just seems to make things worse.

But here is Jesus, right now, walking alongside you, approaching your front door with you. Do you ask Him in? Do you invite Him to stay? In Revelation 3:20 (MSG), He said, "Look at me. I stand at the door. I knock. If you hear me call and open the door, I'll come right in and sit down to supper with you."

Jesus will not impose Himself into your life. He won't break down the door.

But He will respond to an invitation.

And when He does, hope reignites. Life changes forever from that moment.

CHAPTER FORTY-ONE
THE GRAND FINALE

S ometimes we wonder what God is really like, and we look here and look there for glimpses into His personality and character.

But we really don't have to look very far. In one of the last conversations the disciples had with the Lord before His death, Philip and Jesus had this exchange.

Philip said, "Lord, show us the Father, and we will be satisfied."

Jesus replied, "Have I been with you all this time, Philip, and yet you still don't know who I am? Anyone who has seen me has seen the Father! So why are you asking me to show him to you? Don't you believe that I am in the Father and the Father is in me?" (John 14:8-10, NLT)

If you want to know who God is, look at Jesus. Jesus was God walking among us—God who became a man, not man becoming God. He walked in our shoes, breathed our air, lived our life, and died our death. Truly, God came near. In Jesus, God spelled Himself out in language that every one of us can understand. Jesus was God with skin on.

The writer of the book of Hebrews underlined this when he wrote, "This Son perfectly mirrors God, and is stamped with God's nature. He holds everything together by what he says—powerful words!" (1:3, MSG).

In this chapter, we will look at three encounters three different people had with the resurrected Christ. We might title these three vignettes Jesus and the Skeptic, Jesus and the Failure, and, finally, Jesus and You.

Jesus and the Skeptic

The events in John 20 take place after Jesus was crucified and raised from the dead. That Sunday night, a group of dazed, frightened, emotionally frazzled disciples had gathered behind closed doors. Suddenly, Jesus showed up in their midst, showed them the wounds in His hands and side, and breathed the Holy Spirit on them, commissioning them for the work ahead. For whatever reason, Thomas wasn't at that meeting. When the rest of the apostles bumped into him the next day, they had incredibly good news for him—but he couldn't really take it in: "When they kept telling him, 'We have seen the Lord,' he replied, 'I won't believe it unless I see the nail wounds in his hands—and put my fingers into them—and place my hand into his side'" (verse 25, TLB).

Eight days later they got together again, with Thomas among them this time. And guess who showed up again? It was the same scenario as before. The disciples were huddled behind closed and locked doors, and Jesus suddenly appeared in their midst, without the benefit of a door.

This time, the Lord went right over to the one who had been absent the time before. It was as though He was making a custom appearance just for Thomas.

Jesus came, the doors being shut, and stood in the midst, and said, "Peace to you!" Then He said to Thomas, "Reach your finger here, and look at My hands; and reach your hand here, and put it into My side. Do not be unbelieving, but believing."

And Thomas answered and said to Him, "My Lord and my God!" (verses 26-28)

Because of this and other incidents, Thomas has been labeled "Doubting Thomas," and the name has stuck down through the centuries. But I'm not sure that's a fair description. I think we could have easily called him "Skeptical Thomas." He really wasn't asking for anything more than what the others had already seen. He wasn't demanding a special revelation; he just wanted the same proof the other disciples had been given. Jesus graciously gave him that proof, and He did it in the presence of the other disciples.

Thomas had missed that first meeting—that mysterious commissioning service when Jesus had breathed the Holy Spirit over them. We don't know why he skipped that Sunday night gathering, but oh what a meeting to miss!

The truth is, we miss a lot when we're not in church, when we neglect to meet with other believers for worship, prayer, and Bible study. We may study and pray on our own, but something special happens when we seek the Lord in the presence of others. In the book of Psalms, a man named Asaph had been struggling with the age-old questions of why the wicked prosper in our world, and why bad things keep happening to good people. Why is it that people who love and serve the Lord lose loved ones or get cancer, when people who hate Christianity and scoff at spiritual realities seem to skate by unscathed?

Asaph could only shake his head and say, "This doesn't make sense to me." But then he went on to say in Psalm 73:16-17 (NIV), "When I tried to understand all this, it troubled me deeply till I entered the sanctuary of God; then I understood their final destiny."

In the sanctuary of God, perhaps in a moment of worship with others, the truth finally dawned on him. I believe it's the same for us today. As we gather together for worship and Bible study with other believers, we gain an eternal perspective on things that we might not come by on our own. Asaph was essentially saying, "I didn't understand why things are the way they are until I came into God's presence to study His Word with His people. Then my questions seemed to snap into focus."

In that second meeting in John 20, Thomas didn't need a sermon or an extended conversation. Jesus came to him in a way he could understand and revealed to him what he needed to know. And in response he simply said, "My Lord and my God."

His skepticism gave way to belief.

Thomas acknowledged Jesus as God and as Lord of his life. As he did, many of the puzzle pieces in his mind came together.

Jesus and the Failure

The failure, of course, was Simon Peter.

He had impulsively boasted in the Upper Room that even if *everyone else* denied the Lord, he, Simon Peter, loyal and true, would *never* deny Him. He would rather die first!

But just as Jesus had warned and predicted, Peter caved in to fear and the pressure of the moment, denying three times that he even knew someone named Jesus! When Scripture says that he cursed and swore on his third denial, it doesn't mean he used profanity. The word used in Scripture indicates that he was swearing an oath. He was effectively saying, "I swear to God I never knew this Man Jesus Christ."

At that very instant, the Bible says, Jesus made eye contact with Peter.

Can you imagine that?

How would you feel if you had just denied even knowing Jesus, and then glanced up to see Jesus looking at you? The Bible says, "Peter went out and wept bitterly." And that's exactly what I would have done as well.

When Jesus rose from the dead, however, an angel at the tomb gave an interesting message to the three women who had come to care for His body: "Do not be alarmed. You seek Jesus of Nazareth, who was crucified. He is risen! He is not here. See the place where they laid Him. But go, tell His disciples—and Peter—that He is going before you into Galilee; there you will see Him, as He said to you" (Mark 16:6-7).

The angel said, "Tell His disciples—*and Peter!*" In other words, especially Peter. The angel didn't say, "Go tell the disciples and Thomas," or "Go tell the disciples and Matthew." He singled out Peter. Why? Because Peter needed some encouraging words at that moment. He was down, down, down. He had failed the Lord, and he knew it.

The Bible hints at a private encounter between the Lord and Peter that is not recorded. But we know it happened because we are told in Luke 24:34, "The Lord is risen indeed, and has appeared to Simon!" It was there, we assume—at that private meeting—that Jesus extended grace and forgiveness to Peter.

After that, I think Simon Peter understood he was forgiven; I just don't think he imagined he could ever be used by God again. He probably told himself, *I had thought of myself as a leader—a spokesman. What a joke. I will never be a leader or His spokesman. How could I be after what I did? I'll just step back from this disciple thing and go back to what I know. Fishing. I started out as a fisherman, and that's probably all I will ever be.*

John 21:3 (NLT) records the incident like this:

Simon Peter said, "I'm going fishing."

"We'll come, too," they all said. So they went out in the boat, but they caught nothing all night.

Have you ever wished you could do that? Just walk away from it all, grab a pole, and sit by a stream somewhere? Hang a little sign on your office door: "Gone fishing." Sometimes you just want to disconnect and get away for a while. And Peter thought he had good reason to do just that.

He really didn't know what to do next. He was out all night with his friends, bobbing around on the Sea of Galilee, without catching a single fish. Then, just as the sun was coming up, the men in the boat heard a voice calling from shore, "Boys, did you catch anything?" That's an interesting phrase. "Boys" was the word used here—not gentlemen. It was almost like a father speaking to his sons.

Peter might have thought to himself, "Who is that? Who is he calling 'boys'? I'm a full-grown adult male."

Then the voice said, "Why don't you throw the net over on the other side of the boat and you will find some!" Did the voice sound familiar to Peter? Did he say to himself, *Where have I heard this before?* The men in the boat complied with the voice of the Stranger on shore, and suddenly their net was so full of fish that it was breaking apart.

John, the most spiritually perceptive one, said, "It is the Lord!"

Without hesitation, Peter jumped into the sea and swam for shore, while the rest of the men came in the boat, towing their bursting net. Meanwhile, Jesus had prepared breakfast for them, and they realized it was He who had been calling out to them.

> *"Now come and have some breakfast!" Jesus said. None of the disciples dared to ask him, "Who are you?" They knew it was the Lord. Then Jesus served them the bread and the fish. This was the third time Jesus had appeared to his disciples since he had been raised from the dead.*
>
> *After breakfast Jesus asked Simon Peter, "Simon son of John, do you love me more than these?"*
>
> *"Yes, Lord," Peter replied, "you know I love you.".*
>
> *"Then feed my lambs," Jesus told him.*
>
> *Jesus repeated the question: "Simon son of John, do you love me?"*
>
> *"Yes, Lord," Peter said, "you know I love you."*
>
> *"Then take care of my sheep," Jesus said.*
>
> *A third time he asked him, "Simon son of John, do you love me?"*
>
> *Peter was hurt that Jesus asked the question a third time. He said, "Lord, you know everything. You know that I love you."*
>
> *Jesus said, "Then feed my sheep." (John 21:12-17, NLT)*

Breakfast with Jesus! How cool is that? I would love to get up in the morning and have the Lord cook me breakfast. Breakfast is my favorite meal of the day (second only to lunch and dinner). I don't understand people who don't want breakfast, because I always wake up hungry. My wife, however, isn't hungry at all in the morning. I will say, "Do you want to go out and get some breakfast?" And she will say, "I'm not hungry." Sometimes she even forgets to eat lunch. How do you forget to eat lunch? That isn't even a remote possibility for me.

But to have breakfast prepared by Christ Himself! How wonderful that would be.

Notice that in John 21:5 Jesus asks, "Did you catch anything?"

Have you noticed how God likes to ask questions? Back in the Garden of Eden, in Genesis chapter 3, after Adam and Eve had eaten the forbidden fruit, God came looking for them. He called out, "Adam, where are you?"

Was God really having trouble finding them, hiding naked in the bushes? Of course not. He knew exactly where Adam was. He was asking the question to prompt a confession from him. He wanted Adam to say, "Lord, I am hiding from You because I have sinned against You."

I think the question here in John 21 is similar. Jesus was saying, "Well, boys, are the fish biting? Have you been successful? Are you satisfied? Are you pleased with the course your lives are taking? Are you willing to admit your failure?"

What if He asked you the same thing? "How is it going for you right now? Are you pleased with your spiritual life? Are you walking with Me in the way you feel you ought to be? Is your life going the way you hoped it would go? Are you failing?"

If you are failing, you can say to God, "I need Your help!"

The boat finally made it to shore with a net full of fish. Someone actually bothered to count them all, because Scripture tells us that there were 153 large fish (see John 21:13). Dripping wet, Peter took a seat by the fire that Jesus had built and began to warm himself. He might have glanced down at the fish and bread cooking over the flames, but probably didn't want to make eye contact with Jesus.

There may have been an awkward silence. Peter may have been thinking, *Let's see, when was the last time I saw Jesus in the glow of a campfire. Oh . . . right. It was when I had just denied Him for the third time.*

Jesus broke the silence with another question.

The Lord said, "Simon son of John, do you love me more than these?" (John 21:15, NLT). Notice that Jesus didn't call him by his new name, Peter. Instead He said, "Simon." Jesus would use these names interchangeably, depending on how Peter was behaving. When he was living and obeying as he should, Jesus called him Peter. When he was misbehaving, Jesus called him Simon. Of course Simon was the name he had been born with. But Peter was the special name Jesus had given him—a name that means "rock."

This meeting with Peter was his recommissioning. He had already been forgiven, but now Jesus was saying, "Your work isn't over, Peter. You have a job to do. I want you to go out there and feed My sheep. Tend My lambs. This is the work I have called you to."

What was true for Peter is also true for us. God can still use us, even when we have failed. He wants us to learn from our mistakes. I like to call it "falling forward." What good is it to fail if we don't learn anything from the failure? But if we are humbled by our failures and draw wisdom and insight from our mistakes, we can advance in our lives. We can fall forward. But if we don't learn anything from our failures, we're just being fools.

Peter had learned, and he was recommissioned.

Jesus and You

The third of the three vignettes I'm presenting in this chapter involves Jesus and you.

You say, "I don't see my name written in the story."

Maybe not, but it's there just the same. What Jesus said to His eleven followers has direct application to our lives as well. I'm thinking particularly of the words He spoke just before He ascended into heaven. This was His final charge to His followers, and He meant this to include you and me as well.

Then the eleven disciples left for Galilee, going to the mountain where Jesus had told them to go. When they saw him, they worshiped him—but some of them doubted!

Jesus came and told his disciples, "I have been given all authority in heaven and on earth. Therefore, go and make disciples of all the nations, baptizing them in the name of the Father and the Son and the Holy Spirit. Teach these new disciples to obey all the commands I have given you. And be sure of this: I am with you always, even to the end of the age."
(Matthew 28:16-20, NLT)

These very familiar words are often called "the Great Commission."

But for many they have become the great *omission*.

Why is it that we don't share our faith with others? I could suggest a couple of reasons here. We might have a *fear of failure*. We are afraid that if we tell someone about our relationship with Jesus they may laugh in our face, make fun of us, or simply walk away in disgust. They might become highly offended. They might even physically assault us—you never know these days.

Then again, we might have a *fear of success*. What if the individual we speak to actually responds? What if God has prepared that person's heart and he or she wants to accept Jesus Christ? Do we know how to help them and lead them? Do we know how to follow up with a new baby Christian? We might shy away from speaking to someone because we lack confidence about what to say and what to do.

Nevertheless, there are two important points we need to consider about this great commission.

First, in the Greek, the words of Jesus are in the form of a command. That's why we don't call Matthew 28:19-20 "the Great Suggestion." It isn't a suggestion at all. The Lord truly commands us to go into all the world and preach the gospel.

Second, the original language implies that these words were given to every follower of Jesus. Not just to the original eleven. Not merely to "professionals," such as preachers, pastors, evangelists, and missionaries. These words are for you. If you are His disciple, you are commanded by God's Son to go and make disciples of others. If you are not making disciples, then you are not being the disciple He wants you to be.

As C. S. Lewis once said, "The Son of God became a man so men might become sons of God." Jesus said specifically that we are to "Go therefore and make disciples of all the nations . . . teaching them to observe all things that I have commanded you" (verses 19-20).

The Great Commission, then, is twofold: preaching the gospel and making disciples. What does that mean? It means that to the best of your ability you share your faith and try to lead people to Jesus. Then, if they do believe in Him, you take them under your wing, get them on their feet spiritually, and help them integrate into the church. Then go out and do it again.

We so overcomplicate this thing we call evangelism. Jesus said, "Wake up and look around. The fields are already ripe for harvest" (John 4:35, NLT). If we are awake and watching, we will see opportunities everywhere.

I was in a restaurant not long ago with a couple of our pastors. We go to lunch every Wednesday at the same place, and a particular waitress has served us many times. We always have a lot of banter going on, but this time she said, "I want to talk to you guys about something, and it is serious. I want to know when your church services are."

I said, "Eight, ten, and twelve o'clock on Sundays. Why do you ask?"

"I want to come to church," she replied.

"Fantastic. We'll hold a seat for you. We're glad you're coming."

"I really need to get right with God, and I want to do it this Sunday."

"No," I said, to everyone's surprise. "You are not going to do it this Sunday."

She looked at me with a "why?" expression on her face.

I said, "You are going to do it right here. Right now. Let's do it."

"Here?"

"Right here." (Now, the good news is that I know the owner of the restaurant, and he is a Christian. So I knew he would be okay with this.)

"We are going to pray right now," I told her. "Are you ready?"

"Yes," she said. So I led her in a prayer and she asked Jesus Christ to come into her life right there on the spot.

I relate this story simply to illustrate that there are opportunities wherever we go, if we just lift our eyes, look around, and ask the Lord to lead us to people who are already looking for Him.

Making disciples is simply helping people come to faith and establish a daily walk with their Lord.

"But Greg," you might say, "if I lead some guy to Jesus—doesn't that make him, um, my responsibility?"

Yes, to a certain extent it does.

"But what do I do?"

You need to help him. Invite him to church—to go with you, if possible. Introduce him to your Christian friends. Make him a part of your life.

Discipling someone isn't just preaching to a person. It is modeling for a person what a Christian looks like—how Christians live, drive, work, relax, relate to their families, and function in the real world. New believers need that example, and this is what we are called to do.

Jesus loves every man and woman you know. He loves them if they are doubters and skeptics, like Thomas, and He knows how to turn skeptics into believers. He loves them if they have failed over and over again, like Peter, and He can give them a fresh start, renewed hope, and strong help to walk a new path.

Whether we realize it or not or admit to ourselves or not, there are people on all sides of us who would draw close to Jesus and maybe even give their lives to Jesus if they only knew how to do it and where to start.

And that's where you and I come in.

ABOUT THE AUTHOR

Greg Laurie is the senior pastor of Harvest Christian Fellowship in Riverside and Orange County in California. Harvest is one of the largest churches in the United States and consistently ranks among the most influential churches in the country. He recently celebrated forty years as the senior pastor. In 1990, he began holding large-scale public evangelistic events called Harvest Crusades. More than five million people have attended Harvest events around the world, and more than 421,800 people have registered professions of faith through these outreaches.

He is the featured speaker of the nationally syndicated radio program, *A New Beginning*, which is broadcast on more than seven hundred radio outlets worldwide. Along with his work at Harvest Ministries, he served as the 2013 honorary chairman of the National Day of Prayer and also serves on the board of directors of the Billy Graham Evangelistic Association.

He has authored over seventy books, including *As It Is in Heaven; Revelation: the Next Dimension; As I See It; Hope for Hurting Hearts; Married. Happily; Every Day with Jesus; Signs of the Times; Hope for America;* and many more.

He has been married to Cathe Laurie for more than forty years, and they have two sons, Christopher and Jonathan. Christopher went to be with the Lord in 2008. They also have five grandchildren.

For more information visit www.allendavidbooks.com.

NOTES

1   (*Mere Christianity* [New York: Touchstone, 1996], 100.)

2   (*Mere Christianity* [New York: Macmillan, 1952], 54.)

3   www.livescience.com/33895-human-eye.html.

4   http://articles.chicagotribune.com/2006-10-29/Entertainment/0610280136
    _1_cosmetic-surgery-plastic-surgeons-cosmetic-enhancement.

5   Woody Allen, cited in Greg Laurie, *Why Believe?* (Wheaton, IL: Tyndale,
    2002), 76.

6   ThinkExist.com Quotations. "Jim Carrey quotes."
    ThinkExist.com Quotations Online 1 Feb. 2010. 1 Mar. 2010. http://einstein/
    quotes/jim_carrey.

7   J. I. Packer, "endless hell."

8   Rosemarie Jarski, *Words from the Wise: Over 6,000 of the Smartest Things
    Ever Said* (New York: Skyhorse, 2007), 162.

9   J. I. Packer, *Concise Theology: A Guide to Historic Christian Beliefs*
    (Wheaton, IL: Tyndale, 2001), 263–264.

10 C. S. Lewis, *The Problem of Pain* (Macmillan, 1961), 116; *The Great Divorce*
    (Macmillan, 1963), 69.

11 "Madonna on . . ." *USA Today*, April 17, 2003, retrieved from http://
    usatoday30.usatoday.com/life/2003-04-17-madonna-side_x.htm.

12 http://www.washingtonpost.com/blogs/wonkblog/wp/2013/08/13/
    wonkbook-11-facts-about-americas-prison-population/.

13 (*The Wiersbe Bible Commentary: Old Testament* [Colorado Springs: David
    C. Cook, 2007], 1471.)

14 http://www.oswaldchambers.co.uk/classic/the-sphere-of-exaltation-classic/.

15 http://utmost.org/beware-of-the-least-likely-temptation/.

16 (*The Weight of Glory and Other Addresses* [New York: HarperCollins, 1981], 26.)

17 http://www.usatoday.com/story/life/books/2015/01/16/the-boy-who
    -came-back-from-heaven-untrue-alex-malarkey/21855709/.

18 (*Mark: Jesus, Servant and Savior* [Wheaton, IL: Crossway, 2015], np.)

Greg Laurie Books with Study Guides

www.allendavidbooks.com

Other Books by Greg Laurie

A Fresh Look at the Book of Jonah
As I See It (Greg Laurie)
As I See It (Cathe Laurie)
Better Than Happiness
Daily Hope for Hurting Hearts
Dealing with Giants
Deepening Your Faith
Discipleship: Start! to Follow
Essentials
Essentials 2
Essentials Bible Study
Essentials 2 Bible Study
Every Day with Jesus
Following Jesus in the Modern World
Following Jesus in the Modern World Bible Study
For Every Season, volumes 1, 2, and 3
God's Design for Christian Dating
The Great Compromise
The Greatest Stories Ever Told, volumes 1, 2, and 3
Hope
Hope for America
Hope for Hurting Hearts
How to Know God
Living Out Your Faith
Lost Boy
Making God Known
Married. Happily.
Married. Happily. Bible Study
Red, 15 Favorite Christmas Messages
Revelation
Revelation: The Next Dimension Bible Study
Run to Win
Secrets to Spritiual Success
Signs of the Times
Strengthening Your Faith
Ten Things You Should Know About God and Life
Upside Down Living
Upside Down Living Bible Study
What Every Christian Needs to Know
Why God?
Worldview

KERYGMA
PUBLISHING

Visit: www.AllenDavidBooks.com